McGraw-Hill Series in Political Science

JOSEPH P. HARRIS, *Consulting Editor*

Readings in International Relations

McGraw-Hill Series in Political Science

JOSEPH P. HARRIS, *Consulting Editor*

BONE American Politics and the Party System

CHASE · The United Nations in Action

FERGUSON AND McHENRY · The American Federal Government

FERGUSON AND McHENRY · The American System of Government

FERGUSON AND McHENRY · Elements of American Government

FIELD · Governments in Modern Society

FRANK · Cases on the Constitution

GROSS · The Legislative Struggle

HARTMANN · Basic Documents of International Relations

HARTMANN · Readings in International Relations

HOLLOWAY · State and Local Government in the United States

LEONARD · Elements of American Foreign Policy

LEONARD · International Organization

MANGONE · A Short History of International Organization

NEUMANN · European and Comparative Government

REED · Municipal Management

RIEMER · Problems of American Government

STRAUSZ-HUPÉ AND POSSONY · International Relations

VANDENBOSH AND HOGAN · The United Nations—Background, Organization, Functions, Activities

WALDO · Ideas and Issues in Public Administration: A Book of Readings

WILSON · The American Political Mind

WILSON · Police Administration

READINGS IN
INTERNATIONAL RELATIONS

Edited by

Frederick H. Hartmann

Assistant Professor of Political Science
The University of Florida

New York   Toronto   London
McGRAW-HILL BOOK COMPANY, INC.
1952

READINGS IN INTERNATIONAL RELATIONS

III

Library of Congress Catalog Card Number: 51-12940

To Lynne Merry

who helped sometimes . . .

PREFACE

It has always seemed to the editor that there are many writings of fundamental and permanent importance in the field of international relations which the beginning student in theory could read but in practice does not read. They are important not because they are ponderous and dry; rather the reverse—they embody provocative ideas clothed in dynamic terms, often expressed with more than a touch of humor. They are, in short, interesting, and the problems they examine, lasting. No one book this size can include them all, but the editor has put many of the best of them within these pages.

He makes no claim that most of the original publications from which they are taken will not be found in any good university library—but in this book they will be found together, related to one another, and available in sufficient quantity for class use. They will be neither "gone to the bindery" nor "lost." The editor offers this collection in the hope that it will be a convenient source for much that the student will want to read if he would understand international relations.

The plan of this book, designed to supplement the standard texts, is simple: the selections cover the content of the average semester or year course in international relations, with some selections for each usual subdivision of the course. The selections have been distributed fairly uniformly over these topics, and a disproportionate emphasis upon the particular crucial problems of the moment has been avoided. These problems are by no means slighted—Part III is avowedly concerned with them, and much of Parts I and II is only relatively less so. Yet fundamentally these readings are intended to be used *throughout* the course rather than be taken up *en masse* only at the course section dealing with the "cold war" to date. They are intended to add depth to the discussions in the classroom and in the text on *all* the major topics with which international relations courses are concerned.

This book is deliberately somewhat different from the usual volume of readings. For one thing, the selections are both fewer and longer. They are fewer in order that they may be longer. By presenting a limited number of interesting views at sufficient length so that their individual flavor and content can be appreciated, the editor has hoped to avoid the confusion of a welter of incompletely expressed ideas, each canceling the other out in a fierce competition for space on the printed page.

Any book of readings is a challenging problem in organization. The presentation of material must be sufficiently flexible so that the readings can be adjusted to the variety of courses existing in international relations. For this reason, the editor has tried to make of each chapter an effective and cohesive unit in itself. Moreover, each selection in a chapter is there not only because it is worth while in its own right but also because by comparison and contrast it underlines the contribution of other selections in the same chapter. The selections in each chapter are therefore introduced consecutively in the chapter introduction so that this effect will be even more accentuated. For the same reason there are no introductory notes immediately preceding each selection. The emphasis, again, is on chapter *cohesiveness.*

There are several advantages to this general method. Not the least of these is in terms of examinations—for they are always with us. The length of the selections simplifies the task of the student; he is not confronted with an overwhelming number of short selections by an equally overwhelming number of writers. Professors can with confidence expect the student to be able to compare and analyze the selections in each chapter in terms of each other and the basic text. This is, after all, the greatest value of a book of readings—to stimulate thought and discussion by presenting material from more points of view than the basic text and the lecture-discussions provide. In the end maturity of viewpoint depends upon depth of understanding, and depth of understanding in turn depends upon the stimulus which such analysis and comparison provide.

The readings in this book have been drawn from a great variety of sources. Thucydides' description of a diplomatic conference taking place long before the time of Christ shares its pages with Lord Vansittart's lament over the decline of contemporary diplomacy; Machiavelli and Martin Wight, separated by five centuries of time, are brought together in a single chapter, because their analyses shed complementary light upon the nature of international relations. An attempt has been made to avoid any great number of selections dealing with historical periods not too well known to most beginning students of international relations in the belief that a predominantly historical approach has limits in effectiveness. Where the historical events are either well known or easily sketched in an introductory note, the analogy to contemporary and similar problems is valuable. But the editor believes that where this is not the case, the student will often be so preoccupied in attempting to understand the historical scene that he will fail to apply the analogy effectively to the present day.

The editor's colleagues at the University of Florida have consistently encouraged him in this work. Professors Manning J. Dauer, chairman of the Department of Political Science, and Alfred Diamant have read and criticized the manuscript and made many constructive suggestions. Dr. Helen D. Reid, visiting professor of Political Science in 1950 to 1951, first called the editor's attention to Madariaga's excellent essay which appears in the chapter on The Elements of National Power; similarly Alfred Diamant suggested the inclusion of Thucydides' provocative account of the diplomatic conference at Melos. Ross Y. Koen, instructor in Social Sciences, also made useful criticisms of the manuscript. This book owes a great deal as well to the fruitful exchange of ideas and critique of teaching materials which the editor has enjoyed with undergraduate and graduate students at the University of Florida over the last several years. Above all he owes much to his wife, who has given both encouragement and aid in the preparation of this book and who (most valuable trait of all!) has never hesitated to disagree with him on the frequent occasions when he has strayed down an inviting intellectual side path which would have led him from his goal.

FREDERICK H. HARTMANN

GAINESVILLE, FLA.
January, 1952

CONTENTS

PART III: THE PRESENT CRISIS
IN INTERNATIONAL RELATIONS

Part I

Forces and Elements of International Relations

CHAPTER 1

THE NATURE OF INTERNATIONAL RELATIONS

BEFORE WE can understand a subject, we must have some idea of the materials and concepts which compose it; we must orient ourselves in the latitude and longitude of a vast sea of ideas if we are to fix our position and progress toward a known port of comprehension. Otherwise we drift helplessly from idea to idea without method or direction. In a subject so complex as international relations, this is particularly true. The present chapter is included for precisely this purpose.

We live in a world which is physically one world and politically, economically, and ideologically many worlds. The component parts of this world, which we call nation-states, have relations with one another characterized by *conflict* and *cooperation*. Although each state is sovereign, it cannot realistically ignore the existence of other states. A nation-state can never afford to ignore or forget that the actions of other states may decisively influence its own destinies. In the *extreme* case one state may be conquered by another and disappear as a separate entity altogether.

In such a world, power is extremely important; a state must be able to defend itself. It must rely upon its own power as the basic element of its defense, but this power is usually augmented by that of allies having a common interest in restraining the aggressive ambitions of states who may, if successful, turn upon them as well. The problem of defense in an insecure world is inseparable from the problem of organizing and concerting measures with dependable allies. But organization necessitates cooperation even though cooperation in such cases is the product of a conflict, actual or potential. There are, however, many subjects of mutual concern to all or most nations which have very little to do with the power-security problem and where cooperation is carried on with little or no regard to any power considerations. The international exchange of mail is a familiar example.

The relations of states, therefore, are a complex of conflict and cooperation embracing hundreds of different kinds of situations in some of which power is vitally at stake and in others of which mutual convenience is the only real issue. It is possible, therefore, in observing international relations to emphasize either the power-conflict relationship or the convenience-cooperation relationship. This dichotomy of view is to be seen in most writings in the field of international relations, and the three selections which follow are especially useful as illustrations of the various ways in which this can occur.

Niccolò Machiavelli, whose reputation for "realism" in international relations is well known, points out in the first selection, "Concerning the Way in Which Princes Should Keep Faith," the basic anarchy of the nation-state system which makes it necessary for each state to look first to its own interests. The extent to which this was true in his day was even more pronounced than in our own. It is highly significant, however, that he urges princes (or governments) to assume that men are bad and deceitful, while simultaneously insisting upon the need for the prince to *appear* to conform to the moral and social values of his contemporaries. Machiavelli recognizes that in the turmoil of his age a world community did not exist in which the Italian city-states shared common values and that the final arbiter in international relations was the threat or use of force. Machiavelli's advice, therefore, was that the prince should act without being himself bound by moral restraints and as power considerations might suggest. But equally important, as he recognizes, is the vital role which moral and social values play in any national policy. He advised that the prince should put these values to use in his own interest but never that the prince should ignore them or think that they were not important.

Professor Carr, in the second selection, "International Politics: Idealism vs. Realism," has provided a stimulating discussion of the nature of international relations. Writing at a time when the world stood upon the brink of World War II and the resurgence of power politics had revealed the weaknesses of the idealists' overly optimistic views, he argues the need for a greater degree of realism. At the same time, Carr is concerned that, in the search for a more realistic appraisal of international events, the opposite error of ruling out idealism be avoided. Realism is the description of what *is;* idealism is the description of what *might be.* The inevitability of change in the relations of nations is a truth whose proof lies always before our eyes, and although more remains unchanged at any one moment than changes, altered conditions eventually produce altered responses. Realism, with its concern for what *is,* is slow to adjust, so that it is ever in danger of becoming a description of what *was.* Sound realism must also describe what is *becoming;* it must be dynamic rather than static. Yet what is in process of becoming depends not only upon the circumstances of a situation but also upon what it is that men and nations are attempting to achieve. Sound realism, Carr says, must itself contain an element of idealism. To the extent that the realist describes international politics as the search for power, he is in danger of blinding himself to the *goals* for which power is sought. These goals are themselves value goals; they describe the ends which nations seek to attain. Although the pursuit of these goals by nations may bring them into conflict, it may equally necessitate and induce their cooperation. Power and force as methods which states use must not be lightly dismissed, but neither must attention be focused on the methods to the exclusion of the ends sought. The reality of today is the synthesis of the reality and idealism of yesterday.

Martin Wight, in the third selection, "Power Politics," written after the close of World War II, reflects the extent to which in our own day power considerations loom large in the affairs of nations by defining power politics as "the relations between independent powers." These relations are, in his view, carried on by sovereign states in terms of power and the threat or use of force. He points out that the world has not always been organized as it is at present and that the nation-state system is of relatively recent origin. His brief historical description of older organizational forms should warn us that immense and important changes do occur and have occurred. Wight remarks that "power politics" *in common usage* means "the conduct of international relations by force or the threat of force" and goes on to say that power politics as "the relations between independent powers . . . is always inexorably approximating toward 'power politics'" in the sense of threat or use of force. That is to say, in an age when force is frequently threatened or used, the relations of states are *largely* conducted in those terms. He then explores the possibility of whether the relations of states are or can be more than power politics as commonly used: to what extent the threat or use of force is or is not a *complete* description of international relations. The answer to this question, Wight says, depends for one thing on how far states have *interests in common* (to what extent a world community exists). Among these common interests he lists a common interest in freedom. But this kind of common interest is not enough "if it is separated from the idea of common obligation." Such an idea underlies international law. Furthermore, morality in international politics is not alone a matter of tradition but of *security* as well. In an age of insecurity the sense of world community or morality tends to be swallowed up by considerations of power. He concludes with the warning that understanding this is realism, which "can be a very good thing: it all depends whether it means the abandonment of high ideals or of foolish expectations."

CONCERNING THE WAY IN WHICH PRINCES SHOULD KEEP FAITH

NICCOLÒ MACHIAVELLI *

Everyone admits how praiseworthy it is in a prince to keep faith, and to live with integrity and not with craft. Nevertheless our experience has been that those princes who have done great things have held good faith of little account, and have known how to circumvent the intellect of men by craft, and in the end have overcome those who have relied on their word. You must know there are two ways of contesting, the one by the law, the other by force; the first method is proper to men, the second to beasts; but because the first is frequently not sufficient, it is necessary to have recourse to the second. Therefore it is necessary for a prince to understand how to avail himself of the beast and the man . . . it is necessary for a prince to know how to make use of both natures, and that one without the other is not durable. A prince, therefore, being compelled knowingly to adopt the beast, ought to choose the fox and the lion; because the lion cannot defend himself against snares and the fox cannot defend himself against wolves. Therefore, it is necessary to be a fox to discover the snares and a lion to terrify the wolves. Those who rely simply on the lion do not understand what they are about. Therefore a wise lord cannot, nor ought he to, keep faith when such observance may be turned against him, and when the reasons that caused him to pledge it exist no longer. If men were entirely good this precept would not hold, but because they are bad, and will not keep faith with you, you too are not bound to observe it with them. Nor will there ever be wanting to a prince legitimate reasons to excuse this non-observance. Of this endless modern examples could be given, showing how many treaties and engagements have been made void and of no effect through the faithlessness of princes; and he who has known best how to employ the fox has succeeded best.

But it is necessary to know well how to disguise this characteristic, and to be a great pretender and dissembler; and men are so simple, and so subject to present necessities, that he who seeks to deceive will always find someone who will allow himself to be deceived. . . .

Therefore it is unnecessary for a prince to have all the good qualities I have enumerated, but it is very necessary to appear to have them. And I shall dare to say this also, that to have them and always to have them is useful; to appear merciful, faithful, humane, religious, upright, and to be so, but with a mind so framed that should you require not to be so, you may be able and know how to change to the opposite.

And you have to understand this, that a prince, especially a new one, cannot observe all those things for which men are esteemed, being often forced, in order to maintain the state, to act contrary to fidelity, friendship, humanity, and religion. Therefore it is necessary for him to have a mind ready to turn itself accordingly as the winds and variations of fortune force it, yet, as I have said above, not to diverge from the good if he can avoid doing so, but, if compelled, then to know how to set about it.

For this reason a prince ought to take care that he never lets anything slip from his lips that is not replete with the above-named five qualities, that he may appear to him who sees and hears him altogether merciful, faithful, humane, upright, and religious. There is nothing more necessary to appear to have than this last quality, inasmuch as men judge generally more by the eye than by the hand, because it belongs to everybody to see you, to few to come in touch with you. Every one sees what you appear to be, few really know what you are, and those few dare not oppose themselves to the opinion of the many, who have the majesty of the state to defend them; and in the actions of all men, and especially of princes, which it is not prudent to challenge, one judges by the result.

INTERNATIONAL POLITICS: IDEALISM VS. REALISM

E. H. CARR *

The exposure by realist criticism of the hollowness of the utopian edifice is the most urgent task of the moment in international thought. It is only when the sham has been demolished that there can be any hope of raising a more solid structure in its place. But we cannot ultimately find a resting place in pure realism; for realism, though logically overwhelming, does not provide us with the springs of action which are necessary even to the pursuit of thought. Indeed, realism itself, if we attack it with its own weapons, often turns out in practice to be just as much conditioned as any other mode of thought. In politics, the belief that certain facts are unalterable or certain trends irresistible commonly reflects a lack of desire or lack of interest to change or resist them. The impossibility of being a consistent and thorough-going realist is one of the most certain and most curious lessons of political science. Consistent realism excludes four things which appear to be essential ingredients of all effective political thinking: a finite goal, an emotional appeal, a right of moral judgment and a ground for action.

The conception of politics as an infinite process seems in the long run uncongenial or incomprehensible to the human mind. Every political thinker who wishes to make an appeal to his contemporaries is consciously or unconsciously led to posit a finite goal. Treitschke declared that the "terrible thing" about Machiavelli's teaching was "not the immorality of the methods he recommends, but the lack of content of the state, which exists only in order to exist." [1] In fact, Machiavelli is not so consistent. His realism breaks down in the last chapter of *The Prince*, which is entitled "An Exhortation to Free Italy from the Barbarians"—a goal whose necessity could be deduced from no realist premise. Marx, having dissolved human thought and action into the relativism of the dialectic, postulates the absolute goal of a classless society where the dialectic no longer operates—that one far-off event towards which, in true Victorian fashion, he believed the whole creation to be moving. The realist thus ends by negating his own postulate and assuming an ultimate reality outside the historical process. Engels was one of the first to level this charge against Hegel. "The whole dogmatic content of the Hegelian system is declared to be absolute truth in contradiction to his dialectical

* E. H. Carr, *The Twenty Years' Crisis, 1919–1939*, pp. 113–119, 125–127, 131–133, 137. Reprinted by permission of The Macmillan Company, Macmillan & Co., Ltd., and E. H. Carr.

[1] Treitschke, *Aufsätze*, iv. p. 428.

method, which dissolves all dogmatism." [2] But Marx lays himself open to precisely the same criticism when he brings the process of dialectical materialism to an end with the victory of the proletariat. Thus utopianism penetrates the citadel of realism; and to envisage a continuing, but not infinite, process towards a finite goal is shewn to be a condition of political thought. The greater the emotional stress, the nearer and more concrete is the goal. The War was rendered tolerable by the belief that it was the last of wars. Woodrow Wilson's moral authority was built up on the conviction, shared by himself, that he possessed the key to a just, comprehensive and final settlement of the political ills of mankind. It is noteworthy that almost all religions agree in postulating an ultimate state of complete blessedness.

The finite goal, assuming the character of an apocalyptic vision, thereby acquires an emotional, irrational appeal which realism itself cannot justify or explain. Everyone knows Marx's famous prediction of the future classless paradise:

"When work ceases to be merely a means of life and becomes the first living need; when, with the all-round development of the individual, productive forces also develop, and all the sources of collective wealth flow in free abundance—then only will it be possible to transcend completely the narrow horizon of *bourgeois* right, and society can inscribe on its banner: From each according to his capacities, to each according to his needs." [3]

Sorel proclaimed the necessity of a "myth" to make revolutionary teaching effective; and Soviet Russia has exploited for this purpose the myth, first of world revolution, and more recently of the "socialist fatherland." There is much to be said for Professor Laski's view that "communism has made its way by its idealism, and not by its realism, by its spiritual promise, not by its materialistic prospects." [4] A modern theologian has analyzed the situation with almost cynical clear-sightedness:

"Without the ultrarational hopes and passions of religion, no society will have the courage to conquer despair and attempt the impossible; for the vision of a just society is an impossible one, which can be approximated only by those who do not regard it as impossible. The truest visions of religion are illusions, which may be partly realised by being resolutely believed." [5]

And this again closely echoes a passage in *Mein Kampf* in which Herr Hitler contrasts the "programme-maker" with the politician:

[2] Engels, *Ludwig Feuerbach* (Engl. transl.), p. 23.
[3] Marx and Engels, *Works* (Russian ed.), xv. p. 275.
[4] Laski, *Communism*, p. 250.
[5] R. Neibuhr, *Moral Man and Immoral Society*, p. 81.

"His [*i.e.*, the programme-maker's] significance lies almost wholly in the future, and he is often what one means by the word *'weltfremd'* [unpractical, utopian]. For if the art of the politician is really the art of the possible, then the programme-maker belongs to those of whom it is said that they please the gods only if they ask and demand from them the impossible." [6]

Credo quia impossible becomes a category of political thinking.

Consistent realism, as has already been noted, involves acceptance of the whole historical process and precludes moral judgments on it. As we have seen, men are generally prepared to accept the judgment of history on the past, praising success and condemning failure. This test is also widely applied to contemporary politics. Such institutions as the League of Nations, or the Soviet or Fascist régimes, are to a considerable extent judged by their capacity to achieve what they profess to achieve; and the legitimacy of this test is implicitly admitted by their own propaganda, which constantly seeks to exaggerate their successes and minimise their failures. Yet it is clear that mankind as a whole is not prepared to accept this rational test as a universally valid basis of political judgment. The belief that whatever succeeds is right, and has only to be understood to be approved, must, if consistently held, empty thought of purpose, and thereby sterilise and ultimately destroy it. Nor do those whose philosophy appears to exclude the possibility of moral judgments in fact refrain from pronouncing them. Frederick the Great, having explained that treaties should be observed for the reason that "one can trick only once," goes on to call the breaking of treaties "a bad and knavish policy," though there is nothing in his thesis to justify the moral epithet. Marx, whose philosophy appeared to demonstrate that capitalists could only act in a certain way, spends many pages—some of the most effective in *Capital*—in denouncing the wickedness of capitalists for behaving in precisely that way. The necessity, recognized by all politicians, both in domestic and in international affairs, for cloaking interests in a guise of moral principles is in itself a symptom of the inadequacy of realism. Every age claims the right to create its own values, and to pass judgments in the light of them; and even if it uses realist weapons to dissolve other values, it still believes in the absolute character of its own. It refuses to accept the implication of realism that the word "ought" is meaningless.

Most of all, consistent realism breaks down because it fails to provide any ground for purposive or meaningful action. If the sequence of cause and effect is sufficiently rigid to permit of the "scientific prediction" of events, if our thought is irrevocably conditioned by our status and our interests, then both action and thought become devoid of purpose. If,

[6] Hitler, *Mein Kampf*, p. 231.

as Schopenhauer maintains, "the true philosophy of history consists of the insight that, throughout the jumble of all these ceaseless changes, we have ever before our eyes the same unchanging being, pursuing the same course to-day, yesterday and for ever," [7] then passive contemplation is all that remains to the individual. Such a conclusion is plainly repugnant to the most deep-seated belief of man about himself. That human affairs can be directed and modified by human action and human thought is a postulate so fundamental that its rejection seems scarcely compatible with existence as a human being. Nor is it in fact rejected by those realists who have left their mark on history. Machiavelli, when he exhorted his compatriots to be good Italians, clearly assumed that they were free to follow or ignore his advice. Marx, by birth and training a *bourgeois*, believed himself free to think and act like a proletarian, and regarded it as his mission to persuade others, whom he assumed to be equally free, to think and act likewise. Lenin, who wrote of the imminence of world revolution as a "scientific prediction," admitted elsewhere that "no situations exist from which there is absolutely no way out." [8] In moments of crisis, Lenin appealed to his followers in terms which might equally well have been used by so thorough-going a believer in the power of the human will as Signor Mussolini or by any other leader of any period: "At the decisive moment and in the decisive place, you *must prove the stronger*, you must *be victorious*." [9] Every realist, whatever his professions, is ultimately compelled to believe not only that there is something which man ought to think and do, but that his thought and action are neither mechanical nor meaningless.

We return therefore to the conclusion that any sound political thought must be based on elements of both utopia and reality. In international politics, post-War utopianism became a hollow and intolerable sham, which served merely as a disguise for the interests of the privileged Powers; and the realist performs an indispensable service in unmasking it. But pure realism can offer us nothing but a naked struggle for power which makes any kind of international society impossible. Having demolished the current utopia with the weapons of realism, we still need to build a new utopia of our own, which will one day fall to the same weapons. The human will will continue to seek an escape from the logical consequences of realism in the vision of an international order which, as soon as it crystallises itself into concrete political form, becomes tainted with

[7] Schopenhauer, *Welt als Wille und Vorstellung,* ii. ch. 38.
[8] Lenin, *Works* (2d Russian ed.), xxv. p. 340.
[9] Lenin, *Collected Works* (Engl. transl.), xxi. i. p. 68.

self-interest and hypocrisy, and must once more be attacked with the instruments of realism.

Here, then, is the complexity, the fascination and the tragedy of all political life. Politics are made up of two elements—utopia and reality —belonging to two different planes which can never meet. There is no greater barrier to clear political thinking than failure to distinguish between ideals, which are utopia, and institutions, which are reality. The communist who sets communism against democracy is usually thinking of communism as a pure ideal of equality and brotherhood, and of democracy as an institution which exists in Great Britain, France or the United States and which exhibits the vested interests, the inequalities and the oppression inherent in all political institutions. The democrat who makes the same comparison is in fact comparing an ideal pattern of democracy laid up in heaven with communism as an institution existing in Soviet Russia with its class-divisions, its heresy hunts and its concentration camps. The comparison, made in each case between an ideal and an institution, is irrelevant and makes no sense. The ideal, once it is embodied in an institution, ceases to be an ideal and becomes the expression of a selfish interest, which must be destroyed in the name of a new ideal. This constant interaction of irreconcilable forces is the stuff of politics. Every political situation contains mutually incompatible elements of utopia and reality, of morality and power.

This point will emerge more clearly from the analysis of the nature of politics which we have now to undertake.

. . . The utopian who dreams that it is possible to eliminate self-assertion from politics and to base a political system on morality alone is just as wide of the mark as the realist who believes that altruism is an illusion and that all political action is based on self-seeking. These errors have both left their mark on popular terminology. The phrase "power politics" is often used in an invidious sense, as if the element of power or self-assertion in politics were something abnormal and susceptible of elimination from a healthy political life. Conversely, there is a disposition, even among some writers who are not strictly speaking realists, to treat politics as the science of power and self-assertion and exclude from it by definition actions inspired by the moral consciousness. . . . Such terminological implications are misleading. Politics cannot be divorced from power. But the *homo politicus* who pursues nothing but power is as unreal a myth as the *homo economicus* who pursues nothing but gain. Political action must be based on a co-ordination of morality and power.

This truth is of practical as well as theoretical importance. It is as fatal in politics to ignore power as it is to ignore morality. The fate of China in the nineteenth century is an illustration of what happens to a country which is content to believe in the moral superiority of its own civilization and to despise the ways of power. . . . The utopian, who believes that democracy is not based on force, refuses to look these unwelcome facts in the face.

On the other hand, the realist, who believes that, if you look after the power, the moral authority will look after itself, is equally in error. The most recent form of this doctrine is embodied in the much quoted phrase: "The function of force is to give moral ideas time to take root." Internationally, this argument was used in 1919 by those who, unable to defend the Versailles Treaty on moral grounds, maintained that this initial act of power would pave the way for subsequent moral appeasement. Experience has done little to confirm this comfortable belief. The same fallacy is implicit in the now commonly held view that the aim of our policy should be "to rebuild the League of Nations, to make it capable of holding a political aggressor in restraint by armed power, and thereafter to labour faithfully for the mitigation of just and real grievances." [10] Once the enemy has been crushed or the "aggressor" restrained by force, the "thereafter" fails to arrive. The illusion that priority can be given to power and that morality will follow, is just as dangerous as the illusion that priority can be given to moral authority and that power will follow. . . .

Politics are, then, in one sense always power politics. Common usage applies the term "political" not to all activities of the state, but to issues involving a conflict of interests. Once this conflict has been resolved, the issue ceases to be "political" and becomes a matter of administrative routine. Nor is all business transacted between states "political." When states co-operate with one another to maintain postal or transport services, or to prevent the spread of epidemics or suppress the traffic in drugs, these activities are described as "non-political" or "technical." But as soon as an issue arises which involves, or is thought to involve, the power of one state in relation to another, the matter at once becomes "political." While politics cannot be satisfactorily defined exclusively in terms of power, it is safe to say that power is always an essential element of politics. In order to understand a political issue, it is not enough (as it would be in the case of a technical or a legal issue) to know what the point at issue is. It is necessary also to know between whom it has arisen. An issue raised by a small number of isolated individuals is not

[10] Winston Churchill, *Arms and the Covenant*, p. 368. The argument that power is a necessary motive force for the remedy of "just" grievances is further developed on pp. 266–277 [of Carr's book].

the same political fact as the same issue raised by a powerful and well-organised trade union. A political issue arising between Great Britain and Japan is something quite different from what may be formally the same issue between Great Britain and Nicaragua. "Politics begin where the masses are," said Lenin, "not where there are thousands, but where there are millions, that is where serious politics begin." [11]

There have been periods of history when it might have been superfluous to dwell on this obvious fact, and when Engels' dictum that "without force and iron ruthlessness nothing is achieved in history" [12] would have passed as a platitude. But in the comparatively well-ordered world of nineteenth-century liberalism, subtler forms of compulsion successfully concealed from the unsophisticated the continuous but silent workings of political power; and in democracies, at any rate, this concealment is still partially effective. After the War, the liberal tradition was carried into international politics. Utopian writers from the English-speaking countries seriously believed that the establishment of the League of Nations meant the elimination of power from international relations, and the substitution of discussion for armies and navies. "Power politics" were regarded as a mark of the bad old times, and became a term of abuse. That this belief should have persisted for more than ten years was due to the circumstance that the Great Powers whose main interest was the preservation of the *status quo* enjoyed throughout that time a virtual monopoly of power. A game of chess between a world-champion and a schoolboy would be so rapidly and so effortlessly won that the innocent onlooker might be pardoned for assuming that little skill was necessary to play chess. In the same way, the simple-minded spectator of the game of international politics could assume, between 1920 and 1931, that power played little part in the game. What has commonly been called the "return to power politics" in 1931 was, in fact, the termination of the monopoly of power enjoyed by the *status quo* Powers. Stalin's lament that *"in our days* it is not the custom to reckon with the weak," and Mr. Chamberlain's remark that *"in the world as we find it to-day* an unarmed nation has little chance of making its voice heard," [13] are curious tributes—more surprising in the professed Marxist than in the inheritor of a British nineteenth-century tradition—to the illusion that there was once a time when weak and unarmed countries played an effective role in international politics.

[11] Lenin, *Selected Works* (Engl. transl.), vii. p. 295.

[12] Marx and Engels, *Works* (Russian ed.), vii. p. 212.

[13] Report to the Sixteenth Congress of the Russian Communist Party reprinted in *L'Union Soviétique et la Cause de la Paix,* p. 25; *The Times,* June 26, 1939. The italics have been inserted in both cases.

The post-War assumption of the elimination of power from politics could only result from a wholly uncritical attitude towards political problems. In the affairs of the League of Nations, formal equality and the participation of all in debate did not render the power factor any less decisive. The founders of the League themselves entertained no such illusion. . . .

Failure to recognise that power is an essential element of politics has hitherto vitiated all attempts to establish international forms of government, and confused nearly every attempt to discuss the subject. Power is an indispensable instrument of government. To internationalise government in any real sense means to internationalise power; and since independent power is the basis of the nation-state, the internationalisation of power is really a contradiction in terms. International government is, in effect, government by that state which supplies the power necessary for the purpose of governing.

POWER POLITICS

MARTIN WIGHT *

Power politics means the relations between independent Powers. This implies two conditions: independent units which acknowledge no political superior, and continuous and organized relations between them. We take this state of affairs for granted. We have the independent units, which we call states, nations, countries or *Powers,* and we have a complicated system of relationships between them, now peace, now war.

It will however help us to understand this state of affairs better if we recall that it is by no means the rule in history. The present system in Europe has existed roughly since the Reformation, and we have the illusion that it is normal. But looking farther back, we can see it preceded by something quite different. In the twelfth century there was a single juridical unit in Western Europe, where in 1920 there were twenty-six: a single unit known as Christendom or the Christian Republic, which was ruled by two authorities, the Pope in religious affairs and the Emperor in secular affairs. The innumerable principalities and feudatories and cities of which it was composed, despite their constant strife, were

* Martin Wight, *Power Politics,* "Looking Forward" Pamphlets, No. 8, Royal Institute of International Affairs, London, pp. 7–11, 61–66. Copyright 1946, by Royal Institute of International Affairs. Reprinted by permission.

not independent units acknowledging no superior. Again, Christendom had relationships—trade and war—with the Mohammedan Powers across the Mediterranean and with the Byzantine Empire across the Ionian Sea; and these relationships showed glimmerings of the same principles as those of modern nations; but they were not continuous and organized. Looking still farther back (across an interval of confusion and migrations) we see something quite different again: another single unit, occupying a rather different geographical position from Christendom—the Roman Empire. This was a highly organized and centralized state instead of a loose confederation, with a single, absolute, divine ruler instead of two equal, limited rulers. It too had diplomatic relations and wars with the Parthian and Persian Empires across the Euphrates, and it traded with China; but these contacts, like those of Christendom with the Byzantines and Moslems, were distant and irregular. But looking back once more beyond the Roman Empire we see the familiar sight of a multitude of independent units, brilliant cities and large kingdoms, each jealous of its freedom and ambitious to expand, fighting and intriguing, making alliances and holding conferences, and all of them, in the end, conquered, pacified and swallowed up by Rome, which had begun by being one of them. This political kaleidoscope of the great Greek and Hellenistic ages looks modern to our eyes, while the immense majesty of the Roman peace, and the religious culture of medieval Christendom, seem remote and alien. But a similar sequence of periods can be traced in the histories of Islam, India, China and other parts of the world.

What we mean by power politics, then, came into existence when medieval Christendom dissolved and the modern sovereign state was born. But what was the revolution in politics that occurred at this time? In the medieval world there were already growing up feudal, tribal and national authorities which developed into the modern nations of Europe; these fought constantly among themselves; and the two highest authorities, the Pope and the Emperor, waged an almost continuous two hundred years' war at the zenith of the Middle Ages to decide which of them was supreme. The change that culminated in the Reformation (it had begun about two centuries earlier) was fundamentally moral and psychological. First, it was a revolution in loyalties. Medieval man had a customary loyalty to his immediate feudal superior, with whose authority he was in direct contact; and a customary religious obedience to the Church under the Pope, which presided over every aspect of his life; but his loyalty to the king, whom he probably never saw and was seldom aware of, was weaker than either. In due course the king suppressed the feudal barons and challenged the power of the Pope, becoming the protector and champion against oppression and disorder at home and against a corrupt and exacting authority abroad. The common man's inner circle of loyalty expanded, his outer circle of loyalty shrank, and the two met and coincided in a doubly definite circle between, where loyalty before had been vague. Thus the modern state came into existence: a narrower, and at the same time a stronger, unit of loyalty than medieval Christendom. Modern man is in general far more conscious of loyalty to the state than to church or class or race or anything else. A Power is a modern sovereign state in its international aspect, and it might almost be defined as that ultimate loyalty for which men today will fight. With this shift in loyalties came a change in the character of politics. Medieval Christendom was a static, agrarian society whose politics were concerned with defining and interpreting a system which everybody theoretically agreed upon, and in which Pope, feudal lord, burgher and peasant each had his place. Modern times have been a dynamic, tumultuous period of economic expansion and social change, during which agreed moral standards and political beliefs have became increasingly rarefied, as a multitude of Powers have each claimed independence of the rest and driven forward upon their own paths. 'Medieval history,' said the historian Stubbs, 'is a history of rights and wrongs; modern history as contrasted with medieval is a history of *powers,* forces, dynasties and ideas. . . . Medieval wars are, as a rule, wars of rights: they are seldom wars of unprovoked, never wars of absolutely unjustifiable, aggression; they are not wars of idea, of liberation, or of glory, or of nationality, or of propagandism.' The contrast has not become less remarkable in the sixty years since he wrote.

There are several misunderstandings against which we must guard at the outset. First, a Power is not identical with a nation. Nationalism was the main force that broke up Christendom, and most European Powers have in fact been nations; but nationality has not always crystallized into a state, and states have not always been the political expression of a single nationality. . . . The identification of Powers with nations reached its climax in the Peace Settlement of 1919, which was based on the principle of national self-determination, *i.e.* the right of every nationality to form a state. But subsequent history has largely undone this. The three surviving Great Powers today, Russia, the United States and the British Empire are, each in its different way, multi-national units; indeed Britain itself is the political union of the English, Welsh and Scottish nations.

Secondly, it must be emphasized that when we personify Powers, saying that *Britain's* policy is this, *America* demands that and the *Soviet Union* does something else, we are in fact using mythological language just as much as if we speak of John Bull, Uncle Sam or the Russian Bear. 'Britain' in such a connection is a kind of algebraical symbol to denote an immensely complex process which includes the permanent officials of the Foreign Office, the Diplomatic Service, the Foreign Secretary, the Prime Minister, the Cabinet, the House of Commons, the living electorate, and the dead generations who have made the national tradition, combining and re-combining in an infinite number of variations of mutual influence. These shorthand terms are of course unavoidable in political writing, but they are dangerous if they lead us into thinking that Powers are inscrutable and awesome monsters following predestined laws of their own. A Power is simply a collection of human beings following certain traditional ways of action, and if a sufficient number of them choose to alter their collective behavior they may succeed in doing so.

Thirdly, we must note the significance of the fact that the phrase 'power politics' in common usage means, not just the relations between independent Powers, but something more sinister. It is indeed a translation of the German word *Machtpolitik,* which means the politics of force —the conduct of international relations by force or the threat of force without consideration of right and justice. As Mr. Roosevelt said in his last Annual Message to Congress, 'In the future world *the misuse of power* as implied in the term "power politics" must not be the controlling factor in international relations.' It would be foolish to suppose that international relations are governed exclusively by force, and that statesmen are not moved by considerations of right and law and justice. But as we have seen, what distinguishes modern history from medieval history is the predominance of the idea of power over the idea of right; the very term 'Power' to describe a state in its international aspect is significant; and the view of the man in the street, who is perhaps inclined to take it for granted that foreign politics are inevitably 'power politics,' is not without a shrewd insight. It is wisest to start from the recognition that power politics as we defined it at the outset is always inexorably approximating towards 'power politics' in the immoral sense, and to analyze it in this light. When we have done this we can more usefully assess the moral problem. . . .

In the study of international politics we are dogged by the insistent problem, whether the relations between Powers are in fact more than 'power politics' in the popular sense of the term, and whether they can become more. From one point of view, the central question is how far Powers can be said to have interests in common. We have seen that the international anarchy is restrained and to some extent systematized in practice by two opposing kinds of common interest, pulling alternately to and fro. The first is the common interest of all Powers in their freedom, of which they are faintly conscious in peace, and assert at the eleventh hour in war by an armed coalition against a common danger.

The second is the kind of common interest represented by successive Dominant Powers. For their predominance has generally safeguarded real values, and offered real benefits, for other nations, and sometimes they have wielded an international ideology as their most potent weapon —as the Hapsburg Powers were the protagonists of the Counter-Reformation, as Napoleonic France was the carrier of the French Revolution throughout feudal Europe, as Britain in the nineteenth century was the champion of liberalism. In the same way Russia in the twentieth century has represented the ideal of socialism. A Dominant Power that is thus able to give its policies the added momentum of an international ideal becomes a tremendous force, whose limits are reached only if it provokes the counter-interest of general freedom. Nor is it impossible that Powers may henceforward increasingly regard their deepest common interest as being the prevention of war and liberation from anarchy, and that this will only prove obtainable by acquiescence in a common government provided by the strongest Power.

But the idea of common interest can never have much vitality if it is separated from the idea of common obligation, and here we touch a more fundamental issue. There has always existed a theory of international relations which asserts the primacy of common conceptions of justice, right and law. There was an ancient tradition, dating back through the jurists and theologians of the Middle Ages to the jurists and philosophers of antiquity, of Natural Law or the Law of Nature. It taught that man is a rational and social animal, that there is a moral order in the universe to which his rational nature bids him always and everywhere to conform, that the true interests of human societies therefore do not conflict, and that they are bound together by obligations of law and morality. This tradition was the source of international law, which was developed in the seventeenth century to restrain the anarchy into which the states of Europe had fallen, and which used to appeal to 'the common standard of right prevailing throughout the Christian world.' But it was eclipsed by the new revolutionary creed of progress at the end of the eighteenth century, just at the time when the European Powers, as a consequence of the industrial revolution, were beginning to establish a material unification of the world.

The expansion of Europe itself weakened the tradition of Natural Law, by admitting states that had not been schooled in it to the international community. Of the two new Great Powers of the eighteenth century, Prussia was at the extreme limit of Western Christendom, and had been in many ways scarcely touched by its characteristic culture; and Russia is the heir and champion of the very different traditions of Byzantine Christendom. In the nineteenth century international intercourse was extended far beyond the Christian world, at the same time that Christian political theory was at a greater discount inside the Christian world than it had ever been before. In 1856, at the conclusion of the Crimean War, Turkey was admitted for the first time to the community of nations; but it was a passive and not an active member; and it is from the emergence of Japan as a Great Power—the first Great Power that was wholly non-European and non-Christian in its traditions—that we may date the effective transformation of the international community from one based on a common ethos to one whose principle is inclusiveness. Attempts have been made since the French Revolution to find an alternative common ethos in political creed instead of moral tradition. The Vienna Settlement was based on the principle of legitimacy; the Versailles Settlement was based on the principle of self-determination; the Yalta Declaration of 1945 enshrined the principle of 'democracy.' But in each case these formulae have reflected only a transient moment on the surface of affairs, concealing differences rather than expressing 'a common standard of right,' and they have soon dissolved and been superseded. It may indeed be asked whether an effective common ethos is likely to grow up again without an effective common government.

Though the tradition of an international community with a common standard of obligation and justice has faded, however, it has not altogether disappeared. It is the main influence that has modified, and can yet modify, the operations of power politics, and it still gleams faintly in the preamble to the Charter of the United Nations. In countries whose culture and politics are favourable to its survival, it can create a 'moral climate' of opinion that will affect politicians who are quite ignorant of any traditional political theories. The extent to which it may do so in practice is highly controversial, and every historical example that may be brought forward in this light will lead to the kind of argument in which there can be no clear-cut and final conclusion, because it depends not on the establishment of facts but on the exercise of moral insight and political judgement.

It is sufficient to instance two statesmen whose beliefs were saturated with conceptions of Natural Law, and whose politics were grounded on its traditions, Gladstone in nineteenth-century England, and Franklin Roosevelt in twentieth-century America; nor is it any accident that each of these men in his generation had a moral ascendancy and a power over the public opinion of the world, evoking a trust and loyalty far beyond his own country, which was unapproached by any other contemporary political figure. (The devotion inspired abroad in the intervening generation by the supreme revolutionary statesman, Lenin, was perhaps more passionate in its quality, but it was limited and sectional by comparison in its range.) This is not to say that Gladstone and Roosevelt were not assiduous, subtle and far-sighted power-politicians. But their politics had overtones that are absent from the politics of a Theodore Roosevelt or a Cecil Rhodes, a Lloyd George or a Clemenceau, a Bismarck or a Cavour. When we consider the foreign policies of the latter we think in terms of patriotism, of grandeur of conception, of brilliance, of virtuosity, above all of success or failure. Most people would agree that Gladstone's Irish policy or Roosevelt's Latin-American policy (like, in another way, Lincoln's Civil War policy) were different in quality from these, the fruit of a richer conception of politics, which made power an instrument and not an end, and subordinated national interest to public justice.

Nevertheless it is always well to be sceptical of statesmen, and as Lord Acton insisted, to 'suspect power more than vice.' It is particularly necessary to guard against the notion that morality in politics is a flower that blooms especially or exclusively in Anglo-Saxon gardens. The first thing to remember about the policies of Gladstone and Franklin Roosevelt is that Gladstone's Britain and Roosevelt's America were Dominant Powers. This will remind us of the great truth that morality in international politics is not simply a matter of civilized tradition, but is equally the result of security. If British policy in the nineteenth century showed in general perhaps a greater degree of enlightened self-interest than that of any other Great Power in modern history, it was because Britain then enjoyed perfect security. 'We could afford the luxury of gentleness,' as Mr. Harold Nicolson had said, 'because we were completely unafraid.' [1]

Once security is destroyed, all the higher objects of politics are swallowed up in the struggle for self-preservation, a tendency seen in every war. 'A great and civilized Power like England,' said a distinguished writer before the War, 'should strive for a margin of security big enough to make a certain bias in favour of an ideal policy possible, a bias that may never show itself in any specific political action but will inform the manner or spirit of her international conduct.' [2] Yet since it ceased to be Dominant Power, Britain's margin of security has shrunk, and the possibility of an *independent* ideal policy has correspondingly dwindled. This is the vicious circle of power politics: morality is the fruit of security, but lasting security as between many Powers depends on their observing a certain common standard of morality. The League of Nations in theory transformed it into a virtuous circle, by making collective security a moral obligation. But the solution presupposed a degree of enlightened self-interest among the Great Powers that did not exist.

The modern substitute for the Law of Nature might be called the Law

1 *The Meaning of Prestige*, p. 35.
2 F. A. Voigt, *Unto Caesar* (1938 ed.), pp. 272-3.

of Common Material Interest. Contemporary writers on international politics are increasingly driven to place their hopes for future peace on the universal demand for social justice and a rising standard of living, which implies the growth of new economic and social relationships between peoples, and cooperation between Powers 'for the planned development of the economies of geographical areas and groups of nations.' [3] The reality of this common interest is profound, but it does not touch the problem of power. The world communty is still an anarchy, lacking a common superior, and international politics are still power politics. Every Power has an interest greater than welfare, an interest on which it believes that welfare depends and to which welfare must in the last resort be sacrificed—the maintenance of power itself.

It is true that there was equally anarchy in the period when men talked in terms of the Law of Nature, so that its influence upon politics was tenuous and remote. Yet in the long run the idea of a common moral obligation is probably a more fruitful social doctrine than the idea of a common material interest. As the French philosopher Julien Benda has said, mankind has always betrayed its obligations, but so long as it continues to acknowledge and believe in them, the crack is kept open through which civilization can creep. Powers will continue to seek security without reference to justice, and to pursue their vital interests irrespective of common interests, but in the fraction that they may be deflected lies the difference between the jungle and the traditions of Europe. The outstanding contrast between the mood of 1945 and the mood of 1918, which is reflected in the contrast between the United Nations Charter and the League Covenant, is the absence of optimism, the greater realism. Realism can be a very good thing: it all depends whether it means the abandonment of high ideals or of foolish expectations.

[3] Carr, *Nationalism and After*, p. 70.

CHAPTER 2

NATIONALISM

WITH THE successful efforts of the kings of Western Europe to exercise exclusive political control over the people within their domains, the history of the modern state system begins. The king not only won out against the universal claims of Pope and Emperor but brought the lords of his own realm under control, so that he came finally to exercise the exclusive and complete power within his domain which we call sovereignty. In its inception the modern state, therefore, was in many respects simply a greatly enlarged feudal unit governed arbitrarily as the possession of the king. Territory, people, cattle, and goods—all belonged to the king. Modern doctrines of the will of the people, "popular" sovereignty, and nationalism itself were unknown.

The *multistate* system preceded the *nation-state* system which exists today. The transition from the one to the other was the product of several centuries of slow development during which the people in each state gradually came to share a sense of community with one another—the feeling which we call nationalism. This process did not occur at an equal rate in all the states of Europe but was furthest advanced in England and France. The national revolutions in these two states in the seventeenth and eighteenth centuries reflected the new political awareness of the people, their conviction that they were culturally a unique group, and their determination to share power with the king or supplant him altogether.

In the national movements which swept Europe in the wake of the French Revolution, the middle class spearheaded and gained control of the drive to power. Nationalism in its revolutionary beginnings was internally and externally a *liberal* movement designed to limit if not to eliminate the absolute power of kings. Political power was to be shared by the people, as a consequence, on a broader scale. As the middle class gained power, they threw their support to similar movements in "unliberated" states, considering absolute monarchy anywhere in Europe an ultimate threat to their own power. Once this process had been carried to the ultimate extent, the liberal nationalists envisaged that a basic cause of war—monarchial intrigue and ambition—would be eliminated. The middle class had no great sympathy with "power politics," which they equated with monarchial ambition. They wanted to create conditions under which free peoples could trade with one another freely and prosperity for all would be fostered.

When absolute monarchy *did* pass into the dustbins of history, conflicts of a severe nature continued to occur between nation-states, and the expectations of the liberal nationalists were not realized. Indeed, as the people generally came to participate actively in the state and the middle class, forced to extend the suffrage, came to share political power with the masses, the character of nationalism in these states began to alter. A new *integral* nationalism began to make its influence felt, characterized by an intense emphasis upon loyalty to the state in exclusive and particular terms strangely at variance with the liberal, international, world-community ideas of the earlier period. The people began to identify the national prestige with their individual prestige, and as imperialist ventures were embarked upon and the policies of the great powers brought them into conflicts with one another, popular reaction and public opinion came to play an increasingly important role in international relations. Where liberal nationalism dominated much of the nineteenth century, by the twentieth century the new highly patriotic and ofttimes jingoistic integral nationalism had made its impact felt in Western civilization. In the Far East and in other areas now experiencing nationalist feeling for the first time, nationalism has come to mean a curious blend of liberal and integral objectives. At the same time, the rise of ideologies of universal pretensions, including democracy as a mass movement, but especially communism, has raised the question whether nationalism has not itself become obsolete.

The basic questions which are raised by a study of nationalism are therefore two. One is why nationalism has passed in many states where it has long been established from a liberal into an integral phase and why in some cases this process has been carried further than in others. The second question is whether nationalism as the product of the nation-state system is in process of being displaced by larger loyalties on a regional or world basis, whether ideologies are replacing the older loyalties to the sovereign state. It is these questions which the following selections discuss.

The first selection, "Nationalism: What It Is and What It Means," a group study by the Royal Institute of International Affairs, examines the anatomy of nationalism—its trends and tendencies. It points out that nationalism is typically expressed in the beginning as the desire of the cultural group to establish a state which will be under national control. In an earlier day this usually involved limiting the power of the king in a state already existing as a monarchy. Later it came to mean the throwing off of foreign domination and the establishment of a new state altogether. Once this process occurred, the typical goal of nationalism in its liberal form was realized.

The new nation-state possessed a monopoly of the organized force within its frontiers. In democratic states the people controlled the government and set limits on the power of the government to coerce the people. Where this did not occur, totalitarianism easily took root and the nation became an organized community in which the state manipulated public opinion as an instrument of state power for state purposes. Under democracy the power of the state is similarly a perpetual threat of potential dictatorship. It is held in precarious check by the democratic tradition of the dignity of the individual and a zealous concern over civil liberties. Significantly, in the nation-states in the twentieth century there has been a great increase in state control, a tendency to manipulate public opinion, and a corresponding tendency toward integral nationalism as the product of aroused popular passions.

The study points out that the extent to which integral nationalism gains sway is related to the security or insecurity of the nation domestically and internationally. Germany, ravaged by inflation following defeat in war, became the foremost example of this trend. Nazism was extreme integral nationalism. Even the older democracies have not been exempt from a similar tendency on a smaller scale.

In conclusion, the question is examined whether nationalism is inherently bellicose and leads to conflict among men. This view tends to overlook the fact that, as long as men have conflicts, the root of the trouble is not in nationalism but in man. The modern state, as the vehicle of nationalism, is simply the instrument rather than the cause of conflict. If in the future men are politically organized other than in nation-states, the conflicts will not disappear but will be continued through other means and other instruments. This may or may not bring improvement. This is true of regional federations; it would be equally true of a world organized along ideological lines.

In the second selection, "Liberal vs. Integral Nationalism," Professor Hayes examines the development of liberal into integral nationalism, concluding that integral nationalism is implicit in liberal nationalism. This is true, in his view, not only of totalitarian nations but of democracies as well. Three factors, in his opinion, account for this development. One is the militarist spirit engendered by the wars of national unification fought by the liberal nationalists, which encouraged a readiness to use armed force. A second is the feeling of superiority brought about by the success of the liberal nationalists, which convinced them of their own superiority and the necessity for ruling "inferior" peoples. The third factor is the increasing diversion of education from its original purpose of training youth and raising literacy for self-government to inculcation of nationalistic propaganda. These he conceives as world-wide trends.

NATIONALISM: WHAT IT IS AND WHAT IT MEANS

Royal Institute of International Affairs *

In any systematic study of nationalism, the first question which presents itself is that of the relation of nationalism to other forms of group feeling. Is nationalism something *sui generis*, or is it merely a variant of the feeling which binds together Londoners, Trade Unionists, cricketers, or Wesleyan Methodists? The answer . . . is that nationalism is clearly related to those other kinds of group feeling in respect of the emotional impulse underlying it. But it is at the same time differentiated from them in certain important respects. The source of this differentiation is to be found in the peculiar features of the group, the nation, to which the sentiment of nationalism is attached. For the nation is, in the first place, a community rather than an association; that is to say, it covers a comprehensive range of human activities instead of being restricted to a single end, or related groups of ends, as is a Trade Union. A nation combines width and depth and many-sidedness of appeal to an extent unprecedented in other groups. Further, the nation is concerned with political power—a special factor which produces several results. Nobody can place himself outside the bounds of the national activities; voluntary resignation, which is generally open as of right to members of other kinds of groups, or expulsion, which is in other

* A Study Group of the Royal Institute of International Affairs, *Nationalism*, pp. 329–335, 337–340. Reprinted by permission of the Royal Institute of International Affairs, London.

kinds of groups the normal retribution for lack of loyalty, entails in this case the sacrifices and penalties of exile and fundamentally affects every aspect of life. The possibility of either is in any case strictly limited owing to the unwillingness of other nations to accept refugees, while active disloyalty to the nation is met by penalties so drastic as to be a certain deterrent in all but the most exceptional cases. Moreover, the nation, being bound up with the State, is bound up with an insistence on a monopoly of organized force; relations within a nation and between nations ultimately depend on the possibility of coercion, and there is to-day no higher authority overriding this power. Finally, there is the fact that each nation exists not as an isolated unit but as one of a number of other nations similarly constituted. This fact largely explains why it is differentiated, both in form and idea, from earlier organizations such as the Roman and Holy Roman Empires.

Nations are therefore a specific type of group, and it follows that there has grown up round the nation a characteristic system of beliefs or ideology which is unlike that of any other group. That is not to say that all nations will have an ideology identical in all respects, for each nation will clearly have its own geographical and historical environment, which will exercise a decisive influence in moulding the content of its ideology. The relation between two nations and their nationalisms may be compared to that between two languages which, while differing widely in vocabulary, display formal similarities of grammar and syntax which justify the philologist in classifying them in the same language-group.

If the nation and the phenomenon of nationalism which attaches to it is *sui generis,* it is natural to ask whether any distinct species of nationalism can be discerned. Now it is true that there is an apparent difference between nationalism in the nineteenth and twentieth centuries respectively, and between the different forms of nationalism at the present time; and it might be argued, from one point of view, that these differences are so marked as to justify us in making a distinction in kind between two definite species of nationalism. The one emphasizes the value of the nation as distinct from the State. It is based on pride of national culture, and its aim is to create political States on the basis of the national group, by the destruction of dynastic States, and to bring about cultural uniformity within these newly created national States. This type of nationalism was primarily characteristic of those peoples of Central and Eastern Europe which were struggling for national emancipation during the nineteenth century; but its theories and aims were often adopted by the statesmen and philosophers of nations such as Great Britain and France which had already achieved statehood, because it seemed to offer a principle of international organizations suited to their own interests. It was a form of nationalism which seemed at that time to be by no means incompatible with the preservation of world peace or even the attainment of world federation.

This type of nationalism can be clearly distinguished, according to the point of view under discussion, from another type which has largely, but by no means entirely, superseded it in the twentieth century—the more aggressive type of nationalism, the essential characteristics of which are the view of the State as a moral absolute, economic nationalism, and territorial expansion at the expense of alien peoples. Such characteristics clearly render this second type of nationalism incompatible with the peaceful co-existence of nation-States, since it implies the right of any one nation-State to increase its power and wealth by any methods irrespective of the effect on other States. These are the tendencies which have produced in many quarters criticism of the whole national idea: it has been one of the chief purposes of the present study to discover how inseparably they are bound up with nationalism.

Now it is to be observed that this second type of nationalism is integrally bound up with the idea of the State: and it is from the ideology of the State rather than from that of the nation, according to the view under discussion, that the characteristics which have recently brought nationalism into disrepute are derived. They are typical of recurring phases of State development and State philosophy; they have often been exemplified by States which were in no sense nation-States, while there have been periods when nation-States with a mature and well-developed nationalism have been free from one or other of them. They are not therefore to be regarded as being in any way of the essence of nationalism, though they no doubt derive an impetus from their association with nationalism in certain States.

But there is another point of view which, while admitting a *prima facie* difference between these two types of nationalism, would maintain that they are not in reality two different classes of phenomena, but two different phases in the development of the same phenomenon; that as soon as the first type of nationalism has attained its primary object in the identification of nation and State, it is, as a result of that very fact, liable, given certain favouring conditions, to take on the characteristics of the second type. As a result of the very logic of the national idea, which implies that the nation as such has certain indefeasible rights, the ideology of nation and that of State are then fused in a single whole in which the original ingredients are indistinguishable. This is in fact the process which has occurred in the case of some of the more important nations which achieved statehood in the course of the nineteenth century, and whose nationalism has, partly in consequence of that fact, undergone a significant transformation in recent years.

This second point of view is perhaps more consistent with what has been said in previous chapters. Strong arguments were there brought forward for supposing that apparent differences between different types of nationalism are in reality only differences of degree and of historical context, which have affected the conditions under which the various nations have come into being. It was suggested that the character of any nationalism is determined by its environment; that nations as a whole in one century will differ from nations as a whole in another century, while at the same period of time one nation will differ from another as a result of differences in social and economic structure and degree of political development.

If this view is accepted, it will follow that there are infinite gradations of national feeling; and one kind of nationalism will easily and rapidly, in suitable conditions, develop into another. Broadly speaking, the longer a nation has been established and the more secure it feels itself, the more profound and the less demonstrative its nationalism will be. Highly demonstrative nationalism is apt to be the mark of a young and imperfectly integrated nation. On the other hand, periods of crisis in which the national existence or national prestige appears to be threatened, whether from without or from within, may provoke all the symptoms of extreme nationalism even in the oldest established nations. In particular, the popular distinction between 'good' and 'bad' nationalism, or between 'pacific' or 'aggressive' nationalism, should be treated with great caution. Nationalism, as a form of group feeling invoked to justify coercion, is always potentially 'bad' and 'aggressive.' The alleged difference between 'pacific' and 'aggressive' nationalism is attributable, not to any inherent difference either in the character or in the intensity of the feeling, but to a difference in the internal or external circumstances of the nation. It is not the character of the group loyalty, but the situation of the group at any given time, which determines the complexion of its nationalism. The nationalism of nations which are either content in the main with things as they are or are too weak to hope to achieve any improvement by their own strength is 'pacific'; that of dissatisfied nations strong enough to aspire to modify the *status quo* to their own advantage is 'aggressive.'

Or again, the nationalism of those nations whose internal unity is ensured by long tradition and prosperity at home is likely to be more moderate than that of nations whose unity is of recent origin, artificially imposed, or threatened by unfavourable economic conditions. This analysis has an important bearing on the present situation in Europe. It suggests that the violent transformation of the moderate spirit of nationalism in the totalitarian States contains a serious warning for the democratic States of Western Europe; that the moderate spirit which the nationalism of these States has hitherto displayed has been due, not to any innate virtue, but to their highly favourable internal and external circumstances. In recent years their external circumstances have deteriorated, thanks in part to the challenge of the totalitarian States, and at the same time the favourable economic conditions at home, which enabled them to found their national unity on spontaneous cohesion, are rapidly passing away. Is there not a serious danger that, faced with these new conditions, they will be forced to emulate the totalitarian States, not only in their attempts to maintain their external security, but also in their efforts to replace by artificial means the spontaneous cohesion which has hitherto ensured their national unity at home, and that in doing so they will have to abandon the spirit of toleration and moderation and adopt, both at home and abroad, the more ruthless and aggressive spirit of the totalitarian States?

Yet this danger should not be exaggerated. Tradition dies hard, and the tradition of moderation and compromise is so deeply ingrained in the democratic States that, even in circumstances which demand subordination to powerful leaders and the temporary limitation of popular liberties, public opinion will insist that their leaders do not become irresponsible nor popular liberties totally suppressed. Moreover, though their external security is challenged, these States are after all, unlike the totalitarian States, on the defensive. They are seeking to maintain what they have, and not to expand. Their nationalism is therefore likely to retain the moderate and conciliatory quality which befits the defender of his rights. And finally it should be remembered that man is not the blind victim of natural forces. The very awareness of these dangers itself provides the possibility of overcoming them and of ensuring that the democracies shall maintain the virtues of the old type of nationalism without contracting the vices of the new.

Related to the problem of distinguishing different types of nationalism is that of determining the extent to which nationalism is connected with any particular form of government. At the present time, one school of thought emphasizes the historical and philosophical connexion of nationalism with liberal democracy, while another associates nationalism with the modern totalitarian State. The adherents of the first school contend that nationalism is organically connected with the current of thought which found expression in the various declarations of the rights of man in the latter half of the eighteenth century, and which gave birth to the various democratic revolutions. This current of thought was a rebellion against the conception of the dynastic State, and set up in its place the conception of the State as a free association of free men for the development of their natural rights. Its keynote was a protest against every kind of tyrannical interference, and it was therefore logical for the nineteenth-century nationalist to combine his nationalism with hatred for all kinds of forcible control. The creed of such a nationalist implicitly negatived both the idea of 'territorial expansion at the expense of alien peoples' and 'the view of the State as the moral absolute'—in other words, two of the attributes most commonly associated with nationalism as understood at the present time. This school maintains that the autocratic and intolerant manifestations with which nationalism tends at present to be associated are due to the reactions of particular states and their environment upon nationalism *per se*. So far from accepting the identification of nationalism with totalitarian dictatorship, this school considers it a paradox that the modern nationalist should have acquiesced in such a form of government.

The second school would argue that there is a logical necessity by which nationalism develops in the direction of authoritarian collectivism; that the association between nationalism and liberal democracy in the nineteenth century was an association of two ideas which were fundamentally incompatible, and that the development of nationalism in the twentieth century in an authoritarian direction has simply been a revelation in practice of this fundamental incompatibility. This view would seem to be borne out by the study of the development of political ideas from Rousseau through Hegel to Mussolini and Hitler. Democracy claims that there are certain values, such as individual liberty, which are absolute and which cannot therefore be overridden even by the claims of nation or state. Nationalism, in its extreme form, claims that the nation is itself the highest value, and that every other value, even that of individual liberty, must be subordinated to it. This suggests that the more intense forms of nationalism will tend to be associated with authoritarian, or rather with totalitarian, forms of governments; and that association might in a sense be described as necessary.

There is yet a third school, which doubts whether we are justified in associating nationalism either with the democratic philosophy which popularized it in the nineteenth century, or with the totalitarians who claim to be its exponents today. It is possible to hold that nationalism is not necessarily associated with any particular form of government, but that in each case the form of government is decided by the environment of the particular nation and by the general characteristics of the period. The adherents of this view, while agreeing as to the underlying incompatibility between liberal democracy and a fully developed nationalism, would deny the thesis that *all* forms of nationalism necessarily tend to become associated with authoritarian forms of government. This would only follow if it could be shown that nationalism *necessarily* tends to its most extreme form, which does not in fact seem to be the case. Nationalism tends to grow in intensity as a result, not of any inherent logic, but of peculiar circumstances which are only present in certain cases (*e.g.* Germany and Italy), and certain conditions (*e.g.* war). . . .

A matter on which there is at the present moment a particular degree of confusion in popular thought concerns the supposed 'bellicosity' of nationalism. For it is not so much that nationalism leads inevitably to conflict as that the nation, in the present phase of history, is the political unit in which men organize themselves for defending and promoting their most important interests in rivalry with other groups. Ever since the dawn of history—and probably before—human beings have been organized in groups which use force in their dealings with one another. The nation is the political group, and nationalism the political group loyalty, of the present phase of civilization. No doubt the fact that the nation seems to evoke a more intense enthusiasm than other groups gives the resulting conflicts a peculiar intensity. This is the result of the range and complexity of modern social and economic organization. The necessity of conflict resides neither in nationalism nor in the nation, but in the nature of man. It seems Utopian to anticipate a period in which men will cease to organize themselves in groups for the purpose of conflict with other groups. Any hope of progress seems to lie in the possibility of so organizing this conflict as to eliminate or minimize the actual recourse to violence. . . .

. . . The question then arises not merely whether the intensity of nationalism is likely to increase or diminish, but whether nationalism itself is likely to be neutralized or superseded. In this connexion the analogy of religion is frequently quoted. . . . Religion was taken out of politics and 'neutralized,' not through an intellectual conviction that religious wars were ill-advised, and not through a moral conviction that they were wrong, but because political power, and the control of wealth which goes with it, passed, in the countries concerned, from the Church to the rising nation-States. The 'neutralization' of nationalism will occur, if it does occur, not through the growth of an intellectual conviction that nationalism and national wars are ill-advised, or even through the moral conviction that such wars are wrong—these are only factors making for the moderation of nationalism and cannot, of themselves, effect its neutralization or supersession—but through a fundamental change in the basis of political organization, *i.e.* the transference of political power and control over wealth to some kind of political group other than the nation. . . .

If the political group of the future is to be organized on a territorial basis, it will possess many, if not all, of the characteristics which distinguish the contemporary nation-State. Indeed, it may be suggested that, under modern technical conditions, any centralized political unit which is larger than a city-state and yet not world-wide must either develop among its citizens a feeling of a type which may fairly be described as national, or else remain a mechanical conglomeration such as the Hapsburg or Ottoman Empires, unable to make headway against its more integrated competitors, and in perpetual danger of disruption. The States of the present day may well give way, in face of pressure from common enemies or some other stimulus, to larger 'multi-national' political and economic units. But, on the present argument, these new units, if they are to be effective in advancing the welfare of their citizens, will have to develop a common feeling inside their boundaries; and it may be held that this common feeling will in the process of time come to differ from current nationalism merely by the scale on which it operates, and perhaps by the particular slogans which it uses. . . .

As a general conclusion, it may be said that to condemn nationalism as the cause of our present discontents is just as absurd as to exalt the nation into the permanent unit of human society, possessing absolute and eternal values of its own. The nation is the political unit, and nationalism the group symbol, of the present stage of civilization.

LIBERAL VS. INTEGRAL NATIONALISM

C. J. H. Hayes *

Liberal nationalism, arising in the nineteenth century . . . is still with us, very much with us. It nowadays arouses the "oppressed" nationalities of Asia and Africa, as formerly it aroused the "oppressed" nationalities of Europe. . . .

In the twentieth century, however, particularly in Europe and America, has come clearly to light yet another and novel brand of nationalism, a brand which rather arbitrarily may be designated as "integral nationalism." The designation is what Charles Maurras employs to describe the nationalist doctrine of his small and hysterical political party in France—the "Action Française"—but it may conveniently be used, without undue imagination or ambiguity, to indicate certain significant elements in Italian Fascism and even Russian Bolshevism and, curiously enough, in the attitude and behavior of millions of nationalists throughout the world who do not indulge in much theorizing and who are certainly unaware that they are integral nationalists.

* Carlton J. H. Hayes, *The Historical Evolution of Modern Nationalism*, Richard R. Smith, New York, 1931, pp. 164–166, 224–230. Copyright 1931, by Carlton J. H. Hayes. Reprinted by permission of The Macmillan Company.

Integral nationalism may be defined, in the words of Maurras himself, as "the exclusive pursuit of national policies, the absolute maintenance of national integrity, and the steady increase of national power—for a nation declines when it loses military might." It has to do, it will be noted, not with "oppressed" or "subject" nationalities, but rather with nationalities which have already gained their political unity and independence. It is applicable, therefore, to the contemporary nations of Europe and America more than to those of Asia and Africa. Among the latter, liberal nationalism is in the ascendant; among the former, though liberal nationalism is still an active force, integral nationalism has been superimposed upon it and in many minds has actually supplanted it.

Integral nationalism is hostile to the internationalism preached by humanitarians and liberals. It makes the nation, not a means to humanity, not a stepping-stone to a new world order, but an end in itself. It puts national interests alike above those of the individual and above those of humanity. It refuses cooperation with other nations except as such cooperation may serve its own interests real or fancied. It is jingoistic, distrusts other nations, labors to exalt one nation at the expense of others, and relies on physical force. It is militarist and tends to be imperialist. In the face of it, a league of nations or any international sense of peace and security is threatened with sterility and destruction. Besides, in domestic affairs, integral nationalism is highly illiberal and tyrannical. It would oblige all citizens to conform to a common standard of manners and morals and to share the same unreasoning enthusiasm for it. It would subordinate all personal liberties to its own purpose, and if the common people should murmur it would abridge democracy and gag it. All these things it would do "in the national interest."

Such a summary of the teachings of integral nationalism is not derived from the study of a few theorists but, rather, from the observation of hard cold facts in the contemporary world. . . . But integral nationalism could hardly be the living force that it is among the masses in contemporary Europe and even in contemporary America, giving them attitudes and moving them to action, were it not for certain historical factors which, apart from theories, have prepared the way for popular acceptance of a more intensive and forceful nationalism. Of course, the "masses" do not know that they are "integral nationalists," and many of them would probably profess admiration for "liberal" principles and detestation of "integral" principles, if these should be frankly and fully explained to them. Yet the fact remains . . . that the "masses" in most national states today acquiesce in, and on occasion applaud, public policies which partake of the nature of integral nationalism. Even in countries where personal liberties are still guaranteed, where a republican constitution still exists, and where democratic government still functions, the "masses" tend increasingly to evince a chauvinism, an intolerance, and a fanaticism strangely out of keeping with the individualism and internationalism which an older generation of patriots associated with liberal democratic nationalism.

Three factors may be mentioned as specially operating to convert large numbers of Europeans and Americans from the liberal nationalism which was so popular and altruistic at the middle of the nineteenth century into the integral nationalism which is now so widespread and menacing. One has been the militarist spirit engendered by the wars which were undertaken by liberal nationalists in order to free and unify "oppressed" nationalities. Liberal nationalists, it should be recalled, made pacifism an important part of their creed. They desired neither war nor undue preparedness for war. Their pacifist desires, however, they had to reconcile with their paramount desire to redraw the political map along lines of nationality, and they soon discovered that the only way in which they could accomplish this desire, in the existing world of reality, was to incite armed revolts against tyrants and military uprisings against foreign oppressors. Such revolts and uprisings often led to international complications and wars; and liberal nationalists would have been less than human if they had not viewed these struggles as glorious and the military leaders of them as heroic.

Mazzini, for example, was a pacifist at heart, but to realize his dream of a free and united Italy he felt constrained to wage popular insurrections within his country and a series of wars against Austria; and the insurrections, once successful, and the wars, once won, took on a halo in Italian hearts and were naturally glorified by Italian historians and all Italian patriots, liberals included. It was much the same elsewhere. German liberals failed to unify their country without bloodshed in 1848; but when Bismarck succeeded by means of copious bloodletting in three wars from 1864 to 1871, all German nationalists, liberals included, thenceforth looked upon the German army as not only the creator but also the bulwark of German unity and freedom.

In other words, liberal nationalists themselves unwittingly fashioned a martial monster which helped mightily to transform liberal into integral nationalism. For, once "oppressed" nationalities had won their independence by force of arms and accorded enthusiastic praise to their generals and soldiers, they came more and more to feel that only force of arms could maintain their independence and insure their rightful place and prestige in the world. In this way, newly free and erstwhile peace-loving nations armed themselves as they had never been armed when they were unfree, disunited, and less liberal; they now entered into military rivalry with one another on an unprecedented scale; and the World War of 1914–1918 was a result. And the World War itself, in part a consummation of liberal nationalism, has notoriously been, in many places and among many persons, the powerful spark which has ignited the powder-train of integral nationalism.

A second important factor in the transformation has been the feeling of superiority engendered by success. Many a would-be nation, inspired by liberal nationalism, began its struggles for freedom and unity in the nineteenth century with humility and noble resolves; and for its plight and self-sacrificing efforts it won the sympathy and sometimes the active support of foreign nations. But when it actually secured unity and freedom, its success seemed to turn the heads of its people. They grew proud of themselves and self-satisfied. In numerous instances they came to feel that they had acquitted themselves so admirably as to prove their superiority over all other peoples and to justify them in ruling "backward" nations. Having reached the goal of liberal nationalism and being flushed with victory, they treated that goal as a starting-point for a continuing race toward integral nationalism.

This subversive effect of success has been illustrated in the history of Germany, Italy, the United States, and many other nations, and is neatly summarized by Bertrand Russell: " 'I belong,' the oppressed [liberal] nationalist argues, 'by sympathy and tradition to nation A, but I am subject to a government which is in the hands of nation B. This is an injustice, not only because of the general principle of nationalism, but because nation A is generous, progressive, and civilized, while nation B is oppressive, retrograde, and barbarous.' . . . The inhabitants of nation B are naturally deaf to the claims of abstract justice. . . . Presently, however, in the course of war, nation A acquires its freedom. The energy and pride which have achieved freedom generates a momentum which leads on, almost infallibly, to the attempt at foreign conquest, or to the refusal of liberty to some smaller nation. 'What? You say that nation C, which forms part of our state, has the same rights against us as we had against nation B? But that is absurd. Nation C is swinish and turbulent, incapable of good government, needing a strong hand if it is not to be a menace and a disturbance to all its neighbors.' " [1] It is the integral nationalist who here speaks.

A third factor in the transition from liberal to integral nationalism has been the actual operation of certain propagandist instruments which . . . liberal nationalists had devised and employed within unified national states. Those nationalists had established systems of public schools, directed and controlled by the state and compulsorily attended, the original purpose of which was to make the rising generation literate and to train it for liberty and self-government as well as for particular vocations. As such

[1] Bertrand Russell, *Why Men Fight* (1917), 27–28.

school-systems expanded and developed and required more funds for their support, they naturally became both more highly centralized and more responsive to mass prejudices. Soon they were being used for the direct inculcation of nationalism. The majority of their pupils learned enough to be gullible but not enough to be critical. Thus as nationalism became less liberal and more integral, the schools tended at once to reflect and hasten the process. . . .

The freedom of the press and the freedom of association, like free public schools, were advocated by . . . liberals as means of propagating their principles among the masses. But the new freedom was especially utilized by journalists to establish cheap newspapers which, aiming at the widest and greatest possible circulation, catered increasingly to sensationalism and jingoistic nationalism. Thereby these newspapers contributed to the production of integral nationalists. Similarly the new freedom was attended by the founding of many patriotic societies by liberal revolutionaries or veterans of liberal wars, but these very societies in a second or third generation tended to minimize their liberal origins and to emphasize their extreme nationalism. By the end of the nineteenth century all "progressive" national states possessed army leagues or navy leagues, national defense societies, organizations of sons and daughters of veterans, and a multitude of "yellow" journals, all of which helped immeasurably to prepare peoples for the reception of the practices, if not the philosophy of integral nationalism.

Now, in the twentieth century, integral nationalism is essentially religious, fanatically religious. Earlier forms of nationalism, notably the Jacobin and the liberal, were religious, too. But if those earlier forms represented a kind of "New Testament" religion of love and service, with the promise of an apocalypse to the faithful, integral nationalism represents a kind of "Old Testament" religion with jealous and angry gods that insist upon an eye for an eye and a tooth for a tooth.

Integral nationalism involves, according to Maurras, Mussolini, and thousands of other Europeans and Americans, a policy of national selfishness and aggrandizement, a "sacred egoism." Within each national state, its effort is to strengthen and tighten the national bond by every means in its power. Outside, its effort is to make the particular nation feared, or "respected" (as the word goes), by a bold and firm conduct of foreign affairs, backed by military force and accompanied by "prestige." It appeals to the cruder and more exclusively emotional forms of patriotism. Its love of country turns readily into hatred of the alien; its desire for prosperity into competition for territory; and the duty of national service is interpreted as a duty to maintain national unity by unquestioning assent to every decision of government.

CHAPTER 3

THE ELEMENTS OF NATIONAL POWER

In the contemporary world of nation-states, problems of defense and national security are insistent and endless. While nationalism has erected emotional barriers between peoples, and sovereignty, as a legal concept, has divided the powers of government of one nation from that of another, each state remains affected by the acts of other states. Where other states are near and also great in power, the problem becomes particularly acute, since the ability of other states to affect national security adversely is in proportion to these factors. To meet this danger, states have joined in alliances, formed balances of power, and participated in leagues and in efforts at collective security, but their basic and inescapable reliance for security has been on their own national power. In the ultimate sense, the security of a nation depends on the power at its disposal multiplied by the degree of effectiveness with which it brings it to bear upon its problems. This is not only the measure of its chances for survival (in the extreme case of world war); it is also the basis on which its day-by-day diplomacy rests.

In the first selection, "The Fundamentals of National Power," Salvador de Madariaga examines the sources of national strength. The great value of his presentation is that he demonstrates very effectively how many *intangible* factors affect national power. The first element he mentions is mass, but this is in turn affected by the technical capacity of a nation. There is then social discipline, which measures the "coordination of effort" of which the community is capable. These elements comprise the "inherent" strength of the nation, the outward symbol of which is armed forces, but the effect of this power on foreign affairs will vary according to what Madariaga calls "political ability for external affairs." He points out that, when a nation has political ability for internal affairs, it will not necessarily have equal ability for foreign affairs. He then examines what this latter ability consists of—including adequate information on international events and a thorough knowledge of world cultures and therefore the background out of which other foreign policies originate.

Harold Nicolson, in the second selection, "National Character and National Policy," explores this last point raised by Madariaga by inquiring into the effect of national character upon the formulation and implementation of foreign policy. His analysis is both penetrating and amusing. Since he is comparing and contrasting the English and German national characters before an English audience, it is interesting in itself that he feels it possible to dissect the English character so bluntly. His treatment of how Great Britain came to hold Egypt, as seen through foreign eyes and as seen by an Englishman, is particularly revealing. From the foreign point of view it was a diplomatic move "executed with diabolical cunning," while from the English standpoint "We really did not mean to go in; we did really mean to come out." England occupied Egypt not as the foreseen outcome of logical steps but as the result of English "mental indolence." Turning to the Germans, Nicolson asserts that, if the dominant feature of the English character is "mental lethargy," that of the German is "spiritual uncertainty" arising out of "Germany's perpetual lack of outline." By this he means not only geographical outline (Germany is on an exposed plain) but cultural outline as well. This produces what he terms a "warrior conception" of life. Nicolson's analysis of how these national characteristics affect foreign policy and therefore national power has seldom been equaled (particularly on Germany) in the English language.

The third selection, "The Future Population of Europe and the Soviet Union," by Frank W. Notestein and others, is taken from a study done for the League of Nations during World War II. Notestein is concerned with population projections, *i.e.*, with estimates of future populations. Projections of this kind are less open to error than might be supposed, since they are based upon statistical calculations and mortality tables which are fairly reliable. Insurance companies establish their rates on a similar basis. Note that in 1950, for example, allowing statistically for deaths, those who will be fifteen years or older in 1965 are already born. In the same way fertility tables will yield an approximately accurate estimate of future births. Notestein's selection treats particularly future trends in the "prime military" age group, fifteen to thirty-four, and since they furnish the human sinews of war, they are a direct index of national power.

In the fourth selection, "Atomic Energy and National Defence" by Dr. H. E. Wimperis as rapporteur for the Royal Institute of International Affairs study group on atomic energy, the problem of atomic defense is considered. It is one of the most balanced and thoughtful analyses of the effect of atomic energy on national security and power yet written. Dr. Wimperis points out that, although atomic weapons of war are vastly more destructive than conventional weapons, air defense against either variety cannot be predicated for any nation on the basis of "guaranteeing immunity from damage and casualties." The new element which atomic weapons have added to the problem of national defense is that of time—in an atomic war air defense on an adequate basis would have to exist at the outset. He therefore calls for strategic air power at "operational strength as part of ↓ . . permanent forces." Sea power is not, however, obsolete. It is as essential as ever, although changes in hull design and higher speeds may become necessary. In the same way there would still exist a "need for conventional armed forces."

The fifth selection, "Economic Policy and National Security," is taken from three speeches given by Secretary of State Dean Acheson on the relation of international economic policies to national power. They discuss the problems involved in relating "economic, political and social factors . . . to the whole pattern of international life." Acheson points out that "It is hardly possible any longer to draw a sharp dividing line between economic affairs and political affairs." He then examines how American economic strength can be harnessed in America's national interest and enhance national security and power.

In the sixth selection, "Geography and Geopolitics" by Nicholas J. Spykman, the relation of geographic factors to foreign policy and national power is examined. The geographic base of a nation and its physical characteristics have a direct influence on power, since this is vitally affected by size and location. Geography often affects decisively the balance of political forces in the world. The question which Spykman considers, therefore, is the relation of geographic facts to political facts. In form this consideration is an examination of the geopolitical theories of Sir Halford Mackinder, the "father of geopolitics."

THE FUNDAMENTALS OF NATIONAL POWER

SALVADOR DE MADARIAGA *

First as to the inherent power of a nation—apart, let me repeat, from the ability or efficiency with which it is wielded; the inherent power of a nation manifests itself, first, in the guise of such obvious things as the army, the navy, and the air force. A nation from the point of view of its inherent force is generally estimated in the public eye according to whether she possesses one hundred thousand, a million, or five million men. Similarly as to the tonnage of the navy; similarly about the number or power of its airplanes capable of bombing, chasing, or otherwise performing a military activity.

Now this is rather a symptomatic than an essential estimate, for it is evident—it is indeed a truism—that the inherent force of the nation is merely manifested in these forms of power which are its army, its navy, and its air force. It is not there itself. It is the cause of these things; it is not these things themselves. The cause can be traced back from these external appearances to something already more substantial, though not yet quite essential, namely, the economic and financial strength of the nation concerned; for evidently it is only on economic and financial strength that an army, navy, and air force can be efficiently evolved and possessed.

But even this second stage in our analysis of the inherent force of a nation does not go deep enough, and we have to consider now the elements that constitute the force of a nation as manifested, first, in its financial and economic strength or power, and then in its military, naval, and air power.

The first element is mass. If we compare two nations, such as China and Switzerland, we shall at once realize that mass is not an all-powerful element in the estimate of the force of a nation. There is something else than mass. But if you compare Switzerland and the United States you come back at once to realizing that all the same and in spite of your first observation, mass does count. What is then, exactly, the law that emerges from this double comparison, of China and Switzerland on the one hand and Switzerland and the United States on the other? It is that *all things being equal*, as the mathematicians say, the mass does count. I would even go so far as to say that in certain conditions and when the mass is really overwhelming, it is by its sheer presence already an important element in power. May I draw here on a personal recollection? During the Manchurian question, we were once gathered—the members of the Council, except the parties—by Aristide Briand, in his rooms in the Hotel des Bergnes, in Geneva, for

* Salvador de Madariaga, *Theory and Practice in International Relations*, pp. 21-28. Copyright 1937, by University of Pennsylvania Press. Reprinted by permission.

a free and informal discussion. In the course of this gathering, the French Prime Minister and Foreign Secretary, with his inimitable wit and humor, told us he had received the Japanese Ambassador and had said to him, "Mr. Ambassador, I have a friend who is a boxer. He is a very hefty man, a very strong man, and my friend the boxer tells me, 'Well, Mr. Le President, I am afraid of nobody; but I am afraid of a quilt, because I go for the quilt and strike at it with all the might of my fists and the quilt doesn't care at all and I just get tired.' Well, Mr. Ambassador, China is a quilt."

And all that has happened since shows the wisdom of the image struck by the French statesman; the mere fact of mass is already, in itself, an important element of power, of inherent force in the sovereignty of the nation if only because that mass can react in that very efficient way in which its own inertia enables it to react, by passivity. You all remember the enormous effect which the mere mass and distance of Russia produced on the Napoleonic campaigns.

Yet mass of course is not, in spite of all this, the fundamental element in the inherent power of a nation, as shown by the example of very small nations like Belgium and Switzerland, who wield a considerable economic and financial power in spite of their very exiguous mass. What is this, then, due to? It is mostly due to technical capacity, ability, brain-ability, for organizing and leading human beings in the mastering and the controlling of the forces of nature. It is mostly attained through intellectual capacity for the physical, chemical, and mathematical sciences, as well as in the sciences and practical arts of administration and government. This is a force in itself; we need no other definition, and it acts like a powerful factor in the inherent power of a nation.

The next element of power is social discipline; not altogether unconnected with the second, for wherever you find in human beings that technical capacity for controlling the forces of nature, and also for controlling the discoveries of science and even leading them, in which we have seen the second element of power, it generally goes with a predominance of reason over other faculties of the human soul, and therefore an easier coordination of effort in the members of the community, a greater capacity for analyzing events without violence, and consequently the possibility of coordinating all the forces of the community—mass forces and intellectual forces—and enables the government to wield them more firmly in its own hand. With this virtue is very strongly connected the element of patriotism, about which I do not think it is necessary for me to enlarge any further.

So, when closely analyzed, this somewhat dramatic appearance of force, as manifested in the armies, the navies, and the air forces of nations, resolves itself into an individual capacity in the members of those nations for reaching a balance, a government of themselves and of their human relations by reason, excluding violence and therefore a well-organized series of virtues, beginning with the right government of personal affairs which enables the accumulation of financial and economic surpluses in banks, those banks gathering up these surpluses, administering them with wisdom and intelligence, and building up a kind of structure of financial and economic stability which in the end has for its apex the government. The governments in their turn are generally intelligent, since they belong to these advanced nations who are advanced because they themselves are intelligent and technically capable; but moreover, they find already a good deal or most of their work done for them by the fact that the nations which they govern are spontaneously well balanced and well organized. So that they have the immense advantage of possessing in their hand an instrument of force consisting of an element of mass, multiplied by an element of ability.

Quite apart from this inherent force, the ability to wield that force is a most important element toward our estimate of sovereignty. It is evident that the political ability to wield the inherent power of the nation enters already as one of the elements of the inherent force of the nation, since we have admitted—we have indeed put forward—the view that a good deal of this inherent force results from the political capacity of the nation in general to organize itself into a well-built construction of financial, economic, and political forces. But it enters also as a very important element *outside of it,* as a kind of coefficient of efficiency in the manipulation of this force in external affairs. We would then say that political ability for internal affairs is an element of the inherent force of a nation, while political ability for external affairs is a coefficient, and multiplies this inherent force and gives it its efficiency. The coefficient may, as all who have studied arithmetic know, be greater than the unit or lesser than the unit; that is to say, it may increase the inherent force of the nation, or it may decrease it if the political ability for external affairs is not as high as the political ability for internal affairs.

For, and this is a very important point, it does not follow that when a nation has political ability for internal affairs it has an equal amount of it for external affairs. To be sure, certainly it will not be politically stupid for external affairs, for it is not conceivable that ability should altogether change its sign when crossing the frontier; but there are elements in the management of world affairs outside the frontiers of a nation that do not obtain in the management of affairs inside the national frontiers, and therefore it is quite easy to imagine that a government may be more capable of organizing its own inherent force than of wielding it efficiently in the foreign fields.

Without aiming at an exhaustive analysis of the elements that enter into this ability for external affairs, we may enumerate some of them. To begin with, there is a very important element in the knowledge of what is going on, or in other words, in accurate and up-to-date information. Most of the great Powers possess that information as a matter of course. They have the means, the financial means to pay for a sufficient number of foreign representatives, either avowed, such as consuls, or not avowed—they have another name which it is neither necessary nor polite to quote—and these people keep their governments posted with what really is going on.

This factor of accurate information gives to the great powers a tremendous advantage over lesser nations. Take anything that happens in the world nowadays; take, for instance, the Manchurian question; take the Abyssinian question. When the members of the Council gathered in Geneva or Paris or London to discuss these questions, the position of the members of the great Powers who had abundant reports as to what had happened or was going to happen, as to who was who and why he was there, as to the exact financial, economic, political, military background, those members had a considerable advantage over the members of the Council who, belonging to smaller nations, did not possess this accurate and complete information. Here is then an element of efficiency in the wielding of sovereignty in which can at once be seen the considerable difference there is between the big nations and the small nations.

The second element is the capacity for acquiring an adequate knowledge of persons, a knowledge of the persons with whom foreign affairs are actually transacted. This in its turn in great part depends on the knowledge of foreign languages and of foreign cultures, that is to say, on the number of foreign-traveled people at the disposal of the nation in question —that is, foreign-traveled *and* capable of profiting by travel, for there is nothing more traveled than a good portmanteau or trunk, and yet it does not gather much knowledge of foreign people. This assumes that foreign-traveled human beings must be able to see with their eyes and to see with their intellect, and to gather their own conclusions. But not even good observation powers, nor even a good intelligence will be of much avail if behind the people used in foreign employ there is not a sound general outlook, and particularly a sound world culture. The people who are sent abroad—not to *lie* for their country, as runs the famous definition of ambassadors—but to work for the country, must be in a position to pick up what is happening and refer it to a general outlook, a general culture, to what the Germans would call a *Weltanschauung*, which is enlightened and really substantial, so that the observations made refer and coordinate in an harmonious whole.

Finally, a very important element in the control of foreign affairs in the ability to wield the internal force of the nation for foreign purposes is a supply of masterful individuals. Now, masterful individuals cannot be made by machinery. They appear, or they do not appear. They are a kind of person about whom every nation is bound to remain in a kind of Mr. Micawber state of mind, expecting that they will turn up. But here again, we find how unfavored small nations are in comparison with big nations. For it is obvious that a nation with a considerable amount of economic and financial power and with a considerable amount of military power—many soldiers and much tonnage and many airplanes—can, more easily than less developed nations, afford to have a stupid foreign secretary.

NATIONAL CHARACTER AND NATIONAL POLICY

Harold Nicolson *

I now propose to compare the British character and its effect upon British policy with the German character and its effect upon German policy. I take these two instances because they afford me a maximum amount of illustration. . . . I have found that there is a particular quality, or defect if you like, which differentiates the inhabitants of these Islands from the inhabitants of other territories. I have come to the conclusion that the most marked characteristic of the inhabitants of these Islands is mental indolence and mental cowardice. I think that in no country in the world does there exist such cerebral lethargy as there does in England. It always strikes me as strange that the ordinary Englishman who thinks it slightly immoral and decadent not to take physical exercise is apt to regard mental exercises as something Continental and effete. We don't always realise in this country how very lax, how very unformed are our mental biceps. Englishmen are no more cowardly or brave than people in other countries, but mentally they dislike anything that gives them pain, and the whole of English life is largely organised in order to give that very soft shell-fish, the British citizen, spiritual comfort.

If you disagree with me I ask you to consider—though it is rather a digression—the employment not only of the expression "bad taste," but of the expression "affectation." I know very well that if you say anything that might arouse an Englishman's desire to avoid the unpleasant it is said that you have shown bad taste. Anything that makes an Englishman think at all is bad taste; it leaves a nasty taste in his mouth.

* Harold Nicolson, *National Character and National Policy*, Montague Burton International Relations Lecture, 1938, University College. Nottingham, pp. 4, 6–13. Reprinted by permission of the University College, Nottingham, England, and Harold Nicolson.

Then there is the other expression "affectation." I look back upon my boyhood and I remember that when I was seventeen I realized that I was extremely interested in French pictures and deplorably bored by cricket. I felt it ridiculous to waste time hitting one object with another object; had I said that I was bored by this game, but liked French pictures I should at once have been described as "affected."

If you agree about our intellectual indolence you will agree also that it has produced certain effects, some of them good, some of them bad. I will begin with the good. I think mental indolence does produce a distaste for extreme courses. Extreme courses require thinking out, and one thing that no Englishman would ever do is to think anything out. He always stops before he gets to the extreme. That is called "British commonsense."

The second effect is an excellent effect, and I am not going to sneer at it. It is a hatred of hatred and a hatred of fear. I think that is one of the great virtues of the British race—their good humour. But don't let that be put down as an ethical virtue; it comes mainly from moral and mental indolence. A third good point of mental lethargy is its optimism. I don't see how in this climate, in these islands, in these cities which we built during the industrial Revolution—I don't see how a country can survive mentally and spiritually without this tremendous injection of optimism.

Then we pass to the bad effects. Obviously the most serious result of our mental indolence is our incapacity to think. We never plan. Our reliance upon instinct implies a refusal to pry into the future or really to grapple with the facts of the future. Always there is this escape from the unpleasant and especially from any form of long-distance planning. This is a grave intellectual, and I would almost say moral, defect in our nature. It is indeed a curious thing to watch a Scotsman or an Englishman faced either by the really unpleasant or by the conjectural.

These are some of the effects of mental indolence. But we have other characteristics. There is our commercial instinct, our shop-keeping instinct, that love of acquisitiveness and materialism. This leads us to the recognition of the realities of a situation; it leads also to extreme elasticity of policy, and it leads to honesty; not honesty because we "are holier than thou," but because we have learnt the great lesson that honesty means credit, and credit means more money. We are infinitely more honest than other countries in our policy, but is this virtue much more than our old-fashioned shop-keeper point of view?

Then there is a third point. There is what I call roughly Puritanism; by which I mean the continuous search, the perfectly sincere search, for the ethical motive, the power of the idea. The Englishman is not happy unless he can find moral reasons for what he is doing; he is only affected by the real moral idea.

Consider, for instance, British policy towards Egypt since 1882. A for-eigner would say that it was the most brilliant bit of carefully planned imperialism in the whole history of diplomacy, executed with diabolical cunning. We got the French out of Egypt and then we managed to get the Turks out; we then bamboozled the Concert of Europe by means of a sham conference in Constantinople; we then sent Wolseley to suppress the Arabi rising at Telel-Kebir; we then occupied Egypt and have been there ever since. That is the foreigner's point of view. They think it an absolute masterpiece of carefully thought-out Imperialism. But it was not that. We did not know what was happening. We thought it was a noble mission of civilisation. We really did not mean to go in; we did really mean to come out. We gradually slipped into occupying Egypt and then began to search for moral motives. It was quite obvious that we had occupied the country because of the Suez Canal; because of its strategical value as well as its importance to the bond holders. That was the real reason but it did not sound very nice or very pleasant, so we said we were there for the good of the people, which was true. We did the fellaheen a great deal of good. It can only be explained partly through the shop-keeper instinct, partly through the Puritan instinct of always searching for an ethical motive, and partly from our inability to realise what the proposition really was.

Having indicated what the British character is like, how it influences policy, I must consider the question of whether the British character has changed. I do not think that our character has changed at all, or very little; I think our circumstances are changed. Our character and its manifestations in the nineteenth century was based on the fact that we were absolutely unassailable and that the power of supremacy, the power to crush other people, gave us a great virtue. We have lost that; we have lost our invulnerability. There are many people who say that our national character of the eighteenth and nineteenth centuries was based on an alliance between the aristocracy and big business and that this has passed. Aristocracy, it is true, has ceased to be aristocracy, and business to be big. The proletariat has come to complete our character. Our unity is no longer an alliance between the Elizabethan and the Victorian spirit; yet our character is fundamentally and essentially the same. We are still shop-keepers.

Now let me pass to Germany and consider the German character and its effect upon policy. And when I have dealt with that, I shall draw certain conclusions as to the difficulties in Anglo-German relations.

If the dominant feature in the English character is mental lethargy, the dominant feature in the German character is spiritual uncertainty. The main cause of this German uncertainty, diffidence and hesitancy is, to my mind, Germany's perpetual lack of outline. By that I mean not geographical outline only, although being on the edge of other countries does seem to have given the Germans no sharp sense of geographical frontiers. It is also a lack of cultural outline, by which I mean a blurred cultural tradition. It is also a lack of historical outline since Germany suffered much when Augustus withdrew his legions from the Elbe. And it is also a lack of racial outline since the pure German blood has, in the north at least, been diluted by many Slav infiltrations. We who have somewhere at the back of our minds the consciousness that our shores are washed by the silver sea, should try to understand this almost passionate longing of the German to find an outline.

I don't know whether any of you have read a most interesting book on Germany by Frederick Sieburg: it is the most interesting description of the German character I have ever read. The writer says that every German is like a grain of sand blown by the wind, but that in every grain there is a passionate desire to coalesce with others and become one rock. I think that is true. I think if we do not understand this passionate desire for cohesion with other people we shall not for one moment understand the German character. We must always remember that in the German character there are two conflicting tendencies, the one towards international ideas, and the other towards Nationalism. The second tendency was developed by Bismarck and led to extreme concentration. I am afraid that ever since 1870 the Bismarck spirit, the spirit of national concentration, the spirit that might is right, has been the dominating spirit of Germany.

Now what is the result of this uncertainty of outline in Germany? I think we must always try to be sympathetic to their spiritual loneliness, their sense of spiritual forsakenness, their desire to do things with other people, especially with their own people, in what we term the spirit of militarism. You will allow me to tell you a little story. I remember very well when I was in Berlin some five years ago in the Embassy, I found myself sitting next to some banker. I said to him, "How do you keep fit?" He said, "I do physical jerks every morning at seven by wireless. But," he added, "it is rather a bore, because the thing is timed for those people who have to be in their offices by eight. I have not to be in my office till nine. I have therefore to get up an hour earlier than necessary." I said, "But you could get what you want on the gramophone and you could turn it on at eight and it would be all right." And he said, "Oh no, I would not do that because I should not have the pleasure of thinking that thousands of other people were doing it at the same time." Another German, a German educationalist, remarked to me, "How did you organize the week-end movement in England?"

Therefore the first result of this German lack of outline has been to do things with solidarity. Another effect of their uncertainty is their extreme pre-occupation with status. English people never think about status, but the Germans are frightfully pre-occupied with status. That is a point we don't understand.

The final result of their uncertainty and dualism is their militarism; that is a heroic conception of life which is essentially different from our commercial conception. It is important to consider how that affects policy. Let us take first their methods. It is a method of rigid uncertainty, adventurism. It is a method of almost mystical self-sacrifice and the theocracy of the State. It is what Hitler described when he said, "I go forward, inspired by the certainty of a Somnambulist."

There is another thing. It is their extreme sensitiveness. I know we think it funny, frightfully funny, that the German should be so sensitive, but we must remember that the Americans are also sensitive; they are very much closer to the Germans than we are.

The German heroic conception of life leads to what I may call a warrior conception of policy and diplomacy. This warrior conception is one of our great difficulties in dealing with Germany. I believe the ordinary German regards diplomacy as a sort of manoeuvre; that he regards it entirely in military terms; that his method is almost entirely a military method. In fact German diplomacy and policy have all the apparatus of manoeuvres.

Let me now bring this argument, this long argument, back to the point where I started, and illustrate it by certain final suggestions. I started by saying that we can never understand policy unless we understand national character; and I went on to indicate how different characteristics existed with certain fundamental similarities in British and German character, and how important it was to understand those defects and differences in the execution of policy.

I would say further, that national policy is coloured and even governed by national character; and I would say that unless we understand that character we cannot understand the policy. I would say that the approach to diplomacy should be above all a psychological approach; and I would go further and say that we must realise that if we adopt the shop-keeper mentality and approach Germans on a mercantile basis—as we have quite recently done—they then accuse us of *kuhhandel;* they would think that we were not treating them as really respectable people. If, on the other hand—and I would say this to the German—if they approach us from the heroic point of view, we do not understand them, we think they are bullying and blustering. I think it is important for us to realise that in dealing with Germans we should bring our most male qualities to bear—and we have got male qualities—and they should try to bring forward their most feminine qualities. In dealing with the French we should reverse this process, and we should be as quiet, gentle and tolerant as we can be.

I am sure if we approach the foreigner with an understanding of their temperament and nature, and they approach us with an understanding of our temperament and nature we shall achieve a far better, a more reasonable, a more sensible and, I hope, a more hopeful interpretation of foreign policy and foreign diplomacy.

THE FUTURE POPULATION OF EUROPE AND THE SOVIET UNION

FRANK W. NOTESTEIN AND OTHERS *

The population changes of most importance to the economic and political situation of Europe during the next few decades will be those of manpower. Manpower, resources, and technology occupy coordinate positions in determining the economic and political potential of nations. At any given stage of development the number of people, especially men, in the productive ages sets the outer limits of economic productivity. The war has amply demonstrated the reality of this limit, which may be no less apparent in the years of reconstruction to come. . . .

Regional Changes in Manpower Potential

Rapid changes in the distribution of [young] manpower as among the major regions will result from differences in the rates of growth. . . . The situation is similar to that of the total population: rapidly declining proportions of manpower in Northwestern and Central Europe, slightly rising proportions in the South and East, and a rapidly increasing proportion in the Soviet Union.

When consideration is confined to the men of prime military age, the eastward movement of weight of manpower is even greater. At the beginning of a conflict, most of the fighting in modern warfare is done by men between 15 and 35 . . . losses are heavily concentrated in this group because older men are used only when manpower resources run low. . . . Every country in Northwestern and Central Europe [will have] fewer men 15–34 in 1970 than in 1940. Of the Southern countries only Portugal [will have] a larger number at the end of the thirty-year period.

* Frank W. Notestein and Others, *The Future Population of Europe and the Soviet Union*, League of Nations Publication, II. Economic and Financial, 1944, II.A.2., pp. 117, 131–137. Notestein's figures do not include World War II casualties. On the other hand, he is discussing Soviet figures for the 1937 boundaries which were, of course, smaller than those of the U.S.S.R. today. These adjustments tend roughly to counterbalance one another.

Of the Eastern European countries only Lithuania [will show] a decrease, though all except Russia decline between 1955 and 1970. Greece, Roumania, and Yugoslavia [will have] a 20 per cent or more increase in military manpower; the U.S.S.R., a 44 per cent increase. The gain of men 15–34 in the U.S.S.R. [will be] over 13 million as compared with a loss of almost 5 million in Europe west of the Soviet Union. This gain alone is larger than the 1940 manpower of Germany, the Soviet Union's closest rival in Europe.

TABLE 8

RANK ORDER AND NUMBER OF MEN 15–34 YEARS OF AGE IN 1921 AND AS PROJECTED FOR 1940, 1955, AND 1970, FOR THE TEN MOST POPULOUS COUNTRIES OF EUROPE

(In millions)

	1921		1940		1955		1970	
U.S.S.R.	1	24.6 [1]	1	30.1	1	36.9	1	43.3
Germany	2	11.1 [2]	2	11.3	2	10.9	2	9.9
United Kingdom	3	6.7	3	7.6	3	6.9	5	5.7
Italy	4	6.1	4	7.4	4	8.2	3	7.4
France	5	5.6	6	6.0	6	6.1	6	4.8
Poland	6	4.5	5	6.1	5	7.0	4	6.3
Spain	7	3.5 [3]	7	4.3	7	4.8	8	4.1
Roumania	8	3.1 [4]	8	3.4	8	4.3	7	4.2
Czechoslovakia	9	2.2	9	2.6	10	2.5	10	1.9
Yugoslavia	10	1.8	10	2.6	9	3.3	9	3.2

[1] 1926.
[2] 1925.
[3] 1920.
[4] 1930.

The changing relationships between major countries presented in Table 8 reflect regional differences rather than random differential trends. Russia, which two centuries ago probably did not have a much larger manpower potential than France, before the last war had already achieved an overwhelmingly predominant position in Europe as regards sheer numbers. Interwar trends and almost inevitable future developments will further strengthen this position. By 1970 the U.S.S.R., in its 1937 boundaries, has as large a source of primary military manpower as Germany, the United Kingdom, Italy, France, Poland, Spain, and Roumania combined, these being the seven European countries with the greatest forces of manpower outside of the Soviet Union.

In Europe west of the U.S.S.R., Germany has had the largest military manpower since 1871. This position would not be altered by 1970 if the projections were realized and if Germany were maintained with anything approximating the 1937 boundaries. Germany's predominance among Western countries is somewhat increased in the thirty-year period; her position vis-à-vis the East deteriorates rapidly. On the projections the momentum of rapid growth carries Italy and Poland ahead of both France and the United Kingdom, which are in the vanguard of decline. The emerging numerical importance of manpower in Eastern countries is evidenced by rapid increases in Roumania and Yugoslavia. Comparative trends in Czechoslovakia and Yugoslavia reflect the demographic differences between countries of relatively equal population and resources with bonds of common ethnic origin, one of which has been modernized and industrialized, the other of which is still largely a peasant country.

. . . The relationship of manpower to military potential is far too complex to permit the generalization that this shift in manpower balance to the East necessarily means an equivalent shift of military potential. The latter is a composite of manpower, natural resources, technology, economic organization, national psychology, and political alliances. Technological inequality may be so great that manpower is an inconsequential factor, as has been the case in the relation of the Western powers to the more backward areas of the world. Obviously, past political disunity has rendered ineffective overwhelming numerical superiority in such countries as China. The relationship may be generalized in the statement that within the framework of a given stage of political organization and technological development, manpower is an important element in military potential and military achievement; as between different cultures the influence of numerical differences in manpower may be great or insignificant, depending on a multitude of economic, political, and psychological factors. . . .

In Europe population trends and manpower have undoubtedly had a role in the balance of power. The hegemony of France in Europe in the past was certainly not unrelated to the fact that she was the most populous as well as the most advanced of European countries. The rise of German power is certainly in part a function of her predominance in manpower as compared with countries of equivalent technological development.

The eastward movement of the weight of manpower has significance only in company with other elements. Manpower, to be effective, must be implemented with effective economic and military weapons and organized in the context of political unity. However, it seems reasonable to suppose that the past history of diffusing industrial civilization will continue. From its nucleus in England, the Low Countries, Northern France, and Western Germany this technological civilization has spread in widening concentric circles to include Scandinavia, Germany, Bohemia-Moravia, Austria, Northern Italy, and Northern Spain. In embryonic stage, it has become established in the capitals and larger cities of Eastern Europe. In

Russia, through vigorous governmental action, the transition from a feudal to an industrial society has been made in little more than a generation. With political security there is an almost irreversible trend toward an increasingly effective industrialized economy. At the same time that the manpower of Eastern Europe and the U.S.S.R. is becoming much larger relative to that of Western Europe, this formerly backward area is also finding the tools to make its manpower effective.

ATOMIC ENERGY AND NATIONAL DEFENCE

H. E. WIMPERIS *

In the nineteen-thirties, before the development of radar, our chances of intercepting and destroying enemy bombers flying at 200 miles an hour seemed highly precarious. The prospects of successful air defence were very poor; yet radar, even in its early form, multiplied the operational efficiency of our fighter force by ten. When the war came the Battle of Britain was won by a narrow margin. Radar had tipped the scales and had enabled our defence to be conducted successfully.

Now we are confronted with the problem once again in a different form. The size and distribution of the targets remains the same, but speeds in the future may be anything from 300 to 3,000 miles an hour with piloted bombers, automatically-controlled pilotless aircraft, or rockets. In the past, if 10 per cent of piloted bombers could be shot down, the casualties were reckoned as prohibitive to the attackers; over a period this proved broadly to be right. With atomic bombs, if 90 per cent were destroyed and only 10 per cent penetrated the defence, the damage caused would still be very great indeed. Thus, if the air defence organization were to be made capable of producing results of the same order as those of the past, it would have to be far more efficient and able to counter enemy aircraft or missiles travelling at much higher speeds. Consequently, without some unexpected scientific discovery it looks as if the air defence organization of the future would have little chance of attaining anything like an equivalent standard to that of the second world war.

It is not suggested that we need relinquish the idea of an air defence organization that would be highly efficient within its limits; but with all

* H. E. Wimperis, "Nuclear Energy in War," *Atomic Energy, Its International Implications*, Royal Institute of International Affairs (a Discussion by a Chatham House Study Group), pp. 53–59. Copyright 1948, by Royal Institute of International Affairs, London. Reprinted by permission.

the research and development likely to be required the cost might prove enormous. No doubt some form of guided pilotless missile with homing properties would be needed to replace the familiar fighter anti-aircraft gun combination. An improved and more extensive early warning system with very high speed communications, and a much better system of identification of enemy missiles would be requisite. When all these measures had been put into operation, projectiles with nuclear explosives would still be likely to penetrate the defence. There might be no enemy pilots whose morale could be broken down by inflicting casualties and whose attacks could thus be frustrated. Clearly, the problem has assumed different proportions altogether. It needs re-thinking.

Our air defence was never based on the principle of guaranteeing immunity from damage and casualties. The practical limit of what the air defence organization, together with that of civil defence, could do, was to enable us to endure the enemy blows while we developed offensive power great enough to gain a decision in our favour. In the second world war this was a protracted business. The big new factor that differentiates the past from the future is that in another war, if it ever came, there would be no time for a systematic build-up of air power, neither could the air defence organization reach a standard of efficiency good enough to shield us while we slowly built up our forces and accumulated strategically offensive power.

The conclusion appears inescapable. Strategic air power represented by an efficient air force with its bases properly disposed and stocked, together with its communications and supplies, would have to be built up to operational strength as part of our permanent forces. Long range rockets wtih atomic heads might form part of this striking force, if their manufacture had not been banned by international agreement. Whatever the shape and composition of the offensive force, it would have to be ready from the word 'go.' The air defence organization covering vital bases would be its indispensable adjunct, but we should have to rely chiefly on our striking power for defence. This armed power might be invoked, if ever required, under the auspices of the United Nations, or in the last resort it might have to be used under Article 51 of the Charter of the United Nations. In 1943–5 the strategic use of air power appeared as one of the biggest factors in war. In future, if atomic weapons were introduced, it would undoubtedly become the predominant factor, and would govern the planning of all operations at sea, on land, or in the air.

It is not the purpose of this paper, nor would it be appropriate, to try to predict in detail how these strategic requirements might affect our fighting services. The policy and plans concerning these changes would be the business of the professional authorities responsible at the time. The existing conceptions of battleships, armoured land forces, and bombers would be almost bound to undergo extensive change, but their development is largely empirical and has to be threshed out by research and experiment. Even the authorities most intimately concerned could hardly with any confidence forecast developments in equipment and weapons twenty years ahead. Thus, at a time like the present, when the application of recent scientific and technical discovery to armaments is in a state of flux, we can hardly do more than speculate on general tendencies of the kind illustrated by the following example.

The security of our sea communications in war would be just as important as ever to the maintenance of our war potential. It would have to be ensured by the combined exercise of naval and air power. It is evident that naval operations could not be attempted without overriding air superiority, but the fighting ship could not wholly escape the risk of heavy air bombardment, possibly with atomic weapons. It would have to undergo a process of adaptation to new conditions. With the types of radar likely to be developed, retention of the present above-water profile of heavy ships would have to be reconsidered. High speed, manoeuvrability, and a greater resort to submersion would seem to be the only practical antidotes to air attack. Hull design might have to undergo considerable changes. Higher speeds would emphasize the need to suppress hydrodynamic drag. The underwater shock waves produced by atomic weapons would call for appropriate design of hull structures. Substantial protection to crews from gamma radiation would have to be considered. The possible introduction of motive power based on nuclear energy, and the application of reaction propulsion to weapons in the primary armament, might exert a major effect on layout. As a whole, these developments might permit and enforce a considerable reduction in overall dimensions of fighting ships.

It has already been suggested that whatever modifications took place in organization and design, the introduction of atomic weapons would not dispose of the need for conventional armed forces. Nevertheless, it is difficult to resist the conclusion that the new weapons and their operational management would ultimately assume the dominant position. The remaining divisions of the armed forces would become secondary to the newer developments, and the whole perspective of armaments might have to be re-drawn to bring it within the limitations of cost in money and manpower.

In addition to what has been discussed above, there is a further important aspect of defence which must be included. It is evident that the vulnerability of our great industrial and administrative centres in relation to attack by atomic weapons has increased out of all proportion. No defensive measures would be considered adequate if a serious attempt were not made to reduce that vulnerability. In principle the answer is dispersion. Its application under modern conditions is fraught with difficulty.

Hitherto, at any rate in peace-time, the business of defence has been considered mainly a matter for soldiers, sailors, and airmen under the aegis of the government. It has only superficially touched the lives of the civilian population. Admittedly new signs are beginning to be visible. The part that scientists and technicians from outside the services played in the second world war was of major importance. Their collaboration was so productive that it is likely to become permanent.

The threat of atomic weapons is such as to suggest that more far-reaching measures might have to be accepted. It is certain that organization for civil defence and all that the name signified in the second world war would have to be developed on a greater scale. In the struggle for survival, until suitable offensive operations had turned the tables on an enemy, the morale of the people would be a critical question, and it would certainly be braced up by the consciousness that everything possible had been done to insure against unnecessary damage and casualties.

It is commonly supposed that nothing short of a completely troglodytic existence, with its uncivilizing influences, would be any good as a protection against atom bombs. Even then, the effects of deep penetration bombs might be hard to counteract. It is fortunate that such a wholesale transformation is impracticable. On the other hand, less drastic measures which would afford a degree of protection are by no means out of the question.

It is evident that the steel-framed concrete anti-earthquake buildings at Hiroshima and Nagasaki survived remarkably well even at a few hundred yards from the centre of the explosion. Even small shelters stood up against blast effects. In spite of the fact that gamma radiation proved at once the most potent and most insidious cause of casualties, the different effects of neutrons and gamma rays on people who were caught in the open, and on those who were protected in varying degrees inside buildings that did not wholly collapse, were very marked. It was also evident that quite thin clothing provided some protection against burns due to heat flash.

The advantages of dispersion were shown by the percentages of people killed at varying distances from the centre of the explosion. After allowance had been made for better buildings and rescue services in a city like London, it was estimated that with the type of bomb used against Japan, 90 per cent of the casualties would prove fatal at 500 yards from the centre, whereas at 1,500 yards fatalities would be reduced to 28 per cent.

Admittedly the bombs used aginst the Japanese cities were detonated well above the ground, but, allowing for this, suitable cover and dispersion should nevertheless afford a considerable degree of protection.

A fuller appreciation of these factors might exert a strong influence on the planning of public services and utilities with an eye to defence requirements, the design of new buildings more resistant to shock waves and capable of protecting the population against irradiation, and the spacing of buildings with avenues to act as firebreaks. These measures might come to be looked on, not as an unnecessary imposition, but as a matter of common prudence. The extra cost would have to be regarded as a reasonable insurance, if not for this, then for succeeding generations. In brief, defence might have to become the people's affair, a matter of public safety.

Whether a popular appreciation of the threat of atomic weapons might eventually lead to the attainment of a synoptic view such as is implied above is a matter of conjecture. It is hard to imagine that, without public understanding and support in a big way, any democratic government could make appreciable progress in imaginative planning and adaptation of the national structure to accord with the requirements of defence. The present need is a constructive approach to this difficult problem in which all sections of the professions and the business community alike would have to participate. An intelligent compromise between the ideal requirements of defence and those of social and industrial progress could only emerge from an educated and powerful body of public opinion.

ECONOMIC POLICY AND NATIONAL SECURITY

DEAN ACHESON *

There is a character in one of Molière's plays who wondered what prose was and then was surprised and delighted to learn that he had been speaking it all his life.

The process of change in human relations is much like the speaking of prose. All of us are principals in the process of social change, but we seldom see ourselves in this flattering light. Lacking the detached perspective of the historian and preoccupied as we are with the affairs of each day, we are often quite unaware of how different is the way we think, act, and react today from the way we did a few years ago.

* Dean Acheson, *Strengthening the Forces of Freedom*, Department of State Publication 3852, General Foreign Policy Series 28, 1950, pp. 36–37, 42–43, 75–76.

All of us in this country are aware, I think, that the conceptions and convictions that underlie our foreign policies have undergone a momentous transformation in the last decade. Certainly we have had to cast our economic thinking in a new perspective and to see the economic, political and social factors in relation to the whole pattern of international life.

We have come to realize more clearly than ever before that foreign economic policy is not made in a political vacuum. It is hardly possible any longer to draw a sharp dividing line between economic affairs and political affairs. They are related and interacting. Each complements and supplements the other. They must be combined in a single unified and rounded policy designed to serve and advance the national interest.

An affirmative approach to the solution of world economic problems is an imperative need of our times. The United States Government has taken the lead in developing such an approach.

While providing the necessary emergency aid, we have persistently pursued a long-range international economic program. We look forward to the day when the differences between doing business abroad and doing business at home will be much less than at present—when currencies will be generally stable and convertible, trade and travel subject to only moderate restraints, and investment subject to fewer risks. To these ends we have been promoting currency stabilization; we have been negotiating trade-barrier reductions; we have been negotiating simplification of travel arrangements; we have been negotiating treaties and agreements covering investments, commerce, transport, and communications; we have been working on a plan to increase the flow of technology, and we have been working in the United Nations and its specialized agencies in a wide variety of fields. Most particularly, we have been working in that oldest and most important field of economic relations among nations—trade.

We have continued our established and effective policy embodied in the Reciprocal Trade Agreements Act. The usefulness of this principle was greatly extended by means of the General Agreement on Tariffs and Trade concluded by 23 of the world's leading trading nations, in 1947.

The capstone of the economic structure we are seeking to erect is the charter of the International Trade Organization, which President Truman [has] submitted to the Congress for ratification. . . .

The purpose of the proposed [International Trade] Organization is to promote international trade. The charter of the organization establishes for the first time a comprehensive code of international fair trade practices. The organization, to be established within the United Nations structure, will provide a forum where nations can bring their trade grievances and settle their trade problems.

The code of fair trade practices set forth in the charter is a code designed to help achieve an international trading system in which traders may buy and sell where they please—the system economists call "multilateral trade"—the system under which private enterprise and free competition have the best chance to prosper.

This alinement with basic United States principles did not just happen. The United States took the lead in urging the United Nations to bring together representatives of 54 nations to work out an agreed charter. We provided the original document which they used as the basis of their deliberations. We did this because we believed that the world would not achieve economic recovery and world peace unless the unhealthy and chaotic conditions of international trade, resulting from two world wars and a serious depression, could be improved. It was clear that the growth of all sorts of new devices to restrict and channel trade would continue unabated if each country tried to solve its economic problems at the expense of others. Only by joint effort by many countries could we hope to alter the trend toward diminishing trade and bilateralism.

The United States is the leading exponent of free enterprise and free competition. The United States is a leading advocate of the advantages of multilateral trade. The United States believes in the cooperative approach to the settlement of international problems.

It is not enough to believe and to advocate. American leadership in world affairs has always depended on our willingness to translate belief into action, to practice what we preach. In a real and practical way, American action with respect to the International Trade Organization is a test of our leadership. It is a demonstration not only to ourselves but to all other free peoples that we really believe in free enterprise, competition, and multilateral trade. Such a practical demonstration is sorely needed at this time, when freedom is hanging in the balance in many parts of the world and millions of people are looking in our direction for assurance that we really mean what we say.

We have learned the bitter lesson that freedom is often a fragile thing —that it may wither, especially when its roots are shallow, under the stress of privation and economic crisis. It is where the people of a free nation can see the prospect of achieving a fuller and more satisfying material existence that the institutions of freedom are most likely to be secure and the advocates of peace are most likely to hold firmly the reins of government.

The European nations have made great strides toward restoration of their production and economic health, by their own efforts and with our help through the European Recovery Program. They need to do much more.

In the Point Four Program we hope to help in the long process of building production and bringing about higher standards of living in under-developed areas.

But increase in production is not enough. Countries must be able to exchange the goods they produce for the goods of others which they need. In other words, production and trade are two sides of the same coin, both necessary to its value.

If the European countries are to retain the ground they have gained and stand on their own feet, they must be able to trade as freely as possible with each other, with us, and with the rest of the world.

If the underdeveloped countries are to grow in economic strength they must have the greatest possible access to the supplies and markets of the rest of the world.

If the United States is to remain strong and prosperous and secure, it needs a healthy and expanding export and import trade.

If the channels of world trade are not cleared, the economic recovery and the economic development of other countries will be impeded: our own goods will not be able to find markets abroad; we will be hindered in our efforts to get many of the things we need or want from abroad; and economic frictions between nations will be generated as they vie with each other in the manipulation of restrictions on each other's trade. . . .

The fundamental answer is, therefore, to build a successfully functioning political and economic society of free nations. This is the positive task in the doing of which we create the spiritual and material base essential to our defense and to the preservation of the integrity of our way of life.

It is a very difficult job to build a successfully functioning system. It requires adjustments to the changed and changing facts of international life. And it is hard to make adjustments—people tend to resist change and to stick to old ways of doing things. A conscious effort of will is necessary to overcome our native inertia.

We must decide what we need to do and are prepared to do to help carry forward the recovery gains which have been achieved and to help create a secure and firm foundation for the future.

The Europeans must not only expand their productive capacities but must, through greater efficiency, through lower costs and improved marketing methods, improve the competitive position of their products in the markets of the United States and the rest of the world.

This is the reason why we favor the closer association of the free countries of Europe in the economic field as we do in the political and military fields. Such association is necessary if they are to put their economies on a sound, competitive, self-supporting basis. If Germany, instead of being a threat to world peace, is to be a constructive partner in Europe, it is necessary to build a European framework within which her skills and energies can be used for the benefit of all. We hope this drawing together of the European countries will take place within a framework of closer association of all the free countries of the world, including our own. Unity in Europe requires the continuing association and support of the United States. Without it, free Europe would split apart.

GEOGRAPHY AND GEOPOLITICS

NICHOLAS J. SPYKMAN *

Any attempt to consider the geopolitical relationships among . . . states . . . must first emphasize the fact that the total earth's surface has, today, become a single field for the play of political forces. The whole world is now known geographically and changes in the arrangement of forces in one region must affect the alignment of forces in others. The development of sea power has given the political power of the states of Western Europe access to the coasts of the farthest continents. The conditions of power on one continent are inevitably reflected in the distribution of power on another and the foreign policy of any state may be affected by events taking place throughout the world.

The fundamental fact which is responsible for the conditions of this age of world politics is the development of ocean navigation and the discovery of sea routes to India and America. Maritime mobility is the basis for a new type of geopolitical structure, the overseas empire. Formerly, history had given us the pattern of great land powers based on the control of contiguous land masses such as the Roman, Chinese, and Russian empires. Now the sea has become a great artery of communication and we have been given a new structure of great power and enormous extent. The British, French, and Japanese empires and the sea power of the United States have all contributed to the development of a modern world which is a single field for the interplay of political forces. It is sea power which has made it possible to conceive of the Eurasian Continent as a unit and it is sea power which governs the relationships between the Old and the New Worlds.

This important change in the organization of power was first comprehensively recognized and analyzed in 1890 by Alfred Thayer Mahan. . . .

* Nicholas J. Spykman (edited by Helen R. Nicholl), *The Geography of the Peace*, pp. 35–37, 38, 40–43. Copyright 1944, by Harcourt, Brace and Company, Inc. Reprinted by permission.

It was, however, the British geographer Sir Halford Mackinder who, in 1904, first studied in detail the relations between land and sea power on a truly global scale. He used a map centered on Siberia . . . and treated Europe, not as the center of the world, but as one of the many peninsulas of the Eurasian land mass. . . .

The Mackinder analysis began with the idea of the heartland. The vast expanse of Siberia was considered as a unit in terms of internal drainage and access to the sea. This enormous area can be treated as a unit because all its rivers drain into the Arctic Ocean or the inland waters of the Caspian and Aral Seas and no part of it touches the open ocean at any point. The nomadic tribes who have always inhabited this region have been intermittently engaged in trying to reach the sea and have, consequently, exerted a tremendous military pressure on the states that have at various times occupied the coastal regions. This latter territory Mackinder calls the inner crescent and includes within its boundaries all those continental states which had direct access to the sea and thus exercised both maritime and land power. Beyond lie the islands and off-shore continents of the outer crescent while the fringes of the oceans are occupied by the overseas continents of the Western Hemisphere.

From this point of view, the continuity of the land masses of the Western Hemisphere is broken up because the Siberia-centered map shows the Atlantic seaboard of the North and South American Continents facing Europe, while the Pacific seaboard faces the Far East. At the time Mackinder first published his map, in 1904, it was prophetic rather than true to the realities of the day for it was not until the Panama Canal was completed that the full power potential of the United States was made available in the Western Pacific. Today, however, a map with the Eurasian Continent in the center has a definite validity because the Western Hemisphere has a vital interest in and connection with both the European and Far Eastern sections of the Old World.

The constellation of power in the Eastern Hemisphere was defined by Mackinder in terms of the relation between the land power of the heartland and the sea power of Great Britain. Security for the British Empire depended on the preservation of a power equilibrium between the maritime and continental states of the world island. If either of the two gained the ascendancy, the whole continent would be dominated and the pivot area controlled by a single power. With this vast land mass as a base, a sea power could be developed which could defeat Great Britain with ease. It was, therefore, the task of British foreign policy to prevent any integration of power on the continent of Europe and, particularly, to see that nothing would lead to an effective military alliance between Germany and Russia. . . .

The importance of the heartland region was first suggested to Mackinder by his conception of the value of a central position with interior lines of communication made powerful and unified by the development of land transportation to a point where it could begin to compete with sea communication. He also envisaged the transformation of the steppe land from an area of low economic potential to one of high economic potential. . . .

The significance of this region was also defined by Mackinder in terms of position. The fact that the core of the heartland lies in the center of the Eurasian land mass gives it the advantage of interior communication with the lands of the inner crescent. It is obvious that the problems of an army which is working along the diameters of a circle of territory will be less difficult than those of forces which have to function along the circumference of that same region. In comparison with the exterior lines of British naval power running from Great Britain through the circumferential highway around the Eurasian rimlands, Russia has interior lines of communication. The transportation lines between Russian Turkestan and Northwest India are certainly interior as compared with the sea route from Southampton to Karachi.

It must be pointed out, however, that interior lines function in terms of two points of reference rather than one. The relations between the center and the circumference may easily be changed if a point on the circumference becomes in turn the center of another circle of communication. Thus, the strategic implications of the position of the heartland in relation to the British Empire have meaning only if the military strength to be applied at the Indian frontier originates in Great Britain. The moment the defense of that frontier or the Persian frontier or the Chinese frontier rests on a locally developed war potential, the whole concept of interior and exterior lines is changed. What is true for India and China if they have to be defended by British sea power is no longer true if their military strength can be made a by-product of their own industrial development. In this case, unless the raw materials of power in the central Asiatic regions of Russia turn out to be great enough to balance those of the rimland regions, Soviet strength will remain west of the Urals and it will not be exerted overpoweringly against the coast lands to the east, south, and southwest. . . .

The general pattern of political action on the Eurasian Continent has been defined by Mackinder in terms of the pressure of nomadic peoples in the heartland outward against the states of the rimland. When the nomads who roamed the grasslands of the central lowland were replaced by the organized power of the Russian state, the same pattern was continued. The empire sought access to the sea and found its road blocked in the nineteenth century by British sea power which had expanded across the Eurasian littoral. The British imperial position rested on a maritime encirclement of the Eurasian land mass which was maintained by the predominance of her naval power along the circumferential maritime highway. This position could be threatened by the emergence of a competing sea power on the littoral of the continent, or by the penetration of Russian land power to the coast.

So convinced was Mackinder of the fact that any conflict in Europe must follow the pattern of land power–sea power opposition that he declared, in 1919, that the true character of the war which had just been concluded was not visible until after Russia had been defeated. British sea power could then be considered to be fighting against a land power which dominated the heartland. This interpretation would seem to be a little hard on the role of France as a land power, and it is strange to ignore the three years of Russian resistance on the eastern front.

Like all good geopolitical analyses, however, the Mackinder study represented a picture of the constellation of forces which existed at a particular time and within a particular frame of reference. It was first elaborated in 1904 before the conclusion of the British-Russian Entente of 1907 and was strongly influenced by the previous century of conflict between Russia and Great Britain. When, in 1919, his book *Democratic Ideals and Reality* was published, the conception of an inevitable historical opposition between Russian land power and British sea power was re-emphasized. The fallacy of this blanket application of a theory of history is seen when we realize that the opposition between these two states has never, in fact, been inevitable. Actually, in the three great world wars of the nineteenth and twentieth centuries, the Napoleonic Wars, the First World War, and the Second World War, the British and Russian empires have lined up together against an intervening rimland power as led by Napoleon, Wilhelm II, and Hitler.

In other words, there has never really been a simple land power–sea power opposition. The historical alignment has always been in terms of some members of the rimland with Great Britain against some members of the rimland with Russia, or Great Britain and Russia together against a dominating rimland power. The Mackinder dictum "Who controls eastern Europe rules the Heartland; who rules the Heartland rules the World Island; and who rules the World Island rules the World" is false. If there is to be a slogan for the power politics of the Old World, it must be "Who controls the rimland rules Eurasia; who rules Eurasia controls the destinies of the world."

CHAPTER 4

IMPERIALISM AND WAR

AMONG THE most prevalent and recurring phenomena in recorded history are those of imperialism and war. These phenomena antedate the present nation-state system although we customarily tend to discuss them in terms of that system. Their close interrelationship has often been remarked, and the following selections bring out the link between them clearly.

By imperialism we generally mean the attempted or actual acquisition of new territories which an imperialist power wishes to control. This control may be obvious and admitted, symbolized by raising the national flag over the new domain or formally annexing it; it may be less overt and more subtle, taking the form of "concessions" and "spheres of influence" with the fiction maintained, often because of the reactions of other powers, that the territory in question is still independent. Imperialism in its most obvious form is characterized by naked aggression; however, territories may be controlled without being occupied. The effects are much the same.

Until recently imperialism was often regarded as the gaining of, or the attempt to gain, *colonial* domain. In the first selection, "Imperialism and World Politics," Parker T. Moon, in a notable statement describes imperialism from this point of view. The great value of this analysis is that, while Moon accepts the traditional view of the classical writers on imperialism (that "the dominant directive motive was the demand for markets and for profitable investment by the exporting and financial classes" [1]), he insists upon investigating why the masses of the people followed their leadership. He points out that "it requires ideas, attuned to instinctive emotions, to make modern nations fight." Even though Moon accepts the economic motivation of financial and other groups interested in imperialism, he recognizes that even by the nineteenth century the reactions of the people as a whole to proposed policies were decisive in the shaping of the foreign policies of the

[1] Hobson, *Imperialism*, pp. v–vi.

great powers and that the people did not support imperialist adventure out of a conviction that they would *personally* gain economically. Their reward was rather an enhanced national prestige. Moon describes the ideas which have been "particularly potent" in imperialism as resting upon and springing from the instincts of fear, self-preservation, self-aggrandizement, and innate pride. Although Moon does not apply these instincts to an inquiry into the causes of war in general, it is revealing how readily they do apply. The instincts which explain colonial imperialism also explain the phenomenon of war.

The second selection, "Imperialism, the Highest Stage of Capitalism," Lenin's best known and most frequently quoted writing, analyzes what he calls "capitalist imperialism." He admits that imperialism and co'onialism existed "even before capitalism"; he does not make the point often attributed to him that capitalism *causes* imperialism but states merely that imperialism under capitalism is an "essentially different" kind of imperialism in its *effects*. He visualizes a world of capitalist powers, their actions in foreign policies dictated by the financiers in control of the governments. As an industrialized power expands production, it must seek new markets to absorb the surplus; equally important, it must find new and profitable (as well as safe) places in which to invest its surplus capital for large profits. The safest p'ace to invest is one in which the territory is under the financiers' own control, *i.e.*, under the control of the government which they dominate. As the governments seek to annex these new colonial domains, they engage in intense rivalries with one another which create tensions. As the supply of unclaimed lands is exhausted, this rivalry reaches the critical point: to make further gains one great power can succeed only by despoiling another great power of its territories. There is thus no doubt in Lenin's mind of the connection between imperialism and war. Capitalism breeds imperialism, and because the profit motive cannot be denied, wars are inevitable.

Lenin's significant contribution to the theory of imperialism is the direct linking of imperialism and war. Although Lenin wrote during an era of *colonial* imperialism, he forecast a time when imperialism would take the form—as it did under Nazism—of aggression by civilized states on other civilized states, designed to enslave them and convert them into new co'onial areas within Europe itself.

The classical writers on imperialism—both Marxist and non-Marxist—agree upon the essentially economic motivation of imperialism. Moon, unlike Lenin, who conceived of the masses under capitalism as an enslaved proletariat, understood the active and essential part which the emotional willingness of the people to participate p'ays in modern imperialism. The Marxists and classical non-Marxists differ, however, in their analysis of the *ultimate* effects of imperialism, the non-Marxists generally emphasizing the decline of colonial imperialism and the Marxists emphasizing the universal increase in tensions between nations that in the twentieth century have frequently produced the threat or actuality of universal war. This they ascribe to capitalism, since they are forced by the limits of their dogma to assume that the politically inactive and "enslaved masses" could not be at the root of it. Integral nationalism as one explanation of modern war is therefore lost upon the Marxists.[2]

In the third selection, "The Non-economic Roots of Imperialism," E. M. Winslow repudiates both these interpretations of imperialism to the extent that they rest upon economic explanations of causation. Winslow penetratingly analyzes the relation of imperialism to war and the substitution of economic causation for the primeval notion that wars were a catastrophe wrought by God's anger upon sinful men. He points out that there is no "conceivable economic cause in the vicious circle wherein war itself engenders more war." He does not distinguish between colonial imperialism and imperialism as aggression and war between great powers. Where the battlefield or scene of conflicts occurs is immaterial in his view. Similar causes bring war whatever its pretext—colonial domain or the rectification of a European frontier. He explores the part which ideas play in bringing on conflict between states as well as whether or not nations struggle for power as an end in itself or as a means to an end. It is his contention that we instinctively shy away from the idea that nations seek power for the sake of power and that the economic explanations as to why nations come into conflict has been widely accepted precisely because of its rationalization of the power struggle in terms of the sought end of amassing profits or wea'th. In short, Winslow is arguing that imperialism and war are caused by man's struggle for power, using the modern nation-state as the vehicle for conflict and that economic motivation plays at best a minor role.

The fourth selection, "The Causes of War" by Wi'lard Waller, is devoted to war itself as a political and social phenomenon—to the

[2] See the introduction to Chapter 2 for a discussion of integral nationalism.

causes of war. It is revealing to note how closely his description of the emotional "milling process" which the people of a nation preparing for war go through compares with the emotional processes which Moon analyzes in a nation embarking upon imperialism. Waller examines various purported causes of war: the moralistic theory, which on the simplest level claims that wars occur because bad men cause them; a more sophisticated moralistic version, that wars are made to correct wrongs and remedy evils; the psychological theory, that men fight because of an instinct of pugnacity; the demographic theory, that overpopulation necessitates expansion; the economic interpretation, that war springs out of economic causes; and the "primitivized economic interpretation," that wars are instigated by the "merchants of death." While Waller is prepared to admit the importance of economic causes in creating conditions conducive to war, he advances the theory that wars are really caused by "movements of public opinion" which all these factors combine to create. He asserts that we have wars because we develop "war fever"—a cumulative psychological-emotional reaction which, although originating in a clash of interests between nations, is self-sustaining once started and cumulatively builds up tensions which dispose peoples to fight.

In conclusion it should be noted that current writers on imperialism and war make no distinction between the cause of imperialism and the cause of war. They place responsibility on the tendency of man to seek power, which leads to conflicts between states, or else, as with writers to be considered in later chapters, they assert that war is implicit in the anarchy of the nation-state system and can be done away with only by terminating the existence of sovereign states.

IMPERIALISM AND WORLD POLITICS

Parker T. Moon [*]

. . . Imposing as the array of importers, exporters, shippers, financiers, admirals, generals, officials, diplomats, missionaries, explorers, and poli-

[*] Parker T. Moon, *Imperialism and World Politics*, pp. 67–74. Copyright 1926, by The Macmillan Company. Reprinted by permission.

ticians may appear when reviewed in detail, still it remains true that these active imperialist interests are minority interests. The overwhelming majority of a nation has no direct business, or professional, or military interest in colonial empire. Not only is this true of the poorer classes, who of course have no colonial investments, but it applies also to many, probably a majority, of capitalists and business men. Indeed, imperialism might appear to be directly contrary to the economic interests of many business men. For instance, American ownership of Hawaii injures the beet-sugar producers, by admitting Hawaiian cane sugar free of duty. French ownership of Algeria may injure French wine-producers by developing the production of Algerian wine, much of which is used to slake the thirst of Frenchmen, in substitution for domestic vintages. The issue is not between "capital" and "the masses"; capital is divided, one section against another, one industry against another. Why, then, does the majority so cheerfully follow the leadership of the imperialist minorities?

Not direct interests, but ideas, not property or profession, but principles, actuate the public at large. The theories spread broadcast by imperialist propaganda are the dynamic factors impelling nations to send out armies, defray expenditures, risk wars, for the conquest of distant colonies and protectorates. It requires ideas, attuned to instinctive emotions, to make modern nations fight. The ideas which have been particularly potent in imperialism are the idea of preventive self-defense, which awakens the primitive emotion of fear; the idea of surplus population, resting on the instinct of self-preservation; the ideas of economic nationalism, and national prestige, appealing to instincts of gregariousness and self-aggrandizement; and an aggressive sort of altruism, which gratifies our innate pride. These ideas require analysis.

Fear, so easily aroused in the human soul, and so powerful when once awakened, is a cardinal factor in imperialist world politics. The citizens of modern nations fear attack, defeat, conquest. To persuade them that such calamities may be prevented by preparedness for war, is a relatively easy task, as the universality of armies and navies all too convincingly testifies. But of what use is a navy without coaling stations and naval bases? Thus the argument proceeds. If hostile fleets are to be held off from a vulnerable coast, the nation must have outlying naval bases and defeat the enemy's squadrons before they approach. That Great Britain has secured naval bases in all the seven seas, every schoolboy knows. But Great Britain is not unique in this respect. The need of naval bases was one of the chief arguments used by Jules Ferry in the eighties to justify French annexations. It is one of the most popular justifications for American ownership of the Philippines, Hawaii, Samoa, Porto Rico, the Danish

West Indies. It has given anxiety to the Japanese, the Germans, the Dutch, the Italians.

A kindred theory, springing from the same motive of self-protection, is that a nation must control raw material in time of war. It is all very well, imperialists argue, to purchase iron, and coal, and cotton, and rubber, and nitrate, and oil from neighbors in time of peace, but in war a nation must have its own supplies, else its cannon will lack shells, its arsenals will stand idle without coal, its warships, tanks, and airplanes will have no fuel, its laboratories will look in vain for ingredients of explosives. What argument could be more plausible, or more moving? The unimpassioned student may perhaps inquire whether ownership of oil wells in some distant colony will be of value, in war, to any except the supreme naval power, that is, England. But to the "man in the street" such doubt rarely occurs.

Even more influential has been the idea that the great civilized nations, being "overpopulated," need colonies as outlets for their "surplus population." To France, of course, no such argument could be applied, nor was it much used in England; but it has enjoyed an extraordinary vogue in Germany, Japan, and Italy, and it is not unfamiliar in the United States. In a densely populated country, where competition for employment is keen and the cost of living is rising, it is easy to believe that overcrowding is responsible for unemployment and poverty, and that additional breathing-room for the teeming millions is an absolute necessity. The case is all the more convincing, if thousands of emigrants are annually leaving their "overcrowded" mother-country, to find homes in more spacious lands. . . .

A little reflection reveals the fallacy of using "surplus population" as an argument for imperialism. Development of industry and commerce enables supposedly overpopulated countries to support ever-increasing populations. For such development, a country needs increased investment of capital at home. Emigrants leave, not because there is no room for them, but because they believe they can earn more money, or enjoy greater freedom, elsewhere, and they seek prosperity, regardless of flag or nationality, in the country that seems to offer the most attractive opportunities. The colonies that were to be had, and were taken, during the imperialist age from 1875 to the present, have been unsuitable for European colonization, and have failed to attract immigrants. We shall return to this problem later on, but for the present the point to be made is, that the idea of surplus population, fallacious as it may be, has been and still is a vital factor in popularizing imperialism.

The third popular belief, which we have called economic nationalism, has already been elucidated but needs practical application here. The teachings of economists and arguments of List and Fabri and Ferry and

Chamberlain and their compeers have sunk so deeply into popular consciousness, that Europeans, except Socialists, and many Americans take
it for granted that there is such a thing as "national wealth," and that
this thing is increased if a rich colony or a profitable concession is secured
overseas. The diamond and gold mines of South Africa are regarded
as an addition to Britain's store of wealth; the resources of North Africa
are added to those of France; the profits to be made by an oil concession
in the Near East or in Mexico are added to the income of the American
nation. Germany, it has been generally assumed, was made poorer by the
loss of her colonies in 1919.

There might be other ways of looking at such matters. Norman Angell
and other persuasive pacifists have endeavored to prove that conquests
do not profit a nation. A sceptic may ask whether "national wealth" is
more than a phrase; certainly the profits of Cecil Rhodes were not shared
by the denizens of the London slums, nor have the dividends from Mexican oil been distributed equally throughout the American nation. One
might even go further, and inquire whether the Boer War, while profitable
to mine-owners, did not prove an actual loss, in money, to the bulk of
English taxpayers. But national sentiment stills all such doubts, and perhaps even a pauper may have some share in the glorious consciousness
that "we" own rich mines here and fertile fields there; that "we" have
billions invested in tropical lands. And certainly national sentiment re-
sponds with instant thrill when one's fellow-countrymen clash with for-
eigners in rivalry for a railway concession in some backward country, or
for the commerce of a colony. So strong is this sentiment, that applause
rather than surprise greets the action of the foreign minister or secretary
of state who officially takes up diplomatic cudgels to defend against foreign
competitors the business interests of certain citizens belonging to his
nation, albeit he would not think of giving the same governmental support to a private business interest at home.

Quite as subtle, and as potent, is the complex of imperialist ideas
clustering around the notion that a nation's honor and prestige must
be zealously cherished. The fundamental impulse is primitive enough to
be easily comprehended. Each of us naturally desires any group or organization with which he is identified to be better than rival groups. Our
own egotism, or vanity, may perhaps be at the bottom of the desire, for
we enjoy the prestige, whether it is reflected by our family, our fraternity,
our college, our club, our team, our city, our state, or our nation. Most
of all our nation. We are willing to die for that, but not for club or
college. The impulse may be simple, but the applications in imperialism
are subtle. For example, the desire for prestige, for greatness, impels
Italian taxpayers to pour out hundreds of millions of lire on a relatively

barren African empire. Possessing unprofitable and rebellious but impressively extensive colonies, enables Italians to feel that they belong to a Great Power; that theirs is one of the imperial races. The hearts of true Britons beat faster at the thought of England's world empire and world mission, at the sight of world-maps showing Britain's vast possessions all colored in conspicuous red. Germans—before the great defeat—demanded their "place in the sun," meaning a large share of tropical Africa and Asia, as the rightful heritage of a great nation, and eagerly published maps showing Germany's ambitious claims. Frenchmen, learning the phrases of Ferry, repeated the prophecy that unless France built up a great African empire she would become a second or third-rate power. And what patriot desires his nation to be third-rate?

The same solicitude for prestige is responsible for the belief that a nation, a great nation, must punish atrocities or insults to the flag, and protect its citizens and their property in other countries. To refuse protection, most of us feel, is to sacrifice national honor. No proud nation can tolerate affronts. The blowing-up of the United States battleship *Maine* had to be avenged in blood. . . .

National honor is at stake also when two imperialist nations contend for the dubious privilege of conquering a backward nation. When, for example, Germany questions the right of France to subject the unruly and bankrupt African empire of Morocco, it would be humiliating for France to yield, and no less humiliating for Germany: national honor is involved. Even though a compromise may be affected, there will be widespread resentment in both countries, for national honor admits of no compromise.

Finally, some attention must be given to what may be called, for lack of a better name, aggressive altruism. Kipling styled it "The White Man's Burden" . . . to govern and civilize the Asiatics and Africans, the backward peoples who are half devil and half child, sullen and wild. Jules Ferry made it plainer; the "superior races" (including France, naturally) have "the duty of civilizing the inferior races." France has a *mission civilisatrice* in Africa. Germans devoutly believed in their call to give German Kultur to the hapless negroes of Africa,—or, more accurately, to impose it upon them by force. Americans, to a lesser degree, take pride in the sanitary, educational, and other reforms which they have achieved in conquered islands of the Caribbean and Pacific. President McKinley declared, as a reason for annexing the Philippine Islands, that "there was nothing left for us to do but to take them all, and to educate the Filipinos, and uplift and civilize and christianize them as our fellow-men for whom Christ also died." Wilson's Mexican policy was, as Ambassador Page told the British government, "shooting men into self-government." The British foreign secretary found this phrase difficult to grasp, but he had no difficulty in appreciating England's beneficent task of keeping order in India and other disorderly countries.

This is altruism and aggressive altruism, because it means using force, brutal force, to impose on unwilling native peoples the blessings of . . . civilization. . . . An altruism so earnest as this is a very important factor in the popular support for imperialism.

Altruism, national honor, economic nationalism, surplus population, self-protection—such are the principles or ideas which nerve nations to valiant feats of empire-building. The initiative, to be sure, is taken by interests; but the support is given by ideas. When a colony or a protectorate is acquired, the first steps are taken, as a rule, by the business or naval or missionary interests . . . not infrequently the public, ignorant not only of what has been going on, but even of the geographical location of the region about to be annexed, is confronted with an accomplished deed, a *fait accompli*, which needs only to be officially solemnified, popularly applauded, and, perchance, defended. Then the ideas function. The public rallies to the support of importer, exporter, banker, or shipper, missionary, administrator, admiral, or explorer. Imperialism, nay, all history, is made by the dynamic alliance of interests and ideas.

IMPERIALISM, THE HIGHEST STAGE OF CAPITALISM

V. I. LENIN *

We see . . . how "complete" was the partition of the world at the end of the nineteenth and beginning of the twentieth centuries. After 1876 colonial possessions increased to an enormous degree, more than one and a half times, from 40,000,000 to 65,000,000 square kilometres, that is, one and a half times greater than the area of the "home" countries, which have a total of 16,500,000 square kilometres. In 1876 three powers had no colonies, and a fourth, France, had scarcely any. In 1914 these four powers had 14,100,000 square kilometres of colonies, or an area one and a half times greater than that of Europe, with a population of nearly 100,000,000. The unevenness in the rate of expansion of colonial possessions is very marked. . . .

Alongside the colonial possessions of these great powers, we have placed the small colonies of the small states, which are, so to speak, the next pos-

* V. I. Lenin, *Imperialism, the Highest Stage of Capitalism*, pp. 80–84, 88–89, 123–124, 126. Copyright 1939, by International Publishers Co., Inc. Reprinted by permission.

sible and probable objects of a new colonial "share-out." Most of these little states are able to retain their colonies only because of the conflicting interests, frictions, etc., among the big powers, which prevent them from coming to an agreement in regard to the division of the spoils. The "semi-colonial states" provide an example of the transitional forms which are to be found in all spheres of nature and society. Finance capital is such a great, it may be said, such a decisive force in all economic and international relations, that it is capable of subordinating to itself, and actually does subordinate to itself, even states enjoying complete political independence. We shall shortly see examples of this. Naturally, however, finance capital finds it most "convenient," and is able to extract the greatest profit from a subordination which involves the loss of the political independence of the subjected countries and peoples. In this connection, the semi-colonial countries provide a typical example of the "middle stage." It is natural that the struggle for these semi-dependent countries should have become particularly bitter during the period of finance capital, when the rest of the world had already been divided up.

Colonial policy and imperialism existed before this latest stage of capitalism and even before capitalism. Rome, founded on slavery, pursued a colonial policy and achieved imperialism. But "general" arguments about imperialism, which ignore, or put into the background the fundamental difference of social-economic systems, inevitably degenerate into absolutely empty banalities, or into grandiloquent comparisons like "Greater Rome and Greater Britain." Even the colonial policy of capitalism in its *previous* stages is essentially different from the colonial policy of finance capital.

The principal feature of modern capitalism is the domination of monopolist combines of the big capitalists. These monopolies are most firmly established when *all* the sources of raw materials are controlled by the one group. And we have seen with what zeal the international capitalist combines exert every effort to make it impossible for their rivals to compete with them; for example, by buying up mineral lands, oil fields, etc. Colonial possession alone gives complete guarantee of success to the monopolies against all the risks of the struggle with competitors, including the risk that the latter will defend themselves by means of a law establishing a state monopoly. The more capitalism is developed, the more the need for raw materials is felt, the more bitter competition becomes, and the more feverishly the hunt for raw materials proceeds throughout the whole world, the more desperate becomes the struggle for the acquisition of colonies. . . .

Finance capital is not only interested in the already known sources of raw materials; it is also interested in potential sources of raw materials, because present-day technical development is extremely rapid, and because land which is useless today may be made fertile tomorrow if new methods are applied . . . and large amounts of capital are invested. This also applies to prospecting for minerals, to new methods of working up and utilising raw materials, etc., etc. Hence, the inevitable striving of finance capital to extend its economic territory and even its territory in general. In the same way that the trusts capitalise their property by estimating it at two or three times its value, taking into account its "potential" (and not present) returns, and the further results of monopoly, so finance capital strives to seize the largest possible amount of land of all kinds and in any place it can, and by any means, counting on the possibilities of finding raw materials there, and fearing to be left behind in the insensate struggle for the last available scraps of undivided territory, or for the repartition of that which has been already divided. . . .

If it were necessary to give the briefest possible definition of imperialism we should have to say that imperialism is the monopoly stage of capitalism. Such a definition would include what is most important, for, on the one hand, finance capital is the bank capital of a few big monopolist banks, merged with the capital of the monopolist combines of manufacturers; and, on the other hand, the division of the world is the transition from a colonial policy which has extended without hindrance to territories unoccupied by any capitalist power, to a colonial policy of monopolistic possession of the territory of the world which has been completely divided up.

But very brief definitions, although convenient, for they sum up the main points, are nevertheless inadequate, because very important features of the phenomenon that has to be defined have to be especially deduced. And so, without forgetting the conditional and relative value of all definitions . . . we must give a definition of imperialism that will embrace the . . . essential features: . . . .

Imperialism is capitalism in that stage of development in which the dominance of monopolies and finance capital has established itself; in which the export of capital has acquired pronounced importance; in which the division of the world among the international trusts has begun; in which the division of all territories of the globe among the great capitalist powers has been completed. . . .

We have seen that the economic quintessence of imperialism is monopoly capitalism. This very fact determines its place in history, for monopoly that grew up on the basis of free competition, and precisely out of free competition, is the transition from the capitalist system to a higher social-economic order. We must take special note of the four principal forms of monopoly, or the four principal manifestations of monopoly capitalism, which are characteristic of the epoch under review.

Firstly, monopoly arose out of the concentration of production at a very advanced stage of development. This refers to the monopolist capitalist combines, cartels, syndicates and trusts. We have seen the important part that these play in modern economic life. At the beginning of the twentieth century, monopolies acquired complete supremacy in the advanced countries. And although the first steps towards the formation of the cartels were first taken by countries enjoying the protection of high tariffs (Germany, America), Great Britain, with her system of free trade, was not far behind in revealing the same basic phenomenon, namely, the birth of monopoly out of the concentration of production.

Secondly, monopolies have accelerated the capture of the most important sources of raw materials, especially for the coal and iron industries, which are the basic and most highly cartelised industries in capitalist society. The monopoly of the most important sources of raw materials has enormously increased the power of big capital, and has sharpened the antagonism between cartelised and non-cartelised industry.

Thirdly, monopoly has sprung from the banks. The banks have developed from modest intermediary enterprises into the monopolists of finance capital. Some three or five of the biggest banks in each of the foremost capitalist countries have achieved the "personal union" of industrial and bank capital, and have concentrated in their hands the disposal of thousands upon thousands of millions which form the greater part of the capital and income of entire countries. A financial oligarchy, which throws a close net of relations of dependence over all the economic and political institutions of contemporary bourgeois society without exception—such is the most striking manifestation of this monopoly.

Fourthly, monopoly has grown out of colonial policy. To the numerous "old" motives of colonial policy, finance capital has added the struggle for the sources of raw materials, for the export of capital, for "spheres of influence," i.e., for spheres for profitable deals, concessions, monopolist profits and so on; in fine, for economic territory in general. When the colonies of the European powers in Africa, for instance, comprised only one-tenth of that territory (as was the case in 1876), colonial policy was able to develop by methods other than those of monopoly—by the "free grabbing" of territories, so to speak. But when nine-tenths of Africa had been seized (approximately by 1900), when the whole world had been divided up, there was inevitably ushered in a period of colonial monopoly and, consequently, a period of particularly intense struggle for the division and the redivision of the world. . . .

Monopolies, oligarchy, the striving for domination instead of the striving for liberty, the exploitation of an increasing number of small or weak nations by an extremely small group of the richest or most powerful nations —all these have given birth to those distinctive characteristics of imperialism which compel us to define it as parasitic or decaying capitalism. . . .

The receipt of high monopoly profits by the capitalists . . . makes it economically possible for them to corrupt certain sections of the working class, and for a time a fairly considerable minority, and win them to the side of the bourgeoisie of a given industry or nation against all the others. The intensification of antagonisms between imperialist nations for the division of the world increases this striving. And so there is created that bond between imperialism and opportunism, which revealed itself first and most clearly in England, owing to the fact that certain features of imperialist development were observable there much earlier than in other countries. . . .

From all that has been said in this book on the economic nature of imperialism, it follows that we must define it as capitalism in transition, or, more precisely, as moribund capitalism.

THE NON-ECONOMIC ROOTS OF IMPERIALISM

E. M. WINSLOW *

It is now the fashion to deride the old simple unilateral explanations of imperialism and war—those which single out the sinful nature of men, their wickedness and pure cussedness, the fighting instinct, race hatreds— because they are too vague, too general, and give no practical clues as to remedies. They are regarded as almost, but not quite, as naive as the reasons supposedly assigned universally by primitive man—that supernatural forces such as gods and devils impose war upon sinful man. From the external and supernatural, emphasis shifted to natural causes, and from this to social forces. . . .

In contrast with the potency of social forces, of which economic factors are declared to be the most important in causing war, the idea of war being caused by forces which have no conceivable dependence on economic activities and motives must, indeed, seem blind and superficial. And from this point of view the thesis that "the cause of war is war," or that war and imperialism are ancient behavior patterns appearing as atavisms in a modern society, where the weight of economic activity is against such conflicts, or that political causes can stand independently of economic motives, is likely to be dismissed as a thesis to be shunned by the scientific mind.

Yet precisely because it is possible to define economic activity in terms of something more than human selfishness and deadly rivalries, it is also pos-

* E. M. Winslow, *The Pattern of Imperialism*, pp. 65–70. Copyright 1948, by Columbia University Press. Reprinted by permission.

sible to consider the interpretation of imperialism and war in terms other than economic terms. In the modern age, regardless of how much economic causation there may have been at first, imperialism and war may represent behavior patterns which have little or nothing to do with economic activity in the sense of cause and effect. It is entirely possible to think of them as institutions capable of standing independently as ends in themselves. That they use economic resources is another matter, entirely different from the question whether imperialism and war are caused by the desire to acquire economic resources.

Much as we may be forced to criticize the economic interpretation of history, the fact remains that it marked a big advance over the notion that war and conquest are mere visitations upon man for his wickedness—catastrophes ordained by God and carried out by the devil; it was "a healthy antidote to some of the romantic, political, military, or other unilinear or surface interpretations; it was even a good antidote to the refusal to interpret at all." [1] But in going all out for the theory that man's actions can be traced to the fact of his dependence on material things, the new interpreters of history went too far in the other direction and forgot that the pursuit of power can arise from a number of causes in which economic motives play no evident or conceivable part. Fear, the father of hate, has certainly played an enormous role in sending armies and navies against an enemy possessed of similar emotional qualities, across lands and seas which of necessity become the pawns of conquest. And those familiar stand-bys of the history books (which generally are given a place considerably below the economic factors)—love of adventure, prestige ("face"), strategy, civilizing missions, and political and ideological clashes—have certainly been potent causes of imperialism and war. Nor is there any conceivable economic cause in the vicious circle wherein war itself engenders more war. Militarism as a profession, feeding upon and perpetuating itself, combined with the love of power can be a delight and an end in itself, an all-consuming passion capable of perverting the material bases of welfare to the services of war and conquest. And there is truth also in the simple conclusion which history has taught some of its chroniclers, that imperialism is a demonstration of the principle that the more you have the more you have to have to hold what you have. Simplest of all, yet who can deny it some hearing, is the blunt view that imperialism and war are results of pure human cussedness.

These powerful, yet uncomplex, motives and vicious circles, simple as they are, seem somehow to elude most of the modern interpreters of history. Their place has been so largely taken by the economic—essentially capital-

[1] Heaton, "The Economic Impact on History," in Strayer, ed., *The Interpretation of History,* p. 105.

istic—interpretation of modern imperialism and war, that one can only conclude that the scientific mind feels obligated to forswear obvious causes and seek the underlying and mysterious, the hidden and complex forces. This would be all right were it not for the danger that these forces, particularly the economic ones, may be imagined rather than real—supplied by the interpreter rather than merely uncovered. As such they may also be dangerous in that they create conflict and cause war, for these are the stuff of which ideologies are made; the clash of nations over ideological differences itself attests to the reality and power of ideas and notions, compared with which real economic forces may be as nothing.

It is not easy to accept the idea that power is an effective end in itself; it is much easier to regard it as a means to some other end. Power regarded as an end leaves nothing more to be said except that its users employ all available means to accomplish the end. But power regarded as a means opens up enormous possibilities for identifying it with political power, economic power, and every other field of human activity which strengthens the hand of the seekers after power. There is a great confusion here in the tendency to identify economic power with "naked power," yet nearly all the interpretative history written in the past two or three generations has been based on the assumption that economic power and naked power are identical. This assumption, erroneous though it is, gives the interpreter of history something tangible to grasp, because the concept of economic power adds to the general concept of power a dimension which enables the interpreter to talk in terms of tangibles such as economic surpluses, the struggle for markets, and the defense of territory, with a feeling that he is on the track of real and analyzable forces. Armed with these concepts, the interpreter of history has much to talk about; he can go far beyond the simple thesis that power as an end in itself uses all available means to accomplish the end.

If the theory of war and conflict were as simple as this, and if it were accepted by historical writers as a self-evident truth, there would be no need to bolster it with an economic formula. If men fight for perfectly obvious reasons, the historian can hardly be expected to supply the reasons. It would hardly occur to him to account for every battle in a war; therefore, why should it seem any more necessary to account for every war in the universal business of fighting?

Through its doctrine of class warfare, based on the clash of economic rivalries between capitalist and worker, and its accompanying parade of economic "inevitables" flowing from the operation of the profit motive and the accumulation of capital, plus the grinding movement of its business-cycle mechanism, which transmutes competition into monopoly, the economic interpretation of history, regardless of whether or not it describes and explains real events, has captivated the minds of untold millions and set them marching towards the socialist victory which from the first is promised as the inevitable end. The climax of this view of history, growing inevitably out of its doctrine of the class struggle, is the doctrine of the struggle between nations. The logic from here on, granting all the past assumptions, is so powerful as to convince its numberless devotees that there can be no other assumptions and no further argument. The whole thing behaves like a law of nature, and who is man to question it, let alone to oppose it?

Once the class struggle is made to appear incontrovertible, it is only a step to the struggle of nations for supremacy. There have been class struggles and international wars, ever since there were classes and nations, but whether they were inevitable or not is immaterial. The whole force of the modern economic interpretation is that they are made inevitable once all the forces which spring from hunger, the scramble for the earth's resources, and human selfishness converge and congeal in capitalist society. Therefore, modern imperialism, say these economic interpreters, is unavoidable, because it is a natural consequence of capitalist institutions. War is, in turn, the inescapable end-product of this imperialism.

Even if it be granted that all wars have had some sort of imperialistic base (they have been fought mostly on land, if not over it), the point made is that only modern imperialism has had a capitalistic base. Consequently, it is not sufficient to answer the economic interpreters by saying that because imperialism and war are eons older than capitalism their modern manifestations cannot be blamed on capitalism. This may have a point, but it is not their point, which is that capitalism not only has not prevented imperialism and war, but indeed at long last has made both inescapable. The final pay-off is that capitalism must be abolished and socialism must become triumphant before we can hope to see an end to these troubles.

The philosopher of history who created this astonishing way of looking at history was, of course, Karl Marx. Neither he nor the majority of his disciples were professional historians; they were practitioners of economic analysis. Not "economists" in the traditional and classical sense, but—in their own minds—endowed with a special insight which the orthodox economists never dreamed of. What they invented and preached was a formula of history regarded by them as a key to its complete understanding. It was left to the historians to make use of the key, and curiously enough many historians who were far from professing any attachment to Marxism or any other brand of socialism have been its most energetic advocates. At least, many have used an interpretation which looks very much like that of Marx, probably without in the least being conscious of the kinship. We need not be too surprised at this, however, because, shorn of all the mysteries and convolutions of Marx's underlying reasoning, the economic interpretation of history is one of the easiest ways of thinking that modern man can acquire. Surrounded as he is with industrialism, money-making, and aggressive business practices, all of which seem to be readily identifiable with capitalism, modern man in general and the historian in particular have reason to be impressed by the impact of these forces upon history.

THE CAUSES OF WAR

WILLARD WALLER *

What most of us would like to know about war is why it happens and whether it can be prevented. This is a simple and very important query, and one to which the social sciences have not sufficiently applied themselves. There are a great many theories about the causes of war, each of which has some merit. Let us examine each of these theories in turn, and see whether we can arrive at an understanding of war.

Perhaps the simplest theory and the most widely held is what we may call the moralistic theory. Wars are made because bad men make them. When a people goes to war, it commonly believes that it is fighting because the wicked leaders of the other people have precipitated the battle by an attack upon a peaceable folk. When the war is over, it often turns out that the supposedly wicked leader of the enemy was only an intensely patriotic citizen who tried to further what he considered the legitimate interest of his country in the way that seemed to him best. Sometimes, indeed, a wicked leader or an irresponsible fanatic does come to power and does start a war, but there are still many things that require explanation in such a situation. What peculiar set of political processes, what extraordinary moral or economic factors, brought such a person into power? How was he able to impose his will upon other leaders? Why did the masses follow him into war? What delusions did they harbor and how did they come by them? There are, in fact, enough of these subsidiary questions to invalidate the moralistic theory of war altogether. Such a theory is valid only for purposes of propaganda. To say that wicked men make wars does not help us very much. It is well to remember that we nearly always find out afterwards that such beliefs were false.

* Willard Waller, "War in the Twentieth Century," from Willard Waller, editor, *War in the Twentieth Century,* pp. 3-10, 12, 17-21. Copyright 1940, by Willard Waller and The Dryden Press, Inc. Reprinted by permission.

Another moralistic view is that wars are made to right wrongs and to remedy evils. Germany precipitated the War of 1939 in order to redress the wrongs perpetrated by the Versailles Treaty. The North fought the South in our own United States in order to free the Negro and abolish the institution of slavery. There is some merit in this explanation, at least as regards the participation of the average man. Most men must believe their cause is just if they are to be good soldiers. This moralistic explanation, however, calls for another explanation before it tells us very much: How did men come to have these moral ideas and to consider them worth fighting for? Why did the northern half of the United States discover that slavery was wrong? The fact is that in most wars both sides passionately believe in the justice of their cause. There are earnest and God-fearing men on both sides; neither side has a monopoly of right. If we are to understand war, we must seek to discover the forces behind morality.

A second theory may be labelled the psychological theory. Men fight, it is said, because they have an instinct of pugnacity. It is born in them: men fight for the same reason that bulls fight, because they are fighting animals. A major weakness of this instinctivist explanation is that it is certainly very doubtful that there are any instincts at all in human beings. Even if we have instincts, there is little evidence of an instinct of pugnacity. Suppose we grant that there is an instinct of pugnacity—a very large concession— it still does not follow that this instinct causes wars. There are many channels by which the instinct of pugnacity might be expressed much better than in war. The pattern of conflict pervades our lives. If we wish to find an outlet for our alleged instinct of pugnacity we may do so by quarrelling with our families, falling out with our colleagues, writing a letter to the newspaper, booing somebody on the screen, bullying a waitress, attending a prize fight, by suing somebody for something, or in countless other ways.

War itself, as anybody knows who has seen military service, is an extremely poor way of fulfilling one's combative instincts. Many soldiers never see the enemy; most of them never come to grips with him in close quarters. When fighting occurs, it is a mass affair, with little opportunity for individual hates or heroics. The soldier usually does not see the man he kills. He fights men he has never seen before, men whose very names he does not know, men for whom he can hardly have an intense personal hatred. The soldier's life is for the most part spent in a rather dull routine of training, physical labor, movement from place to place, and waiting. And it is marked throughout by subjection to discipline. Modern soldiers have little chance to "drink delight of battle with their peers." Indeed, if a soldier has a highly developed instinct of pugnacity, it probably does not make him a better soldier but a worse one. A soldier is always under orders; if he gets angry easily, he becomes a discipline problem to his officers. Nor is his lot a happy one if he cannot stand the rough give-and-take with his fellows. Furthermore, if there is an instinct of pugnacity, we must suppose that it is universal among men—but there are peoples which do not know war. And we must suppose, if wars are caused by the instinct of pugnacity, that a once-warlike people will always be so—and yet we know that this is not true. The Scandinavians, for example, were once the scourge of Europe, but now they have become pacific. What has happened to their instinct of pugnacity? Suppose, however, that we pass over all these objections, it still remains true that the theory of an instinct of pugnacity explains only one small part of war. It explains why men fight. It does not explain why nations go to war, which is an important part of the problem.

If war is the result of an instinct, then we must always have wars, because it is not feasible to change the instincts of man. If, however, there is no instinct of pugnacity, or that instinct is not indissolubly tied to war, then it may be that in a better organized society there will sometime be no war. Proponents of the instinct theory of war are chiefly found in very conservative groups. Such persons are so well satisfied with the world as it is that they dislike to think that it could ever be changed in even the smallest particulars. If it would be possible to have a world without war, then who knows what other innovations might come?

Another theory of war is that it results from the pressure of population upon the food supply. A group of people with an unrestricted birth rate remains for some generations within the same territory, which in time becomes crowded. The population then flows over into surrounding regions under the impulsion of hunger. There is a measure of truth in this theory. There have been wars for which the pressure of population furnished a principal cause. The great tribal migrations and far-flung conquests at the dawn of history seem to have been conditioned in large part by population pressure. There have been a great many wars in which the pressure of population was a contributing factor. More often than not the pressure of starvation is the ostensible reason for a war, while other and more decisive reasons lie hidden in the background. We remember the case of the Helvetians in the day of Julius Caesar. Their reason for disturbing the peace was that such a mighty people should not be confined within such narrow boundaries, but behind all this was the scheming of the crafty Orgetorix and who knows what other practitioners of power politics. This situation, in essence, has been repeated many times in human history.

Before we regard population pressure as a principal factor in war, we must explain a number of facts which seem, to say the least, peculiar. In the first place the nations which have the greatest amount of population pressure are often singularly pacific. China and India are densely populated, and, by common report, overpopulated, but, at least in recent times, they have bred no swashbucklers to demand *Lebensraum* with a rattle of the sword. Again, the nations which give population pressure as a reason for aggression frequently proceed to relieve the pressure by annexing or subjugating some even poorer and more populous region. How does this remedy the pressure of population upon food supply? Further, those very nations which profess to need room for their existing population are most anxious to keep up the birth rate. It is also quite possible for such nations to relieve the pressure of population by encouraging permanent emigration to other less populous nations, with, of course, loss of nationality, but in fact every attempt is made to combat permanent settlement of nationals abroad. How does this make sense?

The fact is that population pressure alone does not make a people war-like. When a nation experiences some pressure of population on the food supply, and has also the peculiar economic and social structure of militarism, imperialism, and nationalism, the pressure of population becomes an important factor in the causation of war.

A pseudo-Darwinian theory of war perhaps deserves passing mention, although it is less an attempt to understand the causation of war than a justification and glorification of it. The essential notion of this theory is that war aids the survival of the fit, and is therefore a eugenic factor of the first importance. This is quite untrue. War kills off the fit, and leaves the lame, the blind, and the halt to reproduce the race. Only the physically fit can get into the armies and run the risks of combat. A long series of wars may, therefore, lower the physical standards of a population considerably. War is not a eugenic factor in human society.

The so-called economic interpretation of war is widely accepted, and in fact has considerable merit. It is more nearly able to stand on its own feet than any of the interpretations examined so far. Unfortunately, a great many people believe that the economic interpretation of war is a complete explanation which stands in no need of supplementation from other sources, that it contains all that need be known about the causation of war, that it is, in short, the one and only valid theory of war.

The proponents of the economic interpretation of war usually begin their argument by demonstrating the necessary connection between capitalism and imperialism. Capitalism, the system of production for private profit, developed in the highly industrialized nations, necessarily leads to the production in every nation of more goods than can be sold there. Under the spur of competition and production for profit, capitalism expands the productive plant almost infinitely, so that it becomes necessary to find foreign markets. This surplus, composed not of more goods than can be used within the nation but of more than can be disposed of on the domestic market, must be sold in some way; it is therefore urgently necessary to find a market abroad. But foreign trade with other highly industrialized nations results in a mere exchange of goods; it does not dispose of the surplus of manufactured goods. The search for markets therefore turns to the less developed regions of the world, to predominantly agricultural countries, to peoples who lack manufacturing and machine guns. Several reasons conspire to cause the capitalists of industrial nations to strive to control the trade of these less developed portions of the earth's surface: the desire to dispose of a surplus of manufactured goods, to secure raw materials at a low price, to exploit the labor and economic naïvete of less sophisticated races, and to build up highly profitable investments in the virgin natural resources of countries on the edge of civilization. There is thus a powerful drive toward the control of less advanced regions implicit in the structure of industrial capitalism. This is the reason for the desire for colonies; this is what is behind the demand for "a place in the sun."

The economic interpretation of war then goes on to show that where business interest leads, the state must follow, for the state is only the "executive organ of the ruling class." And the ruling class, of course, is composed of the nation's leading businessmen. It happens inevitably that the business interests of leading nations must often clash in the attempt to control particular areas. When two imperialistic powers come into serious competition, war frequently results. And when the less developed nations resist the rule of the great powers, war may also result from that.

There is certainly a great deal of truth in this interpretation of war. There have been many imperialistic wars in the past few centuries. A principal cause, certainly, of the World War of 1914 was the clash of British imperialism and German imperial aspirations. The European nations have also fought countless big and little wars in order to reduce other peoples to colonial status, for the task of ruling all races was thought to be "the white man's burden."

Some wars fit this classic picture of imperialism perfectly; others show fragments of it. In other words, the economic interpretation of war fits many of the facts of some wars, and it fits some of the facts of nearly all wars. The American Revolution was a war by means of which colonies which had developed some economic independence finally put an end to their colonial status. The Civil War involved, among other things, a conflict between rival economic systems; the industrialism of the North, whose leaders wanted a tariff, and the plantation economy of the South, whose leaders demanded free trade. In order to get the Civil War into the picture of imperialistic conflict, we should have to regard it as a clash between the industrialists of the North and those of Great Britain for the control of the South; and this is certainly a bit strained. The War of 1812 and the Mexican War were motivated in part by imperialism, but in each case it was largely an agrarian imperialism; industrial leaders and merchants had little part in either conflict. In yet other wars, we can find only traces of the generally accepted picture of imperialistic war. We may find one class controlling national policy in terms of its own self-interest, either by precipitating or avoiding war. An economic analysis of the political process is often revealing in the extreme, showing as it so often does that men vote as they believe their interest indicates. This is true not only of issues of war and peace but of other issues as well.

In recent years we have heard much of a sort of primitivized economic interpretation of war. Wars, it is said, are promoted by munitions makers in order to create a market for their wares; these merchants of death gladly sell arms to the enemies of their country and even stir up national rivalries in order to promote business. For other writers, international bankers play the same Satanic role. Enough unsavory facts are known about members of each group to lend some credibility to this view, but it may be doubted that their influence has ever been sufficient to start a major war. We must remember that both the munitions makers and the international bankers of the United States were recently investigated by the Senate, and that this investigation, in the judgment of most observers, disclosed little evidence that either group had very much to do with involving the United States in the first World War.

We must concede that the clash of rival economic systems frequently initiates the friction between nations which later leads to war and that it also sustains this conflict by affording a fresh supply of incidents. Economic interest also supplies influential groups with a powerful motive to promote war. While admitting all this, we must insist that economic factors are not the only factors involved in war. A multitude of things not covered by this theory must necessarily enter into any war. There are always moral and sentimental elements, for men must love their country before they are willing to die for it; most soldiers are not very brave unless they feel that their cause is just. . . .

Although the economic interpretation of war affords some illumination, its popularity is greater than its merits seem to warrant. It is popular, no doubt, partly because of its simplicity and because its proponents are kind enough to advance it in a way which does not invite doubt or inflict upon the listener the pain of a divided mind or the torture of suspended judgment. Again, it is a theory which supplies for some persons the need for a personal devil; the men who make wars, the merchants of death, the grasping traders and the international bankers, are obviously very wicked men, and it is a pleasure to hate them. Perhaps the greatest advantage of the economic interpretation is its essentially hopeful character. If wars are the product of capitalistic imperialism, then we may hope to do away with them in a society in which capitalism has been replaced by another form of economic organization. The economic interpretation is thus justified in part by its relation to a program of action rather than on purely intellectual grounds. . . .

All of the elements which we have mentioned undoubtedly have something to do with the causation of wars. They set off processes of change in society which unite with one another to form the major process of going to war. We may say that in the last analysis wars result from movements of public opinion which the factors mentioned combine to create. We have wars because we develop war fever. The process of going to war may be thought of as a sort of spiral movement of public opinion which is largely beyond control. The war process is like certain phases of the economic system: no one wills it, and yet the totality of the process is the result of the inter-action of many wills. No one wills that prices shall go up or down, as a rule, and yet they move in response to certain conditions created by a multitude of individual choices. Nobody effectively wills that we shall go to war, and perhaps nearly everyone ardently desires that we shall not, but everyone does his part in bringing a war about. A newspaper, for example, writes headlines and publishes pictures which inflame the public mind, and at the same time argues strongly for peace on its editorial pages; no doubt the editorial comment represents the editor's sincere belief, but in the end the headlines and the pictures win.

The interpretation of war as produced by the development of war fever in a people is, of course, subject to numerous qualifications. It is most true of democratic nations, for in such countries war occurs only when the majority of the people demand it. But even in a dictatorship, a war must be sold to the populace. A modern dictator is only a kind of demagogue who adds the arts of the propagandist to the ancient weapons of the tyrant. He rules by consent and sufferance under the Damoclean sword. So that he, too, can wage only those wars which his people can be induced to support.

It is obvious, too, that the growth of war fever is subject to law. It is a response to economic, cultural, political, social, psychological, and other factors. We may say that these factors co-operate in producing war in more or less the way in which chemicals combine to produce different compounds. We may gain a clearer idea of the process of combination by studying the way in which wars usually start. The typical process of going to war may be described as follows:

Conflict begins (if under the international conditions of the past few years it may be said that it ever has a beginning or an end) with certain crises between nations, "incidents," in which there is a definite clash of the power systems of two or more nations. Such incidents are usually occasioned, directly or indirectly, by economic competition, but other than economic elements rapidly become involved in them.

These incidents set off definite conflict, which, however, remains within bounds, that is, it is not so great that diplomatic machinery is unable to handle it. The power systems of the two nations confront one another for a time, and there is difficulty in preventing conflict without loss of face by one side or the other. Public opinion in each nation comes to regard the other nation as a potential enemy. When the conflict subsides into diplomatic interchange, it leaves the situation substantially changed. Each side has now acquired a heightened sensitivity to affronts or challenges from the other. On each side the public appetite for news of conflict has been stimulated. One or both sides may feel that they have lost face. In consequence it is much easier for new incidents to occur.

As a result of such a crisis preparations for war increase on both sides. This helps to build a war machine which in time stimulates the war psychology. In addition, this program is interpreted by other nations as a threat to their security.

There now ensues a series of "incidents," each of which leaves the nations involved somewhat closer to war. There is a recognized drift toward war, a process which we may compare to the milling of a herd of cattle getting ready to stampede. In each nation the following changes of public opinion tend to take place:

The agencies which control public opinion fall in line in favor of war. Newspapers print an increasing amount of news in which the conflict is featured; headline writers and makeup men give prominence to news which previously went on the inside pages, and editors blue-pencil domestic news in favor of news of the current crisis. Politicians make issues on the basis of foreign policy; domestic issues are forgotten. Self-appointed agitators keep the populace stirred up; they create what the politicians call a ground-swell of opinion. Among the agencies controlling opinion, the church and the school are probably the last to take a stand for war. Sooner or later, however, the ministers and the teachers discover that this war is different; this is a holy war.

There is a gradual growth of myths about the other people, a depersonalization of the people and a personification of their government. A vicious stereotype is substituted for other conceptions of the potential enemy; cartoons portray him as a bestial figure; he often comes to be known by names denoting derision and hatred. The first atrocity stories often appear at this time.

War fever gradually takes possession of the masses. There is an increasing loss of objectivity in discussing the issue of war or peace. Attention is rapidly deflected from discussing internal affairs and directed to foreign affairs. Needed internal reforms go by the board because they come to seem of minor importance. Individuals identify themselves increasingly with the nation, and feel that each new incident is an affront to their quite personal selves.

This process may be hastened by propaganda emanating from interested parties. In any case, war fever affects different classes, regions, interest groups, religious and cultural groups, in different ways and to different degrees. Some groups necessarily take the lead in the agitation for strong measures or for war. A vociferous minority often forces into line a majority which at first regards the war passively.

What apparently happens when a warlike climate of opinion develops is that certain propositions get established as unquestioned truths, and everyone accepts them because everybody else accepts them, and it comes to be regarded as bad form to question them. Biased news reports and propaganda furnish a multitude of suggestions which are hard to resist. In addition, these suggestions are reenforced by the powerful sentiments of loyalty to one's country. It becomes a sort of patriotic duty to believe the current slogans. Gradually people become angry, and as anger mounts, their minds close, and they hear arguments against their wrath most reluctantly: they believe ill of the enemy because they ardently desire to believe it. It is not strange that the average citizen should be helpless in such a situation. It is quite understandable that he should be caught up and swept along. It does seem a little odd that the leaders of the people should apparently offer so little resistance to the winds of opinion. In general, the intellectual leaders of the various peoples do not cover themselves with glory when war is in the offing. The disturbance of reasoning during the milling process is seemingly so subtle and insidious that even those persons who but a few years or a few months before were violently opposed to war now come to believe that this particular war is both necessary and desirable. None of their beliefs concerning war in general has changed, but this war is an exception to the rules. This war is different. Like the man who has been in love ten times before, they believe that this time it is real.

Part II

Forms and Organizations of the World State System

CHAPTER 5

DIPLOMACY

BECAUSE OF THE vital role it plays in the affairs of states, diplomacy is one of the most fascinating and controversial subjects in the study of international relations. The diplomat has often been painted, in our democratic age, in the dark role of a villain "secretly" committing his fellow countrymen to perilous treaties or, alternately, as a social dilettante, occupied with an endless round of parties, dances, and banquets in the company of very important people. In this stereotyped view the diplomat is pictured as either scoundrel or wastrel.

Yet the main business of diplomacy is discussion and negotiation; it is often a tedious business and always a serious one, for upon its success the national interest of a state depends. The diplomat must not only thoroughly understand the aims and intentions of his own state; he must be eternally alert to draw correct conclusions about the intentions of others, often from insufficient and frequently disconnected evidence. He must know how far to go and when. In over two thousand years, despite new techniques, new participants, and new conditions, these fundamentals have not changed.

The timeless nature of diplomatic negotiations between states is well illustrated by the first selection, "The Old Diplomacy," drawn from Thucydides' account of the conference in 416 B.C. between Athens (then a great or even superpower) and Melos (a small power). Melos was attempting to ward off the impending danger of Athenian attack; the arguments their delegates advance are rich in principle and high in moral content. Unfortunately they were backed by little real power as the Athenians well knew. Brushing aside the arguments of the Melians, the Athenians, in a famous passage, remark: ". . . you know as well as we do that right, as the world goes, is only in question between equals in power, while the strong do what they can and the weak suffer what they must." How similar to our own age! Were the place names and those of the participating states suitably changed, the conversation would easily pass for one between Hitler, Mussolini, or Stalin and the representative of some less powerful state. And Athens was reputedly the most "civilized" nation of the day.

In this classic example of a conference the traditional gambits of diplomacy appear: the veiled and open threat, the appeal to justice, the counterthreat (as when the Melians hint that Athens is not immune to a possible balance-of-power combination of weaker states against her), the attempt to strike a bargain, and the final deadlock signaling the imminent war.

In the second selection, "The New Diplomacy," taken from Harold Nicolson's *Curzon: The Last Phase,* the so-called "new" democratic diplomacy is compared and contrasted with traditional diplomacy. The "old" diplomacy has passed under a cloud of disrepute in the democracies because it was widely believed by 1919 that the secret character of traditional negotiations had helped to bring on World War I and that "open covenants, . . . openly arrived at," in Wilson's phrase, would make for a more secure and peaceful world. From this idea it was one short step in logic to holding diplomatic conferences in the full public view replete with press photographers and radio and television broadcasts. Not only temporary conferences to deal with particular issues underwent this transformation but also the permanent conferences which characterized the League of Nations and United Nations. As another innovation of the "new" diplomacy, the professional diplomats were displaced at crucial times by *elected* officials highly aware of public opinion at home and always pressed for time (since they could not be away from the capital long). As such they were eternally tempted to accept a "formula" representing temporary publicity value rather than a real step forward. A formula did away with prolonged negotiation and the consumption of much time even though it actually disguised disagreement rather than composed it. How these procedures disrupted and vitiated diplomatic progress during the interwar period is penetratingly analyzed by Nicolson, and his conclusions are equally significant in terms of today.

Nicolson believes that the basic weakness of democratic diplomacy lies in the fact that the people, although they play an important part in the formulation and execution of foreign policy, have not developed a sufficient sense of responsibility. Although the word of the nation is pledged in a treaty which has become inconvenient, the people and press ask for its denunciation, unaware that such an action would put the word of the citizen, too, in doubt. In a democracy the people *are* sovereign, and it is *their* honor which is at stake.

In the last decade this weakness of democratic diplomacy has been more than equalled by the notorious unreliability of totalitarian regimes in respect to their pledged word. Hitler made his name a synonym for diplomatic perfidy.

The effects of democratic and dictatorial diplomacy and their interaction are discussed by Lord Vansittart in the third selection, "The Decline of Dip'omacy." His analysis is witty but nostalgic, and his point of view is influenced by what Nicolson would call the characteristics of the professional dip'omat. Vansittart believes the basic cause for the decline of diplomacy is communism; the traditional aim of diplomacy he describes as the maintenance of good international relations, and since the Communists believe in bad relations as "an article of faith," the effect is a general deterioration of confidence and therefore of progress. He devotes the greater part of his analysis to the effects of tota'itarian diplomacy. Since he comments on several of the issues raised by Nicolson in the second selection, it is interesting to compare their views.

But whether it is "new" or "old" or even in "decline," it remains true that dip'omacy arises out of the fact that sovereign states exist who, being independent of one another, must meet to adjust their common and conflicting interests as best they can. The interests which these states have will determine whether the result is "good" international relations or "bad." Despite Lord Vansittart's pessimism, diplomacy is not likely to disappear as long as the multistate system which gave it birth persists.

THE OLD DIPLOMACY

THUCYDIDES *

The next summer . . . the Athenians also made an expedition against the isle of Melos with thirty ships of their own, six Chian, and two Lesbian vessels, sixteen hundred heavy infantry, three hundred archers, and twenty mounted archers from Athens, and about fifteen hundred heavy infantry

* Thucydides, *The Complete Writings of Thucydides—The Peloponnesian War,* Modern Library, Inc., New York, 1934, pp. 330–337. Copyright 1934, by The Modern Library, Inc. Reprinted by permission.

from the allies and the islanders. The Melians are a colony of Lacedaemon that would not submit to the Athenians like the other islanders, and at first remained neutral and took no part in the struggle, but afterwards upon the Athenians using violence and plundering their territory, assumed an attitude of open hostility. Cleomedes, son of Lycomedes, and Tisias, son of Tisimachus, the [Athenian] generals, encamping in their territory with the above armament, before doing any harm to their land, sent envoys to negotiate. These the Melians did not bring before the people, but bade them state the object of their mission to the magistrates and the few; upon which the Athenian envoys spoke as follows:—

Athenians.—'Since the negotiations are not to go on before the people, in order that we may not be able to speak straight on without interruption, and deceive the ears of the multitude by seductive arguments which would pass without refutation (for we know that this is the meaning of our being brought before the few), what if you who sit there were to pursue a method more cautious still! Make no set speech yourselves, but take us up at whatever you do not like, and settle that before going any farther. And first tell us if this proposition of ours suits you.'

The Melian commissioners answered:—

Melians.—'To the fairness of quietly instructing each other as you propose there is nothing to object; but your military preparations are too far advanced to agree with what you say, as we see you are come to be judges in your own cause, and that all we can reasonably expect from this negotiation is war, if we prove to have right on our side and refuse to submit, and in the contrary case, slavery.'

Athenians.—'If you have met to reason about presentiments of the future, or for anything else than to consult for the safety of your state upon the facts that you see before you, we will give over; otherwise we will go on.'

Melians.—'It is natural and excusable for men in our position to turn more ways than one both in thought and utterance. However, the question in this conference, is, as you say, the safety of our country; and the discussion, if you please, can proceed in the way which you propose.'

Athenians.—'For ourselves, we shall not trouble you with specious pretences—either of how we have a right to our empire because we overthrew the Mede, or are now attacking you because of wrong that you have done us—and make a long speech which would not be believed; and in return we hope that you, instead of thinking to influence us by saying that you did not join the Lacedaemonians, although their colonists, or that you have done us no wrong, will aim at what is feasible, holding in view the real sentiments of us both; since you know as well as we do that right, as the world goes, is only in question between equals in power, while the strong do what they can and the weak suffer what they must.'

Melians.—'As we think, at any rate, it is expedient—we speak as we are obliged, since you enjoin us to let right alone and talk only of interest— that you should not destroy what is our common protection, the privilege of being allowed in danger to invoke what is fair and right, and even to profit by arguments not strictly valid if they can be got to pass current. And you are as much interested in this as any, as your fall would be a signal for the heaviest vengeance and an example for the world to meditate upon.'

Athenians.—'The end of our empire, if end it should, does not frighten us: a rival empire like Lacedaemon, even if Lacedaemon was our real antagonist, is not so terrible to the vanquished as subjects who by themselves attack and overpower their rulers. This, however, is a risk that we are content to take. We will now proceed to show you that we are come here in the interest of our empire, and that we shall say what we are now going to say, for the preservation of your country; as we would fain exercise that empire over you without trouble, and see you preserved for the good of us both.'

Melians.—'And how, pray, could it turn out as good for us to serve as for you to rule?'

Athenians.—'Because you would have the advantage of submitting before suffering the worst, and we should gain by not destroying you.'

Melians.—'So that you would not consent to our being neutral, friends instead of enemies, but allies of neither side.'

Athenians.—'No; for your hostility cannot so much hurt us as your friendship will be an argument to our subjects of our weakness, and your enmity of our power.'

Melians.—'Is that your subjects' idea of equity, to put those who have nothing to do with you in the same category with peoples that are most of them your own colonists, and some conquered rebels?'

Athenians.—'As far as right goes they think one has as much of it as the other, and that if any maintain their independence it is because they are strong, and that if we do not molest them it is because we are afraid; so that besides extending our empire we should gain in security by your subjection; the fact that you are islanders and weaker than others rendering it all the more important that you should not succeed in baffling the masters of the sea.'

Melians.—'But do you consider that there is no security in the policy which we indicate? For here again if you debar us from talking about justice and invite us to obey your interest, we also must explain ours, and try to persuade you, if the two happen to coincide. How can you avoid making enemies of all existing neutrals who shall look at our case and conclude from it that one day or another you will attack them? And what is this but to make greater the enemies that you have already, and to force others to become so who would otherwise have never thought of it?'

Athenians.—'Why, the fact is that continentals generally give us but little alarm; the liberty which they enjoy will long prevent their taking precautions against us; it is rather islanders like yourselves, outside our empire, and subjects smarting under the yoke, who would be the most likely to take a rash step and lead themselves and us into obvious danger.'

Melians.—'Well then, if you risk so much to retain your empire, and your subjects to get rid of it, it were surely great baseness and cowardice in us who are still free not to try everything that can be tried, before submitting to your yoke.'

Athenians.—'Not if you are well advised, the contest not being an equal one, with honour as the prize and shame as the penalty, but a question of self-preservation and of not resisting those who are far stronger than you are.'

Melians.—'But we know that the fortune of war is sometimes more impartial than the disproportion of numbers might lead one to suppose; to submit is to give ourselves over to despair, while action still preserves for us a hope that we may stand erect.'

Athenians.—'Hope, danger's comforter, may be indulged in by those who have abundant resources, if not without loss at all events without ruin; but its nature is to be extravagant, and those who go so far as to put their all upon the venture see it in its true colours only when they are ruined; but so long as the discovery would enable them to guard against it, it is never found wanting. Let not this be the case with you, who are weak and hang on a single turn of the scale; nor be like the vulgar, who, abandoning such security as human means may still afford, when visible hopes fail them in extremity, turn to invisible, to prophecies and oracles, and other such inventions that delude men with hopes to their destruction.'

Melians.—'You may be sure that we are as well aware as you of the difficulty of contending against your power and fortune, unless the terms be equal. But we trust that the gods may grant us fortune as good as yours, since we are just men fighting against unjust, and that what we want in power will be made up by the alliance of the Lacedaemonians, who are bound, if only for very shame, to come to the aid of their kindred. Our confidence, therefore, after all is not so utterly irrational.'

Athenians.—'When you speak of the favour of the gods, we may as fairly hope for that as yourselves; neither our pretensions nor our conduct being in any way contrary to what men believe of the gods, or practise among themselves. Of the gods we believe, and of men we know, that by a necessary law of their nature they rule wherever they can. And it is not as if we were the first to make this law, or to act upon it when made: we found it existing before us, and shall leave it to exist for ever after us; all we do is to make use of it, knowing that you and everybody else, having the same power as we have, would do the same as we do. Thus, as far as the gods are concerned, we have no fear and no reason to fear that we shall be at a disadvantage. But when we come to your notion about the Lacedaemonians, which leads you to believe that shame will make them help you, here we bless your simplicity but do not envy your folly. The Lacedaemonians, when their own interests or their country's laws are in question, are the worthiest men alive; of their conduct toward others much might be said, but no clearer idea of it could be given than by shortly saying that of all the men we know they are most conspicuous in considering what is agreeable honourable, and what is expedient just. Such a way of thinking does not promise much for the safety which you now unreasonably count upon.'

Melians.—'But it is for this very reason that we now trust to their respect for expediency to prevent them from betraying the Melians, their colonists, and thereby losing the confidence of their friends in Hellas and helping their enemies.'

Athenians.—'Then you do not adopt the view that expediency goes with security, while justice and honour cannot be followed without danger; and danger the Lacedaemonians generally court as little as possible.'

Melians.—'But we believe that they would be more likely to face even danger for our sake, and with more confidence than for others, as our nearness to Peloponnese makes it easier for them to act, and our common blood insures our fidelity.'

Athenians.—'Yes, but what an intending ally trusts to, is not the goodwill of those who ask his aid, but a decided superiority of power for action; and the Lacedaemonians look to this even more than others. At least, such is their distrust of their home resources that it is only with numerous allies that they attack a neighbour; now is it likely that while we are masters of the sea they will cross over to an island?'

Melians.—'But they would have others to send. The Cretan sea is a wide one, and it is more difficult for those who command it to intercept others, than for those who wish to elude them to do so safely. And should the Lacedaemonians miscarry in this, they would fall upon your land, and upon those left of your allies whom Brasidas did not reach; and instead of places which are not yours, you will have to fight for your own country and your own confederacy.'

Athenians.—'Some diversion of the kind you speak of you may one day experience, only to learn, as others have done, that the Athenians never once yet withdrew from a siege for fear of any. But we are struck by the fact, that after saying you would consult for the safety of your country, in all this discussion you have mentioned nothing which men m'ght trust in and think to be saved by. Your strongest arguments depend upon hope and the future, and your actual resources are too scanty, as compared with those arrayed against you, for you to come out victorious. You will therefore show great blindness of judgment, unless, after allowing us to retire, you can find some counsel more prudent than this. You will surely not be caught by that idea of disgrace, which in dangers that are disgraceful, and at the same time too plain to be mistaken, proves so fatal to mankind; since in too many cases the very men that have their eyes perfectly open to what they are rushing into, let the thing called disgrace, by the mere influence of a seductive name, lead them on to a point at which they become so enslaved by the phrase as in fact to fall wilfully into hopeless disaster, and incur disgrace more disgraceful as the companion of error, than when it comes as the result of misfortune. This, if you are well advised, you will guard against; and you will not think it dishonourable to submit to the greatest city in Hellas, when it makes you the moderate offer of becoming its tributary ally, without ceasing to enjoy the country that belongs to you; nor when you have the choice given you between war and security, will you be so blinded as to choose the worse. And it is certain that those who do not yield to their equals, who keep terms with their superiors, and are moderate towards their inferiors, on the whole succeed best. Think over the matter, therefore, after our withdrawal, and reflect once and again that it is for your country that you are consulting, that you have not more than one, and that upon this one deliberation depends its prosperity or ruin.'

The Athenians now withdrew from the conference; and the Melians, left to themselves, came to a decision corresponding with what they had maintained in the discussion, and answered, 'Our resolution, Athenians, is the same as it was at first. We will not in a moment deprive of freedom a city that has been inhabited these seven hundred years; but we put our trust in the fortune by which the gods have preserved it until now, and in the help of men, that is, of the Lacedaemonians; and so we will try and save ourselves. Meanwhile we invite you to allow us to be friends to you and foes to neither party, and to retire from our country after making such a treaty as shall seem fit to us both.'

Such was the answer of the Melians. The Athenians now departing from the conference said, 'Well, you alone, as it seems to us, judging from these resolutions, regard what is future as more certain than what is before your eyes, and what is out of sight, in your eagerness, as already coming to pass; and as you have staked most on, and trusted most in, the Lacedaemonians, your fortune, and your hopes, so will you be most completely deceived.'

The Athenian envoys now returned to the army; and the Melians show-ing no signs of yielding, the generals at once betook themselves to hostili-ties, and drew a line of circumvallation round the Melians, dividing the work among the different states. Subsequently the Athenians returned with most of their army, leaving behind them a certain number of their own citizens and of the allies to keep guard by land and sea. The force thus left stayed on and besieged the place.

. . . Reinforcements afterwards arriving from Athens in consequence, under the command of Philocrates, son of Demeas, the siege was now pressed vigorously; and some treachery taking place inside, the Melians surrendered at discretion to the Athenians, who put to death all the grown men whom they took, and sold the women and children for slaves, and subsequently sent out five hundred colonists and inhabited the place themselves.

THE NEW DIPLOMACY

HAROLD NICOLSON *

A tendency has arisen in recent years, and especially in the United States, to contrast what is described as 'new' or 'open' diplomacy with what is called 'old' or 'secret' diplomacy. In its more extreme forms this contrast implies a contention that until the coming of President Wilson diplomacy was oligarchic, maleficent and obscure; whereas, after the Revelation of January 8, 1918, it suddenly became democratic, beneficent and limpid. This theory (in that it is often based upon superstitious rather than upon rational conceptions) leads to errors of understanding. It has given rise, for instance, to the idea that there exists some antinomy between demo-cratic control on the one hand; and on the other hand, the secret and ex-pert conduct of negotiation. It has given rise, again, to a widespread con-ception of diplomacy as something which possesses a detached identity of its own—parasitic, and not organic, to the living growth of the State. Such theories are misleading. The history of diplomacy displays no such sudden breaks in continuity: it shows, rather, a constant, if not very im-mediate, process of adjustment to the shifting incidences of sovereignty. A diplomatic service which was unrepresentative of the sovereign authority in its own national State would obviously be an inefficient service. Di-plomacy may thus be defined as that method of international procedure

* Harold Nicolson, *Curzon: The Last Phase, 1919–1925*, pp. 183–186, 391–392, 397–404. Copyright 1939, by Harcourt, Brace and Company, Inc. Reprinted by permission of Harcourt, Brace and Harold Nicolson.

which commends itself to sensible persons of any given epoch, as the most 'representative' and the most 'efficient' for conducting negotiations between States. Its efficiency must be based upon a constant endeavor to secure that international intercourse be conducted in such a manner as to mini-mise the risks of misunderstanding, emotionalism, uncertainty or hasty decision. It is the interaction between the need of exact 'representation' and the impulse towards increased 'efficiency' which has, since the four-teenth century, constituted the main influence formative of diplomatic practice: the conflict between the 'old' and the 'new' diplomacy is thus no sudden phenomenon, but a stage in this long process of adjustment pre-sented (as all modern problems are presented) in an increasingly intricate, impatient and ill-digested form.

Although, therefore, great caution should be exercised when basing any thesis upon some contrast between 'old' and 'new,' between 'pre-war' and 'post-war,' diplomacy, yet it must be confessed that the triumph of the democratic idea (temporary though that triumph may prove) has in fact induced a marked difference of method, even if but a slight difference of purpose. The fact that the people is now sovereign in all democratic countries obliges the negotiator to inform the people of his purposes and to obtain their approval of his decisions. This, in principle, is a wholly admirable necessity. In practice, it is a most irksome obligation. The difficulty of inducing the people to think rapidly and correctly,—the dan-ger that their initial emotion may, although rapid, be incorrect—tempts the modern negotiator to avoid those problems which are likely to prove unpopular and to concentrate on secondary issues which will be more comprehensible, and therefore more welcome, to the popular mind.

The main distinction, therefore, between the methods of the new and those of the old diplomacy is that the former aims at satisfying the *im-mediate* wishes of the electorate, whereas the latter was concerned only with the *ultimate* interests of the nation. It is, very largely, a difference in the time available. The old diplomatist, negotiating as an expert with fellow experts, was able to approach his problems in a scientific spirit, with due deliberation, and without regard to immediate popular support. Such a system was obviously open to abuse and danger. Yet democratic diplomacy is exposed to its own peculiar maladies which, in that they are less apparent, are even more insidious. In its desire to conciliate popular feeling it is apt to subordinate principle to expediency, to substitute the indefinite for the precise, to prefer in place of the central problem (which is often momentarily insoluble) subsidiary issues upon which immediate agreement, and therefore immediate popular approval, can be attained. . . .

The essential defect of democratic policy can be defined in one word, namely *"irresponsibility."* Under a monarchic or oligarchic system the "sovereign" who enters into a contract with some foreign State feels himself personally "responsible" for the execution of that contract. For a monarch or a governing class to repudiate a formal treaty was regarded as a dishonourable thing to do, and would have aroused much criticism both at home and abroad. Now, however, that the people are "sovereign," this sense of individual or corporate responsibilty no longer exists. The people are in no sense aware of their own sovereignty in foreign affairs and have therefore no sense of responsibility in regard to treaties or conventions entered into with other Powers, even when they have themselves, through their elected representatives, approved of those treaties. They are honestly under the impression that their own word has not been pledged and that they are therefore fully entitled to repudiate engagements which they may subsequently feel to be onerous or inconvenient. A state of mind is thus created which (to take an obvious instance) allows a popular newspaper publicly to preach the repudiation of the Locarno Treaties, not on the ground that these treaties were unconstitutionally concluded, but on the ground that their application at the present moment would prove inconvenient and unpopular.

Clearly, if such a state of mind is permitted to continue uncriticised and unchecked, there can be no hope for the future of democratic foreign policy. The foundations of policy, as of diplomacy, are reliability, and under a system of popular repudiation of all national engagements which may eventually prove to be onerous, not even the elements of reliability can exist. Compared with this basic defect in democratic foreign policy, all other dangers are insignificant. Not until the people and the press realise their own sovereignty will they be ready to assume their own responsibility. The period which must inevitably elapse between the fact of popular sovereignty in foreign affairs, and the realisation of that fact by the people themselves; in other words the zone of uncertainty which will have to be traversed before we leave the present quicksands of unconscious public irresponsibility and reach the firm ground of conscious public responsibility, constitute the period or zone of greatest danger. Until that zone has successfully been traversed, no sense of international security can possibly be fostered. The essence of the whole problem is how the danger period is to pass without either disturbance or disintegration. The statesmen of the post-war period have endeavoured to create an artificial sense of security by multiplying security pacts. Yet until the world is convinced that these pacts are regarded by the sovereign democracies as involving their own responsibility they merely serve to inflate the currency of international contract and thereby to diminish certainty rather than to increase confidence. . . .

In spite of the dangers noted above, democratic foreign policy is unquestionably less dangerous than any other form of foreign policy. Democratic diplomacy, on the other hand, is, owing to its disturbing inefficiency, very dangerous indeed.

By "democratic diplomacy" I mean the execution of foreign policy, either by politicians themselves, or through the medium of untrained negotiators whom they have selected from among their own supporters or personal friends.

The failure to differentiate between "policy" and "negotiation" has led to the fallacy that all important negotiation should be carried out, not by persons possessing experience and detachment, but by persons possessing a mandate from the people. In its extreme form this fallacy has led to "Diplomacy by Conference"—perhaps the most unfortunate diplomatic method ever conceived.

(1) *Diplomacy by Conference.* Obviously there are occasions when international agreement can only be achieved by oral discussion between plenipotentiaries. There are occasions, also, when the issues are so vital and immediate that "policy" as well as "negotiation" is involved. On such occasions the negotiators must be identical with the framers of policy, and the resultant congresses and conferences must be attended by the Prime Ministers or Foreign Secretaries of the several Powers.

It should be established, however, that such occasions are exceptional and dangerous. Such conferences should be entered into only after careful preparation, on the basis of a programme elaborated and accepted in advance, against a background of acute public criticism and with full realisation that many months of discussion will be required. The subjects for debate should moreover be rigidly curtailed to those requiring a decision of policy, and all secondary issues, entailing negotiation only, should be left in expert hands.

In the four years immediately following the war these principles were discarded. Innumerable conferences were held without adequate preparation, with no precise programme and within a time limit of three or four days. The subjects discussed were diverse, intricate and suitable only for expert negotiation. The meetings took place in an atmosphere of extreme publicity and uncritical popular expectation. The resultant conclusions, inevitably, were inconclusive, intangible, specious, superficial, and unreal. Compare the expert handling of such conferences as those of Washington, Lausanne and Brussels with the hurried histrionics of Genoa or Cannes.

"Diplomacy by Conference" is to-day so discredited that it may be thought that there is no danger of its revival as a method of international negotiation. The frame of mind which allowed of that method is still, however, a very general frame of mind. It is caused by uncertainty regarding the frontier between democratic control of policy and expert conduct of negotiation. That frontier can only be properly delimitated if we have a clear conception of the dangers of amateurishness on the one hand, and of professionalism on the other.

(2) *The Politician as Negotiator.* It has already been stated that on exceptional occasions, or in dealing with vital issues of policy, the politician must himself negotiate. I should wish, however, to summarise some of the dangers to which, on such occasions, he is exposed.

(a) *Public Opinion.* A politician suffers from the essential disadvantage of being a politician. In other words his position and his future career are dependent upon popular approval. He is acutely sensitive to transitory "opinions" in the House of Commons, his party, or the press. He is apt to reject what he knows to be reasonable because he also knows that it will be difficult to explain; conversely, he is tempted (as Orlando was tempted in the Fiume controversy) to fabricate by propaganda an artificial popular approval in order to strengthen his diplomatic position.

The professional, on the other hand, places ultimate national interest above immediate popular applause.

(b) *Ignorance.* By this I do not mean an ignorance of foreign facts, but an ignorance of foreign psychology. It mattered nothing at all that Mr. Lloyd George should never have heard of Teschen; it mattered very much indeed that he should treat the French or the Germans as he would treat an English trades-union delegation. Those schoolboy levities which might put a Lancashire Labour leader at his ease were regarded by M. Briand as disconcerting; those rhetorical questions, those revivalist dithyrambs which, to the Mayor of Llanberis would appear as usual forms of human speech, were interpreted by Dr. Rathenau or M. Gounaris as signifying either invective or encouragement. Frequent and serious were the misunderstandings which therefrom resulted.

(c) *Vanity.* A British politician, unaccustomed to negotiation with foreign statesmen, is prone to disturbances of vanity. The fact that his general culture, as his knowledge of foreign languages, is generally below the level of that possessed by those with whom he is negotiating gives him a sense of inferiority to which he reacts in unfortunate ways. Either he will air his schoolboy French to the distress of his audience and the confusion of business, or else he will be truculently insular. Upon weaker minds the mere fact of being, although abroad, a centre of public interest, the lavish hospitality of foreign Governments, the actual salutes of people dressed in foreign uniforms, have a most disintegrating effect. Affability, gratitude and general silliness result.

Such subjective forms of vanity are perhaps less dangerous than its more objective manifestations. A Prime Minister, for instance, who is

conscious of a firm majority at home, is apt to acquire an autocratic habit
of mind. Not only is he irritated by the fact that he cannot compel foreign statesmen to obey his behests, but he resents, and thus endeavours
to ignore, those circumstances which he is unable to influence as well
as those areas of knowledge which he can never hope to possess. A tendency
develops in him to deny the existence of those circumstances and that
knowledge and to soar above them on the light wings of obscurantism and
improvisation. Sir Charles Mallet in his *Lloyd George: a Study* (page 156)
has well described the effect of this particular manifestation of human
vanity. "Unvarying self-assurance," he writes, "tempered by an ever-varying
opportunism is perhaps the most dangerous equipment that statesmanship can have."

Democratic diplomacy is very apt to acquire this equipment.

(*d*) *Controversy.* A mind trained in parliamentary or forensic debate
is apt to assume that a conference is a form of controversy. Such people
start from the assumption that the interests of foreign countries are necessarily opposed. They tend to envisage negotiation in the form of a debate
rather than in the form of a consultation. They thus endeavour to "score
points." At many a Conference I have seen a whole hour wasted in purely
artificial dialectics. The politician is always conscious of an audience;
the trained negotiator is conscious only of the negotiation in hand. The
reason why lawyers have always made the worst diplomatists is that their
argumentative faculties are too much on the alert. Negotiation should
never degenerate into an argument; it should be kept always on the level
of a discussion.

(*e*) *Overwork.* The politician, again, is always pressed for time. It
thus results that negotiation is seldom pursued to a precise conclusion,
but is suspended halfway upon the first landing offered for compromise.
This time-pressure, again, leads to impatience. The politician as negotiator is unwilling to listen to information which may tempt him to alter
his own opinion and thus necessitate further discussion. Similarly he is
prone to reject all suggestions, however admirable, which might entail
further study or delay. Time-pressure, in every case, is accompanied by
overwork: the results are expedients, half-solutions, evasion of essentials,
improvisations, and imprecision.

Such are the major disabilities from which even the noblest politician,
when he becomes a diplomatist, is apt to suffer.

The virtues of professional diplomacy are implicit in the above catalogue of the vices of its opposite. The professional diplomatist is indifferent to public applause, has devoted some thirty years to the study of
foreign psychology, is unaffected by vanity, dislikes controversy, eschews
all forms of publicity, and is not subject to acute time-pressure or over-

work. In addition, as a trained expert in a common science working with other experts, he is intent upon producing a piece of work which will satisfy his own professional standards. All that he cares for is the approbation of those whose judgment is worth having. He is completely indifferent to the opinion of those whose judgment is not worth having. This specialised vanity impels him to prefer competent to incompetent work, real achievement to achievements which have only the appearance of reality.

Yet he, also, has his dangers.

(a) *Professionalism.* A man who has spent some thirty years in the diplomatic service acquires, inevitably, an international frame of mind. More specifically he comes to have a masonic feeling for other diplomatists. On occasions he may lack a proper degree of reverence for politicians, or even Press magnates, and an unwarranted contempt for, and suspicion of, their ways and means. In extreme cases he may feel, even, that public and parliamentary opinion is foolish and ill-informed.

Upon himself the effect of these prejudices is seldom serious. Being a civil servant he has been trained to loyalty and obedience, nor would he (I am discussing only British diplomatists) dream of acting contrary to the wishes of the Government in power, and therefore of his democratic sovereign. His prejudices are of negative rather than of positive disadvantage. His experience of democracy in so many lands and in such different forms may induce in him a mood of scepticism. This absence of belief will be interpreted by those politicians with whom he comes into contact as an attitude of superiority. Suspicion and misprisal will result.

(b) *Lethargy.* The professional diplomatist is apt to lack initiative. Important problems, in his opinion, settle themselves; unimportant problems are unimportant. He has seen so much damage done by well-meaning officiousness; he has seen so little damage done by letting well alone. His whole training has tended to convince him that good diplomacy is a slow and cautious business, and he looks with exaggerated suspicion upon all dynamic innovations. For him reality is relative and never absolute: he believes in gradations, in grey zones; he is always impatient of those who think enthusiastically in terms of black and white. Lethargy of judgment descends upon him, a slightly contemptuous disbelief in all forms of human certainty. He is thus more prone to analysis than to synthesis, more ready to indicate doubts than to produce dynamic assurances, more inclined to deny than to affirm. This propensity proves very irritating to the politician anxious to score a rapid popular success.

(c) *Narrowness.* The professional diplomatist suffers also from certain limitations of outlook. He observes widely, but he does not observe deeply. He is inclined to attach to superficial events greater importance than he attaches to underlying causes. He is more interested in overt political

symptoms than in obscure social or economic diseases. He is well aware
that his judgment, if it is to be of any real value to his Government, must
be "sound:" he tends therefore to allow the more imaginative and original
sections of his brain to atrophy. True it is that a brilliant diplomatist
is a grave public menace; the consciousness of this fact is apt to induce
our professional diplomatists to attach exclusive importance to not being
brilliant. This, certainly, is a fault on the right side. Our diplomatic
service is without question (and no foreigner would deny it) the best in
the world. Yet upon the casual observer it may produce a false impression of conservatism and mental rigidity.

(d) *Timidity*. This quality should, perhaps, have been cited in the
category of virtues and not in the category of defects. The British diplomatist is in fact as frightened of "causing trouble" as the British naval
officer is frightened of sinking his ship. Inevitably, the Foreign Office
prefer diplomatists who say soothing and optimistic things to diplomatists
who tell home truths in defiant language. Smugness, rather than out-
spoken realism, is apt to colour many diplomatic reports. A certain nar-
cotic quality thus pervades the information which they supply.

Yet this is but a venial sin.

THE DECLINE OF DIPLOMACY

LORD VANSITTART *

. . . The general decline, in this century, of artificial manners is rather
worse than interesting; and in no sphere has the downward curve been
so steep as in diplomacy. I began my job 47 years ago, and it was a fairly
gentlemanly one on the surface. "The rapine underneath" was there, but
it was relatively war in lace. Some conventions and ostensible courtesies
were preserved.

Occasionally someone exploded in uniform and in dubious French.
(The Americans in their frigid dress-clothes were mostly immune from
even these ebullitions.) Sometimes one ran into quite a bit of dirt. But
life slid along between the clashes and flounderings.

Remnants of the jargon long remained embedded in our language.
Thus, when war came, an Ambassador "asked for his passports" (in the
plural). In fact he had but one, from which he was never parted. I re-

* Lord Vansittart, "The Decline of Diplomacy," *Foreign Affairs*, Vol. 28, No. 2 (January, 1950), pp. 177–188. Copyright 1949, by the Council on Foreign Relations, Inc. Reprinted by permission.

cently saw the old touch taken literally. In the film life of President Wilson the German Ambassador visited the White House at midnight, I think, to "ask for his passports." Author and audience perhaps thought that the President kept them somewhere. I even think that he produced them. The episode recalled a dead world.

Nowadays our diplomatists are booted around incontinent. The tone adopted to and about western diplomatic and consular representatives of all grades by all governments of the Iron Curtain is on the same level as the vituperations of their press. It is the style of an aggressive drunk. Buffon said that "style is the man himself;" but it is, alas, more than that. This is the style of a creed and an era.

In the days when politeness was a tradition, and tradition counted, demands for the recall of diplomatists were unknown save in rare cases of extreme provocation or impropriety. (The expulsion of Lord Sackville from the United States was not really deserved.) Now removal of Ambassadors or Chargés d'Affaires is continually demanded on the flimsiest pretext, and subordinates are simply thrown out in 48 hours. (I have often urged that we should all retaliate more formidably; Communist missions are much more useful to them than ours in Totalitaria are to us.) The excuse for this insolence is usually some stale and fantastic taradiddle on the theme of espionage, which is worked to death like much else by the Cominformants. The simplest conversation with a local citizen is sufficient to start the insanity, which invariably ends in manifold liquidations.

Here it should be stated parenthetically as a quite small cause of disrespect that Ambassadors have been multiplied beyond sense or recognition to gratify *amour propre*. Before 1914 only the Great Powers had Ambassadors, and these had both rank and power. Now they are increasingly mouthpieces; they have lost stature, and braided lightweights have not gained it.

Diplomacy would, however, have changed even without this minor metamorphosis. It is a commonplace that the Iron Curtain exists not only to prevent its inmates from knowing anything of the outside world, but also to bar all understanding from unwelcome but inevitable intruders, which is the totalitarian conception of even the most diplomatic infidel. Here we get nearer to the real causes of the decline in diplomacy during the second quarter of the twentieth century. For, until the First German War at least, diplomatists who knew well the peoples and languages of the countries where they were posted were thought to be an asset to both parties. They were always useful in maintaining good relations; they were often exceedingly popular, and the governments to which they were accredited were loath to let them go. Indeed foreign requests for prolongations of their appointments were sometimes embarrassing. Sometimes they—for instance Herrick—acquired the popularity without acquiring the tongue.

The past put a premium on courtesy. Wherever they went—mainly without let or hindrance—sane diplomatists tried to absorb as much as possible for their real purpose—peace, which they much enjoyed. Contrast this with the real policy of Totalitaria, which is the deepening and widening of ignorance. There is a deliberate aim to get rid of western diplomatists who know the language or nature of the country where they are stationed. There are many cases where this has been the sole reason for expulsion. The change is fundamental.

Here again I must diverge for a moment to complete the picture, and to add in fairness that often where a government had evil intentions its diplomatic representatives were kept in ignorance, the better to play their parts; or sometimes, knowing, they protested. There were bad men in the business, like Holstein, but the novelesque Machiavellis were the exception, not the rule. To the same order of ideas belongs the dramatized cliché of the mid-nineteenth century that "a diplomatist is an honest man paid to lie by his country." With the advent of Nazism and Communism, alike state conspiracies, most of their representatives were involved.

Thus we come to the main cause for the decline of diplomacy; and it will only be fully apparent when we look at its operation from the other end—that is, the composition, activities and purposes of the Communist staffs in foreign capitals. . . .

The change resides in this. The old diplomacy mainly existed to maintain good international relations. When it failed its job was done, and it packed up—"asked for its passports," or more prosaically took a train—for then war had come in spite and not because of it in most instances. Enough official papers from the last century are now available to prove the truth of this assertion. Take, for example, the desperate efforts made to deter Germany from the last two of her five wars. In 1914 both Lichnowsky and Mensdorff did what little they could to milden their evil governments. Broadly speaking, the real charge that can be made against the old diplomacy is that, though sometimes tough or provocative, it was mostly too suave and honeyed on the part of the intending aggressor, too patient and conciliatory on the part of the aggressed. The second tendency issued in appeasement.

Nowadays the diplomacy of an increasing part of the world is thoughtfully calculated to create and maintain *bad* relations. This, of course, is done in no mere *Schadenfreude* or spirit of spite. Bad relations with western democracies and capitalist countries are an article of faith, an accepted condition for the survival of Totalitaria. The successful Communist statesman is therefore he who ensures the permanence and intens'ty of this condition. So the missions of the Cominform are largely stocked with persons who make no pretense of practising diplomacy as previously defined, but are employed solely for hostile propaganda, sabotage, subversion and espionage. I have plenty of evidence and illustration for which I have no space here, and which indeed are unnecessary to demonstrate so notorious a truism.

To revert again to the old diplomacy, espionage was not usually practised from embassies, though they were often the victims of it. They were generally kept apart from such compromising activities—at least by the cautious or respectable Powers. An occasional Military Attaché was mentioned in a scandal like the Dreyfus case. The diplomatic body was, however, practically never involved in such hullabaloos as those now fabricated by ubiquitous secret police disguised in the combinations and permutations of infinite initials. Erstwhile spy-stories rarely attained publicity; when they did there was something in them, but gentlemen in knee-breeches and decorations were seldom implicated. (Of legitimate information they naturally obtained as much as possible.) Sardou's famous play, "Les Pattes de Mouche," often acted in Britain and the United States under the title of "Diplomacy," was a joke in the profession. (Abel Hermant's "La Carrière" was great fun.) Communist diplomatic missions, on the contrary, are everywhere up to the eyes in spying, and "make no bones" about it, though they protest loudly and *pro forma* when detected.

Espionage, however, is only the beginning of the mischief. Sabotage is an even surer way of ensuring the ideal of bad relations, because it is more widely felt. Totalitarian diplomacy now practices two kinds of sabotage, both of which are directed by its missions. The first, of course, is technical preparation for the event of war. The second is the "softening" or undermining of the countries with which war is contemplated. It is essential for the Soviet "Day" that these should first be economically weakened or ruined. The most favored methods are the "unofficial" and "rolling" strikes; but there are many other means of fomenting political disloyalty through industrial disaffection. The details of the technique do not concern us here; the point is that they are a function of the new diplomacy. The old might well turn in its grave. By these openly flaunted means a maximum of resentment is attained by Soviet diplomacy and its satellites. It all sounds like madness, but there is a tireless method in it.

The next activity is more insidious and equally novel, though its advent has been more gradual. It is openly to persuade as many people as possible, in the country whose hospitality is accepted, to hate and revile their own land. This is by far the best way to ensure bad relations. It is achieved partly by Communist press and radio from without, but also by local agencies for publicity (which take orders and subsidies from the Cominform through Communist embassies and legations), and finally by forming and financing "Friendship Societies" to cover the knaves who recruit the fools.

All this leads logically to the next step in the decline. Under the old school, immunity was limited to the diplomatic staff. There were considerable doubts whether it even extended to the consular personnel. Certainly no one would ever have thought of extending the claim to any other body. Such a course would have been impossible, and anyhow it would not have paid, for it would have lowered the status of the greatly self-esteeming plenipotentiaries.

With the vicious extension of the province of diplomacy has come a corresponding exaggeration of the claim for immunity. When all sorts of rogues are part of the machinery, all sorts of devices must be thought up to cover them. The process began in the greatly overstaffed Communist trade agencies—thin concealment indeed, seeing the small trade done by them. Now it has reached the press agencies, and has just produced a *cause célèbre*, which may find its place in international law, if any such thing is preserved in the future—a doubtful hypothesis.

The Soviet Government keeps Tass agencies everywhere for disseminating propaganda. Hitherto these have enjoyed no more privilege than any other undiplomatic body. But recently the London office of Tass brought a foul charge against a most worthy and distinguished exile. He tried to bring a libel action, and Tass at once bolted for cover. It produced to the British court a certificate from the Soviet Ambassador affirming that the news agency is an organ of the Soviet Government. The British court felt bound to accept the certificate. By this trick the agency has hitherto avoided prosecution. I say "hitherto," for I do not mean to let the decision stand unchallenged, and shall attack it when Parliament reassembles. I have already obtained from the Lord Chancellor a public admission that the claim is wholly unprecedented. Just think of the consequences were such a pretension conceded! Any foreign fount of malevolence would then be a law unto itself; there would be no conceivable bound to privilege, which would need only a small further stretch to cast its mantle over espionage as well. Even the most disreputable gangsters would thus be an official part of the new diplomacy. It is typical of the times that such a monstrosity as this Ambassadorial testimony should have been put forward at all. It must be brushed aside, and that gesture also will be symptomatic of a growing disregard for envoys.

Of old, as aforesaid, we diplomatists lived together in apparent comity for enjoyable lapses of time. Even in periods of friction there was some semblance of *esprit de corps*. We were rival practitioners of the same honorable trade. All this is changed. Nowadays these accumulated and exploited elements of discord amount to a state of permanent bad temper. I sometimes think that the degradation of the language of diplomacy is even more sinister than the debasement of its performance. There is a smell of the jungle about these dense growths of words, which smother old conceptions like voluble creepers.

Diplomacy has passed through every phase in its short life, for it only began in the last few centuries, and grew up late. It started with covenants secretly arrived at, less because anyone was ashamed of their contents than because these were of no interest to an illiterate and uninfluential public. The old methods have proved to be no more obnoxious than the new. Similarly, the balance of power, after having been first an ideal and then a punch-bag, is now being practised again and not mentioned by name—which is perhaps sensible, seeing that "human notions are few, not far between."

In the twentieth century, however, President Wilson had a brain-wave. He dreamed of "open diplomacy," and of "open convenants openly arrived at." That really sounded like something. Only after unhappy experience was it discovered that preliminary negotiation cannot profitably be conducted in the open. This glimpse of the obvious was generously assisted by the well-informed activities of the press and by the embarrassing antics of national propaganda and self-advertisement. Wilson was sagely crying for the moon. All right, said some, let us compound for open covenants secretly arrived at. Alas, great chunks of humanity were morally indisposed even to this check on their way to the abyss. The Nazis and the Communists in their *amours* begat a clutch of secret treaties much worse than any that had gone before.

The world of optimists, or even meliorists, thought again, and tended to content itself with diplomacy which could produce decent treaties "any old how." In consequence it got some rather indecent ones after much indecent bickering. The Allies, still so-called, concluded—a verb as inept as the noun—the treaties with Italy and the other ex-satellites, which contained many grave errors and stood no chance of observance, as I pointed out at the time. We have since discovered that the new diplomacy affords no possibility of concluding a German treaty at all; and this is just as well, when we consider the total perfidy of Totalitaria. It is one of history's little jokes that the authors of the Treaty of Versailles were blamed for drafting it in six months. We may be sorry for the Austrians, but even if their desire for a treaty be fulfilled, it will also be an unjust one, which would compromise the little country's prospect of economic survival, and even of territorial integrity. King Log being withdrawn, King Stork may return. No treaty is certainly better than a bad one. I understand this to have been the view of the American representative. I certainly concur in it. I have no wish to see Austria either ruined or reinvaded. In any case even a good treaty would not be kept by the Soviets. The futility of treaties is, however, another matter, which would require a chapter, or even a book, to itself. I will not dwell on it here, beyond observing that all endeavor of diplomacy in treaty-making is stultified by the habitual treaty-breaking of modern despotism.

We have reached the paradox that the decline of diplomacy has synchronized with the increasing equipment of its exponents. The great Ambassadors of the nineteenth century were sometimes not particularly clever men; sometimes they were not even particularly well educated, and owed their positions to favor. I saw at close quarters some who survived into the twentieth. Few of them would have had the least chance of withstanding an examination in any modern sense; but they did their work with authority, partly because there was no organized attempt to prevent them. In the period preceding theirs, an Ambassador's authority was even greater: he sometimes initiated policy and enjoyed considerable latitude, owing to lack of communications. As these improved, Ambassadorial status dwindled to that of mere executant of a policy decided not even in Foreign Offices but in Cabinets.

In complete contrast with a school as extinct as the dodo, our young men today are trained, perhaps overtrained, for a vanishing future, and tested and accoutred with all specialized ingenuity, some of it—in our case—sometimes a little silly. "Too clever by half," my Victorian nurse used to say. Their intellectual attainments greatly, and rightly, exceed those deemed essential in the zenith of diplomacy when the wheels of procedure crunched over the gravel, not always easy going but good enough for carriage folk. Now the surface is made for speed, but the road is usually blocked. Simultaneously the traffic has increased. The staffs of missions have been multiplied tenfold. And all this apparatus has been brought into play in an era which offers less hope for it. The negotiators of the Austrian treaty re-formed, dissolved, returned, mulled over their texts, till they knew them and each other by heart. Nothing happened year after year. Such treaties as have been landed lie instantly in fragments, and all protests are vain. These goings-on would have been deemed impossible in an age less efficient and more affable.

Diplomacy, with all its failings—it had many because it was far too much a class affair, and power politics are never pretty—was an instrument of civilization. It is being paralyzed, but only in common with other previously accepted amenities. It was one of the many veils in which we had sought to soften the outlines of the real harshness of human nature and existence. Now veils have gone out of fashion. I have "done" many conferences in my life, but never went into one without some hope of a fairly quick result. No one could say the same today. Results are often not expected, and often not even desirable, while the technique of negotiation is equally often transformed into a brawling match.

A gallant and pernickety veteran, who had risen to a colonelcy in the First War Against the Germans, immediately volunteered for the Second, and was duly invalided out. Describing his experiences in his club, he said: "My dear fellow, you really can't think what it's like *this* time! The smell . . . the noise . . . and . . . the *people!*" The comment is less applicable to the battlefield than to the conference chamber, for all its new-fangled facilities of earphones and automatic translations.

It may be said that this applies only to the representatives of half mankind. There is no reason why the other half should not behave itself. Part of our species is being conducted by sedulous apes back to the treetops, where it cannot exist; but the rest of *Homo sapiens* can live up to its lightly assumed title. That is perfectly true. And it isn't—not perfectly. We cannot get away from "the noise . . . and the people" of the Iron Curtain leaders so long as we have to meet them in the United Nations or in any more of these shy-making Big Fours—the Apotheosis of Avoirdupois. The pace of a troops was proverbially regulated by the slowest horse; the tone of a conference is set by its noisiest delegation. Diplomacy could flourish only so long as there was a loose, tacit and general agreement to behave *more or less* like gentlemen. There was no snobbery in the notion—only an instinctive recognition of our own limitations. The code was quite vague, and we never used the term "gentlemen's agreement" until it had become anathema to use the word gentleman in any other sense. It survived for a while like an appendix in the diplomatic body. From the moment when the behavior of rowdies became a constant feature, the old body was plainly moribund—for good or evil. We may hope for "somehow good," but the adverse balance is thus far incontestable.

One kind of old diplomacy did cling on until the end of the war; but it was the dubious sort known as personal. From distant days to the present, Very Important Persons have kept up intimate and important correspondences. Then it was time to go, and they mostly took their personal archives with them, salving their public consciences by underlining the word Private in the top left-hand corner. Some valuable material vanished in this way. Only a man as unearthly as Edward Grey kept and left his "private" correspondence in its official place. There is no positive harm in getting off the record, unless the exchanges become unduly secretive, as they sometimes do. Subordinates may then err through ig-norance of vital passages between superiors. In general we may say that it is natural for the great to be on epistolary terms—within limits.

Unhappily, and mechanically, those limits extend themselves. From having their private post offices, the great pass easily to having their private postmen. Thus a rival Foreign Office was run by Lloyd George: it consisted of Lord Lothian. As liaison between Curzon and Lloyd George I had the uneasy task of trying both to contend and cooperate with it. Very Important Persons comprehensibly like to count on a reliable body of assent. They mean to pursue a policy: why weaken themselves by doubts and contradictions? The term yes-men is unnecessarily harsh—indeed unfair—because most henchmen are sincerely fascinated by their chiefs. Thus Chamberlain too had his supporter, Sir Horace Wilson, and the Foreign Office was again overshadowed. As Chief Diplomatic Adviser I saw Chamberlain only thrice in three years, and never once alone. What could be more understandable? He knew that I disagreed with his views. Unhappily neither Lothian nor Wilson had experience of Europe. Nor, for that matter, had Harry Hopkins. Yet it seemed as natural to his patron that he should be sent to cope with Stalin as it seemed natural to Cham-berlain that Halifax should go to Berlin and Berchtesgaden under the amateurish cover of a hunting exhibition.

The V.I.P.'s often love to get rid of experts (which was easier of yore, when there weren't many anyway) and to indulge in a little—which be-comes a lot—of diplomacy "on their own." I fully understand the taste, but—all passion spent—condemn it because it is apt to be attended by favoritism and incompetence. There is something restricted and restrain-ing about an expert, which makes him look narrow to the wide-eyed; and since

"les oreilles des grands
Sont souvent de grandes oreilles,"

he is sometimes compelled, if he has any guts, to adopt the governess touch, which is unfair to him. There is something at once humble and superior about an expert—a trying combination. Consequently some antagonism may arise on *both* sides. But I do comprehend the recurrent itch of the Big Boys (Fours or better) to give rein to their untrammelled inspirations; and it was good entertainment when one day at the Peace Conference M. Clemenceau flared up, and threw out all his own experts plus everyone else's. A little personal diplomacy was impending. Arthur Balfour's chief interest in Lloyd George—and a fascinating one too—was wondering, in his own words, what the Little Man would do next.

In modern times personal diplomacy was much favored by both Church-ill and Roosevelt, who loved to carry on negotiations free from "interference." This predilection was facilitated, and in part necessitated, by war; but such courses are always apt to go too far and to produce errors which might be avoided, given better opportunities for briefing. When it came to personal diplomacy with Stalin, the results were more unfortunate, and to East Europe ruinous. The deals at the expense of Poland and China were as immoral as anything in the ages preceding Ostensible Enlightenment, and were only put over by the weight of unparalleled authority. I do not suppose that there have been many further temptations to personal diplomacy with the Kremlin.

The practice is an essay in omniscience, and it is only sometimes successful, because everyone needs advice. *Nemo sapit omnibus horis* was translated by Mr. Carlter of *The Dolly Dialogues:* "Everyone has been in love at least once." He should have added, "in love with himself." There is nothing new in a tendency which has long roots, but it has grown considerably as the century wears on—perhaps the right expression.

Another modern habit greatly increasing of late is "popular diplomacy." Of course there is really no such thing, just as there is no "popular democracy." There are either democracy and diplomacy without epithets or there are not. In this case the device is an attempt to bypass the governments concerned by appealing over their heads to their people. This has developed into a pernicious usage, and some may point to the fact that the United States virtually started it in the First World War. The answer is that it would have come about anyhow. President Wilson hoped to curtail hostilities by addressing himself to the German people. Most commentators greatly overestimate the effect of this legitimate manoeuvre in wartime. I am not among them. The Germans fought both their great wars to the bitter end. In any case when Wilson later attempted the same tactics with the Italians, the results were admittedly disastrous.

Since then the Totalitarians, in complete control of all their means of communication, have taken over and insensately developed the method. I have already enumerated the nefarious uses for which Communist missions really exist. For true diplomatic considerations they might as well not be there, and we of the democracies might *almost* as well have no representation in Moscow, though there are a few faint arguments for maintaining it in satellite countries. Communist radio is Communist diplomacy, and it has defeated its own ends. While the bellowings go crescendo, the fruits are in marked diminuendo, for no Soviet spokesman seems to have a middle register.

The method is already past its peak, but it has forced itself back upon the democracies by making them resume and improve Wilson's initiative. In the ungraceful German metaphor, we have to do a bit of "howling with the wolves." Here also the effect is small, because so few of the enslaved peoples are able to hear the B.B.C. or the Voice of America owing to jamming and the shortage of receivers. Still we rightly plug along in this duplicate diplomacy; my only comment is that we do not exploit it with sufficient punch and virility. We may as well "make the best of a bad job."

"Everything flows," though not to the pacific. We have lost the belief in automatic progress, and diplomacy is for the nonce among the casualties, through no fault of genuine democracy. It outlasted the parallel practitioners of the League, and could well have coexisted with the United Nations, had they not suffered from trichinosis. It has only wilted under Communist hot air. It may come to its own again in modern dress; indeed it has never fallen into disuse among civilized peoples. But, in common with other advantageous growths, such as Justice, it can never regain worldwide acceptance, so long as the New Barbarians hold sway. We had better make up our minds to that, and conduct ourselves accordingly.

Harold Nicolson calls the life of his father, Lord Carnock, "a study in the Old Diplomacy." There was something to be said for it. Some will say: "Not much." Having experienced both old and new I reply: "More than can be said for its successor."

CHAPTER 6

ALLIANCES AND THE BALANCE OF POWER

WITHIN THE whole field of international politics no concept is super-ficially so capable of definition and yet so elusive and subtle in its workings as the balance of power. The principle involved is easily understood—the balancing of power with power. The fact that decisions can be taken in one or more independent states which may drastically affect the national well-being and vital interests of other nations means that foreign policy must be shaped primarily with the end in view of neutralizing the power threat implicit in such a state system. One solution—indeed, the most frequently adopted solution —is for each nation to seek allies which will counterbalance the power of its principal rival and its allies. In this way an alliance system is created which may preserve national security by the balancing of rival nations and rival power blocs. Under conditions of a true balance neither group could afford to take the decision to attack the other, since it is a first principle of military strategy never to attack without superior force. The fact that victory cannot be certain will, in theory, deter aggression. If the balance of power at all times worked as effectively as its name implies, an end would be put to world wars. The fact that it has not done so stems from certain ambiguities implicit in the concept, as well as from the fact that the alliances which are the sinews of the system may not be honored at the critical point.

In the first reading, "The Balance of Power as Policy" by Nicholas J. Spykman, these ambiguities are discussed. Particularly because nations are not really concerned with *balancing* rival powers but in *overbalancing* them, the balance of power tends at times to become a *race for power*. No nation or group of nations is content to be merely equal to its rival, since the advantage over its rival would be enormous if its own power were only slightly increased, and the reverse would be equally true. In situations where equality has actually been obtained, a slight advantage might prove decisive in the event of war. Moreover, as Spykman points out, the actual task of assessing the power of rival blocs is almost insuperable, since power depends upon a variety of constantly changing factors, many of them purposely shrouded in secrecy (such as the number of atomic bombs possessed by the United States at this moment). Estimates of power are therefore subject to grave error. The resulting uncertainty may either encourage or discourage a potential aggressor, depending upon whether the intended victim's power has been overestimated or underestimated. The possibilities for error and the failure of power rivals to be content with mere equality are only two of the more obvious weaknesses of the balance-of-power theory.

In the second selection, "The Balance of Power in Action," Sir Eyre Crowe, out of his many years' experience as an active participant in foreign affairs, describes the effects of the diplomatic revolution of 1904 when Great Britain, in the face of the growing German threat, came to an understanding with her historic enemy, France. His analysis of Britain's policies sheds much light on the workings of the balance-of-power system in which Britain historically participated. Especially interesting is the way in which Crowe links the balance of power to the necessity for Britain's safe guarding the independence of small states.

Certain points about the balance-of-power theory itself must be clarified if what Crowe is saying is to be fully understood. From an analytical standpoint two main forms of the balance of power exist— the *simple* balance and the *complex* balance. When all the great powers taking an active part in the balance are irrevocably and exclusively committed to one of two rival blocs, the balance becomes simple and *rigid*. When, on the other hand, this has not occurred, the balance remains complex and *flexible*. Before Britain had in effect definitely allied herself with France in 1904, she had sometimes espoused the cause of the Triple Alliance (Austria, Germany, and Italy) and sometimes that of the Dual Entente (France and Russia). As "balancer" she threw her weight to either side with the intention of strengthening the weaker side and preventing the balance from being overturned. Because each group had to consider the possible policy of Britain, they were inclined toward moderation in their policies. Once Britain abandoned her traditional role of "balancer" and permanently associated herself with the Dual Entente, one important reason for moderation in foreign policy was removed. The attitudes of the blocs toward each other became increasingly unyielding. Since there was no longer a great power uncommitted to either side, whose strength when committed could be decisive, each bloc was held in check only by the opposing bloc and each sought to gain an advantage over the other to prevent an advantage being gained over itself. Tests of strength over various issues produced a series of crises ending in war in 1914.

The understanding of 1904 between Britain and France also marked the disappearance of another element which had contributed to the complexity and flexibility of the system. Although at odds on European affairs prior to 1904, France and Germany often cooperated with each other against Britain on colonial questions. While their national interests in Europe brought them into opposition, their interests in Africa and in Asia often induced them to work together. This had a definite moderating effect upon the balance of power, since, although they were rivals within the primary balance of power (in Europe), they were often allies within the secondary balance of power (in Africa and Asia). With the accomplishment of the Franco-British entente, colonial issues which had kept Britain and France opposed were compromised and hence the secondary balance of power largely disappeared. The 1907 rapprochement of Great Britain and Russia completed the destruction of the secondary balance of power. The rigid opposition of the two major blocs in Europe rapidly increased the tensions which culminated in World War I.

The history of the balance-of-power system has again and again reflected these tendencies. When the interests of the powers are sought exclusively through rival blocs that have no elements drawing them together, war becomes likely. When, on the other hand, the system is flexible and complex, war remains unlikely, since the moderating influences mentioned above draw the rivals in some respects into rapprochement.

In addition to the forms of the balance of power already considered, it is important to recognize the connection between isolationism and the balance of power. It is revealing that prior to 1904 Britain followed a policy which she termed "splendid isolation." She was not committed to either group but balanced the balance—"isolated" not from the balance as such but from any one of the two blocs which formed it. On the other hand, during the nineteenth century and spasmodically in the twentieth, the United States held aloof from participation in the balance. Significantly, this policy was followed during the very

period when Britain played the "balancer." Indeed, American isolationism *was made possible* by the stability and complexity of the
nineteenth-century balance of power, Britain's control of the sea lanes,
and Britain's determination to discourage European imperialism in
the Americas. America was free to choose isolationism in *preference*
to a balance-of-power policy only because the balance was stable without her. When the balance of power collapsed in 1914 to 1917 and
again in 1939 to 1941, isolationism, dependent upon a stable balance
for its existence, became completely impossible. The realization that
America must now become an active participant in the balance of
power even before the advent of war is one of the main reasons for the
formation of the Atlantic alliance. Even though the alliance has been
described as a "regional collective security arrangement," it is fundamentally a rejection of universal collective security and a substitution
of a balance-of-power arrangement.

In the third reading, "The Atlantic Pact and International Security," Grayson Kirk analyzes the effects of our participation in the Atlantic alliance. He points out that such alliances also occurred during
League of Nations days and those who made them claimed that they
were compatible with the Covenant, just as it is claimed today that
the Atlantic Pact is compatible with the Charter. The growth of par-
ticularistic alliances in each case reflects a lack of faith in the ability
of the international organization to safeguard national security generally and adequately. Kirk raises the question whether the United
States has actually finally abandoned isolationism. The relative lack
of debate over the alliance may mean that the American people have
not fully understood the implications of the Pact. He points out the
dangers implicit in the fact that America regards the alliance as assuring an advanced base against further Russian expansion, while
Western Europe, reluctant to assume the role of prospective battleground, desires peace and is far less willing to face the prospect of
war. In so far as the Atlantic Pact binds its members more closely to
the United States, Kirk argues that a tendency toward a "global bi-
polar division of influence" (a rigid and simple balance of power) will
occur which is "a path toward ultimate war." This point is well taken,
although subsequent events have demonstrated that the European
members of the alliance have continued to pursue often highly independent foreign policies so that much of the rigidity which might have
been anticipated has not occurred. This diversity of view which has

kept the balance of power flexible is particularly evident in the 1950 to 1951 Anglo-American debate over Communist China.

The fourth selection, "Ideology or Balance of Power?" by William G. Carleton, is concerned with one of the most important issues of our own time, namely, whether the balance of power as an instrument for the preservation of national security is becoming obsolete to the extent that internationalism may be supplanting nationalism. Carleton poses the question whether ideology or the balance of power will in the years ahead exercise the determining influence in the formulation of national foreign policies. Up to the present time alliances have frequently been concluded across ideological frontiers—witness the coalition of the United Nations itself which included both the United States and the Soviet Union. Will the future pattern be different? Will nations henceforth conclude alliances only with other nations having similar ideologies?

The answer to this question is bound up with the future of communism and the prospects of the spread of Titoism. Whether newly communized nations such as China which are both large and distant from the centers of Soviet power and which have not been actually occupied by the Red army will in the long run subordinate their national interests—hitherto sought through the balance of power—to the dictates of Moscow is a riddle which the future alone can unravel.

THE BALANCE OF POWER AS POLICY

NICHOLAS J. SPYKMAN *

. . . The number of cases in which a strong dynamic state has stopped expanding because of satiation or has set modest limits to its power aims has been very few indeed. The policy which aims to restrain growing states and is known as the balance of power policy has been part and parcel of the diplomacy of all successful states. Experience has shown that there is more safety in balanced power than in a declaration of good intention. To preserve the balance requires action not only against the neighbor that becomes too powerful but also against distant states. As a matter of fact, the best period for the application of this policy is before continued ex-

* Nicholas J. Spykman, *America's Strategy in World Politics*, pp. 20–25. Copyright 1942, by Harcourt, Brace and Company, Inc. Reprinted by permission.

pansion makes the growing state a neighbor. A hegemony that has access to the sea can become a menace to far distant shores and the ever-increasing bombing range of modern aircraft is making air power almost as effective a threat as sea power against non-contiguous states.

It is obvious that a balance of power policy is in the first place a policy for the Great Powers. The small states, unless they can successfully combine together, can only be weights in a balance used by others. But although they are stakes rather than players, their interest in the outcome of the game is none the less great. A small state is a vacuum in a political high pressure area. It does not live because of its own strength but because nobody wants its territory or because its preservation as a buffer state or as a weight in the balance of power is of interest to a stronger nation. When the balance disappears, the small states usually disappear with it.

Since the Renaissance and the Reformation, the balance of power has been a favorite topic of speculation among the political philosophers of Europe. After Emperor and Pope had lost their function as keystones in the European political order, a search began for a new integrating principle. It was found in the "balance of power," which became the subject of learned discourses. The philosophers pointed out its relation to the law of nature and the harmony of the spheres and indicated that an equilibrium was not only inherently beautiful but full of practical and ethical implications. If all states were held in check, no state could win a war; and, if no state could win a war, then no state would start a war or threaten war. Equilibrium is balanced power, and balanced power is neutralized power. A society in political equilibrium is a society in which force is useless and in which men will, therefore, live happily by the reign of law and devote themselves to the arts and graces.

To the men of learning it seemed obvious that states ought to pursue a balance of power policy; that the law of nature and Christian ethics both demand such a policy. States ought to direct their diplomacy not merely at counterbalancing specific threats to themselves but at establishing a balanced system for the whole of the international society. They ought to pursue a balance of power policy not merely to preserve their own relative power position but to preserve peace.

Statesmen have always been eager to accept from the theologian and the philosopher the correct formulation of the ethical precepts that should guide foreign policy, and since the seventeenth century all power politics has, therefore, been presented not as a crude attempt to survive in a tough world but as a noble endeavor aimed at the establishment of political equilibrium and the preservation of order.

Formulated in those terms the success has not been overwhelming. We might search for an explanation in the fact that the process is not guaranteed and that not all statesmen are good technicians, but it is perhaps safer to explain the result on the theory that they were not really interested in achieving a balance. There are not many instances in history which show great and powerful states creating alliances and organizations to limit their own strength. States are always engaged in curbing the force of some other state. The truth of the matter is that states are interested only in a balance which is in their favor. Not an equilibrium, but a generous margin is their objective. There is no real security in being just as strong as a potential enemy; there is security only in being a little stronger. There is no possibility of action if one's strength is fully checked; there is a chance for a positive foreign policy only if there is a margin of force which can be freely used. Whatever the theory and the rationalization, the practical objective is the constant improvement of the state's own relative power position. The balance desired is the one which neutralizes other states, leaving the home state free to be the deciding force and the deciding voice.

It would seem that this objective does not require quite the accuracy in measuring which the search for a perfect equilibrium would require, but, even so, the task is full of difficulties. It is easy to balance mechanical forces because they can be measured, but there is no measuring stick for political power. Are two states balanced, is their power equal, is the relationship between the two sets of alliances in equilibrium? On that question there is usually profound disagreement. The relative power remains a purely subjective judgment. Each state always feels that the other one needs balancing. In so far as the power concerned is in the last instance a power to wage war, it might be assumed that the military men would know the answer, but theirs is an opinion equally subjective, even if a little more expert. The most learned generals have disagreed as often as the statesmen. The only objective test of relative strength is to fight the war and see who wins, but this is hardly a helpful guide to the state that wants to decide whether to fight or not.

The second difficulty lies in the fact that the elements contributing to strength are not static but dynamic; they do not stay put. A new economic development, a new raw material, a new weapon, a new martial spirit may produce the most profound inequality between states that only a few years before had been approximately equal. Besides, in a world of states of equal strength, what is there to prevent the combination of two of them against a third?

Another problem which sometimes appears is the discovery that the state selected to be the ally in the opposition to the growing power has already made a deal with the opponent, and the chance for a balance has been missed. Similar unfortunate results may flow from the fact that statesmen occasionally believe in the innocence of other statesmen. This permits some of them to achieve enormous expansion by the accretion of small additions of territory. The state of Lusitania announces that it has only one very limited aim, the incorporation of a little territory of the state of Mauritania after which the true balance will have been established, and it will never aspire to another square foot of land. The demand is so small, the request so modest that it is obviously not worth fighting for. It will, of course, be discovered afterwards that there is still no perfect balance, that there is still need for an additional piece of territory. This even smaller piece is likewise not worth fighting for. It lies perhaps in a region outside the immediate interest of the state which must decide how to act, and so its annexation goes unopposed. It is by this process of gradual conquest that most of the successful hegemonies have been established.

An actual balance of power policy operates along several lines, boundary making, compensation, the creation of alliances, and varying degrees of intervention in wars, grading all the way from slight deviations from neutrality to full participation as an ally. Boundary making is important at the end of a war, and historically the Great Powers have always demanded to be heard at the peace settlement even if they had not participated in the conflict. Under the theory of compensation, states have permitted other states to grow provided they themselves obtained an equal accretion of strength and prestige. It was under this principle of compensation and in the name of the balance of power that the Treaty of Westphalia parceled out the small German principalities among Austria, Bavaria, Brandenburg, and Sweden; that Poland was divided four times; that Africa was carved up; and that plans were laid for the partition of China.

In addition to boundary making and compensation, nations have used systems of alliances to check the growth of a dynamic power. The least expensive and, therefore, the most preferable method would be for a state to encourage an alliance between third parties strong enough to ward off the danger. But this is seldom possible, and the state must be prepared to make its own positive contribution and become part of the alliance. The alliance may stipulate merely a limited contribution in the form of a fixed sum of money, a specific number of ships, or a defined number of soldiers. There is, however, little protection in such limitation. If the survival and continued independence of the ally is really important for the state's own security, its assistance may have to go far beyond the original promises. It will, in fact, have to be increased to whatever is necessary to assure victory and security.

The purpose of the alliance, like the purpose of all power politics, is to achieve the necessary margin of safety in the field of action. But the margin of security for one is the margin of danger for the other, and alliance must, therefore, be met by counter-alliance and armament by counter-armament in an eternal competitive struggle for power. Thus it has been in all periods of history. One state successfully conquers adjacent territory and makes each new conquest the stepping stone for further expansion, each accretion of power the means for further enlargement. Power tends to grow and diffuse through wider areas, and the states in the vicinity have the choice between collective defense and ultimate absorption.

The weak states of the Tigris-Euphrates valley allied themselves against their stronger rivals and preserved their independence for centuries, until Hammurabi finally established the Babylonian Empire. A new and inconclusive struggle for power then emerged over a much wider area between the Egyptians, the Assyrians, the Hittites, and the Persians with the smaller states in the region being used as buffers and weights. The Greek city-states maintained a precarious balance by means of the Delain and Peloponnesian Leagues under the leadership of Athens and Sparta, but they failed to combine against the menace of Macedonia. Rome, the victorious, found no league to stem her vast expansion and defeated her enemies one by one. Had they known how to combine, Carthage, Egypt, and Macedonia might have preserved their independence far longer and confined Rome within the boundaries of Europe.

Modern European history begins with the struggle for power among the Italian city-states which was later transferred to the national states over an ever-widening area eventually including the whole world. When the House of Hapsburg under Charles V attained such vast domains that it threatened to become a menace to other states, these states combined to check its ascendancy. Similar was the fate of the hegemonic aspiration of Spain under Philip II, France under Louis XIV and Napoleon, and Germany under Kaiser Wilhelm II. The fate of Germany's new bid for European domination depends on the outcome of the Second World War.

In this endless story of struggling states, there have been short periods in which an approximation to balanced power prevailed, not because anybody wanted it or tried to achieve it, but because two states or two sets of states were trying to upset it in different directions. Such a situation is inherently unstable because all parties are constantly attempting to destroy it, but while it lasts it brings mankind important benefits as the philosophers had promised. In an international society in which states are intent on preserving their independence, both against world conquest and against world government through federation, balanced power is the only approximation to order. When states are convinced that their strength is inadequate to enforce their will, they become peaceful and reasonable, they discover the benefits of conciliation and arbitration and plead in terms of law and justice instead of demanding in terms of force.

But a political equilibrium is neither a gift of the gods nor an inherently stable condition. It results from the active intervention of man, from the operation of political forces. States cannot afford to wait passively for the happy time when a miraculously achieved balance of power will bring peace and security. If they wish to survive, they must be willing to go to war to preserve a balance against the growing hegemonic power of the period. Balanced power may eventually reduce the prevalence of war, but force remains the most efficient instrument with which to check the expansion of states. Power politics has, therefore, added another reason for going to war to the long list already developed out of the inevitable conflict patterns of international intercourse. States must be ready to fight not only for the defense and the conquest of territory, for the protection and incorporation of nationals living across borders, for the preservation and acquisition of economic benefits, and for the defense and the propagation of national ideologies, but also for the preservation and improvement of their relative power positions.

THE BALANCE OF POWER IN ACTION

SIR EYRE CROWE *

The Anglo-French Agreement of the 8th April, 1904, was the outcome of the honest and ardent desire, freely expressed among all classes and parties of the two countries, that an earnest effort should be made to compose, as far as possible, the many differences which had been a source of perpetual friction between them. . . .

There were two difficulties: It was necessary, in the first instance, that the French Government should realize the benefit which France would derive from a policy of give and take, involving perhaps, from her point of view, some immediate sacrifice, but resulting in the banishment of all occasions for quarrels with a powerful neighbor. It was, secondly, indispensable, if French statesmen were to carry with them the public opinion of their own country, without which they would be powerless to act, that the suspiciousness of English designs and intentions, with which years of hostile feelings and active political rivalry had poisoned the French mind, should give place to confidence in the straightforwardness and loyalty of British Governments not only in meeting present engagements, but also in dealing with any future points of difference, in a conciliatory and neigh-

* Sir Eyre Crowe, "Memorandum." *British Documents on the Outbreak of the War,* edited by Gooch and Temperlev. Vol. III, pp. 397–400, 402–403, 417.

borly spirit. It was natural to believe that the growth of such confidence could not be quickly forced, but that it might slowly emerge by a process of gradual evolution. . . .

The conviction that the removal of causes of friction, apart from having an independent value of its own, as making directly for peace, would also confer on the Governments of both countries greater freedom in regulating their general foreign relations, can hardly be supposed to have been absent from the mind of the British and French negotiators. Whenever the Government of a country is confronted with external difficulties by the opposition of another State on a question of national rights or claims, the probable attitude of third Powers in regard to the point in dispute must always be a matter of anxious concern. The likelihood of other Powers actively taking sides in a quarrel which does not touch them directly may reasonably be expected, and, indeed, is shown by experience, very much to depend, quite apart from the merits of the dispute, on the general trend of relations existing between the several parties. It is impossible to overestimate the importance in such a connection of the existence of a firmly established and broadly based system of friendly intercourse with those Powers whose position would enable them to throw a heavy weight into the balance of strength on the other side. If a country could be imagined whose foreign relations were so favourably disposed that, in the defence of its legitimate interests, it could always count upon the sympathy of its most powerful neighbors, such a country would never—or at least not so long as the national armaments were maintained at the proper standard of efficiency—need to entertain those fears and misgivings which, under the actual conditions of dominant international jealousies and rivalries, only too often compel the abandonment of a just cause as the only alternative to the more serious evil and risk of giving suspicious and unfriendly neighbors a welcome opportunity for aggression or hostile and humiliating interference. If both France and England were acutely conscious that, in the contingency of either of them being involved in a quarrel with this or that Power, an Anglo-French understanding would at least remove one serious danger inherent in such a situation, patriotic self-interest would, on this ground alone, justify and encourage any attempt to settle outstanding differences, if and so far as they were found capable of settlement without jeopardizing vital interests. . . .

The maintenance of a state of tension and antagonism between third Powers had avowedly been one of the principle elements in Bismarck's political combinations by which he first secured and then endeavoured to preserve the predominant position of Germany on the continent. . . . The conclusion of the Franco-Russian alliance some time after Bismarck's fall filled Germany with concern and anxiety, and she never ceased in her efforts at least to neutralize it by establishing the closest possible relations with Russia for herself. . . .

It was, in fact, soon made apparent that, far from welcoming . . . an Anglo-French rapprochement, the Emperor's Government [Germany] had been thoroughly alarmed at the mere disappearance of all causes of friction between the two Western Powers. . . . Nor is it possible to be blind to the fact that Germany is bound to be as strongly opposed to a possible Anglo-Russian understanding. . . .

The general character of England's foreign policy is determined by the immutable conditions of her geographical situation on the ocean flank of Europe as an island State with vast oversea colonies and dependencies, whose existence and survival as an independent community are inseparably bound up with the possession of preponderant sea power. . . . Sea power is more potent than land power, because it is as pervading as the element in which it moves and has its being. Its formidable character makes itself felt the more directly that a maritime State is, in the literal sense of the word, the neighbor of every country accessible by sea. It would, therefore, be but natural that the power of a State supreme at sea should inspire universal jealousy and fear, and be ever exposed to the danger of being overthrown by a general combination of the world. Against such a combination no single nation could in the long run stand, least of all a small island kingdom not possessed of the military strength of a people trained to arms, and dependent for its food supply on oversea commerce. The danger can in practice only be averted—and history shows that it has been so averted—on condition that the national policy of the insular and naval State is so directed as to harmonize with the general desires and ideals common to all mankind, and more particularly that it is closely identified with the primary and vital interests of a majority, or as many as possible, of the other nations. Now, the first interest of all countries is the preservation of national independence. It follows that England, more than any other non-insular Power, has a direct and positive interest in the maintenance of the independence of nations, and therefore must be the natural enemy of any country threatening the independence of others, and the natural protector of the weaker communities. . . .

History shows that the danger threatening the independence of this or that nation has generally arisen, at least in part, out of the momentary predominance of a neighboring State at once militarily powerful, economically efficient, and ambitious to extend its frontiers or spread its influence, the danger being directly proportionate to the degree of its power and efficiency, and to the spontaneity or "inevitableness" of its ambitions. The only check on the abuse of political predominance derived from such a position has always consisted in the opposition of an equally formidable rival, or of a combination of several countries forming leagues of defence. The equilibrium established by such a grouping of forces is technically known as the balance of power, and it has become almost an historical truism to identify England's secular policy with the maintenance of this balance by throwing her weight now in this scale and now in that, but ever on the side opposed to the political dictatorship of the strongest single State or group at a given time.

If this view of British policy is correct, the opposition into which England must inevitably be driven to any country aspiring to such a dictatorship assumes almost the form of a law of nature. . . .

By applying this general law to a particular case, the attempt might be made to ascertain whether, at a given time, some powerful and ambitious State is or is not in a position of natural and necessary enmity towards England; and the present position of Germany might, perhaps, be so tested. . . .

So long as England remains faithful to the general principle of the preservation of the balance of power, her interests would not be served by Germany being reduced to the rank of a weak Power, as this might easily lead to a Franco-Russian predominance equally, if not more, formidable to the British Empire. There are no existing German rights, territorial or other, which this country could wish to see diminished. Therefore, so long as Germany's action does not overstep the line of legitimate protection of existing rights she can always count upon the sympathy and good-will, and even the moral support, of England.

THE ATLANTIC PACT AND INTERNATIONAL SECURITY

GRAYSON KIRK *

I

Current discussion about the Atlantic Pact has given a new emphasis and importance to an old controversy. Ever since the creation of the League of Nations men have disputed bitterly about the relationship of lesser groupings of states to an over-all organization. The view of President Wilson and many of his supporters was that the two were directly opposed to each other. It was argued that such limited security organizations were,

* Grayson Kirk, "The Atlantic Pact and International Security," *International Organization*, Vol. III, No. 2 (May, 1949), pp. 239–251. Copyright 1949, by World Peace Foundation. Reprinted by permission.

in effect, alliances, that they would produce counter-alliances, a revival of the "balance of power," and the destruction of an organization dedicated to the principle of world-wide "collective" security.

But while this view of stern disapproval officially prevailed in the drafting of the Covenant (except for the brief reference to "regional understandings" in Article 21) it did not at any time pass without challenge. Acute discontent soon arose in states, such as France, who felt that the League—with its lack of universality of great-power membership and its feeble provisions for military sanctions—could not be sufficiently effective to be regarded as the only necessary adjunct to their national military establishments. As a result, they made strenuous efforts to get their views officially adopted through such supplementary agreements as the Draft Treaty of Mutual Assistance. This effort failed and they turned their backs upon the official League principle and began to conclude limited mutual assistance pacts. In so doing, it was their argument that, far from weakening the League structure, these subordinate arrangements really would be a source of strength because they would bind together groups of states which had specific security interests in common. Such pacts, they insisted, thus would provide the over-all League with a sound underpinning of limited military obligations to reenforce the obligations of Articles 10 and 16. There is no need here to recount the development of these pacts. Some, like Locarno and the Little Entente, were definitely regional. Others like the Franco-Czech and the Franco-Soviet pacts were regional only in a much broader sense. But, whatever their precise basis or scope, the network of these pacts expanded steadily to meet specific security needs whenever and wherever they developed. And as the League failed to meet effectively the crises which confronted it, emphasis in security planning naturally shifted away from Geneva to an increased reliance on these more limited group agreements. As the crisis of the second world war approached, the nations paid little attention to the League and relied exclusively on their pacts of limited obligation. Indeed, the history of the inter-war period now was interpreted by many to indicate that the principle of universal security obligation was either fundamentally unsound or hopelessly premature. In 1935, for example, Sir Austen Chamberlain made the judgment that ". . . I do not think that we shall find the kind of security that we need . . . in guarantees which are equally binding for every war, wherever, however, on what subject whatsoever it may arise. For obligations so widely spread, so universal, and yet requiring—potentially at least— such immense sacrifices from the nations which undertake them are, I think, beyond the strength of humanity and call for sacrifices that the peoples of the world will not make until the whole outlook of the world has changed. I, therefore, incline . . . to those regional agreements which concentrate the obligations of each country more narrowly in an area where it at once feels that no disturbance of the peace can take place without its own security being in danger." [1]

With this background, it is not surprising that some of the more influential framers of the United Nations Charter should have taken a more generous view of regional arrangements in relation to the new system. Although certain of the League Covenant deficiencies were being remedied —in that the new organization would have universal great-power membership and, presumably, a much stronger sanctions enforcement system— still it was felt that subordinate security pacts could be made to harmonize fully with the general obligations of the Charter. And the Charter-makers did not limit themselves to a mere toleration of these regional associations; they believed that these groupings would be able to contribute positively to the new system in two ways. First, these regional associations might be able to settle local disputes simply and quietly without disturbing the Security Council. Second, they might become useful instruments for local enforcement of Security Council decisions. Finally, and irrespective of such possible contributions to the new order, a place had to be found for regional associations within the Charter framework because the development of the inter-American system had reached such a point that neither the United States nor the Latin American states were prepared to ignore it.

The knotty problem, of course, was the scope of autonomy to be possessed by these regional arrangements. If they were to have powers of action independent of Security Council authorization, they might disrupt the whole enforcement system. On the other hand, it was not possible, for political reasons, to regard them exclusively as enforcement agencies under the direction of the Security Council. Such action might be completely paralyzed by the veto in that body. The compromise was found in the provisions of Articles 52 and 53 and especially in Article 51 which gave Charter blessing to the principle of collective self-defense in the event of an armed attack.

The parallelism between developments after 1919 and after 1945 is striking. Now, as then, but for different reasons, the over-all organization has failed to develop the strength and prestige which its makers had anticipated. Now, as then, and for the same reasons, member states have turned to more limited international security associations to supplement their own national strength. As before, those who enter into such associations proclaim that these new arrangements are supplementary, and in no way antagonistic, to the broader United Nations obligations. A Rip Van Winkle of the early twenties might now rub his eyes, remark, "This is where I came in," and reach again for his trusty flagon.

[1] Maurice Bourquin, ed., *Collective Security*, Paris, 1936, p. 36.

If this observation about historical parallelism is true, then it is important to make a critical examination of present trends, the arguments that are being used to support them, and the direction in which they may lead us. Otherwise, in view of what happened before, we would be guilty of criminal negligence. It may not be possible to do anything about the direction of the trends, but at least we ought to try to estimate them as best we can, even though our only conclusion might be that we can do no better than to join our ancient friend's party in the Catskills.

The following attempt at analysis is directed rather specifically to the Atlantic Pact because it represents by all odds the most significant development to date in the direction of regional associations. It points up clearly and sharply the issues involved, and the stakes as well. Following our democratic tradition, the agreed text of the pact has now (at the time of writing) been submitted to public scrutiny. To undertake this task candidly and in full consciousness of the need to evaluate the pact in terms of its contribution to national security and international peace, is an obligation incumbent on all responsible citizens.

II

The arguments now being used in favor of the pact run somewhat as follows: The Soviet abuse of the veto has so hamstrung the Security Council that the whole United Nations security system remains undeveloped. Article 43 is a dead letter. Behind the wall of secrecy which hides the activities of the Military Staff Committee there is heard the occasional thunder of violent argument followed, apparently, by prolonged siestas of recuperation. Efforts at arms regulation have been frustrated by the atomic energy impasse and by the insistence of the United States and many other powers that security enforcement arrangements must precede arms limitation and regulation. (What a wry satisfaction the French must feel at this particular American and British *volte-face!*)

Meanwhile the general political climate worsens steadily. With the peace of the last war not yet concluded, the dangers of a new and more terrible war assail a frightened mankind on every hand. In such a parlous situation, when the exhausted nations of western Europe live in the darkening shadow of Soviet expansionism, they have a desperate need for external security support—in the form of the Atlantic Pact. With it, they will take heart again, shake off their fears, and renew their strength. At last, they are to have a formal and tangible assurance that the United States will not again watch on the side-lines, cheering them on while they grapple in mortal combat with a new aggressor, and only enter the fray when it is quite clear that they cannot win alone.

Viewed in this way, the pact is a natural and logical supplement to the economic aid being provided to the western European states by the Marshall Plan. Thus the State Department has observed that "People are reluctant to make the strenuous effort and personal sacrifice required for successful economic recovery when they fear that their land will be overrun by alien armies and the fruits of their toil taken from them. . . . If world recovery is to progress, the sense of security must be restored. Since the threat of armed aggression is at the root of insecurity, collective action which will enable free nations to confront a potential aggressor with preponderant power, together with economic recovery and political stability, provides the only satisfactory antidote to fear." [2]

This first argument—that the pact will strengthen western European morale—is followed by a second which is equally significant. This is the view that the formal association of the United States with these countries in a mutual assistance commitment will halt Soviet westward expansion permanently. Such a conclusion rests on the assumption that as long as there is any uncertainty about American policy toward western Europe, the Soviet leaders might be willing to risk an aggressive coup in the direction of the Atlantic, in the belief that the United States, presented with a sudden *fait accompli*, would make the best of it and not resort to retaliatory action. And, even if the United States did act, the Soviet decision-makers might feel that they would be better situated to fight with us on terms which would deny us the use of western Europe. On the other hand, if our policy is made perfectly clear, no such assumptions could be made and no such risks would be taken. As President Truman has said, "If we can make it sufficiently clear, in advance, that any armed attack affecting our national security would be met with overwhelming force, the armed attack might never occur." [3]

Parenthetically, this argument seems to derive from the apparent parallelism between Soviet expansionism and that of Germany in the last two wars, namely, that the German leaders would never have undertaken the war if they had been certain that the United States would have entered the war against them at the outset. Thus, Senator Vandenberg commented recently in a Senate discussion, ". . . in my opinion the mere formal recognition of this community of interest in the event of an armed attack upon the Atlantic community . . . would be an infinite assurance against World War III, because in my opinion if the Kaiser in World War I or the Fuehrer in World War II had been on notice that an armed attack against any of these friendly nations with whom we associate ourselves

---

[2] United States State Department, "Collective Security in the North Atlantic Area," *Foreign Affairs Outlines* 19, Department Publication 3377, January, 1949, p. 2.

[3] As cited by Secretary Acheson in a radio broadcast, March 18, 1949.

would be considered a cause even for us to consider and study and determine whether or not we would enter into the common defense, that would have stopped both of those wars before they occurred." [4]

According to this view, the removal of any possible Russian uncertainty about American policy gradually will lead to better mutual relations between the two superpowers. Being unwilling to bring on a major war with us, Russia will accept her "containment," will give up any hope of reaching the Atlantic, and will eventually settle down into a more cooperative frame of mind. Tension and suspicion will subside, and, little by little, the United Nations security system can begin to function in accordance with original plans.

Also, it is argued that the Atlantic Pact not only is strictly within the framework of the United Nations—being authorized by Articles 51, 52 and 53—but its creation will be a source of considerable support to the United Nations.[5] In the words of the State Department White Paper,

"The Atlantic Pact is a collective self-defense arrangement among countries of the North Atlantic area who, while banding together to resist armed attack against any one of them, specifically reaffirm their obligations under the Charter to settle their disputes with any nations solely by peaceful means. It is aimed at coordinating the exercise of the right of self-defense specifically recognized in Article 51 of the United Nations Charter. It is designed, therefore, to fit precisely into the framework of the United Nations and to assure practical efforts for maintaining peace and security in harmony with the Charter." [6]

Thus, the point is made quite clear that the pact in no way lessens the general Charter obligations of the Atlantic states; it merely supplements them with respect to the area involved. In other words, the official view is that the pact will strengthen western Europe, improve morale, stop Russian expansion westward, and provide a powerful source of support for the future development of the United Nations. If it will do all this, it is clearly a most remarkable document.

III

It is quite possible that all these results may be achieved. If there were not some prospect of such significant success, the proposals could not have aroused the enthusiasm of hard-headed and experienced statesmen in the

[4] *New York Times,* February 15, 1949.

[5] The pact begins with a preamble in which the parties "reaffirm their faith in the purposes and the principles of the Charter of the United Nations" and Article I is virtually identical with the phraseology of Article II, paragraphs 3 and 4 of the Charter.

[6] United States Department of State, *The North Atlantic Pact,* Publication 3462, General Foreign Policy Series 7, p. 5.

countries concerned. There are risks involved both in having a pact and in not having one. But statesmanship always involves risk-taking, and the statesman who is wary of his public necessarily will talk much of the possible advantages of a proposed course of action and less of the risks and dangers involved. Usually, the public can depend on the opposition party to perform the latter function, but when the principle of bi-partisanship is maintained, this source of criticism is apt to be somewhat muffled, and the public is presented with a policy whose virtues are extolled and whose dangers are glossed over with a delicate touch.

It is indeed a striking commentary on the changed position of the United States in the world that the Atlantic Pact thus far has met with so little downright opposition. Here is a proposal that will obligate the United States to give, to some degree, a security guarantee to those European states that traditionally have been the chief objects of American isolationist suspicion and hostility. Did the isolationism of Borah and Lodge and Hiram Johnson die with these men? Have the once-powerful newspapers whose stock in trade was isolationism lost their influence? Merely to raise these questions, is to suggest that there may be a latent, but nonetheless powerful, reaction of opposition which has not yet appeared. Even if it does not appear until after the pact is signed, sealed and ratified, it may still be lurking in the background, and it may appear at some future time with shattering results. The present calm acceptance of an alliance with western Europe might be more deceptive than real. If so, it is the part of wisdom to examine the prospects critically and dispassionately at the present time, for the harm would be incalculable if the United States were to enter into obligations which it might not later be able to carry out as other countries had believed it would.

Thus a first caveat applies to the assumption that our traditional isolationism is now dead. A second one is, perhaps, in order: this is that one may have serious reservations about the wisdom of an Atlantic Pact without being an isolationist, a communist, or even a communist-sympathizer. (The present writer quite obviously belongs to none of these categories.) It would be unfortunate if honest discussion of the pact were to be hindered by a public assumption that criticism necessarily emanated from persons or groups with special ideological interests to defend. The only yardstick by which this—or any other foreign policy proposal—should be judged is that of its prospective contribution to the security of the United States and the peace of the world.

With this criterion in mind, an examination of the pact's prospects can usefully be undertaken by asking, and attempting to answer, a few basic questions. These are: 1) Will the pact actually strengthen western Europe and free these peoples from their present fears? 2) Will the pact tend to bring about a basic improvement in United States–Soviet relations? 3) Will the pact strengthen the United Nations system? Categorical answers, of course, are impossible because the political field is one of probabilities, not certainties, but this is a conclusion which cuts both ways.

The first question, therefore, is that of the ability of the pact to lift the pall of fear from western Europe. The argument in favor of this position has been suggested above. It is that the assurance of prompt and powerful American aid in case of danger will dissipate this fear and provide a new basis for a healthy psychological and political recovery.

Such a conclusion assumes that the western European peoples view the world just as we do, and that the only source of their fears is the Soviet menace. This is undoubtedly true to a considerable extent, but it cannot be wholly true. One of the dangers of American thinking about such matters is to assume that other peoples are like ourselves in their fears, hopes and thought processes, differing from us only in the fact of their physical separation from the United States.

Actually, at least three qualifications to this assumed identity of attitudes must be kept in mind. The first is that these war-weary peoples want security against another war fully as much, if not more, than they want security against Russia. Now, the American people want security against war also, but they want security against Russian expansion still more. It is likely that some American thinking about the pact is based on the notion that, if war should come, the United States would have the inestimable advantage of an advanced base position in western Europe. But we can be very sure that any western European, whatever his political complexion, would take a very dim view of the great service which his country might thus perform. At the present time he favors the pact because it is preferable to standing alone in a dangerous world, but he favors it as an assurance of peace, and not as a strategical maneuver.

The second qualification derives from the first. It seems clear that a considerable number of non-communist Europeans are genuinely disturbed about the possibility of a growing American influence over their countries. Naturally, this feeling is harped upon incessantly by the communists, but aside from Red propaganda there is a discernible European apprehension about the United States. We must not forget that the trend in Europe toward socialism, in one form or another, is not a temporary by-product of the war and its aftermath, but is a deep-seated and long-existing phenomenon whose development has been catalyzed by the war. Thus, to many Europeans, the United States, as the great exponent of Free Enterprise, is a natural object of concern. To the extent that we allow them to believe that association with us will retard their own development, as they wish to have it occur, they will continue to be apprehensive about the effects of our influence. There is a danger that the political implications of the pact will seem to strengthen this fear.

The third qualification arises chiefly out of the German question. It applies chiefly to France, at least for the time being. French interests in Atlantic security are based to a considerable extent on the fear of a future revival of German power. Even if the present division of Germany should persist, the non-Soviet zones have a population greater than that of France. If these Germans should regain control over the Ruhr, there would be, from the French point of view, a serious danger of resurgent German power which might be hostile to French interests. A skeptical Frenchman might well fear that, if American relations with Russia fail to improve, the United States, eyeing the manpower and industrial potential of western Germany, might begin to press for German remilitarization as a powerful adjunct to western European military strength. In such a situation, French security through the Atlantic Pact would diminish sensibly. Of course these events may not happen, but we must not overlook the French fear that they might happen, and the assurance of French opposition if they did.

Another basic issue which relates to the usefulness of the pact in freeing western Europe from fears of aggression is the certainty and promptness of American military aid. The current assumption seems to be that this help will be forthcoming almost immediately in case of need. This may be valid but it requires some examination before any final conclusions can be reached. The point is that instantaneous action cannot be assured. First, while the pact, itself, stipulates that an attack against one party "shall be considered an attack against them all," it binds the signatories only to such action as each deems necessary "including the use of armed force" to restore and maintain security of the area. This may be a moral commitment to use military power promptly whenever necessary, but it is far from an automatic obligation, which is certainly what the European states would like to be able to read into it.

Actually, the commitment could not have been drafted in a more precisely binding fashion. Congress would not be willing—even if there were no constitutional questions—to waive in advance its right to declare war. More important, perhaps, is the consideration, based on the long record of diplomatic history of many countries, that governments will fulfill military obligations in time of crisis only if, at that time, the act of fulfillment definitely and clearly involves a vital national interest. This does not mean that the United States would callously disregard a pledged word; it does mean that if a particular crisis should not be precisely the one originally envisaged, the political situation in this country might force the government to hesitate, to use influence with the other signatories against a decision to take collective action, and in short, to frustrate any speedy or effective military action. It is clear that the pact is being regarded in this country solely as a device to frustrate Russian aggression. Have we asked ourselves what we would do in the event of a clash between two of the European states within the pact?

The practical question is whether we would act more promptly with the pact than without it. To put the matter in a slightly different light, are the European states convinced that we would act more promptly? That we would act to prevent western Europe from being over-run by a single great power is amply attested by our record in the last two world wars. That we would act more quickly because of a pact which did not bind us to automatic action—or even with one that did—is seriously open to question. Unless the answer is emphatically in the affirmative, then the other states involved are not actually receiving any more genuine security because of the pact than they would have without it.

Technically, since the pact will be under Article 51 of the Charter, no joint action could be taken until an armed attack on one of the signatories had occurred. This may be a minor consideration in view of Secretary Acheson's reported judgment that an "armed attack" could be interpreted to include a rebellion planned and directed from abroad, as well as a full-scale invasion across frontiers.[7] It is possible, of course, that such elastic interpretations may be officially adopted, and thus destroy nearly all the limitations contained in the restrictive phrase. If so, the present writer would respectfully submit that such interpretations, while they may be called for by the exigencies of practical politics, are far from the spirit of the Charter or the intentions of most of its framers.

An associated consideration, affecting the security provided by a pact, is the probability that the chief Soviet threat to these states, at least up to a final stage of crisis, is more from subversive activities than from military invasion. If past actions are useful as a guide to the future, then the Soviet policy-makers would do everything possible to use subversive activities to prepare the way for assuming power or for so weakening the state in question that military action might be unnecessary or unimportant. It is clear, from the nature of the problem, that the pact cannot be drafted effectively to insure the European members against the threat of infiltration and subversion. It can be argued that the pact will so strengthen them at home that they will be able to resist this threat but it is not clear that this strength will derive from the pact rather than from the economic aid already being given through the Marshall Plan.

If the pact is to protect these countries from aggression, and not merely to promise to avenge them afterward, then vast military power will have

[7] As reported in the *New York Times*, March 19, 1949.

to be built up in western Europe. In view of the military potential of the Soviet Union, and the distance of the United States from Europe, the pact conceivably might lead to an American policy supporting German military revival. Possible political consequences of such a step have already been mentioned.

IV

The second major question to be asked about the pact is this: will it tend to bring about an improvement in United States–Soviet relations? The argument supporting this position has been summarized earlier in this paper. In effect, it concludes that the Soviet Union will accept this containment, *faute de mieux,* and that a better basis for eventual collaboration between East and West gradually will develop. Such an argument overlooks a point just mentioned, which is that the Russians are likely to continue to rely on subversion as a long-term instrument of their foreign policy. Even more important is the possibility that the pact may worsen relations, not improve them, because it will provide the Russian leaders with what they will profess to regard as tangible evidence of American determination to organize as much of the world as possible against the Soviet Union, with a view to its eventual conquest and annihilation. This is the interpretation already adopted by the Russian press, whose "inspired" comment is that

"The North Atlantic treaty project and the circumstances accompanying its preparation plainly disclose the desire of the Anglo-American bloc for world hegemony. . . . It is clear . . . that the purpose . . . of the Pact is to put the reins of as many states as possible in the hands of U.S. and British ruling circles, depriving the states of the opportunity to conduct an independent foreign and domestic policy and employing these states as auxiliary means for realization of aggressive plans aimed at the establishment of Anglo-American world hegemony." [8]

It would be easy to conclude that since the western powers have no intention of appeasing the Soviet Union, they should be unimpressed by such an angry reaction. Such a view misses the point. No one except those wedded to communism advocates appeasement. But unless we have given up all hope of any *modus vivendi*—in which case we are actually preparing for an eventual and inevitable war—it is important to refrain from deepening the rift between East and West unless the advantages gained by such action are overwhelmingly great. And there would be a gain to both if agreement on any specific issues could be obtained.

Some of the advantages claimed by this policy of formalized opposition have already been dealt with. But some of the disadvantages require brief

[8] *Pravda* and *Izvestia,* January 29, 1949.

attention. First, extra fuel is supplied to Soviet propagandists, as the above citation from the Russian press indicates. Second, European states not behind the Iron Curtain and not included in the pact are left in a particularly exposed position, a fact which is not to be brushed aside by the statement that the over-all United Nations obligations of protection continue to apply to them. If that were considered adequate, then there would have been no need for a special pact. Third, the pact may have the undesirable result of concentrating too much attention on Europe, while Soviet influence reaches out in other parts of the world. Fourth, the pact probably will lead the Soviet Union to reenforce its hold on eastern Germany and Finland. None of these are minor or unimportant issues.

Perhaps the greatest disadvantage of the pact in relation to Soviet-American affairs is its probable effect in frustrating efforts to build up western Europe as a third center of power. Many people believe that such a third center, independent both of the United States and the Soviet Union would be preferable, as a mechanism for preserving future peace, to a bi-polar division of the world between the two. It is true, of course, that western Europe, divided politically as it will continue to be, cannot hope to become a force comparable to that of the two superpowers. But it is not necessary, in order to serve as a useful make-weight, for such a third center to be on the same power level as that of the other two topmost states. If it has reasonable power—and independence of action *vis-à-vis* both—it can still serve as a useful balancing agency in a global equilibrium. But the Atlantic Pact inevitably will tend to bind these European states all the more closely to the United States. In other words, it will foster a global bi-polar division of influence between Russia and the United States. And this is a path toward ultimate war.

V

Our final question—the influence of the pact on the development of the United Nations—has virtually been answered already. Since the United Nations is not a superstate, and is not likely to become one in the near future—despite the pretentious nonsense of most "World Government" advocates—its future success depends on the reestablishment of an equilibrium of world power. That equilibrium necessarily will differ from the situation of the nineteenth century because the number of great powers has been drastically reduced—thereby diminishing the flexibility of the system in adjusting clashes of interest—and we no longer have colonial areas that can be traded off to reduce acute tensions. Therefore, there is all the greater need for developing such areas of agreement as can be found between the two giant powers, for building up a third power center if possible, and for having this center fully independent. These are indispensable conditions for the successful development of the United Nations.

Despite the plethora of official reassurances to the contrary, it is very doubtful if the Atlantic Pact will lead to these. On balance, its influence is likely to diminish the influence of the United Nations. If it intensifies a global division of influence between the United States and the Soviet Union, it will reduce to zero the opportunities for United Nations development. It can scarcely fail to transfer world attention away from the United Nations and toward the rival blocs. It is likely to foster bloc voting in the United Nations General Assembly, and it is quite conceivable that it may cause the Soviet Union to leave the United Nations, as the protective effect —to Russia—of the Security Council veto will no longer have the same value. In any event, it seems far-fetched to assume that the pact can possibly have a beneficial effect upon that growth of community of interests which is the foundation of the United Nations. Whether the advantages gained by the pact can offset these probable disadvantages, is a matter for serious consideration.

It can be argued, of course, that even if the original idea of the pact may have been ill-advised, the political harm which would be produced by any failure to go ahead with it would be far greater than those which may now lie before us. This is an extremely important consideration, and there is much force in it. But two points may be drawn from it. One is that such opportunity as still may remain to make the pact "open-ended," and not merely a closed association of a few states, should be carefully explored. The other point is that even the first steps toward a decision of such magnitude should not be taken until all possible political implications —as distinct from those of a strictly strategic character—should have been given fullest consideration. This may have been done, but at the moment one cannot feel wholly reassured on this point.

IDEOLOGY OR BALANCE OF POWER?

WILLIAM G. CARLETON *

. . . Which is more important—that thing we call 'ideology' or the balance of power? That question raises the fundamental philosophic issue of our time—the issue which goes to the very heart of international relations.

* William G. Carleton, "Ideology or Balance of Power?" *The Yale Review*, Summer, 1947, pp. 590–602. Copyright 1947, by the Yale University Press. Reprinted by permission of Yale University Press and William G. Carleton.

What is the chief element in formulating the foreign policy of a nation? Is it ideology or is it balance of power? Is it both? If both, which weighs the more?

Did Sparta and Athens fight the Peloponnesian War because of the conflict of their social and political systems or because each feared the collective power of the other? Was Whig Britain at war with Bourbon France because of the rivalry of different institutions or because of the clash of competitive imperialisms? Did Burke's Britain fight Revolutionary France because of Tory fear of the Jacobins or because Britain feared for the balance of power? Did the United States go to war with Germany in 1917 and again in 1941 because of a conflict of cultures or a conflict of power?

What is this thing called "ideology"? There are, of course, ideologies and ideologies, and the term needs clarification.

Nations differ from each other in cultural and institutional patterns. But institutions inside nations are forever undergoing changes. These changes bring on institutional conflict within nations. Some fear these changes while others favor them. Very often the institutional conflict taking place inside one nation is at the same time also taking place inside other nations. In other words, the struggle for institutional change often cuts across national boundaries. . . .

The decisive institutional conflict of any age has come to be known as the "ideological" conflict. While, in general, that conflict was in the seventeenth century waged over religion, in the eighteenth century over constitutional and representative government, and in the nineteenth century over political democracy, in the present century it is being waged over Socialism.

That the institutional or ideological conflict is waged inside many nations at the same time, that the new institution struggling to be born is farther advanced in some countries than in others, that this conflict cuts across national lines and leaves people and groups within the various countries with ideological sympathies for similar groups in other countries— all of this enormously complicates international relations. International wars often take on the appearance of deep-seated ideological conflict involving not only national interests but future institutional and cultural development. Men who belong to minority groups are often torn between two loyalties—loyalty to ideology and loyalty to nation. Such men may be damned as "Trojan horses" and "fifth columnists" if they follow their ideological impulse; they may be damned as disloyal to their ideology if they follow their national impulse.

What if a situation arises in international politics in which ideology and national interest do not coincide? In that case, which is put first by those who conduct the nation's foreign policy—ideology or national interest?

As we look back on the past, it seems that, when the hour of decision struck, the national urge was generally stronger than the ideological. . . . Britain fought Bourbon France, Revolutionary France, and Napoleonic France, for while the ideologies shifted and changed, the national rivalry and imperialist conflict did not. In more recent times, Tsarist Russia has been allied with republican France, democratic Britain with oligarchic Japan, democratic America and democratic Britain with Communist Russia, and Communist Russia with Nazi Germany. National interests make strange bedfellows—in the face of a threat to the balance of power, nations will make alliances with the ideological devil.

Where, in general, the dominant ideology within the nation and the national interest do coincide, in what direction have the ideological minorities usually gone? In a crisis, what have these minorities done—have they followed their ideologies or their national patriotisms? In the past, the tug of national loyalty has generally won out over ideological persuasion. . . .

However, it would be a mistake to come to the conclusion that because ideology has not played the leading part in historic international relations it has played no part at all. It has played its part, an important part. Where national interests and dominant ideology within the nation coincide, a national war can be made to appear an ideological one, morale can be strengthened, and enthusiasm intensified. If a nation possesses considerable ideological unity it will be in a stronger position to win a war; if a nation's enemies are ideologically divided those enemies will be more susceptible to fifth-column tactics. When a country is rising to challenge the old balance of power, nations thus threatened will make alliances more easily and earlier if they have similar institutions and cultures; alliances will be more difficult and will come later (perhaps too late!) if the nations thus threatened have dissimilar institutions and cultures.

Just as national interests and balance-of-power considerations seem to have been the most important causes of war, so also they seem to have been most affected by war. The results of international wars seem to have been more significant in their national and balance-of-power aspect than in their ideological aspect. The Grand Alliance against Napoleonic France checked France and saved the European balance of power but did not succeed in arresting the spread of revolutionary ideas. The Grand Alliance won the war nationally but in the end lost it ideologically. However, when nations outside of France became more and more influenced by French Revolutionary ideas, those ideas took on the appearance of being their own—they were assimilated into their own national cultures. Again, at the close of the First World War, it appeared that middle-class democracy would triumph in the world, but now we can see that instead, the First World War marked virtually the end of the advance of middle-class democracy in any large areas of the world. However, the First World War did parry the German threat to the balance of power; it did temporarily satisfy the national interests of the victors; the war was won nationally even though it was lost ideologically. Again, the victory of the United Nations in the Second World War saved the world from a second German threat to the balance of power—that much is certain. Perhaps it will also have hastened Socialism, but, in any event, the ideological results are not so clear as the national ones.

It seems, then, that the influence of great wars on the cultural and institutional trends of the time is exaggerated. These trends arise out of conditions and forces operating within the nations. Wars affect them. Wars may accelerate these trends or slow them up. Wars hardly create them.

The Marxists would claim that what appears to be the national interest has in fact been primarily the interest of the dominant class in control of the state and that class interest has governed the foreign policy of national states and involved national states in wars for class ends. The great national wars, according to Marxist doctrine, have been wars in the interests of the dominant economic classes in the warring nations—conflicts of rival imperialisms. Where, in the past, ideology has seemed to split the dominant class, such ideological conflict, according to the Marxists, has been superficial or at least secondary to that class's economic interest. When a threat has appeared to the economic interest of the dominant class, these secondary ideological ranks have been closed in the class interest masquerading in the name of the nation. . . .

To be sure, the great conflict *is* ideological, say the Marxists—an ideological conflict between the exploiting capitalists and the exploited workers—and when this ideological conflict comes to the fore and cuts across national states, then the conflict between nations will be seen to be a sham and a swindle, the ideological factor will become stronger than the national factor in international relations, national wars will be converted into civil wars, and the erstwhile dominant economic class, now embattled, will find it more and more difficult to cloak its class interests in the garment of nationalism.

It may be that the Marxists are correct as to the future. It may be that the ideological will supersede the national as the number one factor in international relations. It may be that now the great institutional conflict within nations has come to be directly economic (and not indirectly so, as in the case of many of the ideological conflicts of the past) and the fundamental issue easier for all to see, that more and more will men respond to the class and ideological appeal rather than the national appeal. And if men more and more are learning to think as the Marxists do (the post-war elections in Britain and especially in Continental Europe indicate that they are) then it is quite possible that our century will see international relations conducted in fact and in name more along ideological than national lines. . . .

At present, the United States and the Soviet Union face each other as the predominant powers of the earth. Each is viewing world politics in a different light from the other.

Our policy-makers are thinking more in the old terms of nationalism, self-determination, and the balance of power. Soviet influence on Leftist parties the world over is looked upon largely as old-fashioned aggression and imperialism. There is widespread fear that Russia as Russia will upset the balance of power in Europe and Asia. Poland and Rumania and Bulgaria and Yugoslavia and China are appealed to by our government on the basis of national self-determination. (National self-determination, once a liberal rallying cry, has become also a conservative shibboleth.)

The Soviet leaders, on the other hand, are thinking more and more in terms of ideological conflict, class warfare, social politics. To Soviet policy-makers the contest in the world today is not so much one between the United States and Russia as it is between world fascism and world Communism. And those in other countries who follow the Soviet lead take much the same view. Communists and extreme Leftists the world over are giving their allegiance not so much to nations as to ideology. Russia is merely the instrument to be used in spreading ideology. Moscow influences Communist parties in all countries, and Communist parties everywhere influence Moscow. There is common indoctrination, consultation, co-operation. It is a two-way street, though the preeminence of Russia in the movement makes the outgoing counsel from Moscow weightier than the incoming counsel.

If a third world war should come—a war between the United States and the Soviet Union—for millions of Leftists the world over that war would be viewed almost exclusively as an ideological one. In countries where the extreme Left is in control, national policy would be made less on the balance-of-power idea and more on ideological considerations. In the United States, where Marxist ideas have scarcely penetrated at all, the war would be viewed in the old nationalistic terms. It would be a war to protect our shores from invasion, to uphold the balance of power, to save the world from Russian domination. As has already been said, in a final showdown nearly all of us would stand together. Our Communist fifth column would be smothered by the avalanche of nationalistic sentiment. American psychological warfare abroad would naturally reflect our own view of the situation, and we should probably err on the side of making too much appeal to nationalistic sentiments, which in large areas of the world would be effective only in Rightist circles. Our own failure to take into account the enormous strides the ideological point of view has made among the masses of people in Europe and Asia in recent decades, and particularly since the Second World War, might betray us into making very serious mistakes in the conduct of that war.

Should the Communists eventually win control in important countries outside Russia—in China, in Germany, in France, in Italy—it is quite possible that ideology would triumph over nationalism and a new international state emerge. . . . If an international state should come about in this way, then, of course, the old balance of power as played by national states will be relegated to the historical limbo. The Communists still confidently expect that Communism will lead to such an international state.

Of course, the Communists may be wrong about this. Nationalistic forces may be stronger than Communist intentions. When the Communists come into actual power in a country they inherit the national paraphernalia— the nation's history, culture, aspirations—and concessions have to be made to them. . . .

Of one thing, I think, we can be sure: even the creation of an international Communist state would not end the conflict over power. Within the international state would be different social and economic groups with different interests. They would fight for control, just as groups and classes within national states now fight for control. The international state would end the national balance of-power conflict, but it would not end the ideological conflict inside it. The ideological conflict of the future will be different, but it will continue in some form. Even if the Marxists should achieve one-half of their ideal, the international state, they would not succeed in achieving the other half—the abolition of all its internal group differences. Within the international state would be geographical sections, cultural diversities, a wide gamut of different industries and economic enterprises, and various social classes: commissars, managers, engineers, technicians, skilled workers, unskilled workers, farmers, and so forth. These various factors and groups would generate conflict over government policies and there would arise struggles for power which even Communist purges could not keep down. These struggles would cut across the old national boundaries.

In short, evidence is already strong that the Marxists may be able to make the ideological conflict rather than the national conflict the pivot of mid-twentieth-century international politics. . . . If so, then national conflict over the balance of power would disappear, but ideological conflict within the national state would persist.

Should there be a third world war and should the United States, using the old shibboleths of nationalism, win the war, it is doubtful even then if political nationalism and the balance of power would continue as they have done in the past. We are perhaps too close to events of the last thirty years to be able to see just how far the old foundations of nationalism have already been eroded away. In the fifteenth century, participants in the wars of Louis XI and in the Wars of the Roses were too close to those events to realize that feudal power was being overthrown before their very eyes and a strong national power built. So probably with us today. The historians of the twenty-second century, more clear-eyed than we, may look back and see that the great international wars of the twentieth century were in fact dissolving nationalism and building internationalism.

For nationalism today is truly beset from all directions. Among the dissolving agents are: the cumulative impact of technology and science resulting in the continued drastic elimination of distance and space, the atomic bomb, the release of atomic energy, and the overwhelming necessity of having to extend international functionalism to control what in the future will probably be the world's most important source of industrial production. . . . The Communists would put the world together through something like a Communist International; a majority of the people of Britain and the United States would prefer to see the world put together by the slow functional growth of an organization which originated in contract—the United Nations. (Inside the United Nations, too, there would, of course, be power politics, but as international functionalism grew it would come to be less and less power politics based on nationalism and more and more power politics based on ideology, that is, group and class conflicts cutting across the old national lines.) And there are those, like James Burnham and the oversimplifiers and distorters of Arnold Toynbee, who are so impatient with the slower and wiser methods of bringing an international state that they would have America attempt to build a "universal empire" to end "a time of troubles." Whatever method of putting the world together will ultimately prevail is still anybody's guess, but that the world in our time is in painful process of being put together is more than a guess—it is a hypothesis based upon a growing accumulation of evidence.

Thus anyone called upon to answer the crucial question in international relations today would be, I think, on safe ground in saying that, from the rise of national states and up to about now, the chief element in international relations has been nationalism and the national balance of power.

But he should warn the questioner not to be misled by this historic fact or by the superficial aspects of the present diplomatic duel between the United States and the Soviet Union, especially as that duel is generally interpreted in the United States. Because this middle of the twentieth century may be witnessing the epoch-making shift in the foundation of international politics from the nationalistic balance of power to ideology, evidence of which we shall ignore at our peril.

CHAPTER 7

INTERNATIONAL ORGANIZATION:
PEACEFUL SETTLEMENT

IDEAS AND attitudes change with time as do human institutions. The League of Nations and United Nations are illustrations. They have at different times been hailed as harbingers of worldly utopia and dismissed as futile "debating societies." The organizations themselves have changed their character, displayed new strengths or developed new weaknesses, altered in membership, and confronted different conditions. For these reasons, both organizations must be studied in an evolving perspective. The selections in this chapter attempt to do this. Taken together they reflect the subtle changes of viewpoint and performance which time and events have created.

International organizations antedate the creation of the League of Nations. They multiplied during the nineteenth century for the purpose of bringing under effective international supervision a variety of problems of general interest to all or most nation-states. One of the most successful of these, and a typical example of the generally "non-political" character of their functions, is the Universal Postal Union which, in its limited but important sphere, has developed into an efficient and effective limitation on sovereignty. The broad issues of war and peace (the "political" issues) were not confided to the care of these organizations. International peace and security remained purely diplomatic problems, and no permanent organization existed before 1919 designed to handle them.

The League of Nations and United Nations differ from earlier international organizations in their immensely broader scope and function. The great problems of peace and security, once handled exclusively through conventional diplomatic techniques or through an occasional conference convened to dispose of a momentarily troublesome question, have become basic functions of these two general international organizations. It is this factor which makes the League and the UN so different. Instead of excluding vital issues of international politics and power from their jurisdiction, major responsibility for these problems was placed at the very core of the League and UN. These two organizations were by design intended to be the focal point around which the international politics of the era would be centered. It is natural that the selections which follow devote a major part of their analyses to this feature, its ramifications and effects.

The League of Nations and United Nations were designed to preserve both international *peace* and *security*. They were given the task of maintaining international peace by encouraging the settlement of disputes among nations without resort to force. But they were also to create conditions under which international security would be maintained and aggression punished through the collective use of armed force. Both these tasks were collective, but one envisaged conditions of peace and the other those of war (even though, in theory, limited war). The dual functions are difficult to reconcile, for war, no matter how limited, is not peace. For purposes both of analysis and because the League and UN in practice have underlined this distinction, this chapter will be concerned primarily with peaceful settlement and the next with collective security.

Alexandre Parodi, in the first selection, "Peaceful Settlement of Disputes," speaks from the viewpoint of an actual participant in the work of the UN. Parodi believes that the veto has hampered the work of the Security Council but that it nevertheless corresponds "to a kind of necessity" to balance the unreality of giving Iceland and Russia equal votes in the Assembly. He points out that the veto presumed the existence of some degree of harmony among the permanent Security Council members, that, since the Council has so often deadlocked, the Assembly has gained "a sort of moral authority." Even where the Council does act, it is almost exclusively under Chapter VI of the Charter, where it has only the power to *recommend*—a power no greater than that possessed by the Assembly itself. In other words, the Council has in practice shied away from using its greater powers.

Parodi's analysis of this point is extremely penetrating. He links the Council's tendency to refrain from making "decisions" and invoking armed force under Chapter VII to the desire of "a political organ responsible for maintaining peace" to reduce tensions, prevent further irritations, and heal the wounds of national pride—in short, to *conciliate* and settle disputes rather than punish lawbreakers. In his view, the duty of the Council "is to try to calm things down," to keep small disputes from becoming general wars.

In the second selection, "Mutual Understanding—Key to Peace," Dean Rusk, Deputy Under-Secretary of State, sums up the achievements of the UN "in stopping hostilities which would have directly affected 500 million people." In his view (which may be compared to Parodi's) "the principal role of the United Nations is to maintain the peace." This task it discharges by encouraging negotiation designed "to reduce the fever, to find common points of agreement." In the accomplishment of this purpose "a readily available police force is not necessarily a magical panacea." Rusk concludes that the UN has proved its worth and, where Soviet cooperation in particular has not been essential, "has been able to get on with its job."

In the third selection, "Four Years of the United Nations," Erich Hula appraises the work of the UN one year after Parodi. He surveys the record of the UN on peace and security and concludes that the security system, despite differences between the League Covenant and UN Charter, basically resembles the League. He calls it a "melancholy" record and points out that both the United States and the Soviet Union have indicated by the alliance systems they have created that they no longer believe in collective security "as a working substitute for individual self-help." What is needed, Hula says, is more use of the "time-honored diplomatic methods of persuasion and negotiation" conducted *by and through the UN itself*. But if the UN is to discharge this diplomatic function of composing disputes, it will be incumbent upon the United States and the U.S.S.R. to refrain from seeking empty parliamentary victories which actually do not signify progress or from using the UN as a propaganda platform from which to launch tirades. Proposals to abolish the veto are, in Hula's opinion, completely unrealistic in this connection, and his examination of the question leads him to the conclusion that such efforts, carried far enough, will lead to the futile end of confirming the Soviet Union in the belief that the United States intends to use the UN as an instrument of domination over her. On this basis no progress toward diplomatic settlement would be possible at all.

All three selections emphasize the need for and opportunity of mitigating the power rivalry of the United States and the Soviet Union through diplomatic procedures within the UN if international peace is to be maintained.

PEACEFUL SETTLEMENT OF DISPUTES

ALEXANDRE PARODI *

. . . I would like to review rapidly what has been done during this nearly three-year period of the functioning of the United Nations, and try to define what the various legal texts have become with use and what results they have given.

First, concerning the relations . . . between the Security Council and the Assembly, I indicated that the Security Council had a certain practical preëminence, since it is free to retain or not to retain a given question on its agenda, and thus permit or not permit the Assembly to study it. Actually, there has been established between the two organs, between the Security Council and the Assembly, a sort of balance which is really the result of the facts, the result of practice and which is undoubtedly still developing.

The two organs are very different: first, because of their respective size, the number of their members; second, because, as a result of this first factor, there is quite an appreciable difference in the atmosphere of the two organs and their method of work. The Security Council, because it is a body limited in size and composed of permanent representatives who remain at the seat of the United Nations all year long, who know each other and have become accustomed to working together, is more a diplomatic organ. . . .

The Assembly has a different character, I believe, because of its size, because of the number of its members, perhaps also because it is composed of delegations which come only for a short stay and are, therefore, composed more of political men, while the Security Council on the other hand is composed of diplomats and officials. The Assembly tends more or less to take on manners and attributes which are more the customs of parliaments than those purely diplomatic meetings. As a result there is in the Assembly greater freedom of speech. Besides, since the Assembly directly represents the whole group of fifty-eight nations who belong to the Organization, it has a greater authority and represents more fully and in greater measure the weight of public opinion.

On the other hand, the Security Council has been more or less hampered in its functioning by the unanimity rule that you all know so well, the

* Alexandre Parodi, "Peaceful Settlement of Disputes," *International Conciliation*, No. 445 (November, 1948), pp. 624–632. Reprinted by permission of Carnegie Endowment for International Peace.

rule established by Article 27 of the Charter which is commonly called the veto rule. . . .

Upon several occasions I have defended the principle of the veto, not because the veto rule is a very good one in itself—and undoubtedly another solution could have been found—but because it nevertheless corresponds to a kind of necessity. After all, . . . the system set up by the Charter, which gives each country one voice, regardless of its size, its population or the weight that it brings to bear in international life, is a strange system, which may undoubtedly be criticized. It is certainly rather strange to think that a country like Iceland, for example, has the same voting right, has a voice exactly equal to that of the Soviet Union or the United States.

The veto rule is a sort of very imperfect and very rudimentary correction, but a correction nevertheless, of the strange provisions of the Charter on this point. This is so true that, if one wished to eliminate the veto, one would undoubtedly have to find another system of voting which would make it possible to "qualify" the votes, and to give them varying importance depending upon the importance of the countries which cast them.

The veto was also established with the idea, which, alas! has not become a reality, that the great powers would succeed in reaching an understanding, would have the wisdom to reach an understanding, in order to ensure the harmonious functioning of the machinery.

In any case, the veto has certainly been employed much more often than the authors of the Charter thought it would be, and, in a very great number of cases, has resulted in preventing any decision and in seriously hampering or halting the functioning of the Security Council.

I think that all these elements have resulted in giving to the Assembly a sort of moral authority with relation to the Council. In particular, since the veto does not exist within the Assembly, we have been led to bring before it questions which failed of any solution when before the Security Council, because decisions were obstructed by the veto; this practice has contributed to giving in some measure to the Assembly the character of an organ of second recourse, an organ of appeal with relation to the Security Council. To which must be added the fact that the Security Council usually acts under Chapter VI of the Charter, that is to say, finds itself more often employing recommendations and moral pressures than decisions or sanctions, so that, in the last analysis, the Assembly's powers of recommendation do not in practice differ very much from those of the Security Council.

Thus in practice, and especially in quite a number of cases involving the settlement of disputes, we have been obliged to bring before the

Assembly matters which had already been taken up by the Council; the role of the Assembly, in the settlement of disputes, has thus undoubtedly increased beyond that which was envisaged by the authors of the Charter. It is characteristic of living institutions to transform themselves in this way and to complete in practice the texts which first regulated their functioning. Finally, the creation of the Interim Committee,[1] . . . was a complement to the action of the Assembly in the field of the peaceful settlement of disputes. By making it possible for the Assembly to continue to deal with certain matters in the intervals between regular sessions, this Committee also contributed to the enlargement of the Assembly's potentialities for action.

Independent of this question of the balance of the different agencies of the Assembly among themselves, what has been the result of the practical application of the rules which I analyzed a moment ago?

I would like to bring out a first point: the very negligible use that has been made of the International Court of Justice. . . .

I have always found this sort of reluctance of the Security Council to place itself upon a definitely juridical plane very striking. In quite a large number of cases in which serious questions of law were raised, which even involved the authority of the Security Council, it is indisputable that the Council refused to take a position on the ground of law as such. The explanation for this is, undoubtedly, that the maintenance of peace is a very delicate matter in which purely political arrangements must always remain possible, and I think that my colleagues, as a whole, have felt that it might be dangerous to stand intransigently upon the ground of pure law. Solutions dictated by considerations of justice alone probably did not seem sufficiently flexible to them. Nevertheless, the fact remains that among the methods of settlement envisaged by the Charter, the one which provides for recourse to the Court of Justice has been little utilized up to now.

A second characteristic of the Security Council, with regard to the procedures utilized, has been, I believe, its reluctance to stand upon the ground of Chapter VII of the Charter just because of the wide powers which it would have at its disposal in that case. Recently, this was very clearly evident in the Palestine question. We try to put pressure on the parties to the dispute, to persuade them. We use moral pressure. If need be, we threaten them with the possibility that we may have recourse to Chapter VII, but postpone as long as possible the actual moment of giving ourselves access to the redoubtable weapons contained in that

[1] The Interim Committee, also known as "The Little Assembly" was created so that in the intervals between sessions of the entire Assembly, the Assembly could continue to function to some extent.—Ed.

Chapter. We fear to embark upon a path that might some day involve the obligation to go as far as the imposition of economic sanctions, as far as the rupture of diplomatic relations, and then as far as the use of force which, it must be admitted, would have extremely serious consequences.

Perhaps there is a profound difficulty inherent in the very idea of the regulation of international differences: to wit, the sort of contradiction which necessarily appears in certain cases between the desire for justice—which demands that we put completely in the wrong the party that is in the wrong and give the right to the party which is in the right—and the desire that a political organ responsible for maintaining peace must feel, which is to do nothing that might aggravate a state of tension, to do nothing that would create new sources of irritation or leave behind it wounds to the pride of any country that would be difficult to heal.

In reality, therefore, it is essentially Chapter VI of the Charter—that is to say, the stage of arrangements, of arrangements arbitrated or tried by the Council itself—that has been employed.

Finally, I hardly need to recall the fact that all the activity of the Council designed to regulate differences has been gravely hampered by the opposition of great blocs of countries within the body. This is a point with which everyone is familiar and which is quite apparent. . . .

On the whole, what sort of conclusion shall we draw from this experience of nearly three years of regulation of conflicts which I have just reviewed?

I confess that the conclusion to be drawn from the experience in which I have participated during this period is the one about which I am the most hesitant: perhaps because, as one who is participating intimately in the life of the United Nations, I find it difficult to have the perspective necessary for making a judgment, perhaps also because it is still difficult to form a judgment.

It cannot be denied that the conflicts which I have just recalled to you have been, in large part, lessened, even if not completely regulated and if not settled, by texts which state precisely who was wrong and who was right, or indicate that the solution should be thus or thus; nevertheless, on the whole, in a groping fashion these conflicts have been moderated. And if one remembers that the Security Council is not a jurisdictional but a political organ, whose duty it is to try to calm things down, to prevent settlements that might have the merit of being more clear-cut, but that leave memories and rancors in their wake, which would be the cause of new conflicts, I think that, as a whole, the work that has been accomplished—not in a very brilliant manner, perhaps, from the point of view of public opinion—has been effective work nevertheless, work which has healed wounds, calmed conflicts, and saved human lives.

But all the conflicts which I have recalled are minor conflicts, if I may use such an expression; the expression is undoubtedly not a good one because there are, in reality, no minor conflicts. For those who are involved in it, a conflict is never a minor one, and the definition of a conflict as minor always implies the risk that those who thus describe it will not concern themselves with regulating it. And then, on the other hand, we know from too many historical experiences that conflicts which seem limited in their scope may be the cause of very great wars, may be the cause of general conflagrations, so that, in general, to regulate even those conflicts estimated as minor is a great deal.

Furthermore, in the system of the Charter, as I described it to you a moment ago, in connection with the veto, it is to just such conflicts that our texts were intended to apply. The Charter, and the provisions of Article 27 show this, was framed upon the hypothesis of an understanding, of a certain agreement among the great powers, so that one might say, without paradox, that the texts were indeed designed to regulate these secondary conflicts rather than to settle conflicts of the scope of those that now divide whole blocs of countries. . . .

But what is certain is that the United Nations is the only agency to which we can have recourse in the difficult cases where peace is threatened. It is the only organ that has been established to regulate conflicts, and that is why we, the democratic countries—and I understand by that expression the countries where freedom reigns—must remain devoted to it; it is our task, by our common agreement, by our common efforts, to ensure that our Organization survives this crisis, that it emerges victorious from this test, that it develops and grows strong.

MUTUAL UNDERSTANDING—KEY TO PEACE

DEAN RUSK *

When one attempts to assess the work of the United Nations system up to this point, one discovers that the story is difficult to tell. The United Nations has long since outgrown the possibilities of a short and simple account. I am convinced that at least some of the discouragement and some

* Dean Rusk, "Universal, Regional, and Bilateral Patterns of International Organization," The Department of State Bulletin, April 3, 1950, pp. 528–529, reprinted as Department of State Publication 3828, International Organization and Conference Series I, 11. Dean Rusk was then Deputy Under-Secretary of the Department of State.

of the cynicism which has found expression results from a lack of understanding or even information about its activities. . . .

The United Nations has done much more than mobilize world opinion in support of the Charter and against aggression. It has provided in a series of important cases effective machinery for settling disputes which had in them the possibilities of major war. In a number of cases, the United Nations has taken hold of actual fighting and has brought the parties to a peaceful conclusion. In a number of these cases the Great Powers themselves were directly involved. Out of the experience with Iran, Syria and Lebanon, Indonesia, Berlin, Greece, Palestine, Kashmir, and Korea, the United Nations has solved many of the technical problems involved in peaceful settlement and has developed great flexibility in its procedures in order to get on with its task. Thus far, fighting has been prevented or isolated and stopped. The Secretary-General of the United Nations has estimated that in this way the United Nations has helped in stopping hostilities which would have directly affected 500 million people.

It has been said that in many of these disputes "credit" cannot be given to the United Nations because other factors played a major role. That is true, but the principal role of the United Nations is to maintain the peace. It must act on the one hand to overcome factors making for war and on the other hand it must take full advantage of all factors contributing to the settlement, including the determination of many of its members to act in support of peace. If a settlement is reached and peace is maintained, the credit and prestige of the United Nations will take care of itself.

Some have stated that the United Nations is helpless in maintaining the peace because it has no police force and that the result is excessive and fruitless debate. That conclusion is tempting but a little naive. A realistic assessment of the proper role of force and negotiation in the settlement of disputes will show that a readily available police force is not necessarily a magical panacea. Disputes come about in situations where emotions are high, where public opinion is inflamed, where national prestige has been engaged, and where the parties have made commitments from which it is difficult for them to extricate themselves. The role of negotiation and debate is to reduce the fever, to find common points of agreement, to introduce the calming effect of impartial opinion, to mobilize world opinion against the overreaching and excessive view, to bring the contestants into direct touch with each other, to allow public opinion in the disputing countries to subside and to place upon the United Nations as a group political responsibility for results for which the parties could not readily accept political responsibility. These are the processes which are familiar to civilized peoples in both their foreign and domestic affairs and are the badge of sophistication. The onlooker may become bored with tedious debate or a succession of procedural resolutions, or may become scornful of commissions and subcommissions and mediators and observers, but these processes are planned instruments for preventing war and settling disputes. It is important that those who live in compliance with the Charter be strong enough to discourage or resist aggression. But it does not follow that a succession of disputes, even some which involve outbreaks of fighting, could be readily settled by the employment of military means. If Hindu and Moslem or Jew and Arab are to learn to live together in peace, they must do so through the difficult processes of adjustment and mutual understanding and not through military occupation.

It might be said that we are talking about the little troubles and not the big one, our relations with the Soviet Union. Nevertheless, it makes a great difference to the peace and stability of the world that such issues as Indonesia, Kashmir, Palestine, Greece, Korea, and others yield, even if slowly, to the processes of peaceful settlement. The parliamentary veto of the Soviet Union in the Security Council has not been able to block effective action in many situations. The United Nations has developed alternative machinery by which it can proceed with the settlement of disputes despite a veto, except where the Soviet Union holds in fact a veto on the ground. Where the active participation and assistance of the Soviet Union has not been required, the United Nations has been able to get on with its job. Where the direct participation and cooperation of the Soviet Union is essential to a satisfactory result, its work has been frustrated and disappointing.

FOUR YEARS OF THE UNITED NATIONS

ERICH HULA *

The attempt to review and appraise the work of the United Nations on the basis of its four-year record is admittedly a bold and problematic undertaking. Such short experience does not seem to warrant even merely tentative conclusions. And yet, the attempt may actually be less presumptuous than it appears at first sight.

The United Nations is, after all, by no means an entirely novel experi-

* Erich Hula, "Four Years of the United Nations," *Social Research*, Vol. 16, No. 4 (December, 1949), pp. 395–415. Copyright 1949, by *Social Research*. Reprinted by permission.

ment in building an international political organization of projected universal scope. To be sure, it was part of the propaganda employed in selling, or rather overselling, the new organization to the American public, to present the United Nations as a hitherto untested remedy for the evil of war. Inasmuch as references to the defunct League of Nations could not altogether be avoided, they were made only in order to illustrate the constitutional superiority of the new over the old organization. Actually, the United Nations does differ from its predecessor in some, not wholly irrelevant, respects. These differences, moreover, are not confined to the institutional and functional features of the two organizations, but extend to their moral, ideological, and political settings as well. Nevertheless, the United Nations and the League of Nations are, fundamentally, variants of one and the same organizational type—the confederate system. Both were conceived by their founders as international bodies composed of sovereign member states, yet charged with the task of upholding the authority of the community of nations as a whole. The basic identity of structure and purpose has made for a continuity of issues and problems that is already very striking and is bound to become ever more so. Their fundamental unity of structure, purpose, and problems makes it possible —indeed, even imperative—to analyze and weigh the short record of Lake Success and Flushing Meadow in the light of the somewhat longer record of Geneva.

The limits of experience do not present the greatest stumbling block in the way of assessing the accomplishments and failures of the United Nations. A record short in terms of years is not necessarily deficient in terms of work actually undertaken. The Charter assigned to the United Nations and its specialized agencies tasks of a variety and scope unprecedented in the history of international organization. And even the severest critic of the United Nations could not possibly maintain that it has not been eager to make the fullest use of its powers. The formidable number of items on the agenda of each year's General Assembly and the length of its annual sessions clearly testify to a work load that very definitely puts the activities of the League of Nations in the shade. This quantitative difference is no less impressively indicated by the respective staff figures for the League of Nations Secretariat and that of the United Nations. Whereas the maximum number of staff members employed in the former was approximately 800, there are today some 3,000 staff members employed in the latter, not counting the civil service of the specialized agencies. Thus, instead of being frustrated by lack of material, the student of the United Nations finds himself overwhelmed by its abundance.

It would be impossible to evaluate in any one paper all the activities of the United Nations with anything close to accuracy. This holds true especially for the functions assigned to such organs as the Economic and Social Council and the Trusteeship Council. To appraise their actual accomplishments would require not only a careful scrutiny of the whole host of resolutions passed by those bodies and the General Assembly. We would also have to find out to what extent the member governments have taken practical steps to implement the several decisions.

It is not only necessary, but justifiable as well, to limit the following stock-taking to the record of the United Nations as an agency for maintaining international peace and security. Maintenance of international peace and security is the purpose that stands highest in the hierarchy of aims which the United Nations is designed to fulfill. Its success is therefore primarily determined by its actions and failures to act in the political field proper. In fact, all the other activities of the United Nations being of an essentially auxiliary character, they too must be measured in terms of their respective contribution to peace and security.

I

By far the greatest expectations aroused in us by the establishment of the United Nations were based on its alleged merits as a security organization. Chapter VII of the Charter was considered to be its very core. The technical features of the collective security system, incorporated in the Chapter, were supposed to assure the effectiveness of the new peace machinery to a much higher degree than the League of Nations Covenant had done. The powerful protection which the system was presumed to offer the smaller members of the organization was to reconcile them to its hierarchical structure and its authoritarian spirit. Actually, however, not even the legal features of the Charter's security system justified such fervent hopes, quite apart from the doubtful validity of its political assumptions.

According to the concept of collective security, the national security of the individual state is a matter of concern to the community of nations as a whole. A threat to the security of one is a threat to the security of all. The other nations are not only entitled, but obligated, to come to the help of the state threatened. In exchange for receiving protection from the international community, the individual state is expected to give up, or rather accept limitations of, such important attributes of its sovereignty as the right to arm, to form alliances, and to wage war. Collective enforcement of peace and security is to replace individual self-help.

The close interdependence between the obligation of the community and the undertakings of its members is obvious. In fact, it operates as a vicious circle in which any system of collective security is bound to be caught. No nation, including the most peaceable one, can afford or be willing to renounce, without reservation, the paraphernalia of power and the right to employ them, unless it can be virtually certain of effective collective protection. But the confederate structure of the system of collective security precludes the only true guarantee of such efficacy, a supranational authority superior to any and all of the national governments in terms of political, moral, military, and economic strength. The advocates of world government, therefore, are no doubt right in maintaining that the problem of collective security is insoluble within the framework of a confederate system. They are wrong merely in assuming that a world government proper would be attainable or workable.

The short history of the United Nations security system is a melancholy illustration of this vicious circle. It is the more discouraging as it is, *mutatis mutandis,* a repetition of the League of Nations experience, the main difference being the greater rapidity with which the disintegration of the San Francisco system has been consummated. As a matter of fact, it would be more appropriate to say that it has not come into existence.

What are the legal features and political assumptions of that system, and what are the causes and systems of its disintegration?

Universal membership is the ultimate goal of the United Nations. But this was never meant to imply that its coercive powers were to be universally applicable. On the contrary, as a security organization proper, the United Nations to all intents and purposes has had from the very beginning an extremely narrow scope. In view of the right of the permanent members of the Security Council to veto any enforcement measure —a right upon which we insist, even today, as strongly as the Russians do—the organization could not, even in purely legal terms, be expected ever to be in a position to institute enforcement proceedings against any of the great powers. Neither can we count on its support against the Russians, nor can the Russians count on it against us. What is worse yet, none of the smaller powers is entitled to regard collective protection as certain or even likely, if and when its security should be threatened by a great power.

At best it could be hoped that the legal security mechanism of the United Nations might operate in cases of conflict between minor powers. But the veto applies in these cases as well, though its subjective aspect is somewhat different. By exercising it, a permanent member of the Security Council would not stave off collective action against itself, but would refuse to participate in such action against another United Nations Member, thus blocking enforcement procedures against the latter. And it is quite likely to do so if its supposed national interests suggest this course.

To emphasize the restrictive character of the veto is not to imply that the political problems involved in collective security could and should be solved by abolishing the veto in its application to enforcement measures. The veto is a symptom, not the root, of the difficulties that are inherent in the political realities. To remove the legal obstacle which precludes enforcement action against a permanent member of the Security Council would mean to endow the organization with a merely fictitious right, unless it is ready to launch what would be essentially a global war, the very catastrophe which the organization is intended to prevent. Nor would it be any more useful to abolish the veto as a means of blocking collective action against a medium-sized or small Member of the organization. If one of the great powers, and especially if one of the superpowers should consider it, rightly or wrongly, necessary for political reasons to identify itself with the nation against which preventive or repressive collective action is to be taken, such action would again ultimately mean global war. The veto is nothing but the legal form in which a permanent member of the Security Council states what it holds to be the zone of its vital interests on which it is not ready to compromise. Without the veto, it could be legally outvoted, but not actually brought into line.

Given the limited scope of the United Nations security system and the uncertainties of its operation within this scope, the fact that the technique of the enforcement measures provided for in the Charter is an improvement over that of the Covenant has meant very little in a practical way. Moreover, the most important of those improvements has not materialized. As it has been so aptly put, the Security Council "has had its teething troubles, but it has not yet acquired its teeth." According to Article 43 of the Charter, there was to be placed at the disposal of the Security Council a military establishment composed of national contingents. However, owing to the inability of the Big Five to come to an agreement on the character and size of those armed forces, diplomatic and economic measures are still the only coercive powers of the Security Council. The formal authorization to use them, even for merely preventive purposes, is all that is left of the much-praised advance of Chapter VII of the Charter beyond Article 16 of the Covenant.

That the enforcement machinery has not yet been completed weighs in the total balance less heavily than the fact that the political assumptions upon which the security system of the United Nations has been based have failed to come true. The former is rather a mere indication of the latter. The security structure has remained unfinished, because its foundation has fallen apart.

The very word "veto" has today a derogatory connotation. But the actual and potential abuse of the veto privilege should not make us forget that the veto is the reverse of a positive idea of long standing, adapted to the parliamentary procedures of current international politics. The idea that the maintenance of international peace and security depends, primarily and ultimately, upon the existence of what, in the predemocratic age, was called the concert of the leading powers, has not become any less valid because the stubborn facts of world politics displease our tender liberal hearts. Whether we like it or not, far from being a substitute for the concert of powers, the system of collective security has a reasonable chance to work only within a hegemonic framework. The fathers of the United Nations were therefore wise in recognizing the unanimity of the foremost powers as a basic prerequisite for the new security system.

The chances for successful operation of collective security are slim enough when the interests of great powers that otherwise entertain the most cordial relations with one another do not run parallel with regard to enforcement measures called for by the alleged disturbance of peace by a third minor state. The Indonesian case with its alignment in the Security Council of colonial versus anticolonial powers, instead of the usual alignment of east versus west, was a typical illustration of such a situation. That what the French veto defeated was not an enforcement measure proper only corroborates the problematic value of the collective security system even under comparatively auspicious conditions.

But practically speaking, the system is unworkable if the great powers are divided by a deep and permanent rift. To be sure, even within the context of a cold war there might arise situations in which its protagonists are, for one reason or another, willing and able to pursue common enforcement policies. In the Palestinian case, the Security Council went so far as to base its final cease-fire order explicitly upon Chapter VII of the Charter, and to declare that failure to comply with the order would require its immediate consideration with a view to further action. It is an open question, however, whether the Security Council could have ever agreed on actual enforcement proceedings, if subsequent developments in Palestine had called for them. As the record stands, the case testifies to the value of the United Nations as a conciliatory agency rather than as an international policeman. Be that as it may, the case typical of the problem of enforcing peace and security by the collective action of an organization torn by a cold war among its leading members was and still is the Greek case.

The breakdown of the security system of Geneva was dramatically signalized by the failure of the League of Nations in the Sino-Japanese and Italo-Ethiopian conflicts to impose any sanctions in the former case and effective sanctions in the latter. The disintegration of the security system of Lake Success has not followed from any spectacular enforcement experiment, not even one tried on a small nation. But, even so, the symptoms are no less definite and clear. They can be summarized as a return, on almost all sides, to the idea and devices of self-help.

The tempo of the return to international normalcy, as it were, was in each case determined by the length of time for which the belief in collective protection as a working substitute for individual self-help endured. As a matter of fact, the Russians never lost themselves in the pleasant maze of hopes and illusions that nurtured organizational pacifism in the liberal democracies of the west. Being extremely distrustful of the security value, for a socialist state, of international institutions in a world dominated, according to them, by monopoly capitalism, they saw in the establishment of the United Nations no valid reason for discontinuing the game of power politics pure and simple.

This is not to imply that Russian policy can be explained in terms of supposedly realistic security considerations alone. The very dynamism of the communist idea would refute such a simple interpretation of Russia's aggressive actions. It is only to suggest that the obsession about security, deeply rooted in her history, is one of the factors that account for her actual policies. Its force may be the more considerable since Marxist-Leninist doctrine holds that war, international as well as domestic, is the world's inescapable fate, so long as capitalism is working disruption. Unfortunately, wherever there prevails the fatalistic belief in the unavoidable clash of arms, be it founded on religious or scientific conceptions, defensive and offensive motives and actions merge all too easily, as has been amply borne out by history.

Security has become also an American obsession, ever since we fully realized that the political and technological developments of recent years have deprived us of the benefits of an isolated position. Contrary to the Russians, however, in our quest for safety in a shrunken world, we turned to the idea and the contrivances of collective security. True, we hoped to gain our new security at a cheap price, and some of the most important provisions of the Charter, as well as certain omissions in it, all of them tending to emphasize the powers of the Member states over against the authority of the United Nations Organization as a whole, are due to American initiative taken for the sake of American sovereignty. But we were inclined to attribute to the world confederacy a very high security value, because our long liberal tradition had made us prone to believe in the triad of Wilsonian internationalism: the fundamental harmony of divergent opinions and interests, the potency and justness of public opinion, and the effectiveness of rational procedures in settling disputes.

Admittedly, our basically optimistic philosophy has never induced us to neglect completely our actual and potential instruments of national power. The atomic bomb is, after all, hardly a typical expression of the Wilsonian faith. But the pace of our rearmament began to quicken only with the growing realization of the deficiencies of the United Nations security system. The degree which our disillusionment has reached today is ind'cated by the fact that our military planning has caught up with Russian policy in completely disregarding the United Nations as a security factor. In this atmosphere of absolute lack of international confidence, proposals for the regulation of conventional and atomic weapons are, on the part of all powers, likely to be propagandistic gestures rather than serious efforts to arrive at agreements.

Another phase and symptom of the disintegration of the world security system has been the formation of political and military alliances. This trend revealed itself first in the east by a vast network of bilateral treaties between Russia and her satellites as well as between the satellites themselves. The western world soon followed suit with multilateral security agreements. The pattern was set by the Inter-American Treaty of Mutual Assistance, signed at Rio de Janeiro in 1947. Its counterpart in western Europe is the Treaty of Brussels concluded in 1948. The development finally culminated this year in the North Atlantic Treaty and its military implementation.

By far the most momentous of those particular political and military understandings is the Atlantic Pact. It also demonstrates more clearly than any other how far, in spite of ourselves, we have moved away in the brief span of four years from the ideas of Dumbarton Oaks and San Francisco. To be sure, the Pact is based upon and formulated in strict accordance with Article 51 of the Charter, which recognizes the right of individual and collective self-defense. To that extent it can no doubt correctly be called an implementation of a Charter provision. But this does not alter the fact that the Pact is based upon political and legal conceptions that are fundamentally different from those underlying the Charter.

Wilson conceived of the League of Nations as the very negation of the European system of alliances and balance of power, in his opinion one of the main causes of the ever-recurring wars on the Continent. Nor did his heirs who were to build the United Nations hold these devices in any higher esteem. The structure they planned for it and the stress they laid on the paramountcy of the world organization to any regional arrangements were a clear rejection of the allegedly immoral and outdated notions and techniques. It is all the more indicative, therefore, that American statesmen became the main architects of the Atlantic Pact which is, whatever we choose to call it, an alliance based on the balance of power idea.

It signifies that the nation which believed in the efficacy of collective security with almost religious fervor has reluctantly come to the conclusion that the very objective of the system, to check in advance any potential aggression by assembling at least equal or possibly superior forces against it, will be better achieved by the diplomatic methods of olden times. Indeed, it is not entirely unjustifiable to presume that the very concreteness of the system of alliances may well render it a more effective means of assuring peace than the abstract system of collective security with its "twilight zone," where, to quote Mr. Hamilton Fish Armstrong, "one side assumes that collective security exists and the other counts on taking advantage of the fact that it does not." Therein lies our hope that the disintegration of the United Nations security system does not necessarily mean that the cause of peace is lost as well.

No less a discrepancy exists between the legal conceptions that underlie the Charter, on the one hand, and the Atlantic Pact, on the other. In trying to prove to ourselves and others the rightness of our novel policy of alliances, we have recently tended to assign to Article 51, on which the Atlantic Pact is based, a central position in the system of the Charter. Nothing could be more ominous than this attempt to interpret Article 51 as expressing the very essence of the United Nations constitution. The actual position and function of Article 51 in the Charter render it very close to the emergency provisions in a national constitution which authorize, under certain conditions and within more or less clearly defined limits, the suspension of the constitution. In this sense, Article 51 of the Charter might be compared, for example, with the ill-famed Article 48 of the ill-fated Constitution of Weimar.

In accordance with the idea of collective security, the Charter stipulates a general prohibition of war as a means of individual self-help. Any lawful use of force is, under the principal terms of the Charter, the monopoly of the United Nations Organization acting through its central agency, the Security Council. Article 51 establishes the exception, the right of the individual Member states to wage defensive war. True, it also defines the only conditions and limits under and within which the exception may lawfully be considered to apply. But by leaving the previous determination whether a state may in a concrete case resort to self-defense to the discretion of the individual state in question, Article 51, to all practical intents and purposes, restores the right to war to the position it held in modern international law prior to the establishment of an organized international society.

In view of the likelihood of a deadlock in the Security Council in case of an international crisis, which would block collective protection by the organization of the victim of an armed attack, Article 51 is undoubtedly a reservation that no Member of the United Nations can reasonably be expected to renounce. But to shift the emphasis in interpreting and applying the Charter from the provisions that constitute the very core of the system of collective security to the provision which envisages its suspension, and to speak at the same time of implementation of the Charter, is a not very profitable attempt to deceive ourselves and others about the bankruptcy of the political and legal system whose establishment was the primary purpose of the Charter.

II

What are the lessons to be drawn from this disheartening record? The question poses the same basic problems that faced the Members of the League of Nations in 1936 when the failure of its first, and last, sanctions experiment caused them to explore the conclusions to be inferred from that failure. Nor are the types of answers given to the question then and now very different. They recommend either the strengthening of the respective organizations, or adaptation of their methods and procedures to the political realities.

There is no need to comment on the organizational approach to the problem after our lengthy analysis of the United Nations security system. A revised Charter could devise on paper new and broadened legal competencies, but it could not create a political entity willing and able to exercise and enforce them. Moreover, what would have been very sensible from a political point of view between 1936 and 1938 would make no sense and serve no purpose in 1949. The Members of the League were shortly afterward to be the victims of aggression by states outside the League. To strengthen the League would have meant virtually to form, by a free act of will, an alliance that was a few years later imposed on them by their common enemies. It is to Russia's lasting credit that, foreseeing this contingency, she proposed reforms of the League which, if adopted, would in the form of a strengthened Covenant have realized a defensive alliance. The United Nations of today has no common foes, but is split within itself into potentially hostile camps of another world war.

There remains, therefore, only the other alternative, namely, to adapt the methods and procedures of the United Nations to the political realities. This is by no means intended to suggest a policy of passive acquiescence in those explosive realities, and even less a policy based on the belief in the inevitability of an American-Russian war. The proposition suggests resignation only to the unalterable fact that the problems and issues of international politics are not amenable to any novel devices, so long as the structure of international society remains what it is today. But apart from that, it is founded upon the positive and perhaps all too optimistic assumption that the time-honored diplomatic methods of persuasion and negotiation can still be made to contribute to the pacification of the world. If this assumption is correct, at least within those rather narrow limits within which it can reasonably be expected to apply, the chances of the United Nations as a *pacificator orbis terrarum* will be the better, the more it follows diplomatic rather than governmental patterns.

The annual report on the work of the United Nations Organization which Mr. Trygve Lie submitted to the General Assembly this fall points very clearly in the direction of our proposition. After stating that "in the past a somewhat misleading emphasis has sometimes been placed on the enforcement functions of the Security Council," the Secretary-General exhorts the members to concentrate their future efforts on practicing and developing the instruments of Chapter VI of the Charter under which the Security Council has powers of recommendation only. Mr. Lie finally proceeds, in diplomatic language, to enlighten the great powers on the value of diplomacy as a means of making the United Nations a going concern.

In his desire to open up new vistas of hope, Mr. Lie somewhat overstates the successes of the United Nations as a mediatory and conciliatory body. To gauge the actual contribution of the pacific efforts of the United Nations to the positive results achieved in such cases as those of Syria-Lebanon, Iran, Egypt, Palestine, Indonesia, and Kashmir would require a detailed study of each of them in political as well as legal terms. But this qualification is not intended to detract from the credit due the United Nations in this field. The record compares not altogether unfavorably with that of the League of Nations, especially in view of the fact that throughout the twenties the organization of Geneva was an exclusive club of liberal democracies. And it is very definitely better than our over-emphasis on the frustrating effect of the Russian veto would lead us to expect. In point of fact, as far as political disputes proper are concerned, the Russian veto has had a decisive negative effect only in the Greek question.

The good record of the United Nations is the more remarkable because the legal provisions of Chapter VI of the Charter would have easily lent themselves to efforts at paralyzing the Security Council for good. What has actually happened is that the Security Council, in dealing with the political disputes, has developed a body of rules, of customary law, procedural and substantive, that tends to strengthen considerably its legal authority as a pacific agency. To be sure, this authority will be of no practical avail whenever a dispute is engineered with the connivance of, if not directly instigated by, one of the great powers, as is illustrated by the Greek case. But the significance of this development in regard to disputes on the periphery, as it were, of international politics is therefore no less great.

It would hardly be justifiable to ascribe to any of the great powers, or even to the minor ones, a consistent policy in this process of constitutional growth by usage of either Jeffersonian strict or Hamiltonian loose construction. National interests prevail in international politics over considerations of consistency as surely as party interests do in national politics. The one and the same state, or even representative of state, may in one case urge the members of the Security Council to stick to the text of the Charter, and in the other, to apply logic and common sense. All that can safely be said and presumed to hold valid for the future as well is the following: Russia, forming with her satellites a permanent minority bloc, has shown and will continue to show a much greater reluctance to agree to procedures and decisions that seem to touch upon the basic structure of the United Nations than is displayed by the members of the permanent majority bloc. Four of Russia's forty-one vetoes were directed at preventing the strengthening of the General Assembly over against the Security Council, the citadel of Soviet voting power in the United Nations.

<h2 style="text-align:center">III</h2>

It is hardly surprising that the good record of the United Nations as a mediatory and conciliatory body includes no achievements in the cold war between the United States and Soviet Russia. To think and speak of the United Nations as if it were a political entity is a fallacy, though the United Nations does have a legal personality. The name signifies a political relationship, not a substance, and the character of the relationship depends primarily upon the attitude of its leading Members toward one another. It would therefore not be reasonable to assume that the organization could have prevented or halted the cold war. It can, on the other hand, point to some resolutions and actions, especially in relation to the Berlin issue, that were due to the initiative of the minor powers, and may even have exerted some mitigating influence.

But one may wonder why, in the total balance of the cold war, the United Nations has heightened rather than lessened the international tension. This poses the question whether and to what extent the specific procedures practiced by the United Nations might have been conducive to that deplorable effect. Since the United States has played the decisive role in determining, shaping, and employing those methods, it poses also the question of our own responsibility for that unfortunate result.

The United Nations has gone to extremes in trying to replace secret diplomatic negotiation by public discussion and parliamentary procedures based upon the majority principle. It is the most radical attempt made thus far to apply to international politics the methods of domestic democratic politics. Measured in terms of this experiment, the League of Nations looks like the incarnation of old-time diplomacy. The unanimity principle prevailing in both Assembly and Council, the League Members felt compelled to come to an agreement before they proceeded to vote. Secret negotiation preceded and shaped the public discussion, at least in the Council. To put it in Paul-Henri Spaak's revealing words: ". . . the atmosphere of Geneva was very different from that now at Lake Success. It was more prearranged. There were some public debates from time to time, but I do not think I am betraying any secrets or saying anything unpleasant when I say that the public debate, in which the opposing theses were presented, were quite carefully prepared in the corridors, and that in reality everyone there was playing a role which he had learned in advance. When anyone deviated from the role which had been written by the authors, he was immediately considered to be a very bad character." Public discussion and voting thus served only to underline and express a diplomatic agreement.

Since the unanimity principle of long standing still prevails among the permanent members of the Security Council, one should have expected that voting in the Security Council would more or less regularly be prearranged by negotiations among them. Actually, no previous consultation approaching a serious effort to reach agreement seems ever to have taken place. Certainly there are no indications that the speeches of Mr. Austin and Mr. Gromyko or Mr. Malik have been the product of cooperative efforts in the corridors.

It would be naive to suggest that the methods of Geneva might in all cases have positive results at Lake Success as well. The point I am driving at is, rather, that in international politics, and especially in dealings among great powers, parliamentary proceedings cannot replace diplomacy proper, but depend for their part upon the successful operation of diplomacy. If diplomatic agreement proves to be impossible, outvoting the recalcitrant state, whose cooperation is probably necessary for carrying out a recommendation of the Security Council or General Assembly, serves no practical purpose with regard to the matter at hand. Its only effect is to deepen the rift between the powers concerned, the avoidance of which—if it can be avoided at not too high a price—is the main function of the art of diplomacy.

Instead of dealing with the individual cases as they arise in the councils of the United Nations exclusively with a view to our long-range interests, we, as a power certain of majority support, have often succumbed to the temptation to score parliamentary triumphs, expressed in what are, in terms of international power, imaginary figures. Public discussion and voting are, on all sides, no longer regarded as procedures serving primarily the integration of divergent opinions and interests; they are, on the contrary, in danger of degenerating into weapons of the ideological and political cold war.

The adoption by the Charter of the majority principle, side by side with the principle of concurrent majority applying to the permanent members of the Security Council, has charged the United Nations atmosphere with an explosive constitutional issue that is apt to intensify the cold war. "The Nature of the Union" could very well serve as the title of quite a few chapters in the history of the United Nations.

The constitutional controversy over the nature of the union centers on the veto issue, though that is not the only one to fall under this heading. Speaking precisely, it is a dispute over the scope and exercise of the veto rather than its existence and legitimacy. For we are as little ready today to subject our foreign or domestic policy to majority decisions of the United Nations, as we were at the time of Dumbarton Oaks, Yalta, and San Francisco. Commenting upon the veto in the Senate discussion on the Charter in 1945, Mr. Vandenberg said: "It is our defense against what I venture to believe would be bitterly condemned in many quarters as our 'involuntary servitude' if our veto power did not exist. It is the complete answer to any rational fears that we may be subordinating our destiny to alien commands. . . . It guarantees our perpetuated independence of international dictation." In the meantime we have, of course, learned from Russia's two vetoes in the Czechoslovakian case that the veto can also be abused to facilitate the imposition upon a free nation of "involuntary servitude." But we still neither have any reason, nor have we declared any intention, to forgo the veto as a protection of what we rightly consider to be our vital interests. Nor do we want any other of the great powers to renounce the privilege altogether. If the limitations upon the veto which we have proposed were to be adopted, the flag, to paraphrase Mr. Vandenberg, would still fly from the dome of the Capitol as well as from the Kremlin.

We should not, however, be surprised that the Soviet Union, as a minority power, is not ready to accept even minor limitations upon what is essentially a minority privilege. In fact, never in history has the majority principle appealed to permanent minorities that could not expect ever to profit from a free swing of the political pendulum. The Soviet Union is, therefore, inclined to see even in innocent and well-meant attempts to smooth the operation of the Security Council by limiting the scope and exercise of the veto the first axe-stroke against what she considers to be the democratic foundation of the United Nations.

Her suspicion, in this case, is the easier to understand since we have not—I regret to say—been fair to the Russians with regard to her veto policy. If the Russians have abused the veto, we have not failed to abuse their abuse. To be sure, in six cases the exercise of the veto was clearly intended to protect the Soviet satellites, and it blocked United Nations action that would have been justified or required under the Charter. In the great majority of the forty-one vetoes, however, Russia's motive was to maintain her relative power position in the United Nations rather than to obstruct its activities. It is only natural that this is a concern as dear to the Russians as it is to us, though as a majority power we need not for its sake employ the veto. No less than twenty-two vetoes were directed against the admission of new members in order to prevent an increase in the size of the majority in the General Assembly. And at least four vetoes, as has already been mentioned, can be interpreted as "the prevention of any formal action which, directly or by implication, would increase the competence of the General Assembly."

The constitutional controversies in the United Nations thus make one thing abundantly clear. Any move on our part in the direction of extending the application of the majority principle, be it directly by limiting the veto or indirectly by strengthening the General Assembly, will confirm the Soviet Union in her belief—a belief that is, unfortunately, based on a *Weltanschauung*—that we intend to transform the United Nations, originally planned as an organization within which the great powers would deal with one another on an equal footing, into an instrument of domination over Russia. Nor can we actually deny that this policy does fit our national interests better than those of Soviet Russia, at least as understood by her present rulers. They feel confident that they see through to the purely ideological roots of this policy. What they cannot see, what their very *Weltanschauung* prevents them from realizing, is that this policy, rather than being primarily inspired by utilitarian motives, is deeply rooted in our national history, and in our idealistic desire to see the governmental procedures of domestic democracy extended and applied to international politics, not for our sake alone, but for mankind's sake as well.

Dreaming of the Parliament of Man, we, for our part, find it no less hard to realize that any thing coming close to an attempt to make the dream come true is bound to nurture Russia's suspicion of encirclement. But we cannot any longer afford to ignore the evidence, if we want our United Nations policy to fulfill what is the main purpose and function of diplomacy: to remove unfounded suspicions and thus to decrease international tension. Reliance on ideas and techniques of diplomacy proper will better serve this end than any move toward world government.

CHAPTER 8

INTERNATIONAL ORGANIZATION:
COLLECTIVE SECURITY

THE LEAGUE of Nations and the United Nations were both designed to bring about conditions conducive to international peace and security. They were to dispose of the great issues of peace and war— composing international disputes amicably wherever possible and averting armed struggle, restoring peace by collective force against any aggressor who defied efforts at peaceful settlement.

The previous chapter selections were primarily concerned with the peaceful settlement of disputes by general international organizations such as the League and the United Nations; the present chapter selections discuss the use of armed force to restore peace through collective security when efforts at peaceful settlement fail.

In the first selection, "Collective Security versus Balance of Power," Woodrow Wilson, speaking of Germany, asserts that the Germans "never would have begun the war" (World War I) if they could have foreseen the great coalition which eventually was created to oppose them. Wilson was certain that neither isolationism nor the balance of power could prevent new wars. While he did not believe that the use of force by nations could be abolished, he did think that force could be collectivized so as to bring maximum pressure against an aggressor from the outset of hostilities. If an aggressor was almost certain of the armed opposition of a world-wide coalition *from the beginning,* in most cases aggression would not even occur. Where it did occur, it could be suppressed more readily and effectively.

Edwin Borchard, in the second selection, "The Impracticability of 'Enforcing' Peace," takes the opposite point of view from Wilson on collective security. Borchard contends that collective security is an illusion believed in by "romantic chasers of the international rainbow." He calls it "a counsel of despair." Borchard says that the rules of neutrality, evolved by states in an effort to keep out of wars which did not concern them, resulted in localized wars. Abolishing neutrality and insisting as a consequence that every war must become a gen-

172

eral world war would not furnish "the desired key to international tranqui'ity." He points out the difficulty of defining "aggression" and distinguishing it from self-defense. The outlawing of aggression, Borchard states, in effect freezes the legal *status quo*. Instead of attempting to adjust international problems to changed conditions, the *status quo* powers would be encouraged to reject such demands and threaten collective security against nations which find the *status quo* "intolerable" without some changes. These dissatisfied nations, if armed, would not be likely to submit to the "intolerable" situation for long, and in the end war would result.

Professor Edward H. Buehrig, in the third se'ection, "Collective Security in a Bi-Polar World," examines the UN after five years of its existence. Buehrig begins by saying that the UN "cannot be expected to abolish the balancing process . . . in international politics." The existence of an international organization does not abolish international politics but presents a new framework within which politics (or "the balancing process") may continue with potentially less dangerous effects upon world peace. Buehrig believes that the balancing process naturally reduces itself to "a pair of opposites, thereby crystallizing into a tense balance of power." This effect he calls polarization, and he proceeds to examine how it has affected the UN. Since American-Soviet rivalry has transformed the UN into "a house divided against itself," col'ective security in the true sense of *all* nations acting against *any* aggressor cannot be expected. At best there can be "collective security among friends" as is the case in the North Atlantic Pact. (This is another way of saying that in the present divided state of the wor'd, collective security has been in fact abandoned in favor of a return to ba'ance-of-power alliances.) Buehrig calls the action taken in the Korean case "short of being a satisfactory exemplification of collective security," since the burden of the fighting has been carried by American forces. This has resulted in the Korean case taking on "the aspect of a coa'ition led by the United States in opposition to the expansion of Soviet influence" and is another proof of how the UN is divided against itself.

That the UN is divided cannot be disputed, but collective security always must take place in an atmosphere of division—between the aggressor and the "police" force. Until China's recent intervention in Korea the possibility of effective collective security existed, since the forces at the disposal of the UN were in fact able to destroy the North

Korean armies. After China's entry, however, the action began more and more to resemble a typical balance-of-power test of strength, since the UN no longer possessed, vis-à-vis the aggressor, the overwhelming power which collective security assumes as basic to successful action. Successful "police" action in these circumstances could not have been distinguished from war, and since collective security is supposed to avert war, it could hardly achieve its objective. The Korean case above all shows the difficulty of using collective security against even a single major power, and in this case China had Russia's backing as well.

Would it be better under such circumstances to have a UN without Soviet participation? Buehrig points out the difficulty which the United States would experience in maintaining an international organization "whose chief preoccupation was opposition to the Soviet Union in particular and communism in general," since the solidarity of the non-Communist nations can easily be overrated. He says further that, if the Soviet Union left the UN, the satellite nations would too, and this would severely limit any hope of the further spread of Titoism. Altogether, Buehrig is convinced that, since the balancing process is inevitable, it is least dangerous "among multiple centers of power in shifting relationships of friction and cooperation"—in short, within the UN.

COLLECTIVE SECURITY VERSUS BALANCE OF POWER

WOODROW WILSON *

If Germany had dreamed that anything like the greater part of the world would combine against her, she never would have begun the war, and she did not dare to let the opinion of mankind crystallize against her by the discussion of the purposes which she had in mind. What I want to point out to you to-night is that we are making a fundamental choice. You have either got to have the old system, of which Germany was the perfect flower, or you have got to have a new system. You cannot have a new system unless you provide a substitute, an adequate substitute, for the old, and when certain of our fellow citizens take the position that we do not want to go into any combination at all but want to take care of

* Woodrow Wilson, Address at Coliseum, Sioux Falls, South Dakota, Sept. 8, 1919, from *Addresses of President Wilson*, Senate Document No. 120, 66th Congress, 1st Session, Government Printing Office, Washington, 1919, pp. 83, 85–86, 88.

ourselves, all I have to say to them is that that is exactly the German position. . . .

The old system was, Be ready, and we can be ready. I have heard gentlemen say, "America can take care of herself." Yes, she can take care of herself. Every man would have to train to arms. We would have to have a great standing army. We would have to have accumulations of military material such as Germany used to have. We would enjoy the luxuries of taxes even higher than we pay now. We could accumulate our force, and then our force would have to be directed by some kind of sufficiently vigorous central power. You would have a military gov ernment in spirit if not in form. No use having a fighting Nation if there is not somebody to swing it. If you do not want your President to be a representative of the civil purposes of this country, you can turn him into merely a commander in chief, ready to fight the world. But if you did nobody would recognize America in those strange and altered circumstances. All the world would stand at amaze and say, "Has America forgotten everything that she ever professed?" The picture is one that every American repudiates; and I challenge any man who has that purpose at the back of his thought to avow it. If he comes and tells you that America must stand alone and take care of herself, ask him how it is going to be done, and he will not dare tell you, because you would show him the door and say, "We do not know any such America."

Yet we cannot do without force. You cannot establish land titles, as I have expressed it, and not maintain them. Suppose that the land titles of South Dakota were disturbed. Suppose the farm lines were moved, say, ten feet. You know what would happen. Along every fence line you would see farmers perching with guns on their knees. The only reason they are not perching now is that there are land deeds deposited in a particular place, and the whole majesty and force and judicial system of the State of South Dakota are behind the titles. Very well, we have got to do something like that internationally. You cannot set up Poland, whom all the world through centuries has pitied and sympathized with, as the owner of her property and not have somebody take care that her title deeds are respected. You cannot establish freedom, my fellow citizens, without force, and the only force you can substitute for an armed mankind is the concerted force of the combined action of mankind through the instrumentality of all the enlightened Governments of the world. This is the only conceivable system that you can substitute for the old order of things which brought the calamity of another war upon us. Your choice is between the League of Nations and Germanism. I have told you what I mean by Germanism—taking care of yourselves, being armed and ready, having a chip on your shoulder, thinking of nothing but your own rights and never thinking of the rights of anybody else, thinking that you were put into this world to see that American might was asserted and forgetting that American might ought never to be used against the weak, ought never to be used in an unjust cause, ought never to be used for aggression; ought to be used with the heart of humanity beating behind it.

Sometimes people call me an idealist. Well, that is the way I know I am an American. America, my fellow citizens—I do not say it in disparagement of any other great people—America is the only idealistic Nation in the world. When I speak practical judgments about business affairs, I can only guess whether I am speaking the voice of America or not, but when I speak the ideal purposes of history I know that I am speaking the voice of America, because I have saturated myself since I was a boy in the records of that spirit, and everywhere in them there is this authentic tone of the love of justice and the service of humanity. If by any mysterious influence of error America should not take the leading part in this new enterprise of concerted power, the world would experience one of those reversals of sentiment, one of those penetrating chills of reaction, which would lead to a universal cynicism, for if America goes back upon mankind, mankind has no other place to turn. It is the hope of Nations all over the world that America will do this great thing. . . .

I can not understand the psychology of men who are resisting it. I can not understand what they are afraid of, unless it is that they know physical force and do not understand moral force. Moral force is a great deal more powerful than physical. Govern the sentiments of mankind and you govern mankind. Govern their fears, govern their hopes, determine their fortunes, get them together in concerted masses, and the whole thing sways like a team. Once get them suspecting one another, once get them antagonizing one another, and society itself goes to pieces. We are trying to make a society instead of a set of barbarians out of the governments of the world.

THE IMPRACTICABILITY OF "ENFORCING" PEACE

EDWIN BORCHARD *

Just in what respect is the United Nations an improvement over the League of Nations? Both of them have their justification in the assurance

* Edwin Borchard, "The Impracticability of 'Enforcing' Peace," *The Yale Law Journal,* Vol. 55, No. 5 (August, 1946), pp. 966–971. Copyright 1946, by Yale Law Journal Co., Inc. Reprinted by permission.

of peace which a bewildered humanity anxiously seeks. Both of them purport to advance the cause by enforcing peace upon the so-called "aggressor." When the League sought to accomplish this aim in Manchuria (1931), in Ethiopia (1935), in German reoccupation of the Rhineland (1936), it found itself hampered by the fact that various constituent members declined to go along. But the idea that force was the "Open, Sesame" to peace was not abandoned. Finally, in 1939, after Hitler had absorbed Austria (1938) and—despite the Munich appeasement—Czechoslovakia as well (1939), while the League stood by helpless, Russia invaded Finland, and the League manifested its impotent displeasure and frustration by expelling the Soviet Government. That seems to have been the last important activity of the League.

Why it is assumed that the membership of the United States would have changed this picture is not altogether clear, unless it be thought that in the name of righteousness the United States can be induced to fight on any and all occasions. At all events, when the time came to organize a new League, because of Soviet disapproval of the old and its waning prestige, the United States took the lead in organizing it under the name of the United Nations. Its aims are the same as those of the old League, except that the Military Staff Committee (Art. 47) is to symbolize the military potency of the organization, and the acknowledged exercise of the veto power by one of the Big Five assures that nation of an immunity from the ministrations of the organization machinery. . . .

The proposals for enforcing the peace announced at San Francisco in 1945 are founded on the theory that peace can be "enforced" by "peace-loving," "sovereign" nations on recalcitrant states, called "aggressors," in the same way that the non-conformist within a state is subjected to arrest, judicial control and punishment. The fact that states in the international constellation differ fundamentally from individuals in a municipal community, and that the method of and procedure for controlling them must of necessity be entirely different, has not been recognized by the seekers of a new world order, romantic chasers of the international rainbow.

Enforcement under the Charter rests essentially upon armed coercion by the Big Three, drawing support from the smaller member states. The theorists, in their attempt to produce the new order by coercion, are driving out of existence international law, the only law that is able to survive among a congeries of states, none of whom is entitled to pass judgment on others, and none of whom is able to enforce its judgment without inviting war. The theorists thus propose to "enforce" peace by war at a time when international relations are more irreconcilable than ever; yet they expect the promotion of law to accompany this essentially anarchistic process. This is the state of mind that the 20th century has attained. Perhaps two world wars, with their destruction of human values, were too great a shock to permit the survival of reason.

What is now happening follows from the acceptance of an assumption, made by gentlemen like Woodrow Wilson, that the world and its processes can be changed by a new charter or league. That the world's distant places are now more accessible has promoted the propaganda that an international organization is essential to the world's survival. The world has undoubtedly shrunk, but the nature of the state and the relations between states have not thereby been changed. Indeed, international propinquity has promoted nationalism and thus increased the dangers of conflict. Instead of methods to allay the growing distemper, predominant force or compulsion, a counsel of despair, is the only solution offered to us. . . .

Many schemes for organizing peace have dotted the centuries since the Abbé de St. Pierre announced his unworkable plan. These schemes differed from the League of Nations in that the latter was adopted by statesmen and not in that it was any more valid. Such schemes fail because of contradictions inherent in "enforcing" peace and because they falsely assume that sovereign states can sit in judgment or agree on the meaning of such an undefinable term as "aggressor" and then carry out the judgment without upsetting the world. Nations perhaps *should* abandon their sovereignty, which in many respects is outdated, but no nations seem ready to do so, least of all the great powers who have sponsored the United Nations. As Elihu Root once said about a sensible solution to another problem, "they just won't do it."

Whereas international law was built on the theory of the equality of states, the new scheme involves an essential denial of this equality by making power the test of rank. Yet the maintenance of sovereignty, upon which the constituent states insist, is incompatible with regulating the conduct of states by strengthening the sinews of dictated law. On the contrary, the law that can prevail among sovereign states is not a law dictated by superior to inferior, as is the case inside a state, or in municipal law, as we call it, but only a system to which states agree, whether created by custom or by treaty among equals. The rules of neutrality, so created, but now flouted as never before, constituted a means by which society could control wars, limit their area, and restore a healthy peace. This time-tested protection of society against mutual destruction is now ostensibly abandoned, although no nation seems to have abrogated its neutrality laws, and the survivors are likely to insist upon neutrality in the civil wars that are in the offing. Whereas non-intervention was the keynote both of international law and American policy, universal intervention in other people's local affairs and in matters of which an understanding is quite wanting is now presented as the desired key to international tranquility. The idea of enforcing peace in analogy to a municipal system is only theoretically tolerable when a superstate controls all others, a condition which it is impossible to assume. There can be no superstate unless the Big Three fight it out for supremacy, and, as yet, even our wild theorists have produced no school to suggest this course. In fact, we are dealing with a congeries of sovereign states, and if the Big Three profess to be above the law, laying down the rules—most likely their whims—for states of lesser breed, long docility can hardly be assumed.

The other alternative is that sovereignty be abandoned to a federation, such as the United States, with the federation having power to enforce upon individuals the constitutional rules of the federation. Since Europe is unable to organize such a sensible organization inside a continent which should be cohesive, it is hardly to be assumed that the disparate states of the world are ready to form a federation. Only blind faith supports the belief that order can be maintained in the world by a thinly disguised military alliance of the three largest Powers. It takes such faith to believe, against history's clear warnings, that Great Britain, Russia, and the United States, facing the problems that their financial and social conditions make inexorable, are likely long to see the future in the same light. Early renewal of war is not probable; of this, exhaustion is the principal guaranty, but the growth of regionalism seems likely, with small states, while still boasting of their sovereignty, diminishing to the position of protectorates of larger units. That imperialism will suffer a serious check under this power system seems unlikely. As force grows in importance, the law recedes.

The assumption of numerous theorists that the weakness of international law is due to the lack of force behind it is responsible for much of the sorry thinking of the present day. International law is a primitive system, not because it lacks the support of force but because it deals with sovereign states who cannot be coerced by other states without entailing war. There must be a certain agreement on the law, at least among the majority. But the law gains its strength through practice, invocation by foreign offices and application by tribunals.

If such an epithet as "aggressor" under the new theory is made the test of status and action, it must be assumed that the judging nations in the Security Council—at least the large ones—will be able to agree on the meaning of such an uncertain term, not merely when applied to a particular nation, now, but also when applied to nations behaving similarly in the long future. Yet experience teaches us that agreement is exceedingly doubtful, since the judgment is reached not on impartial criteria but on subjective if political grounds, including self-interest, association, commitments, alliances, and other considerations far from legal. It is not possible to conceive that Great Britain would consider one of its dominions an "aggressor." It is not possible to imagine that Russia would find one of its satellite states to be an "aggressor," which presupposes Russian inability to control the recalcitrant itself. It is not possible to assume the continuance of the inter-American system if the United States should declare one of the constituent states to be an "aggressor." . . .

Another weakness inherent in "enforcing" peace is revealed by recognition that "to outlaw aggression" is, by and large, an attractive formulation of "to maintain the status quo." The peace to be "enforced," under the facts of economic life, present as well as historic, must perforce be the result of war, and must immobilize geography as it emerged from war. In so far as the peace imposed upon the vanquished be not statesmanlike, *i.e.*, conforming to the new political conditions, it must create malaise and discontent certain to break out into open dissatisfaction and conflict. The nullification of conquest as a source of title cannot be effective without the creation of a substitute method for effecting boundary and economic adjustments.

The philosophy which identifies the preservation of peace with the maintenance of the status quo and favors hounding the non-conformist has, however, disastrous consequences. A good physician attempts first to establish the nature of his patient, his constitution, his allergies, his habits, his weaknesses, and then fashions his therapeutics to harmonize with the natural tendencies of the patient. But by prescribing the use or threat of force against a nation that finds the status quo intolerable, the international physicians are abandoning diagnosis. Independent national entities do not naturally have the same political objectives, internal or external, and are likely to drift into a balance of power—where there is political interest—and not unity. Coercion or its threat promotes disunity. Compulsion to observe a status quo—whether called "peace" or "international law"—is a politically comprehensible device, but experience shows the device has had no success as a conciliator or pacifier. If employed against a nation in possession of arms or capable of resistance, it is likely to have unhappy results. International relations cannot be mechanized or regimented. Especially is this true if peace treaties are drawn, like many European treaties, not to reflect prevailing political trends, heal wounds and restore the lost equilibrium, but to impose unnatural conditions. In an industrial age such treaties tend to produce social diseases, peculiarly cancerous in their virulence. In the quest for peace a study of history and psychology is a more important asset than a knowledge of law or political mechanics; the emphasis on enforcement gives it a misplaced role in the drama.

The identification of peace with the status quo has other results. It is responsible for muddying intellectual clarity and the understanding of history. To it we owe the chameleonic epithet "aggressor," which is applied selectively to those particular disturbers of the status quo whom the dominant states happen to dislike. It is responsible for the war-spreading conception that by remaining out of wars, when the dominant states are in, the neutral is in some way guilty of immorality. Veneration of the status quo, backed by coercion, adds up to the practice of intervention, now common to many nations in spite of lip-service occasionally paid to non-intervention. It is responsible for the doctrine of non-recognition of political facts, however inexorable, if unwelcome to the ruling nations. It is responsible for the doctrine of sanctions, designed to bend nations to the will of the ruling group and carrying behind it a whole flood of evils. It is responsible for that rigidity and inflexibility of diplomacy, spiced by invective, which regards every proposal to alter the status quo as prima facie intolerable, though there is no exit in peaceful change. Such inflexibility is likely to be associated with self-righteousness, calculated to evoke desperation and desperate men. As an incident to discountenancing neutrality—which over the centuries had demonstrated its utility—the concept of an enforced peace introduced into the language such ambiguous conceptions as "non-belligerency," which seems to justify violations of neutrality (*i.e.,* law) while purporting to escape the risks of war and legal liability. Thus, the confusion of peace with war, which at least the traditional law had sought to distinguish clearly, is now accompanied by a whole conglomeration of ambiguities, like "international police force," "just war," "concern"—the jargon of "collective security"—which have made political life uncertain and hardly encourage hope of a profitable cooperation.

COLLECTIVE SECURITY IN A BI-POLAR WORLD

EDWARD H. BUEHRIG *

The United Nations cannot be expected to abolish the balancing process, which is the natural expression of the struggle for advantage and influence in international politics. It does, however, endeavor to modify the process. What are the methods which it employs? What actual effect have they had in promoting security? Above all, what relevance do they have for the conduct of American foreign policy?

* Edward H. Buehrig, "The United States, the United Nations and Bi-Polar Politics," *International Organization,* Vol. IV, No. 4 (November, 1950), pp. 573–584. Copyright 1950, by World Peace Foundation. Reprinted by permission.

The United Nations is chiefly reliant not on authority but on the disposition of its members to cooperate. With certain notable exceptions in the political field, the Charter places no considerable legal obligations on governments, nor does it, apart from the organization's control over its own officials and headquarters and the rather equivocal control which is exercised over trusteeship areas, establish jurisdiction over individuals or territory.

However, it should be pointed out that authority of the three types just mentioned may be and, in fact, has been elaborated in varying degrees in agreements concluded at Lake Success. Moreover, the constitutions of regional and functional agencies and various agreements arrived at through these agencies, have also extended the range of international law and administration. The International Refugee Organization, the International Bank and the International Monetary Fund—to take some examples—approach a position which is tantamount to, if it does not actually involve, an independent policy-making function. Such a centralization of decision making has the advantage of bringing to bear in full and fair discussion the different interests and viewpoints which are relevant to the treatment of a problem and of encouraging any disposition to yield to the convenience of an overall authority.

The charge is made that the United Nations is too conservative in its estimate of the degree to which uniformity, central direction and world authority are feasible and desirable. This poses a large and abstract issue about which much more has been said than has been digested. The contemporary world, no less than the world of the past, presents tremendous contrasts in economic development, political values and social patterns which no supreme authority, whether by virtue or convenience, persuasion or force, can be expected to dominate. This observation is notably true for the differences that separate communism and democracy, and for those between the Orient and the Occident. But it is relevant also as regards the western democracies among whom too ambitious machinery for centralized decision making might result in distraction rather than in the promotion of solidarity. This is a subject about which it is helpful (certainly it is less polemical) to be specific rather than general and experimental rather than doctrinal. An examination of the remarkable proliferation of international organization since 1945 shows that it has developed along regional and functional lines. Regionalism rather than universalism will continue to be the trend for the future; and whatever authority is vested at the international level is likely to be in pin-pointed functional organizations rather than conferred on bodies with broad governmental powers.

In the political field the Charter lays two legal obligations on its members: to settle disputes by peaceful means in conformance with the requirements of justice; and to refrain from the use of force, except in accordance with the principles of the Charter. These principles and the machinery for their implementation are an attempt to deal immediately and directly with the hostile manifestations of the balancing process which are so emergent as not to be subject to alleviation by long range economic and social measures.

Policy Decisions and the Balancing Process

Presumably politics in a perfectly harmonious society would consist of nothing more than administration. Such a society, however, is beyond human experience, and politics retains its dynamic and tragic, and even comic, qualities. Since the clash of opposing views and wills is an abiding feature of society, the expectation of future conflict is one of the conditions under which the policy-maker operates; power, therefore, is a consideration affecting the character of his decisions.

In the first instance the policy-maker is confronted with a specific situation, such as the future of Korea (or, at the domestic level, such commonplace situations as those involving wages, administrative organization, etc.), which has given rise to differing viewpoints and opposing demands. The conflict involved in such a situation is susceptible of being resolved by application of such criteria as welfare, law, public opinion— which in varying degrees in different areas can be defined with an approach to objectivity—thus presenting to the interested parties the opportunity of agreeing on a mutually acceptable course of action. However, there is seldom such a complete identity of interest as to exclude an arbitrary, or at least fortuitous, element in a settlement, which is an invitation to quarrel over advantage.

Another factor enters to further complicate the making of decisions. The policy maker must take into account more than the immediate situation; he is obliged to judge what effect his action will have on the general fund of prestige and influence available to him in future conflict situations. Power relates not alone to the outcome of the immediate controversy but also to controversies still in prospect; it is not only a means to an end but also an end in itself, thus becoming a separate criterion of policy. It is not merely the amount of money in the pay envelope which is at stake in a strike but also the future bargaining power of the union and management. Or, to take an example from international politics, Korea is tragically involved in a situation which transcends local and immediate issues. Coming to a focus in that unhappy land is the question of prestige as it affects communism and democracy, the Soviet Union and the United States and the United Nations. A dispute which "on its merits" may seem capable of easy settlement may actually become intractable because of uncertainties and apprehensions regarding the future. The balancing process, which is manifest in a great variety of forms throughout the whole of society, is oriented toward future contingencies and is concerned with the broad objective of security. It is the expression of the ceaseless search for security through influence. The concept of balance is involved because the sufficiency of one's influence is measured by an estimation of the strength and intention of others.

It frequently happens that the long range and short range criteria fail to point in the same direction. What seems to be required by law, or welfare, or public opinion may be at odds with what seems prudent or mandatory from the standpoint of power. This dilemma, which is at the basis of the Machiavellian reputation of politics, makes politics a difficult art. All of the common human weaknesses are involved; politics is a dark terrain where impulses of vanity, greed and fear may operate without being easily detected, and where, quite as easily, their presence may be mistakenly or maliciously ascribed. But it is not these psychological hazards alone which plague the decision making process. Even in circumstances permitting of the utmost objectivity, calculations about the future may go wrong. This is the most frustrating aspect of the matter, for there is no wholly persuasive test of the wrongness or correctness of a decision, even in retrospect. A course of action once taken excludes alternative choices, and what the results would have been of embarking on one of the latter remains forever a matter of speculation. History is not a laboratory in which the less likely alternatives can be methodically discarded; it teaches only from living experience. A choice once made begins forthwith to influence events; the original premises cannot again be recaptured.

At the risk of making politics appear to be wholly a game of chance, still another aspect of the balancing process must be pointed out. Even with the best will and the most cogent analytical aids the policy-maker may be frustrated, for the limits within which he can influence the other participants in the direction of forebearance and accommodation are narrow at best. Always in some degree one is at the mercy of his opponent. There is a kind of Gresham's law of politics whereby the bad drives out the good.

The discomfort, the perils and the pathology of the balancing process are forbidding. But it cannot be interdicted. Nor can it be ignored. It is rooted in the anxieties of human nature and the tensions of history. If Utopia essays the abolition of insecurity—a condition in society which underlies creativeness no less than catastrophe—it is not only improbable but inhuman.

The United Nations and Polarized Power

The balancing process seems naturally to want to reduce itself to a pair of opposites, thereby crystallizing into a tense balance of power. It is paradoxical that the search for security should be susceptible to this dangerous tendency which is so directly opposed to what is ostensibly sought. Institutions of government seek to prevent this gathering of hostility in two opposing camps. Liberal political institutions seek to frustrate such a crystallization by keeping the balancing process many sided and flexible. Neither polarized nor monolithic, a multiple power pattern, by virtue of its very lack of predictable alignments, maximizes both stability and liberty. The United Nations was constructed on the assumption of a constantly shifting configuration of friction and cooperation among independent governments.

The dilemma of the United Nations is that it was launched in an already polarized world. The weakness of western Europe, the turmoil of the Orient, and the ruthless determination of the Soviet Union to expand its influence were conditions which already made themselves manifest at the first meetings in London, preventing the United Nations from establishing a firm footing. The United States, which was in a mood for relaxation and rather naively inclined to let the United Nations stand for its foreign policy was presently galvanized into the Truman Doctrine and the Marshall Plan, becoming, by virtue of its own great power and distaste for communism, the counter-attraction to the Soviet Union. This calamitous split resulted in confusion and consternation within the organization and has had its counterpart outside in a wild search for new answers, ranging all the way from preventive war to world government.

The present purpose is to observe how this polarization of power, which so rapidly overtook the United Nations, has resulted in skewing the assumptions and operations of the organization.

In all the organs of the United Nations there is a continuous contention with the Soviet Union over the nature and significance of the assumptions underlying the organization. This propensity of the Charter to be caught in the crossfire is related to the fact that its aims and principles and procedures are reflections of democratic assumptions about the nature of politics. Indeed international organization is a projection of the attitudes and patterns which flourished in nineteenth century democracy, of which the United States is a leading prototype. The United States was the chief architect of the Charter, and was the constitution-maker for practically all of the postwar international organizations. The Charter views the balancing process as a normal and inevitable aspect of politics; assuming the restraint which such an attitude recommends, it is optimistic about the outcome. The attitude of the Soviet Union toward the balancing process is at once less tolerant and more optimistic. The Soviet Union maintains that nothing less momentous than a classless world society and the abolition of politics are at stake in the struggle for power. It is understandable, therefore, that the foundations of the Charter itself have become a battleground. So far as relations with the Soviet Union are concerned, the democratic assumptions underlying the United Nations are not acting as buffers for the balancing process. Whereas in the domestic politics of countries in which the democratic pattern is firmly established the attitudes and procedures of democracy actually mitigate the struggle for power, their validity in the United Nations has become the subject of acid debate.

There are chasms which cannot be bridged by parliamentary debate and the casting of ballots. This situation frequently is characteristic of the kind of differences which arise in international politics; it is a predicament which confronts the United Nations in the most acute form as regards the gulf between the Soviet orbit and the rest of the world. It is rather comparable to placing a group of highly articulate Catholics and Protestants in a public forum and demanding that they come to agreement by discussion. There are circumstances in which discussion, which necessarily presumes a large area of common understanding, might actually inflame a conflict situation. In such circumstances the admittedly cruder, but also more rugged and less easily stultified, bargaining techniques of traditional diplomacy might be more appropriate —although in this case too there is no guarantee that the balancing process can be contained. Such methods of gross adjustment are not excluded by the United Nations.

So long as the Soviet Union remains within its own universe of discourse, disdainful of fact and logic as conceived by the "bourgeois" world and intent on ceaseless verbal attack, there is no choice but for its opponents to exploit the United Nations as an anti-Soviet weapon. In the process the United Nations becomes, paradoxically, a forum in which to demonstrate how formidable an obstacle the Soviet Union is to the internationalized and normative approach to world politics. The resulting fireworks are a caricature of open diplomacy. They contribute nothing to the development of a consensus.

The hostilities in Korea invite an examination of the manner in which those aspects of the Charter relating to force have been affected by the split in the United Nations.

The first World War tentatively, and the second one more compellingly, prompted the United States to advocate a new departure in international law and organization through which the legitimate use of force in world politics would be internationally determined and directed. By the recognition and development of the collective point of view it has been hoped that the United States would escape the vicious circle of measuring and testing power in terms of fighting effectiveness.

Wilson's attempt to do this failed, in part through the myopia of his own countrymen. In the present postwar period a similar attempt is confronted with two formidable conditions which have gathered strength out of the failure of the first. In the first place, not only has Europe ceased to be the hub of world politics, but this historic center of the western state system has itself become a bone of contention between the superpowers occupying the periphery in Asia and America. Secondly, this new, polarized, distribution of power, which in itself presents a difficult problem of adjustment, is paralleled by ideological differences which are not confined to questions of organization and procedure in the economic and political realms, but which penetrate to the very heart of religious and philosophical assumptions about the nature of man and society. Both the material and psychological bases of power are undergoing an upheaval which has obscured or undermined the old landmarks.

These circumstances of mid-twentieth century politics have proved to be unpropitious for the implementation of a program of collective security. Meantime, still another circumstance, the change in the character of warfare imposed by technology, has given an unprecedented urgency to the most elemental aspect of security—that of physical safety. The dilemma is further compounded by the fact that total war, because of its intolerable encroachment on civilian life and the institutions of civil society, has lost the quality of an instrument of policy. In an indeterminate conflict such as now exists force cannot be employed with the slightest degree of rational calculation. The inordinate effort and destruction exacted by total war, in conjunction with the unpredictability which has always characterized warfare, has rendered the use of force less an act of policy than the initiation of a convulsion. Aside from conscience and the legal prohibitions of the Charter, this is in itself a powerful argument against preventive war.

If, in this fantastic situation, the role of force in international politics could be reduced, by disarmament and international government, to that of police action, history would have shown a welcome considerateness. But it seems not to be so disposed. The hopefulness and ingenuity of the Charter to the contrary notwithstanding, the American Government is urgently faced with the necessity for a military policy—if for no other reason, because indifference on this score would have the effect of making the force at the disposal of the Soviet Union a useful instrument of policy.

This necessity does not arise from the failure to implement Article 43, a failure which is a symptom rather than the cause of the difficulty. The armed forces, assistance and facilities there envisaged are designed for police action, which clearly can be effective only as regards isolated disturbances involving relatively weak countries. In any event Article 43 would have been vitiated in the Korean situation, where the split with the Soviet Union would have paralyzed the Military Staff Committee. Fundamental to any constitutional document is the assumption of a disposition to cooperate. So long as the attitudes and policies of the Soviet Union belie such an assumption, the United States will not find in the institutions of the United Nations, or in any form of international organization, the basis for a relaxation of its military policy.

A logical consequence of the Charter's outlawing of force is the outmoding of the military alliance, which is incompatible with the requirements of collective security. We do not have to look far to see that the split in the United Nations has subjected the Charter to a very severe strain on this point. As a consequence Articles 51 and 53 have come into a special prominence, which, as a matter of fact, was foreshadowed by the care and difficulty with which they were originally negotiated.

Article 53 in embracing regional "arrangements" as well as "agencies" legitimizes the Soviet military agreements with neighboring states, some of which had already been concluded at the time of the San Francisco Conference. Moreover, the Article frees military action under these agreements from the necessity of prior authorization by the Security Council insofar as such action is directed against the "renewal of aggressive policy" on the part of an ex-enemy state. This provision of Article 53 is a crack in the structure of the Charter which the Soviet Union has employed as the point of departure for its postwar system of alliances. The Soviet-Chinese treaty of February 14, 1950, for example, contains a formula which with variations is to be found in agreements with all of the satellites: the parties are bound jointly to resist "any repetition of aggression and violation of peace on the part of Japan or any other state which directly or indirectly would unite with Japan in acts of aggression." Thus the independence from Security Council authority reserved to the victors by Articles 53 and 107 as regards action against former enemy states is stretched to include the possibility of such action against an ex-ally.

Whether the Atlantic Pact fits any more comfortably in Article 51 than the Soviet's satellite treaties do in Article 53 is a question which invites much refinement of argument, but which we shall endeavor to treat with brevity. Article 51 is designed to cover the awkward situation in which an attack occurs without the Security Council for one reason or another, including the veto, taking action. One effect of this provision is to enable a regional agency (which by Article 53 is prohibited from taking enforcement action without the authorization of the Security Council) to take prompt measures against attack, by one of its own members or from without, should the Security Council be stalemated. In its bearing on the Organization of American States, Article 51 has a particular significance by virtue of the veto power possessed by the United States, which assures the possibility in all circumstances of maintaining the autonomy of the inter-American system. At San Francisco this was considered to be the chief consequence of Article 51.

The question whether the Atlantic Pact does or does not constitute a regional organization has been much discussed, but still remains unclear notwithstanding the talent expended on its elucidation. If it is based on Article 52, its restricted membership despite the lack of a clear geographical focus, and the fact that it is directed exclusively against the possibility of attack from outside its own circle, emerge as incongruities. If it is based solely on Article 51, it then takes on the nature of a permanent hedge against the United Nations itself, involving the same illogicality contained in wanting one's cake and eating it too. This ambiguity surrounding the pact emphasizes that it is not an instrument of collective security (at best it is collective security among friends), but is a defensive arrangement, tied negatively rather than positively to the Charter, which lies essentially outside the purview of the organization. Despite the international organization aspects of its internal structure, the pact is a manifestation of the traditional balancing process. Like the Soviet system of alliances, it is a military policy of the kind which the Charter is designed to discourage and which it was hoped would be outmoded.

However the pact may be classified from a legal point of view, it is, from the political point of view, an attempt to compensate for and eventually, it is hoped, to assist in remedying the weakness of western Europe, which is a basic cause of tension between the United States and the Soviet Union. There is a certain irony in the shifting incidence of the balancing process. Up to the first World War the internal difficulties of Europe were a condition which redounded to the freedom of action and security of the rest of the world. Today these difficulties, having descended below what one might wryly call the optimum point, invite quarrels among outsiders over the future of Europe. This is a state of affairs unprecedented in the history of the western state system, and one which was not anticipated in the postwar planning. In the best of circumstances there would have been a pronounced tendency for the Soviet Union and the United States to disagree. But, even more than the disorder in the Orient, it has been the economic debility, military weakness and political instability of Europe which has provided the occasion for the heavy clash of Soviet and American power. An imbalance of such magnitude is one which is beyond the capacity of the principles and procedures of a constitutional document to redress.

Meanwhile the United Nations has had in the Korean affair its first experience with a clear-cut case of aggression. Although the Security Council, owing to the fortuitous absence of the Soviet Union, was able to take prompt action, thereby making it unnecessary, for the time being at any rate, to refer the matter to the General Assembly, the action of the United Nations falls short of being a satisfactory exemplification of collective security. The previous failure to implement Article 43, together with the straitened circumstances, militarily and economically, of most members of the United Nations (combined as well with a certain willingness to let the powerful play the game in accordance with the old pattern) resulted in an overwhelming preponderance of American fighting personnel. Moreover the campaign has been under exclusively American direction. While the fact that American forces have fought under the clear authority of the Charter is of great mutual benefit to the United Nations and the United States, the effect of American predominance in the military effort has been to make the United Nations excessively dependent on American government and opinion. As a consequence the United Nations, even though in the Korean case no extra-Charter security pacts are involved, takes on the aspect of a coalition led by the United States in opposition to the expansion of Soviet influence. This is another demonstration of how the United Nations is a house divided against itself.

The Soviet Union in the United Nations

It was recognized from the beginning of the United Nations that a major split among the leading powers was not likely to be healed or suppressed by anything internal to the organization itself. Or, to express the obvious more simply: there is no way of guaranteeing that the strong stuff of international politics can be contained within the bounds of a constitutional document. Feelings of frustration, growing out of the conviction that the Soviet Union has stalled the United Nations on dead center, have called forth numerous proposals which would fundamentally alter the organization. The program advocated by ex-President Herbert Hoover is a recent and striking example. Admittedly the burden of proof is on those who see in the participation of the Soviet Union in the United Nations a factor which contributes to international stability. Yet there are certain considerations which suggest that such may actually be the effect.

There was no alternative to the inclusion of the Soviet Union as a planning participant and original member of the United Nations. This was based on a genuine hopefulness for the future and there was no suggestion in any quarter that it be excluded. Even in the light of subsequent events, the original inclusion of the Soviet Union was a sound course of action, for two reasons: 1) only in the perspective thereby afforded can the meaning of its postwar policy be rightly judged. Any failure on the part of the western allies "to keep the record straight" would have been a plausible explanation of the Soviet Union's subsequent hostility, which would have confused world opinion—perhaps to the point of paralysis. 2) Had the exclusion of the Soviet Union been demanded by Great Britain and the United States, or even had the Soviet Union decided independently to remain aloof, few governments outside the western hemisphere would have been inclined to join the organization, for it straightway would have had the character of an alliance. To these observations must be added another. The Soviet Union was impelled to associate itself with the idea of a permanent United Nations because it could not afford in the highly fluid situation at the war's end to risk the future of its own influence by frustrating a project whose objectives were so widely and fervently approved.

If judged only from the point of view of the convenience and future advantage of the west, the initial identification of the Soviet Union with the United Nations has had an important influence on the development of postwar events. It has enabled the balancing process to proceed, however equivocally, in a universal framework. From the standpoint of the United States this has had a special value which could not have been adequately appreciated at the time of drafting the Charter, when the enormous accrual of strength with which the United States was to emerge from the war had not yet been fully revealed.

The power and well-being of the United States impose responsibility for leadership, but, owing to the very sharp contrast with most of the rest of the world, the carrying out of that responsibility is made exceptionally difficult. No matter how benevolent its intentions, power repels as well as attracts. This is a dilemma which confronts the United States in even more acute form than that experienced by Great Britain in the nineteenth century. The comparative difficulty of the American task is greater for other reasons as well. The growth in political awareness of nearly all peoples; the great role played by propagandized mass opinion; and the serious economic maladjustment between the United States and the rest of the world make contemporary international politics highly intractable. Since the United States can do much about many things which need doing, yet is not omnipotent or free from its own bias, it is a ready target for the discharge of resentment. As a channel for the expression of American policy, the United Nations tends to spread participation and responsibility, thus serving the American government, and the international community, in the useful capacity of a lightning rod.

After inadvertently facilitating the establishment of machinery for the democratic internationalization of American policy, has Soviet membership in the United Nations now ceased to have a salutary influence on international politics? There is reason to believe that, judged from the standpoint of both the external and internal circumstances of American leadership, the presence of the Soviet Union in the organization has tended, at least up to this point, to be helpful.

It would be extremely difficult for the United States to keep in order a coalition whose chief preoccupation was opposition to the Soviet Union in particular and communism in general. It should be pointed out in this regard that the solidarity of the inter-American system and of the Atlantic community can be easily overrated. A similar combination in the east, if it were decided upon, would have even less coherence. The placing of such combinations, however loosely, in the larger framework of the United Nations minimizes the embarrassment of dependence on American power; moreover, by being related to the purposes and principles of the Charter, which are positive and dynamic, they are less exposed to the danger of assuming a merely defensive posture. For the vast and crucial areas which have not received the direct imprint of European civilization, the United Nations is particularly important as a supra-national symbol. Conceivably, anti-Americanism (which in many cases does not imply pro-Sovietism) and neutralism would receive a strong impetus if the United Nations were to become exclusively identified with American power and policy.

Viewed in this light, the propaganda and obstructionism of the Soviet Union have not been an unmixed evil. The Soviet Union rushed headlong into the game of vituperation and pettifoggery, giving satisfaction to already confirmed believers and no doubt influencing those who are restricted in their access to information. But the net result has probably been unfavorable for the expansion of Soviet influence. The irritation and frightening implications of such tactics have contributed to the solidarity of the free world. But even more interesting and ironical, has been the effect of Soviet behavior in precluding the possibility of the postwar policy of the United States falling into confusion and impotency from internal causes. For two decades between the wars the United States was immobilized in world politics by the bewilderment and contention which beset American opinion. As regards the present period, it is probable, even if regrettable, that the statesmanlike policy thus far pursued by the United States has been sustained in part by the crude drama enacted by the Soviet Union at Lake Success.

In judging the future incidence of Soviet membership in the United Nations we are on less firm ground than when judging the past and present effect. Obviously there are limits to the usefulness of the Soviet Union as a foil for the United States. However, two additional factors suggest that her continued membership serves the interests of the international community. Participation in the United Nations affords a contact with reality which would be almost wholly lacking were the relations of the Soviet Union with foreign governments confined to the conspiratorial atmosphere of her diplomatic establishments. But a consequence still more important than the breaking of this contact would result from Soviet departure from the organization. The exit of the Soviet Union would involve also the departure of the satellites, which would be unfortunate in two respects. It would reinforce the isolation which Moscow seeks to impose upon them, thus further inhibiting the spread of Titoism. Also, if the waters were to close completely over the identity of the eastern European governments, the tendency toward further encroachment in Europe would probably be quickened. It is not improbable that the satellite governments are aware of the strengthened position vis-à-vis Moscow which is implicit in their membership in the United Nations and would for that reason be reluctant to withdraw. If this presents a dilemma to the Kremlin (and that body is not as free from predicament as we may be inclined to believe), it is a situation to be encouraged. There are many practical as well as imponderable factors which enter the question of admitting the Chinese communist government into the United Nations. It is appropriate to suggest in the present connection that in all probability the Soviet Union actually views such a prospect with disfavor—despite the surface appearances to the contrary, which serve as propaganda for Asiatic consumption.

If, as the case of Yugoslavia suggests, the United Nations can, in the capacity of a half-way house, help to loosen the bonds of the Soviet satellites, it also has the effect of promoting reciprocity in the relations between the United States and the governments outside the Soviet orbit. In this it serves the best interests of the American government. In its long range policy of building strength abroad, the United States is not asking subserviency, but is aiming at the establishment of independence from outside subversion and control. In undertaking this difficult task, the American government is engaged in an attempt to stabilize international politics in accordance with the original assumption of the Charter: namely, that the balancing process is least dangerous when it occurs among multiple centers of power in shifting relationships of friction and cooperation.

CHAPTER 9

INTERNATIONAL LAW

THE FUNCTIONS and possibilities of international law are among the most discussed aspects of international relations. A vast variety of opinions has been expressed which, in the popular mind, has served to confuse and distort its true nature. These opinions vary from cynical rejection of international law as impotent to enthusiastic and evangelical fervor about it as the instrument for obtaining enduring world peace. More sober consideration must lead away from these opposite extremes and toward a more balanced evaluation, as evidenced in the following selections.

In the first selection, "The Outlook for International Law," Professor Brierly clearly and concisely delineates the role of international law in international relations. As he insists, any analysis of international law must bear in mind that it is an existing system of law which is being discussed, that law is an instrument having not only uses but limitations, and that advances in international law can come only to the extent that sovereign states are willing to make them. Brierly says that international law is an inevitable consequence of the coexistence of sovereign states. Precisely because each state is sovereign in its own domain, there must be law to regulate and adjust the relations among them. The fact that international law is on occasion violated does not mean that it has no real existence any more than the same would be true for domestic law. International law originated in custom, and its rules are elaborated and modified by treaties which are a form of legislation. The uncertainty and impreciseness of many of these rules are often criticized, and much progress can yet be made in avoiding ambiguities. Nevertheless, while law is necessarily "stated in the form of general principles," facts are never general but particular, and the circumstances of their concrete application are often unforeseen and subject to dispute. International law works effectively in most cases, but the public is primarily aware of the exceptions, the great political issues which are not controlled by law. It is worth noting that national law also fails to control political issues effectively within the state. In this regard national and international law reveal similar tendencies. Brierly points out that political questions are not settled through legal procedures, because states are not willing to do so—"vital interests" of states remain in the realm of international politics and will continue so until and unless the observance of international law becomes "compulsory and unconditional."

The second selection, "The Feasibility of Compulsory Legal Settlement" by Grant Gilmore, is concerned in form with an analysis of the International Court of Justice; in actual effect it is an examination into the feasibility of converting international law into a compulsory system—the basic question which Brierly suggests is at the root of any survey of international law in international relations.

Gilmore examines the Court in terms of its contentious and advisory functions. In its contentious jurisdiction it settles cases voluntarily submitted to it by the parties to a dispute; the decision is handed down and is binding. In its advisory capacity the Court gives legal advice upon the merits of a dispute being heard by the United Nations Security Council or General Assembly. This advice is not binding, technically, but it nevertheless carries great weight in influencing public opinion. States which take what they consider to be a political dispute to the political bodies, the Council or the Assembly, usually do so precisely because they did not wish to go to the Court for a legal settlement in the first place. While they cannot be forced to go to Court under the present rules of international law, they may be much more easily persuaded to submit their dispute to the scrutiny of an international political organization; otherwise the organization may decide on measures adverse to their interests in their absence. But if the political body requests legal advice from the Court in the form of an advisory opinion, the disputants are put in the position of having their political problems settled legally through the back door.

In practice nations draw a distinction between disputes which they are willing to regard as legal questions and those which they desire to settle politically. Political settlement means settlement not on a basis of law but on a basis of national interest. Gilmore points out that, where advisory opinions were requested for the settlement of political problems in League days, dissension over the opinion clearly revealed that such a distinction exists. Legal decisions in contentious jurisdiction are customarily and voluntarily observed *because* the states concerned are willing to carry out the verdict of the Court; they are prepared to accept the verdict, win or lose. Where the issues touch the fundamentals of power, however, they are not prepared to do so. If they will not do so of their own free will or out of a fear of retaliation, force is the only alternative. But where issues of power are concerned, the international community of states becomes deeply divided along lines of interests and the balance of power, and enforcement becomes difficult. It is these facts which, in his opinion, serve to underline a distinction between legal and political disputes, each of which needs settlement through different procedures. In so far as theorists advance plans for compulsory jurisdiction of a world court, they overlook this distinction which all states powerful enough to do so insist upon: legal disputes are disputes which states are prepared to settle legally; all others are political disputes.

THE OUTLOOK FOR INTERNATIONAL LAW

J. L. BRIERLY *

When the international order is rebuilt after the present war, international law will be one of the instruments that the architects will use. They will be bound to use it, if only because the settlement will involve the making of treaties, and treaties raise questions of drafting, of interpretation, of enforcement, and other questions, the answers to which belong to international law. But the part that international law can play, or the conditions on which we can hope to make it one of the pillars of a more stable world, can not be determined by reasoning in the void or by wishful thinking. . . .

That is not to say that international law is a mystery about which only professed international lawyers have a right to express opinions. On the contrary, one of the handicaps that it has always suffered from is the lack of general interest in its problems and of informed criticism of its defects. But no reasonable estimate either of its present value or its future prospects can be formed without a certain amount of serious thought, and there are three matters in particular to which it is necessary that this thought should be directed. In the first place, we have to re-

* J. L. Brierly, *The Outlook for International Law*, pp. 1–11, 15–18. Copyright 1944, by The Clarendon Press, Oxford. Reprinted by permission.

member that we do not start with a clean slate but with an existing system, such as it is, and we need to make some examination of the part that that system is playing, as things are, in international relations. Secondly, law is not, as some laymen seem to imagine, a sort of sociological maid of all work, but a highly specialized instrument, and it is essential to have before our minds not only the uses that it may serve but even more the limitations upon its usefulness as a means of controlling human conduct. Thirdly, we are concerned with the problems of a system of law in which the subjects are not individual men and women, as they are in the law with which we are all brought into contact in our daily lives, but independent states, and we have perpetually to be asking ourselves how far, and on what conditions, independent states can be expected to be amenable to the special kind of control that it is in the nature of law to provide. All this is but to say that our best laid schemes will be likely to go agley unless we have taken account of the data which are given us, the instrument we have to use, and the subject matter we hope to mould.

The present system of international law is about four hundred years old. Some of its rules are much older than this; but it was only in the sixteenth century that men began to study the rules that states followed in their relations with one another systematically and as a separate branch of learning, and to treat them as rules of law rather than of ethics. The rise of international law was in fact one of the consequences of that great political change which marks the dividing line between the medieval and the modern eras; it is one of the results on the secular side of the Reformation movement. It assumes the abandonment of the medieval ideal of the unity of Christendom, and the substitution for it of the modern system of sovereign states, each independent of the others in its system of government and law, and each acknowledging no authority outside itself. But that this modern conception of the sovereignty or independence of states is not inconsistent with their subordination to law was and is its fundamental postulate.

There are of course versions of the doctrine of sovereignty which deny this, and assert that it is of the very essence of sovereignty to be absolute and illimitable. If states were indeed sovereign in that sense, it would follow that they cannot be limited in their behaviour by law or anything else but superior force, and international law would be impossible in the nature of things; at most the term might describe certain practices which states do normally follow, not because they have any obligation to follow them, but because they find it convenient to do so. The defect of all such theories, however, is that they are reached by *a priori* reasoning, by arguing that a state as such *must* have certain attributes, and therefore we ought to conclude without more ado that actual states do have them. But that is a thoroughly unscientific method of approach to any object of study. States are facts in the world in which we live, and there is no way of understanding their nature except by observing them as they are and as they behave. If we do that, we see at once that one of the conditions under which every actual state exists, and from which it can never escape, is the coexistence with itself in the same world of other states with which it is brought into constant relations. To neglect this condition of state existence and to profess to explain what a state is and what its attributes are without reference to it, as political philosophers have too often done, is like trying to explain human nature by studying the behaviour of Robinson Crusoe before the arrival on the scene of Man Friday.

The existence of some kind of international law is simply one of the inevitable consequences of this coexistence in the world of a plurality of states necessarily brought into relations one with another. It is one illustration of a truth with which all students of law are familiar and to which there are no exceptions, that when there is a society there is necessarily law, and when there is law there we can be sure a society will exist. The reason that law and society are linked together in this way is quite simple; it is that men who are living together cannot avoid making claims on one another; they must demand that their neighbour should act or refrain from acting towards them in some particular way; and they learn by experience that these claims will not be recognized, that is to say, they will not be treated as rights, except on terms of reciprocity, unless each for his part recognizes a correlative duty to do towards others as he would be done to by them. Even a hermit state, such as Tibet used to be, must at least claim as its right that other states should leave it alone, and must admit its own corresponding duty not to interfere with them. It is not a bad definition of international law to say that it is the sum of rights that a state may claim for itself and its nationals from other states, and of the duties which in consequence it must observe towards them.

The best evidence for the existence of international law is that every actual state recognizes that it does exist and that it is itself under obligation to observe it. States may often violate international law, just as individuals often violate municipal law; but no more than individuals do states defend their violations by claiming that they are above the law. It is only the philosopher in his study who sometimes makes that claim on their behalf. States may defend their conduct in all sorts of other ways, by denying that the rule they are alleged to have broken is a rule of law, by appealing to a supposed right of self-preservation superior to the ordinary law, and by other excuses more or less sincerely believed in as the case may be; but they do not use the explanation which would obviously be the natural one if there were any doubt that international law has a real existence and that they are bound by it.

The rules of international law have never been embodied in any formal code; they still derive their authority from unwritten custom. Customary law is typical of an early stage in the devlopment of any legal system, for it is only in a fairly mature system of law, such as we have within a modern state, that most legal rules come to be expressed either in formal legislation or in judicial decisions, and international law has not yet reached that stage. But to say that it is essentially a system of customary law does not mean that all the rights and duties of states are derived directly from customary rules. On the contrary, the greater number of any state's rights and duties to-day come from treaties into which it has entered with another state or states. But indirectly even these treaty rights and duties depend on custom, for what makes a treaty binding is a customary rule that when it has been duly entered into its terms shall bind the states that make it. This rule is the most fundamental of the whole system. For owing to the defective condition of international law on the institutional side treaties have to fulfil functions which are much wider than those of the contracts which are their most obvious counterpart in a municipal system, and in particular they provide the most effective of the means whereby international law develops. A purely customary law can only grow in a slow and haphazard way; it has no regular procedure by which it can be adapted to new situations, however urgently these may require to be regulated by law. But treaties, especially those to which large numbers of states are parties, 'multi-lateral' treaties, as they are called, provide a substitute, though not a completely satisfactory one, for the legislative processes of municipal law, and thus supply international law with a principle of growth which is necessary for the health of any legal system.

The function that international law tries to fulfil in the world of states is not always clearly understood. It is a more limited and specialized function than is sometimes supposed. We hear so much today of the ever-growing interdependence of the different countries of the world, and of those manifold contacts in trade and finance and social and cultural relations of all kinds, which are always taking place across national frontiers, that it is perhaps natural that people should expect that international law would be a system having for its function, or at least for its ideal aim, the co-ordination and regulation of this great volume of intercourse. . . .

But certainly if international law did profess to regulate the innumerable contacts to which intercourse across national frontiers gives rise in a way at all comparable to the way in which municipal law regulates the life of society within a modern state, it would be almost a complete sham. That, however, is not the function, or at any rate it is as yet only a subordinate and little developed function, of international law. It is true, as Sir Alfred Zimmern mentions, that it does contain regulations for some few of the contacts that take place across frontiers; it does so because states have made arrangements among themselves on these matters by means of multilateral treaties. This is a very important movement, but it is quite a recent one, less than a hundred years old, and it covers as yet only a small part of international intercourse. Most of that intercourse is not between states but between individuals, and with this international law has as a rule nothing to do. If, for instance, legal questions arise out of a contract which business men in different countries have made with one another, these will be decided by the municipal law of one or other of these countries, and not by international law. It is true that the court which decides such questions may take the principle which will determine the case from a branch of law which is sometimes called 'private international law,' but this kind of law is quite distinct from the 'public international law' with which we are concerned here. Private international law is not international, but municipal, law, in spite of its name; it denotes the rules that the municipal law of each state directs its courts to apply when the case before them has some foreign element in it, but these rules are 'international' only in the sense that there is, as it is obviously desirable that there should be, a large measure of uniformity in the rules that different systems of municipal law provide for such cases.

There need be no mystery about the primary function at least of international law. Stated quite simply, what it tries to do is to define or delimit the respective spheres within which each of the sixty-odd states into which the world is divided for political purposes is entitled to exercise its authority. Each of these states is independent of the others, and each has its own governmental and legal system; if there is not to be a clash between their respective competences there must clearly be some principles to determine where the competence of one state ends and that of another begins. These principles are given by international law, and once that is understood, most of those topics that wear an appearance of formalism and remoteness from the real life of the world in the textbooks fall into their place. Thus inasmuch as we are concerned with the respective competences of states, a primary question is to determine the conditions that entitle an organized association of human beings to rank as a state for international purposes, and that is not a simple question; it will be answered in the text-books under such headings as 'the subjects of international law' or 'international persons.' When we know what a state is, we must know how in a legal sense it 'acts'; for it is only individual human beings that can ever act in any literal sense, and there must therefore be rules to determine the circumstances in which the act of an individual is to be regarded in law as the act of his state, and these rules will be found under such headings as the 'responsibility of states,' 'diplomatic agents,' and others. When we know what acts are to be regarded in law as the acts of a state, there must be rules to demarcate the scope of their validity, both by reference to the territory, by land, sea, and air, over which a state may extend its authority to the exclusion of that of other states, and by reference to the persons who may be subjected to that authority. Rules of this kind will occupy many chapters in any exposition of the contents of international law; they will comprise, to name only a few of the usual chapter headings, discussions of the open sea, territorial waters, the air, the various modes of acquiring territory such as occupation, cession, or prescription, nationality, extradition, aliens, and many other topics. Another big heading will relate to treaties, showing how they must be made if they are to be binding on the states that make them, the conditions in which they become void, and so on, and still another to the machinery for settling differences between states when they arise.

This short catalogue of some of the main topics to which the rules of international law relate shows how far it is from being a system of law for the regulation of international life in general. The fact is that international law is still very definitely in the *laissez-faire* stage of social development. In most modern states men have ceased to believe that the function of law ought to be limited to the marking out of separate spheres within which each individual member of society is to be free to act as he pleases so long as his acts do not lead to collisions between the sphere of one man and that of his neighbour, and they have begun to see that in law a society has a valuable instrument for positive action aiming to promote the general social welfare. This revolution in thought has gone farther in some countries than in others, but it is comparatively recent in all, and it is as yet only beginning to make headway in international relations. There have, as has been already mentioned, been a few tentative efforts in this direction in modern times, but these would have to be developed on a far greater scale before it would be accurate to describe international law as a system of rules for the general regulation of the relations of states with one another, and not even the most farreaching development on these lines would convert it into a system for the regulation of international life as a whole. . . .

One of the difficulties that is often supposed to be a particularly formidable obstacle to the use of international law as a practical instrument is the alleged vagueness and uncertainty of its principles. There is some substance in this objection, but not very much. The customary part of the law does consist of rules which are often vague or disputed, and, unlike the rules of the English Common Law, which in origin were also customary rules, they have not had the advantage of being worked out by many generations of judges into a rich store of detailed and very practical principles. That is a defect which one may hope will be gradually reduced in importance by the development of international adjudication. But it is also true—and this is more serious—that some of the uncertainties of the customary law are not historical accidents; they are the reflection in the law of divergencies, not always avowed or superficially apparent, between the interests of different nations, and this is a defect which is only likely to be cured by a closer integration of the society of states, which at the best will be a slow process. But these difficulties do not apply to the bulk of international legal business, which does not arise out of the customary law but out of treaties, and in respect of clearness treaties are very like Acts of Parliament, that is to say, if they are not always conspicuously clear, they can at least be made to yield up a meaning to a properly equipped court. But when international law, or for that matter any other kind of law, is criticized on the score of uncertainty, the criticism often springs from a misunderstanding. Certainty is an ideal that law must never cease to aim at, but it is also one that it can never realize at all completely; for the main cause of uncertainty in any kind of law is the uncertainty of the facts to which it has to be applied. Law has necessarily to be stated in the form of general principles, but facts are never general; they are always particular, they are often obscure or disputed, and they were very likely not foreseen, and therefore not expressly provided for, at the time when the rule of law received its formulation. It is this intractability of facts that prevents the practice of law from ever becoming a science; it is and always will be an art.

For various reasons this credit side of the balance-sheet of international law is not sufficiently recognized. The facts which show the smooth working of the system are not as a rule made public, partly because foreign offices are temperamentally secretive, but partly too because the public would not be interested in them. What it is interested in, and what it does hear about, are the breaches of international law, and it naturally concludes that breaches are the rule and observance the exception. This one-sided presentation of the facts also has the effect of making it difficult to compare international and municipal law in point of effectiveness. For the failures of the former of which the public hears are failures to control great political issues, and we do not always ask ourselves whether it is law that controls such issues when they arise within the state. We tend therefore to compare two dissimilar things, the political failures of international law with the successes of municipal law in regulating the private affairs of individuals. The contrast would certainly be reduced if we could compare the operation of the two kinds of law, on the one hand, in matters which are not politically important, for there we should find the standard of observance is fairly high in both; and, on the other hand, their capacity to influence issues in which a political element is prominent, which we should find in both cases to be slight.

It is right therefore that we should be reminded that international law, even as things are, is performing a useful function in the relations between states; it is a means for enabling the day-to-day business of states to be conducted in normal times along orderly and predictable lines, and that is no small service. But the debit side of the balance-sheet is a serious one. It is that hitherto states have only allowed law to control their relations in matters which, though they are not unimportant in themselves, are of secondary importance, and therefore present them with no very strong temptation to defy it. When issues of high politics arise between them they do not yet allow law to have the final word in the determination of their policies. A generation ago this used to be expressed quite frankly in arbitration treaties by a clause which excluded from the obligation to arbitrate those differences which affected the 'vital interests' of either party, and it was left to each party to say when a case arose whether it fell within this description or not. The result, as one of the delegates to the Hague Conference of 1907 pointed out, was that, though the treaties began with the imperative 'thou shalt,' they ended with the reassuring words 'if thou wilt.' To-day this 'vital interests' clause has gone out of fashion; no doubt it was almost indecently candid. But there has been no fundamental change in the attitude of states towards the law that it expressed; normally they find it a useful lubricant for their relations and they use it accordingly, but in the last resort they regard its observance as optional rather than, as the nature of true law requires, as compulsory and unconditional. This attitude has its extreme but logical development in the traditional attitude of states to war.

THE FEASIBILITY OF COMPULSORY LEGAL SETTLEMENT

GRANT GILMORE *

The International Court of Justice, "the principal judicial organ of the United Nations," has replaced the League of Nations' Permanent Court of International Justice with little change in the Court's constitution, in its relationship to the parent international organization, in the extent of its jurisdiction, or in the procedure prescribed under its Statute. The new Court has a new name, a technically new Statute, some new judges and, perhaps most important of all, some new members. In matters of substance, however, the new Court is a continuation of the old. It need not be expected, nor was it intended, to add anything new to the structure of international order. . . .

Is the present Court, or could it become, an effective agency for world peace? What is the scope of the Court's jurisdiction or competence, and what should it be? The two questions are interrelated and interdependent. The greater the area of the Court's jurisdiction, the greater the effectiveness of the Court's work, provided always, however, that the jurisdiction conferred is something more than a paper charter. Watered stock can be a judicial as well as a corporate calamity.

When the Permanent Court was established in 1920, the principal innovation was thought to be the creation of a continuing judicial body, which could by virtue of its continuity develop its own traditions, forms, precedents and jurisprudence. Previously each international arbitral tribunal had to be specially constituted by the parties, and performed its task without reference, or with only informal reference, to past decisions of similar tribunals. The Permanent Court was designed to be, and was, a notable procedural advance, in that successive disputes could come before the same Court, composed of judges who sat for relatively long terms, operating under permanent rules. The Court was not designed to bring about any change in the number or gravity of international disputes submitted to arbitration, except insofar as the Court's existence, availability and (it was hoped) growing prestige might induce parties to submit themselves voluntarily to its jurisdiction. The only new jurisdictional element was an almost accidental by-product of the League Covenant: the Court

* Grant Gilmore, "The International Court of Justice," *The Yale Law Journal*, Vol. 55, No. 5 (August, 1946), pp. 1049–1064. Copyright 1946, by Yale Law Journal Co., Inc. Reprinted by permission.

was empowered to give advisory opinions on questions referred to it by the League Council.

The Court's jurisdiction was thus in part contentious, in part advisory. Consideration of what the Court accomplished under its double mandate will clarify what can be expected of the Court in its second, or United Nations phase, and, to some extent, what can be expected of any international court—*i.e.*, what limitations there are to the effectiveness of such a court.

The Court's contentious jurisdiction in both its League of Nations and its United Nations phases is substantially limited to cases which the parties to a dispute are willing to bring before it. Under the so-called "optional compulsory jurisdiction" clause in the original Statute, which has been continued without important change in the revised Statute, States adhering to the Court may, however, declare that they recognize the Court's jurisdiction as "compulsory *ipso facto* and without special agreement, in relation to any other state accepting the same obligation. . . ." During the Court's League period, forty-six States made declarations under this provision. Many of these declarations were, however, so fogged over with reservations and exceptions that they did not in fact notably extend the Court's jurisdiction beyond the caprice and whim of the declarant States. . . .

Under the Court's contentious jurisdiction, some thirty cases were disposed of between 1920 and 1940. None of these cases was of any great significance or importance, if those words be taken to refer to the bright hope of a better world. They were the undramatic, unspectacular run-of-the-mill cases which any court, international or national, is primarily equipped to handle. They were, since the Court's jurisdiction was limited to cases which the disputant States were willing to have adjudicated, cases on which the States concerned were willing to take a chance of losing. . . .

Thus the Court's contentious jurisdiction produced nothing particularly novel and the Court functioned smoothly and efficiently in traditional grooves. Its advisory jurisdiction, however, which turned out to have been booby-trapped, deserves more extended analysis. (It should be noted that one of the few significant changes made in the revised Statute has worked a limitation in this branch of the Court's jurisdiction.) We shall examine two of the cases referred to the Court for its advisory opinion by a League Council which was never notable for its capacity to meet difficult issues squarely.

The *Eastern Carelia* case grew out of hostilities between Russian and Finnish forces following the Russian Revolution. A peace treaty concluded at Dorpat in 1920 provided *inter alia* for the withdrawal of Finnish troops from certain Communes which were to be "reincorporated in the State of Russia and . . . attached to the autonomous territory of Eastern Carelia . . . which shall enjoy the national right of self-determination." . . . In 1921, following an attempted revolt against Russian sovereignty in Eastern Carelia, the Finnish Government brought the matter before the League Council. An attempt, made through the Estonian Government to have Russia submit the matter to the Council as a non-member State, met with Soviet refusal on the ground that the question was purely domestic, the references to Carelian autonomy in the Dorpat Treaty . . . being merely descriptive of an existing situation and not intended to create treaty obligations. After a year's delay the Council, at the suggestion of Finland, referred to the Court the question whether those references in the Treaty . . . constituted "engagements of an international character" which Russia would be under a duty, towards Finland, to carry out. Finland appeared before the Court and submitted a voluminous dossier. Russian participation was limited to a splenetic telegram signed by Tchitcherin, Commissar for Foreign Affairs, which stated that Russia found it impossible to take part in the proceedings before the Court, which were "without legal value either in substance or in form," briefly rehearsed the Russian position in a series of "Whereases," denied the right of the "so-called League of Nations" to intervene, and in conclusion referred to the shabby treatment of Russia by the League Powers in a number of instances as demonstrating the impossibility of an impartial hearing, under League auspices, of any question involving Russia. The resulting opinion, seven of the eleven judges who sat on the case concurring, stated the facts and concluded that, although in form the Court was being asked to give an advisory opinion, nevertheless "answering the question would be substantially equivalent to deciding the dispute between the parties," and, Russia having declined to participate, "the Court, being a Court of Justice, cannot, even in giving advisory opinions, depart from the essential rules guiding their activity as a Court." "The Court therefore finds it impossible to give its opinion on a dispute of this kind." The Council, having received the Court's reply, took note of it, and, after discussion, entered in its minutes a somewhat irritated justification of its own procedure. The Eastern Carelians then retired from the international stage.

The *Austro-German Customs Union* case presented issues notably more serious than those in the *Eastern Carelia* case. Article 88 of the Versailles Treaty provided that "the independence of Austria is inalienable" other than with the consent of the Council of the League of Nations and imposed upon Austria the undertaking "to abstain from any act which might directly or indirectly or by any means whatever compromise her independence." In 1922, in Protocols drafted at Geneva in connection with loans to Austria by the victorious powers, Austria reiterated its undertaking under Article 88. The 1922 Protocols contained language construing the undertaking as not restricting Austrian action in relation to "customs tariffs and commercial or financial agreements," subject to the proviso that no State should be granted "a special regime or exclusive advantages" calculated to threaten Austrian independence. In 1931 Austria and Germany executed a Protocol, dated March 19, under which the two Governments agreed to negotiate for a treaty "to assimilate the tariff and economic policies of their respective countries." Under the Protocol, drafted with considerable technical skill to avoid even the appearance of offending against Article 88 of the Versailles Treaty and the 1922 Geneva Protocols, the projected treaty would, among other things, have prescribed the substantial elimination of duties as between Germany and Austria, a uniform tariff law for their dealings with other countries, and a proration of tariff receipts between them. The League Council, acting with unwonted dispatch, heard French objections to the proposed union on May 18 and 19, and promptly referred the matter to the Court, with a request that the Court act with all possible speed, for its opinion whether the Austro-German Protocol was "compatible" with Article 88 and the Geneva Protocol. Austria, meanwhile, agreed to take no further action pending the Court's opinion. Represented before the Court were the Governments of Austria, Czechoslovakia, France, Germany and Italy. A preliminary question involved the appointment of so-called *ad hoc* judges. Under the Court's Statute, a State, party before the Court and not having a judge of its own nationality on the Court, has a right to have a national appointed judge *ad hoc*. Both Austria and Czechoslovakia, being unrepresented, requested such appointments. The Court, after argument, denied both requests, ten of the fifteen judges concurring, on the ground that, Austria and Germany being in the same interest, Austria was sufficiently represented by the German judge, and Czechoslovakia, being in the same interest as France and Italy, was sufficiently represented by the French and Italian judges. The Court then heard oral argument between July 20 and August 5, written statements having been filed previously.

On September 3, before the Court's opinion had been announced, the Foreign Ministers of Austria and Germany declared that the March 19 Protocol and the idea of a Customs Union had been abandoned by the two Governments. On September 5 the Court, without reference to the announced abandonment, delivered its opinion, widely predicted in advance, that the Austro-German Protocol was, in the wording of the Council's request, "incompatible" with the 1922 Geneva Protocol, although "compatible" with Article 88 of the Versailles Treaty. On Sep-

tember 7 the Council noted the Court's opinion and disposed of the
affair with a statement that, in view of the September 3 renunciations
"there can no longer be any occasion for [the Council] to proceed further
with the consideration of this item of its agenda." Getting "items" on
and off the "agenda" appears to have been, in 1931 and in 1946, the
principal preoccupation of international deliberative bodies.

The Court's division over the point at issue could not, so far as the
Court's prestige was concerned, have been more unhappy. It appears from
the opinions that seven judges (including the German judge) found that
the Austro-German Protocol was "compatible" with both Article 88 and
the 1922 Protocol. Seven others (including the French and Italian judges)
found that it was "incompatible" with both. The Brazilian judge alone
saw that, while it was "compatible" with Article 88, it was "incompatible" with the 1922 Protocol. As odd man on an otherwise evenly divided
Court, his peculiar insight became the opinion of the Court. This line-
up was invitingly open to the charge, promptly formulated, that the
Court had split on nationalistic, political grounds into a "Latin bloc"
and a "Teutonic bloc." The argument in defense of the Court's integrity
was more involved, although on the whole more convincing.

The majority opinion was based on the conclusion that the arrangement contemplated by the Austro-German Protocol (even though no
specific provision of the Protocol itself was tainted with "incompatibility")
would constitute a "special regime" affording Germany in relation to
Austria "advantages" withheld from third Powers—thus a regime forbidden by the language of the 1922 Protocol. The Italian judge, contributing a notable dose of Latin realism, delivered a separate concurring
opinion, premised on the observation that "the answer depends on considerations which are for the most part, if not entirely, of a political and
economic kind," took judicial notice of the movement for political union
between Germany and Austria, and dismissed with polite skepticism the
clauses in the March 19 Protocol designed to safeguard Austrian "independence." The dissenting judges joined in an opinion in which they
professed to be unable to understand how the March 19 Protocol could
be "incompatible" as a whole without being "incompatible" in any detail, found that the "provisions" of the Protocol did not purport in any
way to subordinate Austria to German control, and suggested that the
majority had condemned not the proposed regime itself, but assumed
consequences which might result from the establishment of that regime
—thereby overstepping the limits of the Court's function.

The *Carelia* and *Customs Union* cases have been reviewed, not with
any idea of weighting a conclusion that the Court failed, either in those
cases or generally, but rather for the light they throw on the advisable

limits of an international court's jurisdiction, on the theoretical usefulness of such a court. We have noted that the Court's contentious jurisdiction, dependent on the parties' willingness to gamble on judicial issue, produced a routine crop of cases routinely decided and, without exception, routinely disposed of by the parties in accordance with the Court's mandate. The same statement may be made concerning most of the advisory opinions which the Court delivered.

The *Carelia* case, on the other hand, may be seen as a novel attempt on the part of the League Council, on paper a supra-national body, to accomplish an extension of the Court's compulsory jurisdiction by inviting it to adjudicate the substance of a dispute between two States, only one of which accepted the adjudication—since it was clear at the time when the Council referred the issue that Russia would not recognize the Court's competence. And it was the Council's sense, after the event, that the Court should have gone right ahead and adjudicated no matter what the probable consequences might have been and despite the fact that the Council, when the Court declined, could think of nothing useful that the Council itself might undertake in the premises. In the *Customs Union* case the accused States willingly accepted the Court's jurisdiction, although it is reasonable to infer that the 1931 ratio between French and German armament was relevant to such unsovereign docility. Even in 1931, however, the political issue was politically decided by politicians— the only way it could have been decided—before the Court had even been given the opportunity to pronounce on the legal issues in which the political ones had been wrapped for transmission to the Hague.

The cases are cited, then, to the proposition that there are issues which it is not healthy to bring before an international court—in 1920 or in 1930 or in 1950—because they escape or transcend judicial competence. "Adjudication" of such issues, however court-like the attendant proceedings, will be fruitless and inconclusive at best, and at worst prejudicial not only to the ideas of "law" and "court" but to the continuing and always delicately poised international ordeal of peace. Such issues may be composed, and the composition will reflect the current shift of power; they can be only exacerbated by being subjected to a judicial weighing of rights which must, overtly at least, exclude all counters except the words of treaties and the accepted propositions of international law.

Precisely this inquiry, whether there are issues suitable for international arbitration or adjudication and issues not suitable, has long sparked controversy among theorists and publicists of international law. The standard texts on international law have long been in remarkable agreement that international arbitration or adjudication is competent to dispose of only relatively minor differences between States. It has, however, been correctly pointed out that this is not at all the same thing as saying that international law regulates only minor matters—but rather amounts to saying that international tribunals have been or will be, or ought to be, allowed to dispose only of such matters. The matters that tribunals will be allowed to settle have been designated by the terms "legal" or "justiciable" as opposed to the terms "non-legal," "political," "non-justiciable," which in this context refer to disputes which have not been, or will not be, or should not be, brought before international tribunals.

Difficulty has been found in formulating a workable test for distinguishing "justiciable" from "non-justiciable" issues. An early test, now in disfavor, was based on the assumed incomplete nature of international law: "legal" disputes are those whose subject-matter is adequately governed by existing rules of international law. Another formulation, incorporated by way of reservation in many arbitration treaties, was that "legal" disputes are those which do not affect the vital interests, honor or independence of a State. It is the current fashion to define "legal" disputes as all those involving conflicts between opposing sets of "legal rights;" all others—*i.e.*, conflicts of "interests"—are "non-legal" or "political." When analyzed, the foregoing definitions turn out to be merely false fronts for the statement that a "legal" dispute is one which the States involved are, for whatever reason, willing to have arbitrated and various writers have vigorously and diligently rung changes on the demonstration of such logical insufficiency. Some of these writers have, however, used the demonstration that no one has ever been able to draw a satisfactory—*i.e.*, rigid, invariant, predictable—line between "legal" "justiciable" on the one hand and "political" "non-justiciable" on the other to buttress the conclusion that all disputes between States ought to be judicially determined and resolved. This perilous jump merits consideration.

The most convinced and effective advocate of a court of unlimited jurisdiction has been Professor Hans Kelsen, who has clarified matters by offering a draft Covenant of a Permanent League for the Maintenance of Peace. . . .

The argumentation in favor of such an all-powerful and irresponsible court is learned and ingenious, although it has the defect of being in the form of a series of responses to assumed objections. To the objection that an international court competent to decide any dispute would be hamstrung in the absence of an international legislature to set norms for the court's decisions, is opposed the proposition, assumed as historical or anthropological fact, that courts have always preceded legislatures in the organization of human society. To the objection that international law in its present stage of development is incomplete, fragmentary and, as a system, riddled with gaps, it is answered that no system of law can ever be considered defective since it is axiomatic that any act, not specifically forbidden, is permitted; thus the court can always pronounce for or against any contention. To the objection that certain classes of disputes are not susceptible of judicial determination and resolution—disputes variously referred to as "political," "non-legal," "non-justiciable"—is opposed a flat denial, on the ground that any dispute can be reduced to terms of opposing sets of legal rights, and a State in dispute with another State has only the choice of justifying its position legally or of frankly taking an extra-legal stand, thus impliedly admitting that right is on the other side. By way of illustrating the feasibility of an all-powerful court, reference is finally had to the jurisdiction of the United States Supreme Court over disputes between the several states, and the early case of *Rhode Island v. Massachusetts,* in which a boundary dispute was adjudicated, is favorably commented on.

The proponents of an international court of unlimited jurisdiction have thus run up a neat, tidy, and orderly scaffolding of theory. It is submitted, however, that their logic goes no more than skin deep and that their conclusions are shored up by a series of assumptions which are at best unprovable and at worst false. Thus, inherent in their reasoning is the premise that disputes within a national State are settled within the framework of law and courts—at least so long as the parties lack the strength to resort to civil war. Brief reflection will show how vast is the area of dispute even within the State which is settled extra-judicially or politically—currently, for one example, in the field of labor relations. In this extra-judicial area decision is actually reached between the contending groups; despite the elaborate structure of legality, the organs of government, court and legislature, do little more than transcribe dictation.

Governments govern and courts adjudicate, effectively, only where disputes arise between groups none of which has power to threaten the State, or where disputes arise between power groups on minor issues, which both sides are willing to submit to the arbitrament of chance or justice. The area within which effective government or adjudication is possible is still vast, but it does not improve matters to pretend that it is all-embracing or without limit. It is dangerous to believe that "law" can do something it is not equipped to do, *viz.,* make the less-powerful prevail over the more-powerful on the ground that the less-powerful is "right" —morally, economically, or traditionally—and the more-powerful is "wrong."

When disputes arise, not between groups within the State but between States themselves, the difficulties in the way of any effective "government" or "adjudication" are immediately multiplied to something approaching impossibility. Even were we to assume as fact the proposition that all disputes within the State are regulated by law, the analogy between disputes within a State and disputes between States is hazardous. But if we start with the contrary assumption, that disputes between what we have loosely called "power-groups" will be settled, whether within States or between States, extra-legally, we must conclude that in the class of "disputes between States" there will be alarmingly little room for government and adjudication. As within the national community, certain power groups in the international community are predominantly strong and the weaker units subject to their coercion. Internationally, as nationally, the matters subject to effective adjudication will be those (a) involving Great Powers which the Great Powers are willing to have adjudicated and (b) involving Small Powers which the Small Powers are willing to have adjudicated or which the Great Powers insist on having adjudicated. . . .

The function of courts is essentially conservative—to maintain, or to settle incidental disputes within the framework of, a status quo satisfactory to the majority or to a minority sufficiently strong to impose its will on a disarmed majority. When the existing order is radically altered, courts go out of business for a time. Revolution and war are not justiciable. . . .

CHAPTER 10

WORLD GOVERNMENT

IN THE NAME of peace, men have fought many wars designed to preserve or enhance national security. Until World War I the balance-of-power principle was the main reliance of the great powers to preserve their security. Its failure to avert war in 1914 led the Western world after the war to attempt (although without the participation of the United States) a new method—collective security. For this purpose, among others, they established the League of Nations. Despite the failure of the League to avert war in 1939, the UN was established in 1945 as an "improved" version of the same principle, this time with the United States playing a leading role.

Since the UN resembled the League, which had been a failure, and since the balance of power was equally distrusted as a preserver of peace, many, during and after World War II, began to advocate a new principle altogether—world government. In this way, many believed, the prophecy of Isaiah eight centuries before Christ might be fulfilled and war would disappear from the earth.

One of the most eloquent pleas ever made for world government is to be found in Emery Reves's book *The Anatomy of Peace*. The first selection, "The Need for World Government," is taken from it. Reves rejects as inadequate the many reasons for war that have been advanced and asserts that the problem of the twentieth century is that "conflict is inevitable whenever and wherever sovereign power resides in the individual members . . . and not in society itself." As long as sovereign nation-states exist, war will remain potential in their relations with one another. He believes that the solution can only be "the establishment of constitutional life in world affairs"—in short, a universal society governed by universal law. Reves is impatient with constitutional blueprints for the "new society." He argues that federations are preceded by the acceptance of general principles, and to this task of propagating principles he devotes his efforts.

Reves considers the longing for security which characterizes the

contemporary nation-state system as the "most dangerous of all collective drives," since he believes that security can come only through
law or through conquest. Indeed, Reves believes that the search for
security is the major cause of imperialism and war, since enhanced
security for one means lessened security for another in the chaotic
world of nation-states. His incidental analysis of the then embryonic
cold war and American-Soviet conflict in these terms is particularly
provocative. He is sure the world *will* be united—either through law
or through conquest. If union cannot be achieved by democratic
methods, he prefers that it come by war sooner rather than later, on
the supposition that a war fought now would avoid greater future
bloodshed.

Reves's analysis of the *problem* of the nation-state is acute and accurate. As long as sovereign states exist, war among them is possible if
not probable. He realizes that pious talk of peace by statesmen representing sovereign states is less than meaningless in any absolute sense,
since the peace they seek is always a relative one in which the national
interest and national security can be preserved. They will prefer to
have security and peace if they can; if not they will choose security
and war. But Reves believes that war cannot bring true security unless
it results in a unified world governed by law. If nations will not cooperate to bring about such a world, they must have it imposed upon
them. The analysis of the problem is accurate; the proposed solution
is highly debatable. It is necessary to remember, however, that not all
advocates of world government would agree with Reves's final conclusion.

The second selection, "The Illusion of World Government," by
Reinhold Niebuhr, is devoted to a critique of the ideas advanced by
Reves and others. He believes that the "fallacy of world government"
is that (1) governments are not created by fiat and (2) governments
result from already established communities; they do not *create* communities.

As Niebuhr points out in connection with his first point, most arguments for world government begin with the proposition "that the
desirability of world order proves the attainability of world government." Niebuhr calls attention to the "social contract" idea imp'icit
in proposals to call a world constitutional convention and create a
legal instrument for the world. This idea he considers a "pure fiction."
As to Russian participation, which some world-government advocates

assume would be forthcoming if the proposed constitution were not weighted against her, Niebuhr remarks that constitutions cannot "insure the mutual trust upon which community rests." He then examines the alternative of a "world" government without Russia. As he rightly recognizes, the effects of such a division of the world could not in reason be termed world government at all; it would be a different form of the age-old balance-of-power system. As such it might easily bring on war. "The world federalists who accept the inevitability of war walk bravely up the hill of pure idealism and down again into the realm of pure power politics."

In examining the second "fallacy," Niebuhr analyzes the extent to which a true world community exists at present; he indicates his belief that a feeling of community must precede the creation of any world state. He describes the conflict between the United States and the Soviet Union as "a civil war in the heart of western civilization." The "social tissues" for a world state, freely formed, he concludes, do not exist.

It is highly illuminating to note not only where Reves and Niebuhr disagree but where they agree. They both acknowledge the continual threat of war which hovers over the nation-state system. They both agree that war is always potential where separate sovereignties exist. Neither is opposed to a world government resulting from an actual sense of world community. They disagree basically only on what should be done if no such feeling of world community exists. Reves would bring it about through war if necessary, on the assumption that the world community really does exist but that the intrenched interests in various nation-states willfully obscure the true will of the people. Niebuhr would strive to avert war through diplomacy and the United Nations and await the slow development of the prerequisite "social tissue."

THE NEED FOR WORLD GOVERNMENT

EMERY REVES *

The problem of our twentieth century crisis, seemingly so vastly complex and inextricable with its hundreds of national, territorial, religious, social, economic, political and cultural riddles, can be reduced to a few simple propositions.

1. From the teachings of history we have learned that conflicts and wars between social units are inevitable whenever and wherever groups of men with equal sovereignty come into contact.

2. Whenever and wherever social units in any field, regardless of size and character, have come into contact and the resulting friction has led to war, we have learned that these conflicts have always ceased after some part of the sovereignty of the warring units was transferred to a higher social unit able to create legal order, a government authority under which the previously warring groups became equal members of a broader society and within which conflicts between groups could be controlled and eradicated by legal means without the use of force.

3. From the experience thus gained we know that within any given group of individuals in contact and communication with each other, conflict is inevitable whenever and wherever sovereign power resides in the individual members or groups of members of society, and not in society itself.

4. We further know that, irrespective of the immediate and apparent causes of conflict among warring groups, these causes ceased producing wars and violent conflicts only through the establishment of a legal order, only when the social groups in conflict were subjected to a superior system of law, and that, in all cases and at all times, the effect of such a superior system of law has been the cessation of the use of violence among the previously warring groups.

5. Knowing that wars between nonintegrated social groups in contact are inevitable, that the coexistence of nonintegrated sovereign social groups always and in all cases has led to wars, we must realize that peace among men, among individuals, or among groups of individuals in any sphere, is the result of legal order. Peace is identical with the existence of law.

6. As the twentieth century crisis is a world-wide clash between the

social units of sovereign nation-states, the problem of peace in our time is the establishment of a legal order to regulate relations among men, beyond and above the nation-states. This requires transferring parts of the sovereign authority of the existing warring national institutions to universal institutions capable of creating law and order in human relations beyond and above the nation-states.

These propositions are merely the reduction into elementary formulas of one long line of events in our history. The task before us is nothing unique. It is one step further in the same direction, the next step in our evolution.

That conditions in our present society make it imperative for us to undertake this step without further delay should by now be clear to everybody.

Within a single generation, two world wars have ravaged mankind, interfered with peaceful progress and disrupted the free, democratic way of life of the entire Western world. In spite of the desire of the overwhelming majority of the peoples to live and work in peace, we have been unable to escape war. For more than three decades, we have been witnessing an unprecedented decay and downfall of our civilization.

To wage this stupendous struggle, we have had to submit to a hitherto unknown degree of privation, persecution, degradation, suffering, and have been forced to change drastically our civilized way of life. The great majority of the entire human race has been subjected to regimentation, dictation, fear, serfdom.

Considering this world-shaking catastrophe which directly affects every home and every individual,

We believe that the progress of science and industry have rendered national authorities powerless to safeguard the people against armed aggression or to prevent devastating wars.

We believe that peace in any country of the world cannot be maintained without the existence of an effective universal government organization to prevent crime in the inter-national field.

We believe that independence of a nation does not mean untrammeled and unrestricted freedom to do whatever it wants, and that real independence can be created only if no nation is free to attack another, to drag it into war, and to cause such devastating loss of life and wealth as has been wrought twice in our lifetime.

We believe that security of a nation, just as security of an individual, means the co-operation of all to secure the rights of each.

We believe that the relations between nations, just as the relations between individuals in a community, can be peaceful only if based upon and regulated by Law.

We believe that the only way to prevent future world wars is through regulation of the interrelationship of nations, not by unenforceable treaty obligations, which sovereign nations will always disregard, but by an enforceable legal order, binding all nations, giving all nationals equal rights under the established law, and imposing equal obligations upon each.

We believe that peace and security can be established and assured only if we, the sovereign people, who, for our own safety and well-being have delegated parts of our sovereignty to cities to handle our municipal affairs, to departments, counties, provinces, cantons or states to take care of departmental, county, provincial, cantonal or state issues, to our national governments to attend to our national problems—to protect ourselves against the danger of inter-national wars, now delegate part of our respective sovereignty to bodies capable of creating and applying Law in inter-national relations.

We believe that we can protect ourselves against inter-national wars only through the establishment of constitutional life in world affairs, and that such universal Law must be created in conformity with the democratic process, by freely elected and responsible representatives. Creation, application and execution of the Law must be rigorously controlled by the democratic process.

We believe that only a world-wide legal order can insure freedom from fear, and make possible the unhindered development of economic energies for the achievement of freedom from want.

We believe that the natural and inalienable rights of man must prevail. Under twentieth century realities they can be preserved only if they are protected by Law against destruction from outside forces.

How can these propositions be translated into institutions and become the driving force of political reality?

Nothing is more futile than to work out detailed plans and prepare drafts for a constitutional document of a world government. It would be a simple matter for a competent individual or group of people to sit down and work out scores of plans in all detail and in all variety. Within a few days one could produce twenty constitutional drafts, each completely different from the others, each equally plausible.

Such procedure would only hinder progress. Nothing is more open to criticism than a constitution, unless it be the draft of a constitution.

If at the very inception of democracy, before the democratic nation-states had been created in the eighteenth century, a specific draft of a democratic constitution had been identified with democracy itself, and put forward for general approval and acceptance, we should never have had a democratic nation-state anywhere in the world.

History does not work that way.

The founders of democracy were much wiser and more politic. They first formulated a small number of fundamental principles regarded as self-evident and basic for a democratic society. These principles succeeded in arousing the vision and inflaming the enthusiasm of the peoples who, on the basis of these fundamental principles, empowered their representatives to translate them into reality and create the machinery necessary for a permanent legal order, representing the triumph of these principles.

The constitutions, the fundamental laws of the new democratic order, were debated *after*, not before the acceptance of the elementary principles and the mandate given by the people to their representatives for the realization of those principles. So today we see democracy expressed in systems of great variety in detail, but nonetheless, deriving from identical principles.

Democracy in the United States is different from British democracy. French democracy is different from the Dutch, and Swiss democracy has institutions differing greatly from Swedish democracy. In spite of their differences in detail, they are all workable forms of democracy, expressing the same fundamental social conception, the sovereignty of the people as understood a hundred and fifty years ago.

Regarding the creation of universal democratic legal order, we have not yet reached the stage of conception. We have not yet formulated the principles. We have not yet set the standards.

To put the problem before national governments would be a hopeless enterprise, doomed to failure before even starting. The representatives of the sovereign nation-states are incapable of acting and thinking otherwise than according to their nation-centric conceptions. As such a universal problem cannot be solved along national lines, certainly and naturally they would destroy any plan, any draft, of a universal legal order.

Our national statesmen and legislators, by virtue of their education, mentality and outlook, are completely insensitive to the nature of the reform required. Besides, many high priests of the nation-state cult look upon international war as an admirable instrument of advancement toward wealth, fame, distinction and immortality.

Waging war is the easiest thing in the world. It is a business which has a clearly defined, primitive aim—to destroy the adversary—and is based on simple arithmetic and strategy, easy to learn. To manage an enterprise in which one can spend unlimited amounts of money regardless of income, produce goods irrespective of markets, monopolize newspaper space and radio time for self-advertisement, enjoy dictatorial powers over lives and property, establish an artificial, *ad hoc* hierarchy and a high command that suppresses all criticism, seize all means of production and communication, creates a situation which ought to satisfy the caesarmania of any child. Many of our ministers, generals, diplomats, scientists, engineers, poets and manufacturers—consciously or unconsciously—just adore wars. At no other time is it so easy to achieve success, so easy to obtain the applause and servile adulation of the rabble.

All these people, while constantly paying pious tribute to "peace," are solidly entrenched in the hierarchy of the nation-state, and will defend to the last the fetishes, taboos and superstitions of a society with such unparalleled opportunities for them.

From men who are personal beneficiaries of the old system—incapable of independent thinking and victims of the scandalous method of teaching history in all the civilized countries—we cannot expect constructive ideas, much less constructive measures.

We must therefore begin at the beginning. And the beginning is the Word.

This should in no way be discouraging. In this modern world of ours, with mass-circulation newspapers, motion pictures and radio, capable of reaching the entire civilized population of the earth, a decade is ample time for a movement to bring to triumph the principles of universal law, if such a movement is guided by men who have learned from the churches and the political parties how to propagate ideas and how to build up a dynamic organization behind an idea. . . .

The longing for security within the nation-state structure is the most dangerous of all collective drives. In the small, interdependent world of today, there are only two ways for a nation to achieve security.

Law . . . Conquest.

As the nation-state structure excludes a legal order embracing men living in different sovereign units, the drive for security directly produces the drive for conquest.

The drive for security is the major cause of imperialism.

This has never been admitted by the representatives of those powers who have actually traveled that road.

It is amusing to hear the anti-imperialist diatribes of the representatives of the two most virulently imperialist nations of the middle twentieth century—U.S.A. and U.S.S.R. Both nations are persuaded that they are anti-imperialist and that what they want is nothing but security. To understand this paradox, it is most enlightening to reread the history of the growth of the Roman Empire.

Nobody in Rome wanted an empire, nobody wanted war, nobody was an imperialist. They merely liked and valued their own civilization, their higher culture and standard of living, and were anxious to preserve their own way of life. The dominating conception was as "isolationist" as that of any midwestern Senator in Washington or central Russian Commissar in Moscow. The Romans wanted only to be left alone, to enjoy their higher living standards, their superior civilization.

But unfortunately, the barbarians on their frontiers did not leave them alone and always made trouble for them in one way or another. So their deep desire for security forced the Romans to go beyond their frontiers, to eliminate immediate dangers and to push their frontiers farther away from Rome to protect themselves. This desire for security led them finally to conquer virtually all of the then known world and to subjugate other peoples, until internal decay and new, stronger outside forces finally destroyed the whole structure.

This is the real story of most of the great empires of world history. It is also the story of the British Empire, which has been built up by the desire for security of British commercial investments and interests scattered all over the world, of growing British industrialism, which was essential to the survival of the British Isles.

Today this very same force is the driving element behind the policy of the Soviet Union and the United States. Both are deeply convinced of the superiority of their own values and standards and the primacy of their own civilizations. They have vast territories and are not in need of expansion *per se*. Their sincere desire is to be left alone, to live peacefully and to be able to continue to live their own way of life.

But the globe is shrinking, steppes and oceans are no longer safe frontiers, and other nations are not willing to let them do what they want. Outside forces constantly threaten and occasionally attack them. Therefore, to achieve security they feel obliged to build up huge armed forces, to defeat and conquer their immediate enemies and to push ahead their ramparts, their defense positions, their bases, their spheres of influence, farther and farther.

At the end of the second World War, we are seeing American forces annexing islands and other bases thousands of miles away from the American mainland for reasons of security. And we are seeing the Soviet frontiers pushed forward from the Arctic to the Mediterranean and from Europe to the Far East, also for defensive reasons.

It is no use accusing the Soviet or the American governments of imperialism. They sincerely believe that these measures are purely security measures. Just as sincerely they are convinced that superior armed force in the hands of any other nation would be dangerous to peace, but a guarantee of peace and a benefit for all in their own possession. And they are equally sincere in believing that the dissemination of their own political doctrines in other nations, the acceptance by other nations of their own political and economic conceptions, would strengthen peace and would be beneficial to all.

All these unmistakable symptoms of present-day realities indicate that if we insist upon remaining on the old road of national sovereignty, the drive for security, inherent in all nations, will push us toward more violent clashes between the nation-states, compared to which the first and second world wars will appear as child's play.

After the liquidation of the second World War, there remain only three powers capable of creating and maintaining armed forces in the modern sense: three empires. The small and medium-sized nations will inescapably have to become satellites of one of these three dominating industrial and military powers.

Some incurable dreamers among our statesmen seriously believe that such a triangular power structure of our world is possible—even desirable. Actually, it is the mathematical formula for the next, probably the last phase of the struggle for the conquest of the world.

In spite of the endlessly repeated anti-imperialist catch phrases of the representatives of the great powers, every economic and technological reality of our epoch, every dynamic force in the world today, every law of history and logic, indicates that we are on the verge of a period of empire building—of aggregations more powerful and more centralized than ever before. There is no virtue in relying on obsolete slogans and ignoring the forces that today are pushing mankind toward a more organized control of this earth.

It would be wiser to recognize these realities and to guide the torrent into democratic channels. If we leave the concept of sovereign nationalities enshrined as the test of "freedom" the contradiction between this fiction and the physical facts will only cause greater explosions. Unless interdependence, and hence the need for the centralized rule of law—for the freedom which comes from equality before the law among nations as among individuals—is recognized, we shall suffer further and more devastating wars among the United States, Great Britain, Soviet Russia and whatever other nation-states retain any sizable power, in every possible combination. As in an elimination contest, one of these or a combination will achieve by force that unified control made mandatory by the times we live in. Of course, it will be a strictly anti-imperialist imperialism, a kind of very anti-Fascist Fascism. Intervention will always take place in the name of nonintervention, oppression will be called protection and vassalage will be established by solemnly assuring the conquered nation its right to choose the form of government it wants.

There is something angelic in the simplicity and credulity of professional statesmen.

What the two camps destined to wage the coming struggle for conquest of the world are going to say about each other's political intentions, social and economic systems, how they will explain to others and justify to themselves the causes of the war—fought, naturally, in sheer self-defense and for self-preservation by both sides—will be sentimental claptrap. Pure doggerel. . . . It will have not the slightest relation to facts. . . .

For the first time in human history, *one* power can conquer and rule the world. Indeed but for the industrial potential of the United States, Hitler might have done it! Developments may take a different turn. But technically and militarily, it is a definite possibility.

And politically, it is a definite probability if no legal order is created to satisfy the instinctive desire of peoples for security. A decision upon this crucial issue will probably be reached before the end of the twentieth century.

To put it bluntly, the meaning of the crisis of the twentieth century is that this planet must to some degree be brought under unified control. Our task, our duty, is to attempt to institute this unified control in a democratic way by first proclaiming its principles, and to achieve it by persuasion and with the least possible bloodshed. If we fail to accomplish this, we can be certain that the iron law of history will compel us to wage more and more wars, with more and more powerful weapons, against more and more powerful groups, until unified control is finally attained through conquest.

Political unification of the world by conquest is expensive, painful, bloody. The goal could be achieved so much more easily if it were not for that eternal saboteur of progress—human blindness.

But if it is impossible to cure that blindness and if mankind is unable to face its destiny and to determine by reason and insight the course of our immediate future, if our nationalist dogmatism will not permit us to undertake the organization of a universal legal order, then at least, let us try not to prolong the agony of a decaying, dying system of society.

If we cannot attain to universalism and create union by common consent and democratic methods as a result of rational thinking—then rather than retard the process, let us precipitate unification by conquest. It serves no reasonable purpose to prolong the death throes of our decrepit institutions and to postpone inevitable events only to make the changes more painful and more costly in blood and suffering. It would be better to have done with this operation as quickly as possible so that the fight for the reconquest of lost human liberties can start within the universal state without too much loss of time.

The era of inter-national wars will end, just as everything human ends. It will come to an end with the establishment of universal law to regulate human relationship, either by union or by—conquest.

THE ILLUSION OF WORLD GOVERNMENT

REINHOLD NIEBUHR *

The trustful acceptance of false solutions for our perplexing problems adds a touch of pathos to the tragedy of our age.

The tragic character of our age is revealed in the world-wide insecurity which is the fate of modern man. Technical achievements, which a previous generation had believed capable of solving every ill to which the human flesh is heir, have created, or at least accentuated, our insecurity. For the growth of technics has given the perennial problems of our common life a more complex form and a scope that has grown to be world-wide.

Our problem is that technics have established a rudimentary world community but have not integrated it organically, morally or politically. They have created a community of mutual dependence, but not one of mutual trust and respect. Without this higher integration, advancing technics tend to sharpen economic rivalries within a general framework of economic interdependence; they change the ocean barriers of yesterday into the battlegrounds of today; and they increase the deadly efficacy of the instruments of war so that vicious circles of mutual fear may end in atomic conflicts and mutual destruction. To these perplexities an ideological conflict has been added, which divides the world into hostile camps.

It is both necessary and laudable that men of good will should, in this situation, seek to strengthen every moral and political force which might give a rudimentary world community a higher degree of integration. It was probably inevitable that the desperate plight of our age should persuade some well meaning men that the gap between a technically integrated and politically divided community could be closed by the simple expedient of establishing a world government through the fiat of the human will and creating world community by the fiat of world government. It is this hope which adds a touch of pathos to already tragic experiences. The hope not only beguiles some men from urgent moral

* Reinhold Niebuhr, "The Illusion of World Government," *Foreign Affairs,* Vol. 27, No. 3 (April, 1949), pp. 379–388. Copyright 1949, by the Council on Foreign Relations, Inc. Reprinted by permission.

and political responsibilities. It tempts others into irresponsible criticisms of the necessarily minimal constitutional structure which we have embodied in the United Nations and which is as bad as its critics aver only if a better one is within the realm of possibilities.

Virtually all arguments for world government rest upon the simple presupposition that the desirability of world order proves the attainability of world government. Our precarious situation is unfortunately no proof, either of the moral ability of mankind to create a world government by an act of the will, nor of the political ability of such a government to integrate a world community in advance of a more gradual growth of the "social tissue" which every community requires more than government.

Most advocates of world government also assume that nations need merely follow the alleged example of the individuals of another age who are supposed to have achieved community by codifying their agreements into law and by providing an agency of some kind for law enforcement. This assumption ignores the historic fact that the mutual respect for each other's rights in particular communities is older than any code of law; and that machinery for the enforcement of law can be efficacious only when a community as a whole obeys its laws implicitly, so that coercive enforcement may be limited to a recalcitrant minority.

The fallacy of world government can be stated in two simple propositions. The first is that governments are not created by fiat (though sometimes they can be imposed by tyranny). The second is that governments have only limited efficacy in integrating a community.

II

The advocates of world government talk of calling a world constitutional convention which would set up the machinery of a global constitutional order and would then call upon the nations to abrogate or abridge their sovereignty in order that this newly created universal sovereignty could have unchallenged sway. No such explicit abnegation has ever taken place in the history of the world. Explicit governmental authority has developed historically from the implicit authority of patriarchal or matriarchal tribal forms. Governments, so established, have extended their dominion over weaker neighbors. But the abridgment of sovereignty has always been indirect rather than direct; or it has been attained by the superimposition of power.

The notion that world government is a fairly simple possibility is the final and most absurd form of the "social contract" conception of government which has confused modern political thought since Hobbes. It must certainly be obvious by this time that the conception of a state of nature in which all men were at war with all, and of a subsequent social contract through which men established a power over themselves to avoid mutual annihilation, is a pure fiction. A small human community is as primordial as the individual. No group of individuals has ever created either government or community out of whole cloth. One reason why the social contract conception of government has a particular plausibility with us is because the United States came closer to a birth by "contract" than any other nation. But the preamble of our constitution declares that its purpose is to establish a "more perfect union." That is a very telling phrase which presupposes a previous union. This previous union was in fact established on the battlefield in a common struggle against a common foe; it needed only to be made "more perfect." It may be observed in passing that, though the 13 colonies had never enjoyed sovereignty, they did not find it too easy to submit what had only been potential, and not actual, sovereignty to the authority of the federal union. We fought a civil war before it was proved that they had in fact done this without reservation.

When the question is raised whether the nations of the world would voluntarily first create, and then submit to, a super-national authority, the possible reluctance of nations, other than Russia, to take this step is fortunately or unfortunately obscured by the Russian intransigeance. The Russians have declared again and again that they would leave the United Nations if the veto power were abolished. This means that Russia, as a prospective minority in a world community, is not ready to submit her fate to the will of a majority, even in such a loose organization as the United Nations. It is therefore obvious that she would be even more unwilling to submit her sovereignty to a more highly integrated constitutional order.

The proponents of world government have two answers to the problem posed by Russian intransigeance. One is to assert that the Russians never have had the chance to accept or reject a genuinely constitutional world order; and that there are real possibilities of her acceptance of a constitution which is not weighted against her. This answer contains in a nutshell the rationalist illusion implicit in world government theories. It assumes that constitutions can insure the mutual trust upon which community rests. Actually, even the best constitution must, if it is democratic, set up some kind of majority rule. It is not workable if there is not enough common ground between majority and minority to assure that a majority will not take advantage of a minority, or that the minority will not suspect the majority of injustice, even though without cause. There are republics in South America with quite nice constitutions in which a defeated minority starts conspiracies against the government, usually through military channels, on the day after election.

The other answer to the problem of Russian intransigeance is a proposed creation of a "world" government without Russia. Thus in the name of "one world" the world would be divided in two. Proponents of world government are always ready with criticisms of the ambiguities in the Charter of the United Nations, without recognizing that those ambiguities correspond to the actual historical situation. The Security Council is, for instance, a bridge of a sort between the segments of a divided world. They would destroy that bridge for the sake of creating a more logical constitutional system. This done, they look forward to one of two possibilities.

One is that Russia, faced with a united opposition, and concluding that she would not have to sacrifice her Communist Government but only her ambition to spread Communism, would ultimately capitulate and join the world federation. This abstract approach to political problems is completely oblivious of the dynamism of Communism.

The other course chosen by some advocates of world government is to create such a government without Russia and to divide the world more consistently in the name of the principle of "one" world. If this should lead to a world conflict they believe that the agonies of war will be assuaged for us by our knowledge that we are at least fighting for a principle of ultimate validity.

There is, of course, a possibility that a closer political integration of the non-Communist nations may save the world from war by the creation of an adequate preponderance of power in the west. But such an objective is not to be reached by loftily disavowing "power politics" in favor of "law." The world federalists who accept the inevitability of war walk bravely up the hill of pure idealism and down again into the realm of pure power politics. In this journey they rid themselves of the logical and moral ambiguities of the much despised quasi-constitutional system of the United Nations. Their brethren who are in a less exalted frame of mind will continue to put up with the Charter for the sake of preserving a bridge, however slight, between Russia and the west, making the best arrangements they can to restrain Russia, while trying at the same time to strengthen the existing world security agencies.

The ambiguities in the Charter of the United Nations which so outrage the advocates of world government are in fact the consequence of seeking to guarantee two, rather than one, objectives. The one objective is to preserve the unity of one world, even though it be seriously divided, and to provide a meeting ground between east and west where some of the tensions and frictions may be resolved. The other is to preserve the integrity of our "way of life" against a tyrannical system which we abhor. The Russians, in so far as they are honest devotees of a Marxist dream of world order, are presumably in the same position. Each of us hopes ultimately to create a world order upon the basis of our conception of justice. Neither of us is ready, at the moment, to submit our fate to a world authority without reservation, so long as the possibility remains that such an authority could annul a system of law and justice to which we are deeply committed.

III

So far we have considered only the difficulties of creating a world government by constitutional fiat. But a much more serious defect in world government theories is to be found in their conception of the relation of government to community. Governments cannot create communities for the simple reason that the authority of government is not primarily the authority of law nor the authority of force, but the authority of the community itself. Laws are obeyed because the community accepts them as corresponding, on the whole, to its conception of justice. This is particularly true of democratically-organized communities. But it is well to observe that even in traditional, non-democratic communities of the past there was a discernible difference between tyranny and legitimate government. It consisted precisely in the fact that a legitimate government relied primarily upon the implicit consent of the community.

Even in a national constitutional system, such as our own, we have seen how limited is the power of law whenever a portion of the community adheres to moral standards which differ from those of the total community. We have had this experience both with the prohibition movement and with the question of civil rights for Negroes in southern states. And where is the police force, loyal to a world state, to come from? The police power of a government cannot be a pure political artifact. It is an arm of the community's body. If the body is in pieces, the arm cannot integrate it.

The priority of the community to its laws and its use of force does not mean that both law and force may not have limited efficacy in perfecting the organization and preserving the integrity of the community. Good constitutions provide for the rational arbitrament of many conflicting and competing forces which might otherwise tear the community apart. Preponderant force in one part of the community may also so shape the social forces of the total community that its use need not be perpetual. Thus the preponderant force of the northern states decided the issue whether our nation was a nation or merely a federation of states. But force is no longer necessary to guarantee the loyalty of the southern states to our union. The ancient empires of Egypt, Babylon and Persia were created through the preponderant force of a particular city-state; but they finally achieved a unity which did not require the constant application of force. It must be noted that this pattern of coalescence of communities gives us no analogy for the creation of a world community in democratic terms, that is, without the imposition of preponderant power. The best analogy for our present world situation is to be found in Greece rather than in Egypt or Babylon. The Greek city-states never achieved the imperial unity of the oriental empires. The threat of Persia did finally prompt the organization of the Delian League; but the rivalry of Sparta and Athens for the hegemony in the League resulted in its disintegration. The unity of Greece was finally achieved under Philip and Alexander of Macedon. But this imperial unity was also a tyrannical nemesis for Greek culture. The analogy in present global terms would be the final unification of the world through the preponderant power of either America or Russia, whichever proved herself victorious in a final global struggle. The analogy teaches us nothing about the possibilities of a constitutional world state. It may teach us that though the perils of international anarchy are very great, they may still be preferable to international tyranny.

The coalescence of communities from city-states to empires in the ancient world, and from feudal entities to nations in the modern period, was frequently accomplished only by the imposition of preponderant power. The fact is particularly significant, since all of these communities could rely upon all sorts of "organic" factors for their force of cohesion which the rudimentary world community lacks. By organic factors, I mean such forces as the power of ethnic kinship, the force of a common history—particularly the memory of joint struggles against a common foe—a common language, a common culture and a common religion. We do have examples of ethnically and religiously pluralistic nations and empires, but they possess a basic homogeneity of some kind, underlying the differences. In modern India, where religious differences are thoroughgoing and highly localized, it proved impossible to construct a constitutional system which could allay the mutual fears of Hindus and Moslems. The birth in blood of these two nations, once the unifying force of an imperial power was removed, ought to teach our world planners more about the limited efficacy of constitutions than they have evidently learned. There were certainly more common elements in the situation in India than the world community will possess for a long time to come. Despite these common elements, the unity of India proved to be unattainable.

Sometimes the world planners recognize the absence of organic forces of cohesion in the world community. Thus Erich Kahler [1] sees that a world constitution lacks the "substratum" of organic and historical forces, which characterize the constitutions of national governments. But he draws the conclusion that a world constitution "must create the substratum to which

[1] Erich Kahler, "The Question of a 'Minimum Constitution,'" *Common Cause*, June 1948.

it is to be applied." The proposed method of creating the substratum, according to Mr. Kahler, is to use "regions" rather than "extant states" as electoral units in the world constitution, for "if we base the world government on the states, we will fail in the essential task of creating the substratum." The illusions of omnipotence which infect the thought of this kind of political idealism could not be more vividly portrayed. There is no explanation of how states, who have a sovereign voice, would be persuaded to grant this electoral power to "regions" which would have no such voice in a world constitutional convention. The idea probably is that there would be a nonrepresentative constitutional convention of "experts" and the hope is that sovereign states will meekly accept the dictum of the experts that regions offer a better "substratum" for the world community than extant states. Nor is any attempt made to deal with the difficulty that many of the regions which would hopefully be created are so little integrated that an electoral canvass would be completely meaningless in them.

The fact is that even the wisest statecraft cannot create social tissue. It can cut, sew and redesign social fabric to a limited degree. But the social fabric upon which it works must be "given."

IV

The international community is not totally lacking in social tissue; but it is very scant, compared with that of particular states. Let us briefly assess the various factors in it. Most important as a force of social cohesion in the world community is the increasing economic interdependence of peoples of the world. But it is important to contrast this economic interdependence immediately with the wide disparity in the economic strength of various nations. At the climactic dinner of the World Republic convention, held in Chicago in October 1948, Professor Urey, the atomic scientist, expressed the conviction that the "inclusion of the illiterate, poverty-stricken, overnumerous masses of the Far East" constituted the major problem of the world state. He believed that the white race would not tolerate being outvoted by Asiatics. He therefore proposed a system of weighted votes in favor of nations with high literacy and abundance of raw materials and industrial production. He felt certain that the more "enlightened" Orientals would not object to this procedure. But an objection, from Thomas Tchou, sitting two places to the left of Professor Urey, was immediately forthcoming. Weighted representation, he declared, was immoral.[2] Thus the real problems have an inconvenient habit of peeking through, even at a dinner of a World Republic convention.

A second factor in the social tissue of the world community is the fear of mutual annihilation, heightened in recent years by the new dimension

[2] *Common Cause,* December 1948, p. 199.

which atomic discoveries have given to mankind's instruments of death. We must not underestimate this fear as a social force, even as we must recognize that some culturally pluralistic communities of past history have achieved some cohesion through the minimal conviction that order is to be preferred to anarchy. But the fear of destruction in itself is less potent than the fear of specific peril from a particular foe. There is no record in history of peoples establishing a common community because they feared each other, though there are many instances when the fear of a common foe acted as the cement of cohesion.

The final and most important factor in the social tissue of the world community is a moral one. Enlightened men in all nations have some sense of obligation to their fellow-men, beyond the limits of their nation-state. There is at least an inchoate sense of obligation to the inchoate community of mankind. The desperate necessity for a more integrated world community has undoubtedly increased this sense of obligation, inculcated in the conscience of mankind since the rise of universal, rather than parochial, philosophies and religions. This common moral sense is of tremendous importance for the moral and religious life of mankind; but it does not have as much immediate political relevance as is sometimes supposed. Political cohesion requires common convictions on particular issues of justice; and these are lacking. If there is a "natural law" which is "self-evident" to all men, it certainly does not contain very much specific content beyond such minimal rules as the prohibition of murder and theft and such general principles of justice as the dictum that each man is to have his due. There is little agreement on the criteria by which the due of each man is to be measured.

There is a special irony in the fact that the primary differences in the conceptions of justice in the world do not, however, spring from religious and cultural differences between east and west. They can, therefore, not be resolved by elaborate efforts at cultural syncretism between east and west. The primary differences arise from a civil war in the heart of western civilization, in which a fanatical equalitarian creed has been pitted against a libertarian one. This civil war has become nationally localized. Russia has become the national center of the equalitarian creed, while America is the outstanding proponent of the libertarian one. The common use of the word "democracy," together with the contradictory interpretations of the meaning of that word, is the semantic symbol of the conflict. The idea that this conflict could be resolved by greater semantic accuracy is, however, one of the illusions of a too rationalistic culture which fails to understand the power of the social forces expressed in contradictory symbols.

In short, the forces which are operating to integrate the world community are limited. To call attention to this fact does not mean that all striving for a higher and wider integration of the world community is vain. That task must and will engage the conscience of mankind for ages to come. But the edifice of government which we build will be sound and useful if its height is proportionate to the strength of the materials from which it is constructed. The immediate political situation requires that we seek not only peace, but also the preservation of a civilization which we hold to be preferable to the universal tyranny with which Soviet aggression threatens us. Success in this double task is the goal; let us not be diverted from it by the pretense that there is a simple alternative.

We would, I think, have a better chance of success in our struggle against a fanatical foe if we were less sure of our purity and virtue. The pride and self-righteousness of powerful nations are a greater hazard to their success in statecraft than the machinations of their foes. If we could combine a greater degree of humility with our stubborn resolution, we might not only be more successful in holding the dyke against tyranny, but we might also gradually establish a genuine sense of community with our foe, however small. No matter how stubbornly we resist Russian pressure, we should still have a marginal sense of community with the Soviet Union, derived from our sense of being involved in a common fate of tragic proportions and from a recognition of a common guilt of mutual fear. If community in basic terms is established by various organic forces of history, it must finally be preserved by mutual forbearance and forgiveness.

There is obviously no political program which can offer us, in our situation, perfect security against either war or tyranny. Nevertheless, we are not prisoners of historical destiny. We shall have constant opportunity to perfect instruments of peace and justice if we succeed in creating some communal foundation upon which constitutional structures can rest. We shall exploit our opportunities the more successfully, however, if we have knowledge of the limits of the will in creating government, and of the limits of government in creating community. We may have pity upon, but can have no sympathy with, those who flee to the illusory security of the impossible from the insecurities and ambiguities of the possible.

Part III

The Present Crisis in International Relations

CHAPTER 11

AMERICAN-SOVIET RELATIONS

FOLLOWING World War II a revolution in the status and relations of the great powers has occurred which is in great contrast to the inter-war period. After World War I the United States had limited its co-operation with Europe to spasmodic, irregular occasions—well-meaning but unsustained efforts, which sometimes did more harm than good. On the other side of Europe, the pariah among nations, the Soviet Union, was first excluded from the League and then grudg-ingly recognized and, in the aftermath of Germany's resignation, per-mitted to become a member. Yet within a very few years the U.S.S.R. was expelled as an aggressor nation because of the Soviet invasion of Finland. She thereby achieved the dubious distinction of being the first and only nation to be expelled.

Thus during the very years between the two world wars when in-ternational relations revolved around the actions and policies of the European powers and the organization which they dominated—the League of Nations—the United States and the U.S.S.R. participated only occasionally and irregularly. Each of them was for long periods almost exclusively preoccupied with internal affairs—the United States at first with the great boom and later the great depression, the Soviet Union with the conversion of Russia to the first Communist state, accompanied by vast social upheavals. As actors in the interna-tional drama, they played negative, if important, parts.

The coming of war, however, drew them irresistibly into a promi-nent role in the shaping of the world that was to come. Both were literally forced into the conflict by surprise attacks. In the war years that followed, the great task of allied statesmanship was to forge the bonds of a strong anti-Axis alliance. One of the high points of this collaboration was the organization of the United Nations in 1945. From that time, however, gaps and tears in the fabric of unity began to become increasingly apparent.

As disillusionment set in, the high hopes for fruitful collaboration among the wartime allies, which the American people in particular had entertained, began to be rep'aced by a growing pessimism in the light of Russia's apparent unwi'lingness to cooperate. To pessimism was soon added anger, since the widely accepted thesis that the Soviets acted as they did out of fear of the capitalist world had induced many Americans to believe that a policy of generous concession would convince the Russians of America's good intentions. Yet concessions failed to improve the basic relations between the two states. For this reason American policy tended for a time to waver between obstinate rejection of Soviet demands and a too evident willingness to make compromises. In the first months of 1946 this attitude finally began to crystallize into a firm (or "tough") policy with Russia, to which the Soviets opposed an equally firm policy. Far from the secondary positions which the two countries had occupied in the prewar international crises, the struggle between the two territorial giants began to be itself the primary political fact of postwar international relations.

The power conflict between the United States and the U.S.S.R. was implicit in the structure of the postwar world in that the only grave potential threat to the security of one stemmed from the existence of the other. Comp'etely aside from the ideological issue, no other single nation or even group of nations in the immediate postwar years was in a position to constitute a serious threat to either of them. It is this situation which produced the cold war.

One of the most interesting things which has occurred as a direct result of the conflict is the change of attitude toward Russia on the part of Americans. From an enthusiastic willingness to "get along" with Russia, sentiment in large degree has shifted to fear and suspicion of Soviet motives and intentions. From the most extreme group have been heard voices urging a preventive war, convinced that war with Russia is inevitable. However, if two nations are not "friends," neither need they necessarily become actual "enemies"—they may become simply rivals. Much here depends upon circumstances. In reality, "friendship" and "enmity" between nations or between the peoples of nations are personified expressions of the fact that the vital national interests of the states concerned are readily or with difficulty reconciled. Under the stimulus of a common threat, both nations found their vital interests sufficiently in accord to cooperate on a reasonable basis. When that threat had been disposed of, just as naturally the vital interests of each nation became threatened potentially or actually by those of the other. Their rivalry became overt once the reason for suppressing it was removed.

The readings in this chapter reflect two stages in the development of this cold war. The first stage is that prior to the development of the Soviet atomic bomb; the second stage is the present one, following its creation. Stage one is discussed by Mr. "X" (George F. Kennan, sometime Counselor of the Department of State) in "The Sources of Soviet Conduct." He advocates a policy of "containment" which is, in turn, criticized by Walter Lippmann in the second selection, "A Critique of Containment," from *The Cold War*, particularly on the grounds that to await Soviet collapse as a result of being contained would be highly unrealistic and dangerous. The second stage of the conflict is discussed in the third reading, "Strategy of Error" by Hans J. Morgenthau, who makes the point that the development of the Soviet bomb *ahead of schedule* has actually destroyed the basis on which American foreign policy in recent years has rested and that Russia's military strength now has become equal to that of the United States. In the fourth selection, "Is War with Russia Inevitable?" George F. Kennan appears again. It will be of interest to the reader to compare his views with those of Morgenthau, with whom he disagrees in many important respects, and with his own views of some two years earlier.

The appointment of Mr. Kennan as American Ambassador to the Soviet Union early in 1952 makes the two selections by him in this chapter of more than ordinary interest.

In the fifth selection, "Will There Be War?" by Winston Churchill, the wartime British Prime Minister warns the Western world that, while "it is idle to reason or argue with the Communists . . . it is, however, possible to deal with them on a fair, realistic basis." He argues that the Communists "will keep their bargains as long as it is in their interest to do so" and urges the need to "bring matters to a head" with them. Otherwise, he warns, we may drift into war.

THE SOURCES OF SOVIET CONDUCT

"X" *

So much for the historical background. What does it spell in terms of the political personality of Soviet power as we know it today?

Of the original ideology, nothing has been officially junked. Belief is maintained in the basic badness of capitalism, in the inevitability of its destruction, in the obligation of the proletariat to assist in that destruction and to take power into its own hands. But stress has come to be laid primarily on those concepts which relate most specifically to the Soviet regime itself: to its position as the sole truly Socialist regime in a dark and misguided world, and to the relationships of power within it.

The first of these concepts is that of the innate antagonism between capitalism and Socialism. We have seen how deeply that concept has become imbedded in foundations of Soviet power. It has profound implications for Russia's conduct as a member of international society. It means that there can never be on Moscow's side any sincere assumption of a community of aims between the Soviet Union and powers which are regarded as capitalist. It must invariably be assumed in Moscow that the aims of the capitalist world are antagonistic to the Soviet regime, and therefore to the interests of the peoples it controls. If the Soviet Government occasionally sets its signature to documents which would indicate the contrary, this is to be regarded as a tactical manoeuvre permissible in dealing with the enemy (who is without honor) and should be taken in the spirit of *caveat emptor*. Basically, the antagonism remains. It is postulated. And from it flow many of the phenomena which we find disturbing in the Kremlin's conduct of foreign policy: the secretiveness, the lack of frankness, the duplicity, the wary suspiciousness, and the basic unfriendliness of purpose. These phenomena are there to stay, for the foreseeable future. There can be variations of degree and of emphasis. When there is something the Russians want from us, one or the other of these features of their policy may be thrust temporarily into the background; and when that happens there will always be Americans who will leap forward with gleeful announcements that "the Russians have changed," and some who will even try to take credit for having brought about such "changes." But we should not be misled by tactical manoeuvres. These characteristics of Soviet policy,

* "X," "The Sources of Soviet Conduct," *Foreign Affairs*, Vol. 25, No. 4 (July, 1947), pp. 571–582. Copyright 1947, by the Council on Foreign Relations, Inc. Reprinted by permission. ("X" was subsequently identified as George F. Kennan of the Department of State.)

like the postulate from which they flow, are basic to the internal nature of Soviet power, and will be with us, whether in the foreground or the background, until the internal nature of Soviet power is changed.

This means that we are going to continue for a long time to find the Russians difficult to deal with. It does not mean that they should be considered as embarked upon a do-or-die program to overthrow our society by a given date. The theory of the inevitability of the eventual fall of capitalism has the fortunate connotation that there is no hurry about it. The forces of progress can take their time in preparing the final *coup de grace*. Meanwhile, what is vital is that the "Socialist fatherland"—that oasis of power which has been already won for Socialism in the person of the Soviet Union—should be cherished and defended by all good Communists at home and abroad, its fortunes promoted, its enemies badgered and confounded. The promotion of premature, "adventuristic" revolutionary projects abroad which might embarrass Soviet power in any way would be an inexcusable, even a counter-revolutionary act. The cause of Socialism is the support and promotion of Soviet power, as defined in Moscow.

This brings us to the second of the concepts important to contemporary Soviet outlook. That is the infallibility of the Kremlin. The Soviet concept of power, which permits no focal points of organization outside the Party itself, requires that the Party leadership remain in theory the sole repository of truth. For if truth were to be found elsewhere, there would be justification for its expression in organized activity. But it is precisely that which the Kremlin cannot and will not permit.

The leadership of the Communist Party is therefore always right, and has been always right ever since in 1929 Stalin formalized his personal power by announcing that decisions of the Politburo were being taken unanimously.

On the principle of infallibility there rests the iron discipline of the Communist Party. In fact, the two concepts are mutually self-supporting. Perfect discipline requires recognition of infallibility. Infallibility requires the observance of discipline. And the two together go far to determine the behaviorism of the entire Soviet apparatus of power. But their effect cannot be understood unless a third factor be taken into account: namely, the fact that the leadership is at liberty to put forward for tactical purposes any particular thesis which it finds useful to the cause at any particular moment and to require the faithful and unquestioning acceptance of that thesis by the members of the movement as a whole. This means that truth is not a constant but is actually created, for all intents and purposes, by the Soviet leaders themselves. It may vary from week to week, from month to month. It is nothing absolute and immutable—nothing which flows from objective reality. It is only the most recent manifestation of the wisdom of those in whom the ultimate wisdom is supposed to reside, because they represent the logic of history. The accumulative effect of these factors is to give to the whole subordinate apparatus of Soviet power an unshakeable stubbornness and steadfastness in its orientation. This orientation can be changed at will by the Kremlin but by no other power. Once a given party line has been laid down on a given issue of current policy, the whole Soviet governmental machine, including the mechanism of diplomacy, moves inexorably along the prescribed path, like a persistent toy automobile wound up and headed in a given direction, stopping only when it meets with some unanswerable force. . . . Since there can be no appeal to common purposes, there can be no appeal to common mental approaches. For this reason, facts speak louder than words to the ears of the Kremlin; and words carry the greatest weight when they have the ring of reflecting, or being backed up by, facts of unchallengeable validity.

But we have seen that the Kremlin is under no ideological compulsion to accomplish its purposes in a hurry. Like the Church, it is dealing in ideological concepts which are of long-term validity, and it can afford to be patient. It has no right to risk the existing achievements of the revolution for the sake of vain baubles of the future. The very teachings of Lenin himself require great caution and flexibility in the pursuit of Communist purposes. Again, these precepts are fortified by the lessons of Russian history: of centuries of obscure battles between nomadic forces over the stretches of a vast unfortified plain. Here caution, circumspection, flexibility and deception are the valuable qualities; and their value finds natural appreciation in the Russian or oriental mind. Thus the Kremlin has no compunction about retreating in the face of superior force. And being under the compulsion of no timetable, it does not get panicky under the necessity for such retreat. Its political action is a fluid stream which moves constantly, wherever it is permitted to move, toward a given goal. Its main concern is to make sure that it has filled every nook and cranny available to it in the basin of world power. But if it finds unassailable barriers in its path, it accepts these philosophically and accommodates itself to them. The main thing is that there should always be pressure, unceasing constant pressure, toward the desired goal. There is no trace of any feeling in Soviet psychology that that goal must be reached at any given time.

These considerations make Soviet diplomacy at once easier and more difficult to deal with than the diplomacy of individual aggressive leaders like Napoleon and Hitler. On the one hand it is more sensitive to contrary force, more ready to yield on individual sectors of the diplomatic front when that force is felt to be too strong, and thus more rational in the logic and rhetoric of power. On the other hand it cannot be easily defeated or discouraged by a single victory on the part of its opponents. And the patient persistence by which it is animated means that it can be effectively countered not by sporadic acts which represent the momentary whims of democratic opinion but only by intelligent long-range policies on the part of Russia's adversaries—policies no less steady in their purpose, and no less variegated and resourceful in their application, than those of the Soviet Union itself.

In these circumstances it is clear that the main element of any United States policy toward the Soviet Union must be that of a long-term, patient but firm and vigilant containment of Russian expansive tendencies. It is important to note, however, that such a policy has nothing to do with outward histrionics: with threats or blustering or superfluous gestures of outward "toughness." While the Kremlin is basically flexible in its reaction to political realities, it is by no means unamenable to considerations of prestige. Like almost any other government, it can be placed by tactless and threatening gestures in a position where it cannot afford to yield even though this might be dictated by its sense of realism. The Russian leaders are keen judges of human psychology, and as such they are highly conscious that loss of temper and of self-control is never a source of strength in political affairs. They are quick to exploit such evidences of weakness. For these reasons, it is a *sine qua non* of successful dealing with Russia that the foreign government in question should remain at all times cool and collected and that its demands on Russian policy should be put forward in such a manner as to leave the way open for a compliance not too detrimental to Russian prestige.

In the light of the above, it will be clearly seen that the Soviet pressure against the free institutions of the western world is something that can be contained by the adroit and vigilant application of counter-force at a series of constantly shifting geographical and political points, corresponding to the shifts and manoeuvers of Soviet policy, but which cannot be charmed or talked out of existence. The Russians look forward to a duel of infinite duration, and they see that already they have scored great successes. It must be borne in mind that there was a time when the Communist Party represented far more of a minority in the sphere of Russian national life than Soviet power today represents in the world community.

But if ideology convinces the rulers of Russia that truth is on their side and that they can therefore afford to wait, those of us on whom that ideology has no claim are free to examine objectively the validity of that premise. The Soviet thesis not only implies complete lack of control by the west over its own economic destiny, it likewise assumes Russian unity, discipline and patience over an infinite period. Let us bring this apocalyptic vision down to earth, and suppose that the western world finds the strength and resourcefulness to contain Soviet power over a period of ten or fifteen years. What does that spell for Russia itself?

The Soviet leaders, taking advantage of the contributions of modern technique to the arts of despotism, have solved the question of obedience within the confines of their power. Few challenge their authority; and even those who do are unable to make that challenge valid as against the organs of suppression of the state.

The Kremlin has also proved able to accomplish its purpose of building up in Russia, regardless of the interests of the inhabitants, an industrial foundation of heavy metallurgy, which is, to be sure, not yet complete but which is nevertheless continuing to grow and is approaching those of the other major industrial countries. All of this, however, both the maintenance of internal political security and the building of heavy industry, has been carried out at a terrible cost in human life and in human hopes and energies. . . .

In addition to this, we have the fact that Soviet economic development, while it can list certain formidable achievements, has been precariously spotty and uneven. Russian Communists who speak of the "uneven development of capitalism" should blush at the contemplation of their own national economy. . . . Construction is hasty and poor in quality. Depreciation must be enormous. And in vast sectors of economic life it has not yet been possible to instill into labor anything like that general culture of production and technical self-respect which characterizes the skilled worker of the west.

It is difficult to see how these deficiencies can be corrected at an early date by a tired and dispirited population working largely under the shadow of fear and compulsion. And as long as they are not overcome, Russia will remain economically a vulnerable, and in a certain sense an impotent, nation, capable of exporting its enthusiasms and of radiating the strange charm of its primitive political vitality but unable to back up those articles of export by the real evidences of material power and prosperity.

Meanwhile, a great uncertainty hangs over the political life of the Soviet Union. That is the uncertainty involved in the transfer of power from one individual or group of individuals to others.

This is, of course, outstandingly the problem of the personal position of Stalin. We must remember that his succession to Lenin's pinnacle of preeminence in the Communist movement was the only such transfer of individual authority which the Soviet Union has experienced. That transfer took 12 years to consolidate. It cost the lives of millions of people and shook the state to its foundations. The attendant tremors were felt all through the international revolutionary movement, to the disadvantage of the Kremlin itself.

It is always possible that another transfer of preeminent power may take place quietly and inconspicuously, with no repercussions anywhere. But again, it is possible that the questions involved may unleash, to use some of Lenin's words, one of those "incredibly swift transitions" from "delicate deceit" to "wild violence" which characterize Russian history, and may shake Soviet power to its foundations. . . .

Who can say whether, in these circumstances, the eventual rejuvenation of the higher spheres of authority (which can only be a matter of time) can take place smoothly and peacefully, or whether rivals in the quest for higher power will not eventually reach down into these politically immature and inexperienced masses in order to find support for their respective claims? . . . In Russia there is not even such a thing as local government. The present generation of Russians have never known spontaneity of collective action. If, consequently, anything were ever to occur to disrupt the unity and efficacy of the Party as a political instrument, Soviet Russia might be changed overnight from one of the strongest to one of the weakest and most pitiable of national societies.

Thus the future of Soviet power may not be by any means as secure as Russian capacity for self-delusion would make it appear to the men in the Kremlin. That they can keep power themselves, they have demonstrated. That they can quietly and easily turn it over to others remains to be proved. . . . And who can say with assurance that the strong light still cast by the Kremlin on the dissatisfied peoples of the western world is not the powerful afterglow of a constellation which is in actuality on the wane? This cannot be proved. And it cannot be disproved. But the possibility remains (and in the opinion of this writer it is a strong one) that Soviet power, like the capitalist world of its conception, bears within it the seeds of its own decay, and that the sprouting of these seeds is well advanced.

It is clear that the United States cannot expect in the foreseeable future to enjoy political intimacy with the Soviet regime. It must continue to regard the Soviet Union as a rival, not a partner, in the political arena. It must continue to expect that Soviet policies will reflect no abstract love of peace and stability, no real faith in the possibility of a permanent happy coexistence of the Socialist and capitalist worlds, but rather a cautious, persistent pressure toward the disruption and weakening of all rival influence and rival power.

Balanced against this are the facts that Russia, as opposed to the western world in general, is still by far the weaker party, that Soviet policy is highly flexible, and that Soviet society may well contain deficiencies which will eventually weaken its own total potential. This would of itself warrant the United States entering with reasonable confidence upon a policy of firm containment, designed to confront the Russians with unalterable counter-force at every point where they show signs of encroaching upon the interests of a peaceful and stable world.

But in actuality the possibilities for American policy are by no means limited to holding the line and hoping for the best. It is entirely possible for the United States to influence by its actions the internal developments, both within Russia and throughout the international Communist movement, by which Russian policy is largely determined. This is not only a question of the modest measure of informational activity which this government can conduct in the Soviet Union and elsewhere, although that, too, is important. It is rather a question of the degree to which the United States can create among the peoples of the world generally the impression of a country which knows what it wants, which is coping successfully with the problems of its internal life and with the responsibilities of a World Power, and which has a spiritual vitality capable of holding its own among the major ideological currents of the time. To the extent that such an impression can be created and maintained, the aims of Russian Communism must appear sterile and quixotic, the hopes and enthusiasm of Moscow's supporters must wane, and added strain must be imposed on the Kremlin's foreign policies. For the palsied decrepitude of the capitalist world is the keystone of Communist philosophy. Even the failure of the United States to experience the early economic depression which the ravens of the Red Square have been predicting with such complacent confidence since hostilities ceased would have deep and important repercussions throughout the Communist world.

By the same token, exhibitions of indecision, disunity and internal disintegration within this country have an exhilarating effect on the whole Communist movement. At each evidence of these tendencies, a thrill of hope and excitement goes through the Communist world; a new jauntiness can be noted in the Moscow tread; new groups of foreign supporters climb on to what they can only view as the band wagon of international politics; and Russian pressure increases all along the line in international affairs.

It would be an exaggeration to say that American behavior unassisted and alone could exercise a power of life and death over the Communist movement and bring about the early fall of Soviet power in Russia. But the United States has it in its power to increase enormously the strains under which Soviet policy must operate, to force upon the Kremlin a far greater degree of moderation and circumspection than it has had to observe in recent years, and in this way to promote tendencies which must eventually find their outlet in either the break-up or the gradual mellowing of Soviet power. For no mystical, Messianic movement—and particularly not that of the Kremlin—can face frustration indefinitely without eventually adjusting itself in one way or another to the logic of that state of affairs.

Thus the decision will really fall in large measure in this country itself. The issue of Soviet-American relations is in essence a test of the overall worth of the United States as a nation among nations. To avoid destruction the United States need only measure up to its own best traditions and prove itself worthy of preservation as a great nation.

Surely, there was never a fairer test of national quality than this. In the light of these circumstances, the thoughtful observer of Russian-American relations will find no cause for complaint in the Kremlin's challenge to American society. He will rather experience a certain gratitude to a Providence which, by providing the American people with this implacable challenge, has made their entire security as a nation dependent on their pulling themselves together and accepting the responsibilities of moral and political leadership that history plainly intended them to bear.

A CRITIQUE OF CONTAINMENT

WALTER LIPPMANN *

We must begin with the disturbing fact, which anyone who will reread the article can verify for himself, that Mr. X's conclusions depend upon the optimistic prediction that the "Soviet power . . . bears within itself the seeds of its own decay, and that the sprouting of these seeds is well advanced;" that if "anything were ever to occur to disrupt the unity and the efficacy of the Party as a political instrument, Soviet Russia might be changed overnight (*sic*) from one of the strongest to one of the weakest and most pitiable of national societies;" and "that Soviet society may well (*sic*) contain deficiencies which will eventually weaken its own total potential."

Of this optimistic prediction Mr. X himself says that it "cannot be proved. And it cannot be disproved." Nevertheless, he concludes that the

* Walter Lippmann, *The Cold War*, pp. 11–14, 60–62. Copyright 1947, by Walter Lippmann. Reprinted by permission of Harper & Brothers, and Hamish Hamilton, Ltd., London.

United States should construct its policy on the assumption that the Soviet power is inherently weak and impermanent, and that this un-proved assumption warrants our entering "with reasonable confidence upon a policy of firm containment, designed to confront the Russians with unalterable counterforce at every point where they show signs of encroaching upon the interests of a peaceful and a stable world."

I do not find much ground for reasonable confidence in a policy which can be successful only if the most optimistic prediction should prove to be true. Surely a sound policy must be addressed to the worst and hardest that may be judged to be probable, and not to the best and easiest that may be possible.

As a matter of fact, Mr. X himself betrays a marked lack of confidence in his own diagnosis. For no sooner had he finished describing the policy of firm containment with unalterable counterforce at every point where the Russians show signs of encroaching, when he felt he must defend his conclusions against the criticism, one might almost say the wisecrack, that this is a policy of "holding the line and hoping for the best." His defense is to say that while he is proposing a policy of holding the line and hop-ing for the best, "in actuality the possibilities for American policy are by no means limited to holding the line and hoping for the best." The ad-ditional possibilities are not, however, within the scope of the authority of the Department of State: "the aims of Russian communism must ap-pear sterile and quixotic, the hopes and enthusiasms of Moscow's sup-porters must wane, and added strain must be imposed on the Kremlin's foreign policies" if "the United States can create among the peoples of the world generally the impression of a country which knows what it wants, which is coping successfully with the problems of its internal life and with the responsibilities of a world power, and which has a spiritual vitality capable of holding its own among the major ideological currents of the time."

This surely is a case of bolstering up the wishful thinking of "hoping for the best"—namely, the collapse of the Soviet power—by an extra strong dose of wishful thinking about the United States. There must be something deeply defective in Mr. X's estimates and calculations. For on his own showing, the policy cannot be made to work unless there are miracles and we get all the breaks.

In Mr. X's estimates there are no reserves for a rainy day. There is no margin of safety for bad luck, bad management, error and the unfore-seen. He asks us to assume that the Soviet power is already decaying. He exhorts us to believe that our own highest hopes for ourselves will soon have been realized. Yet the policy he recommends is designed to deal effectively with the Soviet Union "as a rival, not a partner, in the political arena." Do we dare to assume, as we enter the arena and get set to run the race, that the Soviet Union will break its leg while the United States grows a pair of wings to speed it on its way?

Mr. X concludes his article on Soviet conduct and American policy by saying that "the thoughtful observer of Russian-American relations will . . . experience a certain gratitude to a Providence which, by providing the American people with this implacable challenge, has made their entire security as a nation dependent upon their pulling themselves together and accepting the responsibilities of moral and political leadership that history plainly intended them to bear." Perhaps. It may be that Mr. X has read the mind of Providence and that he knows what history plainly intended. But it is asking a good deal that the American people should stake their "entire security as a nation" upon a theory which, as he himself says, cannot be proved and cannot be disproved.

Surely it is by no means proved that the way to lead mankind is to spend the next ten or fifteen years, as Mr. X proposes we should, in reacting at "a series of constantly shifting geographical and political points, corresponding to the shifts and maneuvers of Soviet policy." For if history has indeed intended us to bear the responsibility of leadership, then it is not leadership to adapt ourselves to the shifts and maneuvers of Soviet policy at a series of constantly shifting geographical and political points. For that would mean for ten or fifteen years Moscow, not Washington, would define the issues, would make the challenges, would select the ground where the conflict was to be waged, and would choose the weapons. And the best that Mr. X can say for his own proposal is that if for a long period of time we can prevent the Soviet power from winning, the Soviet power will eventually perish or "mellow" because it has been "frustrated."

This is a dismal conclusion. Mr. X has, I believe, become bogged down in it because as he thought more and more about the conduct of the Soviet, he remembered less and less about the conduct of the other nations of the world. For while it may be true that the Soviet power would perish of frustration, if it were contained for ten or fifteen years, this conclusion is only half baked until he has answered the crucial question which remains: can the western world operate a policy of containment? Mr. X not only does not answer this question. He begs it, saying that it will be very discouraging to the Soviets, if the western world finds the strength and resourcefulness to contain the Soviet power over a period of ten or fifteen years. . . .

At the root of Mr. X's philosophy about Russian-American relations and underlying all the ideas of the Truman Doctrine there is a disbelief in the possibility of a settlement of the issues raised by this war. Having observed, I believe quite correctly, that we cannot expect "to enjoy political intimacy with the Soviet regime," and that we must "regard the Soviet Union as a rival, not a partner in the political arena," and that "there can be no appeal to common purposes," Mr. X has reached the conclusion that all we can do is to "contain" Russia until Russia changes, ceases to to be our rival, and becomes our partner.

The conclusion is, it seems to me, quite unwarranted. The history of diplomacy is the history of relations among rival powers, which did not enjoy political intimacy, and did not respond to appeals to common purposes. Nevertheless, there have been settlements. Some of them did not last very long. Some of them did. For a diplomat to think that rival and unfriendly powers cannot be brought to a settlement is to forget what diplomacy is about. There would be little for diplomats to do if the world consisted of partners, enjoying political intimacy, and responding to common appeals.

The method by which diplomacy deals with a world where there are rival powers is to organize a balance of power which deprives the rivals, however lacking in intimacy and however unresponsive to common appeals, of a good prospect of successful aggression. That is what a diplomat means by the settlement of a conflict among rival powers. He does not mean that they will cease to be rivals. He does not mean that they will all be converted to thinking and wanting the same things. He means that, whatever they think, whatever they want, whatever their ideological purposes, the balance of power is such that they cannot afford to commit aggression.

In our conflict with Russia a policy of settlement—as I have sought to show—would aim to redress the balance of power, which is abnormal and dangerous, because the Red Army has met the British and American armies in the heart of Europe. The division between east and west is at that military boundary line. The meeting of those armies caused the division. No state in eastern Europe can be independent of the Kremlin as long as the Red Army is within it and all around it. No state in western Europe is independent while it is in effect in the rear of this military frontier. The presence of these non-European armies in the continent of Europe perpetuates the division of Europe. The Soviet government has been communist for thirty years. For more than a hundred years all Russian governments have sought to expand over eastern Europe. But only since the Red Army reached the Elbe River have the rulers of Russia been able to realize the ambitions of the Russian Empire and the ideological purposes of communism.

A genuine policy would, therefore, have as its paramount objective a settlement which brought about the evacuation of Europe. That is the settlement which will settle the issue which has arisen out of the war. The communists will continue to be communists. The Russians will continue to be Russians. But if the Red Army is in Russia, and not on the Elbe, the power of the Russian communists and the power of the Russian imperialists to realize their ambitions will have been reduced decisively.

Until a settlement which results in withdrawal is reached, the Red Army at the center of Europe will control eastern Europe and will threaten western Europe. In these circumstances American power must be available, not to "contain" the Russians at scattered points, but to hold the whole Russian military machine in check, and to exert a mounting pressure in support of a diplomatic policy which has as its concrete objective a settlement that means withdrawal.

Then we shall know what we are trying to do. The Russians will know it. Europe will know it. We shall be trying to do a great thing which is simple and necessary: to settle the main actual consequences of this particular war, to put an end to the abnormal situation where Europe, one of the chief centers of civilization, though liberated from the Nazis, is still occupied by its non-European liberators.

We shall be addressing ourselves to an objective to which our own power is suited—be it in diplomacy or in war. We shall be seeking an end that all men can understand, and one which expresses faithfully our oldest and best tradition—to be the friend and the champion of nations seeking independence and an end to the rule of alien powers.

STRATEGY OF ERROR

HANS J. MORGENTHAU *

At the conclusion of the Spanish-American War in 1898, William Graham Sumner published in the *Yale Law Journal* an article under the title "The Conquest of the United States by Spain." Its thesis was that "We have beaten Spain in a military conflict, but we are submitting to be conquered by her on the field of ideas and policies."

For one who has studied and in part witnessed the policies which have led Germany to the catastrophe of two total defeats within a quarter

* Hans J. Morgenthau, "The Conquest of the United States by Germany," *Bulletin of the Atomic Scientists*, Vol. VI (January, 1950), pp. 21–26. Copyright 1950, by the Educational Foundation for Nuclear Science, Inc. Reprinted by permission. (As reprinted in *The University of Chicago Alumni Magazine*, Vol. 42, No. 6 (March, 1950), pp. 9–13.)

of a century, the similarities between the intellectual processes underlying these German policies and those which influence much of American foreign policy today, are indeed as striking as they are disquieting.

We have beaten Germany in a military conflict, but we are submitting to be conquered by her on the field of ideas and policies.

From the dismissal of Bismarck in 1890 to Hitler, the foreign policy of Germany was guided by three fatal propensities: a lack of a sense of proportion in assessing her own strength in comparison with the strength of other nations, an emphasis upon material force to the neglect of those "imponderables" with which Bismarck never failed to be concerned, an exaggerated and misguided sense of mission which equated power with right. To what extent these three delusions have taken possession of our thinking on foreign affairs is clear for any critical observer to see.

We are here concerned only with the first of these delusions, the depth of which a recent event has made manifest. The authoritative reactions to the announcement that an atomic explosion has occurred in the Soviet Union (and the fact that a Russian hydrogen bomb may shortly be fact) have demonstrated the extreme extent to which we have lost our sense of proportion and to which we insist that, regardless of what happens, we are naturally superior to all nations, the Russians included.

A historian, a thousand years hence, writing the story of American foreign policy from 1945 to 1949 on the basis of the contemporary reactions only, would arrive at strange conclusions.

The most important event of that period, touching the national concerns of the United States at their most sensitive, and bringing the world to the verge of war, would appear to him to be the Communist seizure of Czechoslovakia. If he were to use his own judgment, he would not fail to note that this event, while accentuating Russian expansionist tendencies, stabilized the predominance of the Soviet Union over Czechoslovakia which had existed since the end of the second World War and that it did not infringe upon the line of demarcation between East and West which the United States was resolved to defend. The Communist seizure of Czechoslovakia, then, would appear not as an attack on the existing status quo, to the defense of which the United States was committed, but rather as an accentuation of the existing status quo, an event within the preexisting Russian sphere of influence which left the actual distribution of power intact.

Our fictitious historian would find that the United States ranked the trial of Cardinal Mindszenty next in importance for her national interest, while his own judgment would have advised him that, whatever the moral significance of this trial and its importance for the Vatican State, it had no bearing upon our national interest.

The event attracting his attention next would be the Berlin blockade, and he would agree with public opinion that here was an issue which actually affected the distribution of power between the United States and the Soviet Union. Farther down the line our historian would have noticed the shooting-down of American airmen by Yugoslavia, the Greek Civil War, Iran, China, Palestine, etc.

Far down toward the bottom of the list, he would have detected a little item of obviously minor importance, expected, discounted, prepared for by everybody concerned—the fact that an atomic explosion had occurred in the Soviet Union. How did our leaders comment on this event?

U.S. Reaction to the Bomb

An expert of the *New York Times,* Mrs. Anne O'Hare McCormick, who obtains much of her inspiration from Washington, gave an impressive summary of the official reaction. "There is no reason," says Mrs. McCormick, "why the world should be taken by surprise by the President's statement. What was bound to happen sometime happened a little ahead of schedule but not unexpectedly to scientists, soldiers, or even mere observers of the hurrying pace of history." And Mrs. McCormick quotes "experts" to the effect "that in the experiment the Russians destroyed the only bomb they had and probably most of the plutonium in their possession."

The *Economist,* on October 8, summed up the official reaction by stating: "There has been, indeed, no glimmering of a new or original thought since the news broke; everyone is just as he was before—only more so."

This curtain of complacency, flimsy, worn, and full of holes, cannot conceal, and by contrast rather puts into stark relief, the three glaring facts with which the atomic explosion on Russian soil confronts the American people: (1) the national obsession to underrate Russian strength; (2) a decisive change in the world balance of power, and (3) the shattering of the foundations upon which American foreign policy has been built.

Nations have a natural propensity to underrate their enemies and to overrate themselves. These distortions are the weeds in the garden of patriotism and of national pride. They may be harmful, but not seriously so long as a critical intelligence is aware of their existence and applies the corrective of objective analysis to the excesses of self-glorification.

They become fatal, however, if reason refuses to adjust its preconceptions to reality.

Well known to psychiatric literature is the case of the neurotic who is unable to apply the test of reality to his mental picture of the world and is under the compulsion to make the latter the standard of reality. After a number of violent clashes between his conception of the world and the actual world, which have the quality of what is popularly called "hysteria," the patient calms down, retires into himself, seems to be confident, self-reliant, and at peace with the world.

The truth is that he has succeeded in withdrawing completely from reality as it actually is, substituting for it the reality of his delusion. Now he can rest content, for his diseased mind, having created a world all its own, has made it impossible that his picture of the world and the world itself be ever at odds again. Yet whenever the neurotic must act in relation to the real world he fails, and his failure is the more complete in the measure in which he succeeds in substituting the reality of his delusion for the actual world. Frequently, helpless in infantile contentment, he ends his days in an asylum.

There is a frightening parallel between typical neurotic reaction to a reality unpleasant and full of problems and the official reaction to the atomic explosion in Russia. Even the most conservative official estimates expected an atomic explosion in the Soviet Union not earlier than 1952 and, hence, were off the mark, if we date them at about the middle of 1945, by about 40 per cent.

This error is only one in a series which started almost with the Bolshevist regime itself. The Western world has insisted upon underestimating the strength of the Soviet Union, especially in its technological-military aspects, and has done so invariably to its own detriment. The allied intervention in the civil war was based on the assumption that the weakness of the Bolshevist regime would make such intervention successful.

During the thirties, the Soviet Union figured in the calculations of the Western Powers as a negligible quantity not to be taken seriously as a military factor. It was this argument which was generally invoked with success in the debates on the implementation of the Franco-Russian Alliance of 1935, the Russian offer of support to Czechoslovakia in 1938, and the Anglo-French mission to Moscow in 1939. When Germany attacked the Soviet Union in 1941, the best military opinion in the West gave the Soviet Union from six weeks to six months. And when she survived, it was only logical to attribute her survival either to the climate or to her wide open spaces or, and preferably, to American lend-lease.

Passion for Underrating Russia

How wrong all this is, is clearly demonstrated in a recent book which bears a triple mark of respectability. It is written by General Guillaume, division commander in the Second World War and from 1946–48 French

Military Attaché in Moscow. It is published by the Infantry Journal Press.

For the purposes of our discussion the importance of this book is two-fold. First of all, it gives an impressive account of the Russian technological achievements. Let us hear what General Guillaume has to say about the relocation of Russian industries during the war. "The transplanted establishments resumed their activities after a short period for installation. For example, tank factory No. 183 of Kharkov, evacuated in October 1941 to the region of Sverdlovsk, furnished its first tank from the new location on December 18 and reached its prewar level of production by March, 1942. . . . Whenever it could be done, the factories themselves were moved: 75 per cent of the industrial equipment of Leningrad and the numerous factories from Moscow were transferred in this way; and the same was true of the great tractor plants of Stalingrad."

General Guillaume gives the main credit for the victory in the East to the Soviet Union. "Nor was it Allied matériel that stopped the Germans at Leningrad, Moscow, and Stalingrad. By 1943, when the Lend-Lease matériel and tools were first flowing in quantity into the USSR, the German armies had already long been arrested or turned back on the front from the Black Sea to the Arctic Ocean.

"To sum up: Hitler was defeated on the Eastern Front because he never realized the true import of the deep transformation that had occurred in the USSR in every field of endeavor from 1917 on." Underestimation of the Russians is the invariable source of Hitler's misjudgments. "His underestimation of the enemy strength all the way through," says General Heusinger, his chief of operations until July, 1944, "led constantly to false deductions and to errors." This holds true of the West at large.

It is against this background of consistent underestimation that one must consider the official reaction to the atomic explosion in the Soviet Union. It would have been a rational reaction to admit that an error had been committed, to search for the causes of that error, and to resolve not to commit a similar error again.

Nothing of the kind, however, happened. Even those who admit that there was error refuse to admit that the error was of any consequence. After all, what difference does it make if what was bound to happen happens a few years earlier than expected? It makes all the difference in the world, as shall be shown in the course of our discussion. But, then, the plans which have been made in view of that eventuality will simply be put into operation now instead of later. What those plans might be is, of course, a military secret. Yet it is no military secret that the only present defense against atomic bombs is the dispersion and the moving underground of cities and industrial installations, and nothing of the kind is being done.

But is it not true that, if we just keep at it, we will always have more and better atomic bombs than the Russian? Even if this were axiomatic, it would be irrelevant. As I pointed out two years ago in a discussion of atomic disarmament: "The preponderance of the United States in atomic weapons is bound to be temporary. In the not too distant future the Soviet Union will certainly have atomic weapons. If the ratio of $X : O$ is not transformed now into $O : O$, it will inevitably be transformed later into $X : Y$. Yet, concerning atomic weapons, $X = Y$. In other words, once the Soviet Union has atomic weapons, it matters little that the United States will have more atomic weapons than the Soviet Union.

"It requires only a limited number of atomic bombs to destroy the military potential of the United States. This destruction will deprive the United States of the ability to win a war against the Soviet Union, however much damage it might be able to do by dropping a superior number of atomic bombs on Russian territory."

But, perhaps, what exploded in the Soviet Union was not an atomic bomb at all, or the only one the Russians have, consuming the bulk of their fissionable material. And, probably, it was not a particularly good bomb. Anyhow, we have nothing to worry about, let us have confidence in our leaders and forget the whole thing. Here the neurotic mind has succeeded in withdrawing almost completely from reality and in creating a world of its own in which it feels secure. Yet the collective neurosis of a nation does not end in the infantile contentment of the asylum, but in the terror of a national catastrophe.

Biggest Event of Postwar Era

The truth is that the acquisition by Russia of an atomic weapon is an event of the greatest importance. In comparison with it, all the great issues of the postwar period fade into insignificance. Certainly in the short run, and probably for the foreseeable future as well, it overshadows the passing of China into the Soviet camp.

Its importance lies in the decisive change in the world balance of power which it entails, and the production of a Hydrogen bomb by the U.S. will make no difference in this change, since the Russians are supposed to be well on their way to producing one.

However misguided the policy of secrecy with regard to the atomic bomb has been in other respects, it made sense only under the assumption that the monopoly of the atomic bomb was so invaluable an asset of American power that extreme measures and sacrifices were justified to prevent other nations from gaining the knowledge which only the United States was supposed to possess.

If this assumption was correct—as we think it was—then, obviously, the ability of another nation to make atomic bombs is bound to destroy that advantage.

U.S. vs. Russian Strength

There are eight basic factors which determine the power of a nation: geography, natural resources, industrial capacity, military preparedness, population, national character, national morale, and quality of diplomacy. Making due allowance for the necessarily hazardous nature of any such comparative assessment, we venture to suggest that there are rational grounds for believing that the United States has at present an advantage in three factors: industrial capacity, national character, and diplomacy; that the Soviet Union has an advantage in three: geography, population, and military preparedness; that with regard to one, natural resources, both countries are in a roughly similar position; and that one, national morale, is beyond rational calculation, for there is no way of telling in advance how a people will stand up under the conditions of modern warfare.

We have already referred to the over-all superiority of the United States over the Soviet Union in the field of industrial capacity, a superiority which, however, is not the necessary equivalent of superiority in the production of the implements of war.

We would assume that a people whose national character is marked by self-reliance, individual initiative, spontaneous manipulation of social change, and mistrust of government dictation, possess greater intellectual and moral reserves and a greater adaptability to changing circumstances than a people who have for the whole of their history lived under authoritarian, if not totalitarian rule.

We would also assume that a diplomacy which is uncertain of its goals and methods but operates with the method of persuasion and respects the national independence of other nations will in the long run be superior to a diplomacy which prevails only where military and police power have already decided the issue in its favor.

The geographic advantage of the Soviet Union over the United States consists in two factors. The extension of territory allows an unmatched defense in depth, and it makes possible an equally unmatched decentralization of population and industrial centers.

Aside from this geographic advantage and from the superiority in numbers of population, it is in military preparedness that the chief element of Russian strength is to be found. While certain important factors bearing upon the military power of a nation escape objective determination in advance—such as quality of strategic plans, of leadership, of training, and morale—there are others which are susceptible of such determination. Among them two stand out: the fraction of the national effort spent for military preparedness, and the kind of weapons at the disposal of a nation.

It is obvious that a totalitarian government has a potential advantage in being able to give unified direction to the national effort and direct as much of it as seems desirable and feasible into military channels. The Soviet government has made full use of its power and maintains an army and air force superior in numbers to any other existing army and air force or combination of them. This advantage has in the past been thought to be roughly cancelled out by the absolute American superiority in one weapon: the atomic bomb. It was even generally held that the unique destructiveness of this weapon would give the United States an edge in over-all military strength over the Soviet Union. For while in the initial stages of a war with the Soviet Union the atomic bomb would destroy the latter's industrial centers, the whole American national effort, using a vastly superior industrial potential, would be marshalled for military purposes and overcome the initial Russian advantage.

The Russian possession of the atomic bomb not only removes the counterweight to the superior Russian military establishment, constituted by the American monopoly of the atomic bomb, it also removes the edge in the balance of power in favor of the United States. For now the superior industrial plant of the United States is as exposed to destruction by atomic bombs as has been the inferior Russian industrial plant. The atomic bomb is no respecter of technological achievements, and before it all industrial plants are equal.

It is for this reason that we have said that the Russian possession of the atomic bomb constitutes a decisive change in the world balance of power.

It remains now to be shown that postwar American foreign policy has been predicated upon the assumption of the military superiority of the United States over the Soviet Union, a superiority which was supposed to last for a number of years but which, as we have seen, is about to disappear, long before its appointed time. In concrete terms, it was assumed that our superiority, derived mainly from the monopoly of the atomic bomb, would come to an end only after we had gained equality with the Soviet Union on land by enabling Western Europe to withstand a Russian attack at least during the period needed to bring American superiority in other fields into play. This assumption underlay the Marshall Plan and the North Atlantic Pact.

The short-term objective of this foreign policy was the containment of

Russia, that is, the use of our military superiority for the purpose of maintaining the territorial status quo. Its main expression was the Truman Doctrine. The long-term objective of this foreign policy was the imposition upon the Soviet Union of a settlement which would remove the threat of Russian aggression from Western Europe and would bring to an end the exclusive domination by the Soviet Union of Eastern and part of Central Europe. The strategic moment for obtaining that long-term goal was thought to be the one in which the United States became equal to the Soviet Union on land while retaining its superiority in other respects; that is, after Western Europe had recovered militarily and economically and before the Soviet Union had obtained the atomic bomb.

The acquisition by the Soviet Union of the atomic bomb in 1949 instead of much later has completely upset the timetable upon which American foreign policy was based and has seriously impaired the bargaining position of the United States. It necessitates the elaboration of a new foreign policy based upon new assumptions to be formulated in the light of a new balance of power.

Two such assumptions come immediately to mind.

In view of the unknowns and imponderables which go into the assessment of the respective strength of nations under contemporary conditions, it would be safe to start with the assumption that the U.S. and the Soviet Union will in the very near future be roughly equal in military strength.

If this is so, the policy of "getting tough" with Russia and the policy of containment have become obsolete. One can afford to get tough with someone and be able to contain him if one is unquestionably superior in strength. But between equals toughness becomes a two-way street.

The Balance of Power Now Equal

If we believe that the possibilities of negotiating a settlement with the USSR have not been exhausted, then we must ask ourselves:

What are our vital interests vis-à-vis the Soviet Union and how can they be safeguarded by mutual agreement? What are the vital interests of the Soviet Union vis-à-vis ourselves, and how can they be safeguarded by mutual agreement? If these vital interests conflict, how can they be reformulated so as to become compatible? How can the issues of secondary importance outstanding between the two nations be settled by compromise?

To repeat: the choice before the United States is to prepare for war or for peace (or, perhaps, for both). We are doing neither, but continue to drift, hypnotizing ourselves into believing that no such choice needs to be made. We do not prepare for war, but reply to the atomic explosion in the Soviet Union with a reduction of the military budget, continue to think that we can do without a general mobilization plan, leave Alaska open to invasion, and find nothing strange in the expectation that the Russians will passively watch us make Western Europe strong enough to defend itself, which under the conditions of modern warfare is tantamount to making it strong enough to attack. We do not prepare for peace, but refuse to face the one issue from which the conflict with the Soviet Union arose and which still dominates it: the question of the domination of Eastern Europe.

The conflict between the United States and the Soviet Union started with incompatible interpretations of the Yalta agreement. Underlying these interpretations was the question, who shall control Eastern Europe—the Soviet Union, the Western world, or both together? This is the decisive question today. Since Eastern Europe can be liberated from Russian domination only by war and since such liberation would certainly not affect the vital interests of the United States in such a way as to be worth a war, the reaffirmation of the political and military essence of the Yalta Agreement by the Western world in exchange for the military and political evacuation of Central Europe by the Soviet Union appears to be the objective toward which a new American foreign policy should aim.

It is worth recalling the warning which, two years ago, Mr. Churchill uttered in words of profound wisdom:

"It is idle to reason or argue with the Communists. It is, however, possible to deal with them on a fair, realistic basis, and, in my experience, they will keep their bargains as long as it is in their interest to do so, which might, in this grave matter, be a long time, once things are settled. . . .

"There are very grave dangers—that is all I am going to say today—in letting everything run on and pile up until something happens, and it passes, all of a sudden, out of your control."

After his first meeting with Stalin, Mr. Churchill remarked that Stalin left with him "the impression . . . of a complete absence of illusions of any sort." Absence of illusions is indeed one of the marks of the statesman. Politicians, whose horizon is limited by the prospects of the next elections, prefer to delude themselves and their constituents.

The official reaction to the atomic explosion in Russia has given us an indication of the depth of our national illusions. That is the German way of making foreign policy, and the fate that awaits such a policy of illusions is likely to be the fate that was Germany's. In such manner politicians may manage to win the next elections. But they also make sure that there remain few elections to be won.

IS WAR WITH RUSSIA INEVITABLE?
FIVE SOLID ARGUMENTS FOR PEACE

GEORGE F. KENNAN *

Great confusion of thought prevails today with respect to American policy toward the Soviet Union and Russia's real attitude toward us. There is much loose talk going around—on both sides of the ocean—about "preventive war," "the inevitability of the conflict," and "warmongering imperialists." Let us ask, and answer, five basic questions—and see if they do not give a pretty clear answer to all this talk of war.

1. *Are the Russians planning to make war on us?* Naturally, only the Soviet leaders themselves could answer this question with certainty. But the following facts are worth remembering.

It is true that Lenin wrote: "The existence of the Soviet Republic side by side with imperialist states for a long time is unthinkable. One or the other must triumph in the end. And before that end comes, a series of frightful clashes between the Soviet Republic and the bourgeois states is inevitable." And this still remains accepted Communist doctrine.

But current Stalinist doctrine does not demand war. On the contrary, it also teaches that eventually capitalism will fall largely of its own weight, *i.e.,* as a result of the inner "contradictions" which the Communists believe it embodies. They see the role of Communism as one of hastening the collapse of capitalism and assisting, as a midwife, at the birth of the Socialist order. In theory, they seem inclined to regard this as primarily the task of the native Communists in each country, and not of the Soviet Red Army.

There is nothing in Stalinist doctrine which would make it necessarily the main responsibility of the armed forces of the Soviet Union themselves to overthrow capitalism everywhere by direct military action. This premise would actually seem illogical and improper, from the Communist point of view; for it would imply that capitalism, in the absence of such an attack, would be basically sound and capable of coping permanently with its own "contradictions." But this is exactly what good Marxists do not believe.

So much for doctrine. How about Russian tradition? This factor cannot be ignored; for everyone who knows the Russians is sure that Russia has changed Communism more than Communism has changed Russia.

* George F. Kennan, "Is War with Russia Inevitable?" *The Reader's Digest*, March, 1950, pp. 1–9.

Russia has a long history of expansion; but it is generally a history of a sly and cautious expansion, of a readiness to wait patiently for opportunities to extend existing borders without undue risk. Apparent exceptions, such as the Finnish War, seem to have been the results of miscalculations.

The Russians, because of the vastness of their territory and the nature of their geographic position, are land-minded; and this psychology leads them to a preoccupation with their land frontiers and the territories which lie just beyond them. This, on account of their technical and economic backwardness, generally precluded them from ventures which would carry them far afield. Russian imperialism has generally been a process of nibbling, carefully geared to the capacity of the digestive organs of the Russian state. The experience with the present Eastern European satellites indicates that in this case Soviet imperialism bit off more than it could comfortably chew. The resulting discomfort should make the Kremlin more wary, rather than less, about taking on much bigger bites just at this time.

Finally, we must ask ourselves whether the Soviet leaders would have reason, from the standpoint of their internal interests, to want a world war at this time.

Less than five years have elapsed since the termination of the one great war in which the Soviet Union has engaged. For the Russians that war was terribly wearing and destructive. While steady progress is being made, it may be several years before the human and material damages have been entirely remedied.

In addition to repairing the devastations of the war, the Soviet regime is engaged, with deadly seriousness, in implementing a program designed to make the U.S.S.R. a strong and well-rounded industrial state. It will also take several years before some of the basic parts of this program could possibly be completed. World War II set the program back nearly ten years. Another one could not fail to constitute another serious interruption.

Viewed against the background of doctrine, tradition and practical realities, therefore, the picture would look something like this: The Russian leaders believe our downfall is inevitable. They would do anything they could to hasten it, but they would not wish to endanger in any major way the security of the world citadel of Communism, the U.S.S.R.

In these circumstances, where another world war would obviously involve such dangers, it is hardly likely that the Russians are now charting an early military onslaught on the Western World.

2. *How does Russia's development of atomic weapons affect the situation?* From the evidence available today, Russia's development of the atomic bomb does not affect it very much. The bomb is complicated, costly

and difficult to produce. The raw materials required for its production are still not easy to come by.

Alone, the bomb could not win a total war against a great industrial nation unless it were possible to deliver enough bombs to cripple military resistance at the outset and to compel the government to sue for peace on the attacker's terms. The crippling of resistance would in itself require not just one bomb, successfully delivered, but many. And there are no indications that the Soviet Union now possesses anything like the requisite number of bombs and carriers to achieve this effect on the United States.

In 1946 Stalin said: "I do not believe the atomic bomb would be as serious a force as certain politicians are inclined to regard it. Atomic bombs are intended for intimidating weak nerves, but they cannot decide the outcome of war." There is no reason to believe that the Soviet leaders have departed from this view.

Furthermore, an aggressor would have to take account of the factor of retaliation. In a war where your adversary also has bombs and means of delivery, you have to reflect not only upon what you might do to him but also upon what he might do to you. A single bomb will not suffice to cripple a great industrial nation; but a single bomb may suffice to wipe out national landmarks and shrines of inestimable value in the hearts and traditions of a citizenry, to say nothing of individuals whose importance to the nation cannot be measured in any material terms. It is one thing to ask an innocent people to bear such blows when they come, unprovoked, from an arrogant aggressor; it is another to ask people to bear them when they represent the logical and foreseeable consequence of a policy on which their own government has deliberately embarked.

In the past, aggressors have generally had the hope that their own countries might emerge relatively unscathed from the adventure upon which they were embarking. Weapons being what they were, it was technically possible, if your superiority looked good enough, to have such a hope. To-day, if you inaugurate the use of the bomb against civilian-industrial targets, and if your adversary also has atomic bombs and carriers, this hope becomes much dimmer. You may do fearful injury to your adversary; conceivably, if you have enough bombs and the ability to deliver them, you may even inflict upon him damage which would wreck for a time his capacity for large-scale, organized resistance; but only two or three of *his* bombers need get through in order to wreak upon your own country counter-injuries which can make any reports of victories far afield sound to most people like a hollow mockery.

Let us apply these considerations to the purposes and psychology of the men in the Kremlin.

With respect to such retaliation, it is not hard to guess at Soviet reactions. There is no country where the evidences of man's handiwork, both in the cultural monuments of the deep past and in the products of modern industrialization, mean more to people. The cultural monuments are few. They symbolize cultural achievements won with suffering and anguish from the soul of the Russian people. They command deep and general reverence.

The modern industrial plant has also been built up the hard way. Much of it would not compare qualitatively with our own. But to most Russians, regardless of their attitude toward the Communist regime, it symbolizes, again, the potential road of escape from the bondage of Russian backwardness. As for the Russian Communists themselves, it is their outstanding prize and achievement. It was for this, good Communists might privately tell you, that the comfort and the freedoms of at least one generation have been sacrificed.

Now we have already seen that these physical values took a terrible beating in World War II. In these circumstances, further large-scale destruction in Russian cities or industrial communities would constitute a major tragedy from the standpoint of both the regime and the people. This is not to mention the human values; and not even the Kremlin can be oblivious to these, for man power constitutes the core of dictatorship as well as of democracy. The idea that the men in the Kremlin, just because they are tough, "wouldn't care" about atomic destruction in Russia reflects an ignorance of Russian realities.

For the Russians, then, atomic aggression would be an inconclusive and risky venture. It might produce certain momentary favorable effects, but it would also involve considerable dangers. It would begin a war which it alone could not finish. The last two world wars stand as lessons to those who start things they can't finish, and particularly to those who attempt to conquer Europe before they have found some means of permanently neutralizing the military-industrial potential of the North American continent.

In an atomic world, total war remains a possibility, inherent in the susceptibility of men to fallacy. But it is now perhaps even less of a probability than before. For it has become potentially more suicidal; and the masters of the Kremlin, in contradistinction to Hitler and the Japanese, are not suicidally inclined.

3. *Is war possible?* Of course it is, and we must unfortunately always think of it as possible as long as we have the sort of world we have today. As Alexander Hamilton once wrote: "Let us recollect that peace or war will not always be left to our option; that, however moderate or unambitious we may be, we cannot count upon the moderation, or hope to extinguish the ambition, of others."

There are three main reasons why we must reckon with the possibility of war:

(*a*) Wars can arise by accident, even though none of the parties really wants them. Considerations of prestige, and the natural nervousness which surrounds the use of armed forces anywhere, mean that nations can become involved in wars accidentally. This risk is perhaps less than it used to be: people are today well aware of the horror of war, and they have calmer nerves than they used to have in dealing with explosive incidents. . . .

(*b*) War can occur because the Russians may think someone is going to attack them. While their ideology does not say that they must attack us, it does not say that we will not sooner or later attack them. On the contrary, the official doctrine is that most non-Communist statesmen are panting to unleash military attacks on the Soviet Union; that they are restrained temporarily by the might of the Red Army and by the great sympathy and respect which, according to the Soviet press, the U.S.S.R. enjoys among the popular masses throughout the world; but that eventually, unless world revolution or some devastating intercapitalist war intervenes, the attack will come.

The fact that this is nonsense does not make it any the less serious. One of the worst things about totalitarian governments is that they tend to misinform themselves. No one, not even the dictator, can be sure that he is getting honest and reliable information. While we think the Soviet leaders must know that we are neither armed nor arming for aggressive war, we have absolutely no reason to trust the accuracy of the information about our ultimate intentions which is permitted to reach higher authority by the organs of the Soviet secret police. And we have no reason to trust the ability of that higher authority—cut off as it is from normal contact with the world—to evaluate such information as it receives.

The thesis that the outside world is hostile and deceitful and menacing is essential to the maintenance of the internal power and position of the Soviet secret police. They will do everything they can to uphold that thesis, without regard to reality. We can never be entirely sure that they will not someday succeed either in convincing themselves and their masters that a capitalist attack is imminent, in which case they might feel that they had to move in order to get the jump on their enemies, or in causing those masters to make further miscalculations similar to those they have occasionally made in the past, with similar results. . . .

These are all reasons why we must regard war as *possible*. No one of them could be cited, nor all of them together, as a valid reason for regarding war as *probable* at an early date.

4. *Where, in these circumstances, must the accent of U.S. policy lie, with*

respect to the Communist danger? It must continue to lie in a vigorous and hopeful foreign policy which firmly rejects all defeatism about a future war and aims at keeping alive and pursuing vigorously every possibility for solving international differences where possible (and for bearing them where solution is not yet possible) without recourse to war.

The events of the past few months have caused many of us to be concerned primarily with the possibility of military attack on our own territory. But that is not the only way that our security can be menaced. If the Russian Communists should succeed, by means short of war, in bringing progressively under their influence the remaining non-Communist countries of Europe and Asia, our security would be more subtly (but perhaps just as dangerously) undermined than by an atomic attack on our own territory. For the world balance of power would then be turned, at least temporarily, against us.

It is this political expansionism which has been the real Soviet program since the conclusion of World War II. During this period the Soviet Government has not taken one inch of land by outright military aggression. There are easier, less expensive and far less risky means of extending power than aggressive war; and it is on these means that the Kremlin appears to have placed its first reliance. There is no reason to believe that this basic relationship will be changed by Russia's possession of the atomic weapon.

Thus we still have justification for hoping that by continuing the political struggle known as the "cold war" the worst of our present difficulties can eventually be overcome without another great outbreak of international violence. It means that we must continue to take an intelligent and helpful interest in the efforts of people everywhere to withstand the sort of pressures which are brought to bear against them from the Moscow Communist side. It means that we must continue the policy of throwing our weight into the balance wherever there are relatively good chances that it will be effective in preventing the further expansion of the power of international Communism.

This policy has never been guaranteed to be equally successful always and everywhere. There are limits to what a democracy can do in this respect. The result depends invariably not just on what we do but on the interaction between our own policy and the natural powers of resistance which exist among the peoples affected. (No one can force a country to be free which is not itself deeply concerned for its own freedom.) Nothing that has occurred in the recent past has disproven the thesis that such a policy, if resolutely and actively pursued, provides the best chance of carrying us over the peculiar dangers of the present to a more stable and satisfactory condition of international society.

This procedure will not satisfy those impatient spirits who look for some sudden or dramatic solution to the ills which now beset the international community. But these people would find it easier to reconcile themselves to this procedure if they would reflect realistically on the alternatives. There are only two: (*a*) a return to isolation and armed neutrality, or (*b*) war. The first would be accompanied by a disastrous deterioration of conditions in the rest of the world. The second is something which no democratic country could make the objective of its policy.

An attempt at an over-all "agreement" with the Soviet leaders is not really an alternative. The dynamism of world Communism would not be seriously affected by such an agreement. Words would still mean different things to the Russians than they mean to us. The agreement would be worth precisely what the realities of world power made it worth at any particular moment. Unless the free world, including ourselves, maintained a vigorous resistance to Soviet Communist political expansion wherever possibilities for such resistance presented themselves these realities would rapidly deteriorate, from our standpoint, and with them the value of the agreement. Not to mention the fact that in any over-all agreement the Russians would doubtless insist on provisions which would be interpreted everywhere as an acceptance and approval on our part of the system of colonial oppression and exploitation which they have imposed upon other peoples in Eastern Europe and elsewhere.

The "cold war" will not be entirely settled in our favor until those whose aims and decisions now keep the international community in a turmoil have been caused to conclude that efforts to maintain or establish political power over other peoples are detrimental to their own selfish interests and that it is inadvisable for them to pursue those efforts further. They will not be brought to this view by oral persuasion. They must come to it in their own manner in the face of a situation of fact which it is our business to help create. Until they do this, no over-all written agreement will really bind them to act as though they had.

It is evident, then, that there is no escape for us from the long hard road on which we have been advancing with a view to bringing about, by peaceful means, a happier and safer and more stable international society. This is the hardest task our country has ever undertaken. It is one unfamiliar to us by experience or tradition. But it has fallen to us by the logic of history and there is no avoiding it.

5. *On what, then, does our national security really rest in this coming period?* First, our security rests in making sure that military aggression remains improbable if not impossible. We should continue to maintain a military posture which, as Theodore Roosevelt once said, will make fighting us "too expensive and dangerous a task to be undertaken lightly by

anybody." Let us not be diverted from our task by a morbid preoccupation with what *could possibly happen if*. Let us remember that there is no security in a search for the absolute defense. Security lies in accepting moderate risks in order that immoderate ones may be avoided.

Second, our security rests in remembering that the fiber of political resistance among our allies to Moscow Communist pressure will be deeply affected by the extent to which they continue to feel themselves secure in the military sense. Let us give those allies the assurance that we are solidly with them. At the same time, let us help them achieve, for their part, a calm and balanced understanding of the nature of their danger, so that their enemies cannot play on false fears.

Third, our security rests in keeping our flag flying high here at home. Few Americans are aware of the intense and skeptical scrutiny to which our domestic affairs are subjected by the outside world, and of the beneficial effect produced on both our friends and our enemies by evidences that we are seriously tackling the problems of our own society.

This is not just a question of material prosperity. What the outside world is more eager to know is whether we are capable of coping with the sociological and spiritual strains placed upon us by all this abundance. It is eager to know whether we are going to be able to retain, in a mechanized environment, the individuality, the emotional tone and the civic vigor of earlier generations of Americans. Naturally, a nation cannot rely on social and spiritual progress for safety, any more than it can rely on inoffensiveness. But the connection between these things is closer than most of us would think. We will not convince others, or perhaps even ourselves, that we are protecting something precious unless we cultivate that something as assiduously as we prepare to defend it. To make sure that we can fully respect ourselves remains the best way to hold the respect of others.

Fourth, our security rests in continuing to act in a spirit of justice and good will toward others, which will make it possible for us to help a little toward bringing about a general attitude of peaceful cooperation in the world at large. It is here that the present possibilities of the United Nations come into their own.

We should not lose ourselves in vainglorious schemes for changing human nature all over the planet. Rather, we should learn to view ourselves with a sense of proportion and Christian humility before the enormous complexity of the world in which it has been given us to live.

If we do these things, we should be able to go about our international business with our heads high and our eyes clear, untroubled either by overweening ambitions or by panicky anxieties, accepting the risks which are the inevitable concomitant of all real human progress, and keeping our gaze fixed confidently on the distant goals which it is every man's duty always to move toward even though they may never be entirely reached. We will then be doing the best we can in a complex and problematical world. No nation can do more than that.

WILL THERE BE WAR?

WINSTON CHURCHILL *

I am often asked, "Will there be war?", and this is a question I have often asked myself. . . .

Can you doubt that times are grave when the word "sabotage" is used in accusation of one of the greatest Powers of the world, both by Mr. Marshall in the United States and by the Foreign Secretary in this House? Such language in any previous period would have been incompatible with the maintenance of any form of diplomatic relations between the countries affected. I think it quite right to say the things said, but when they are said it is certainly not odd that we should have to ask ourselves this grim and hateful question, "Will there be war?" . . . . I last spoke on these questions in the House in October, 1946, 15 months ago. . . .

Certainly, in the interval that has passed, the Soviet Government have not used their overwhelming military power in Europe to march westward to the North Sea, the Channel and the Atlantic Ocean. Nevertheless, it is common ground between all parties that the situation has deteriorated, especially in the last six months. No, indeed, it is not odd that this ugly question should still be put, and force itself upon us: "Will there be war?" I will only venture now to say that there seems to me to be very real danger in going on drifting too long. I believe that the best chance of preventing a war is to bring matters to a head and come to a settlement with the Soviet Government before it is too late. This would imply that the Western democracies, who should, of course, seek unity among themselves at the earliest moment, would take the initiative in asking the Soviet for a settlement.

It is idle to reason or argue with the Communists. It is, however, possible to deal with them on a fair, realistic basis, and, in my experience, they will keep their bargains as long as it is in their interest to do so, which might, in this grave matter, be a long time, once things were settled. When

* Winston Churchill, House of Commons Speech of Jan. 23, 1948, *Parliamentary Debates* (Hansard), Fifth Series, Vol. 446, House of Commons, Jan. 23, 1948, His Majesty's Stationery Office, London, 1948, pp. 558–561.

this Parliament first assembled, I said that the possession of the atomic bomb would give three or four years' breathing space. Perhaps it may be more than that. But more than two of those years have already gone. I cannot think that any serious discussion which it may be necessary to have with the Soviet Government would be more likely to reach a favourable conclusion if we wait till they have got it too.

We may be absolutely sure that the present situation cannot last. The Foreign Secretary spoke yesterday of the Russian frontier line which runs from Stettin to Trieste. This was exactly the line which I mentioned in my speech at Fulton—Stettin to Trieste. He also mentioned the Elbe, and who can ever believe that there will be a permanent peace in Europe, or in the world, while the frontiers of Asia rest upon the Elbe? But now this line runs farther south along the Adriatic shore, and there is actual fighting now going on in Greece to decide whether it shall not curl round Athens, and so to the Dardanelles and Turkey. Surely, there can be no doubt in our minds that this is highly dangerous, and cannot endure. It is not only here in Europe that there are these iron curtains, and points of actual collision. In China and in Korea there are all kinds of dangers which we here in England find it baffling to measure. There is also much to be considered in the Middle East. There are very grave dangers—that is all I am going to say today—in letting everything run on and pile up until something happens, and it passes, all of a sudden, out of your control.

With all consideration of the facts, I believe it right to say today that the best chance of avoiding war is, in accord with the other Western democracies, to bring matters to a head with the Soviet Government, and, by formal diplomatic processes, with all their privacy and gravity, to arrive at a lasting settlement. There is certainly enough for the interests of all if such a settlement could be reached. Even this method, I must say, however, would not guarantee that war would not come. But I believe it would give the best chance of preventing it, and that, if it came, we should have the best chance of coming out of it alive.

CHAPTER 12

CONTEMPORARY PROBLEMS:
EUROPE AND ASIA

ONE OF THE most important causes of the postwar tension between East and West is rooted in the uncertainty and unsettled conditions of a Europe and Asia torn by war or the fear of war. In Europe these conditions have been decisively influenced and aggravated by the unrest which has characterized Germany since the beginning of the twentieth century and has p'ayed a significant part in bringing to pass two world wars. Although relatively weaker today in power and divided through occupation between East and West, Germany is still the key to Europe's future. The present tension in Europe is inescapably bound up with the uncertain future of Germany. To the extent that this future is uncertain, tension continues; to the extent that tension continues, a settlement of the problem becomes even more difficult.

In the first selection, "Settlement for Germany," written by the editor in 1949, the possibilities of a German settlement are explored, not only in terms of the policies of the great powers, but in terms of the motives and forces at work among the German people themselves. Such an examination leads to the conclusion that the German people cannot in the long run be expected to acquiesce in the continued division of their nation. Should the cold war continue or a third world war appear probable, a struggle for Germany will inevitably ensue. This will make the reunion of Germany more difficult and at the same time force both East and West to offer greater and greater concessions to the Germans in the hope of adding German power to their own side. In this way a situation may easily develop in which the German people and their government or governments will assume a role equivalent to the "balancer" of the European balance of power. In such a case the revolution in power status would become complete, and Germany, defeated in 1945, would hold the keys to war and peace in Europe once more in her hands. Whether Germany remains ostensibly one state or two would not necessarily appreciably influence this result unless she continued to be also an occupied nation. Whether continued occupation is compatible with simultaneous wooing of German power by East and West is highly uncertain.

In Asia, China has experienced an equivalent period of war, revolution, and unrest, which has produced equally unsettled conditions. In a similar fashion China is also a key to war and peace in Asia. As China emerges as a military power, she will more and more contest and may even displace Japan from the position of dominance which Japan was able to hold while China's internal revolution consumed her energies. As in Europe, Asia's keys to war and peace are divided between East and West, with China in the Soviet orbit and Japan in that of the West. In Asia, even more than Europe, the whole situation is extremely fluid and future trends cannot be predicted with certainty. One element of the situation, however, is crystal clear: what the people of China and Japan (and indeed all Asia) desire is going to exercise a determining influence on their foreign policies, regardless of the wishes of the other great powers of the world.

In the second selection, "The Problem of Revolutionary Asia," John K. Fairbank examines the interaction of the policies of the great powers and the desires of the peoples of Asia. He indicates why he believes all Asia to be in the throes of a great revolutionary process brought about by a delayed coming of nationalism, a reaction against imperialism, and the impact of communism. He denies the possibility of bringing this revolution in social, political, and economic ideas to a halt before vast and far-reaching reforms have been consummated and urges the need for the West to avoid placing itself in a position of hostility to reform. His central point is that communism need not be the only avenue to consummation of the desires of Asia's peoples but that, if other avenues are closed, the pattern of events in China and the triumph of communism there may be repeated elsewhere around the extending periphery of Soviet power.

In the third selection, "Crisis in Asia," Dean Acheson provides a concise explanation of why China became Communist. He points out the danger of reducing American policy in the Far East to merely negative terms of opposition to communism. In his view Russia's moves toward incorporation of four of China's provinces will ultimately cause friction between Soviet Russia and China, which will inevitably drive a wedge between them. Therefore, the United States must not deviate from its traditional policy "that anyone who violates the integrity of China is the enemy of China and is acting contrary to our own interest." Although Acheson does not say so, the adoption of this policy by the State Department—a policy of encouraging "Titoism" in China—marked a transition from a policy of containment. Which policy will prevail after the Korean War remains a matter of conjecture.

In the final selection, "A Crossroads in Foreign Policy," the editor examines whether isolationism has been reviving in America since the end of World War II. The discussion over isolationism has been confused owing to the fact that "many of those expressing nominally isolationist views have also called for active intervention in the Far East." The editor concludes that "Americans today are not split into isolationists versus interventionists, but into those who believe the United States should have a policy which it should pursue by itself and alone if need be . . . and those who believe that America must solve its problems collectively with like-minded nations." The former are "unilateralists"—they want to "go it alone." If America seriously attempts such a policy, the editor believes that it will "court defeat in . . . efforts to strengthen the bulwarks of the free world." The future of the world, and particularly the shape of things to come in Europe and in Asia, depends in part upon the ability of the United States to avoid a unilateralist attitude and policy.

SETTLEMENT FOR GERMANY

FREDERICK H. HARTMANN *

It is generally agreed that the German problem is the key problem of Europe today; Europe's future cannot be disentangled from Germany's future. Both East and West know this, but so far they have failed to agree on what kind of settlement for Germany would be mutually acceptable. Some observers have even indicated a disbelief in the likelihood of any settlement at all; they expect to see a permanently divided Germany—a continuing battleground for the power giants of the postwar world.

* Frederick H. Hartmann, "Settlement for Germany," *The Yale Review*, Vol. XXXIX, No. 2 (Winter, 1950), pp. 240–254. Copyright 1949, by Yale University Press. Reprinted by permission.

This view is essentially unrealistic, not because anyone doubts that German politics will be decisively influenced by the East-West tug of war, but because a preoccupation with this one aspect of the problem tends to suppress and distort the other vital element in the situation—what the Germans themselves hope to do. It is inconceivable that the German people will be content to be an inert football in a conflict between two rival teams, tossed back and forth by the impact of the stronger force.

So when we attempt an analysis of the German problem, we must keep in mind that any solution must satisfy not only the United States and the Soviet Union (together with their respective allies); it must also satisfy the German people and their government or governments. While satisfying the great powers is more immediately important and has received the greater share of attention, in the long run what the Germans want will be the determining element.

A permanently divided Germany is no solution; it is unreal even as a concept. With the withdrawal of the occupying armies such an artificial division would collapse, either under the impetus of a patriotic German national unification movement or as the result of international intrigue, with the truncated Germanies seeking to annex each other as the advance agents of conflicting power blocs. A divided Germany would be a state of suspended animation—suspended, not destroyed.

But even for the moment assuming that such a "solution" would prove feasible, it undoubtedly is and will continue to be one of the least attractive possibilities for either power bloc. For both it would represent deadlocked force; each would be compelled to be ever alert to the possibilities of renewed struggle.

What might appear to be the most attractive solution for one bloc is, at the same time, the least attractive for the other—that is, the shifting of Germany into a definite, permanent alignment with either East or West. Obviously, if she could be won to either side, it would be an extremely important acquisition for that side, but at the same time it would bring war much closer, because the pivotal position of Germany would make of such a shift a real upset in the balance of power. A prompt offensive into Germany before the new alliance could be consolidated and implemented would appear imperative to the losing bloc, and that offensive would have to take place immediately. This is certainly one of the lessons of the years just passed; the alteration in the balance of power which followed the elimination of the Czech bastion and the disappearance of the restraining influence of the Czech army upon Hitler's designs is too well remembered to be ignored. The further freedom which the Nazis acquired in the East through their Non-Aggression Pact with Russia in 1939 is also instructive in this regard. Today, with Czechoslovakia already aligned with the Soviet bloc, the addition of a Soviet Germany would seriously menace the West.

Conversely, the definite alliance of Germany with the West would thrust Western power forward to the Polish frontier and would redouble Russian fears of invasion. Although Germany's military potential in the future may very well be substantially below what it was in the recent conflict, its weight would still be decisive. Such considerations reinforce the view that a solution of the German problem by the alignment of Germany with either group would in fact be no solution at all. It would be instead an intensification of the problem.

Some writers point to precedents for Germany's uniting in some degree with the Soviet Union; they recall that the two nations entered into *rapprochement* at Rapallo in 1922. Others point to the fact that Germany has historically vacillated at times between a pro-Russian and an anti-Russian policy. Admittedly history is not an infallible guide to the future, and to argue that what has been must be is to mislead. But in a situation as difficult as this, surely it would be folly not to get what help we can from accumulated experience.

Modern Germany came into existence in 1870 in the aftermath of Prussia's crushing victory over France. Russia contributed to that victory in two ways: by abstaining from any threatening move from the East and by helping to divert England's attention to the Near East. (She was insisting on a revision of the terms of the treaty concluding the Crimean War.) Thus the partnership produced benefits for both Germany and Russia. But in the following years it was subjected to increasingly severe strain, followed, after Bismarck's retirement, by open rupture. Kaiser Wilhelm considered that the obligations of the Triple Alliance (Germany, Austria, Italy) were incompatible with the Reinsurance Treaty (with Russia), and the latter was not renewed. As the European crisis grew worse, Germany's choice of Austria in preference to Russia became irrevocable; Germany was committed to an anti-Russian orientation which subsequently culminated in war. At no time during this previous period of partnership had Russo-German relations been completely untroubled, however. There was always French enmity to consider in the West and the need for Austrian friendship to consider in the East. Cooperation between Russia and Germany was never more than a mutual convenience depending upon transient circumstances. It did not survive severe stress and was largely maintained by Bismarck's astuteness. When the test came, Slav and Teuton fought on opposite sides.

There is a parallel between the pre-World War I and the pre-World War II periods in this respect. Following Germany's defeat and Russia's isolation in 1918, there grew up a temporary and limited cooperation reminiscent of the age of Bismarck. Germany and Russia signed trade agreements to their mutual advantage. Russia permitted German military training on Soviet soil. The grounds for growing friendship seemed fertile. After the advent of Hitler and his open denunciation of Bolshevism, the prospect of accord seemed to disappear; but the Nazis, heeding the lesson of a two-front war which Germany had lost in 1918, showed willingness once again to cooperate with Russia on the eve of hostilities in 1939. This overture was accepted by the Soviets with a complete lack of naïveté. It was purely a marriage of convenience—a fact which was well understood on both sides. In 1941 the arrangement was brusquely, but not unexpectedly, terminated. Again German and Russian fought against each other. Even if we were to go back as far as the days of the Teutonic Knights, we would find the same eventual enmity succeeding periods of temporary coopera-tion.

One of the fundamental elements in recurrent Teutonic-Slav conflict has been the refusal of the Germans to accept a subordinate role in Euro-pean politics, particularly a subordinate role vis-à-vis the "inferior" Slavs. Such cooperation as has occurred between the two nations has been upon a basis of jealously measured mutual advantage. It is highly significant that the Russia which cooperated with Germany previous to World War I was a Russia defeated in war and attempting to regain its freedom from restrictive treaty clauses. It is equally significant that the Russia which cooperated with Germany at Rapallo was an outcast, a pariah among na-tions. In 1870 German victory over France was not considered a threat to Russian interests. In 1922 the strengthening of a weakened and defeated Germany was not considered by the Soviets as constituting any threat to themselves. The Soviet problem was how to keep France and her allies preoccupied elsewhere, and Germany offered a convenient solution. These instances of cooperation are essentially *tactical* examples. The long-range strategic dispositions continued to allow for eventual German-Soviet con-flict—even in the case of the 1939 *rapprochement*. Stalin chose to make a temporary arrangement with Hitler in order to gain time for Russia. He considered that the real intentions of France and England were to provoke war between the Nazi and Soviet powers. None of these arrangements en-visaged the *subordination of one power to the other*.

Precisely here is where current Soviet-German collaboration would have to differ decisively from previous experience. The cooperation of these powers, for the foreseeable future, would entail the recognized subjection of Germany to the Soviet colossus. Far from being temporary, this sub-jection would continue indefinitely, for two reasons: In the first place, it would be the collaboration of a defeated and weakened power with a newly-triumphant and powerfully enlarged Soviet Union. It would be much more like the relationship of Italy and Germany towards the end of the Axis than like a *quid pro quo* arrangement. In the second place, the existence of Communism and the inevitability of Germany's becoming a Communist state under any such settlement would insure that the arrangement, once made, would at best enable Germany to pursue a course akin to that of Tito in Yugoslavia, and at worst could transform her into a mere puppet state. Neither would be a particularly appealing prospect for the German nation.

Some have argued that, regardless of the past, the new frontiers proposed for Germany would ensure German-Soviet collaboration even if Germany had a non-Communist national government (and could continue to have such even during collaboration—which would seem dubious). This argument is based on the circumstance that the West, having stripped only minute sections from pre-Hitlerite Germany, would have almost no territory to offer the reconstituted Reich, while Russia would be in the key position of being able to return East Prussia and Silesia through cession either by herself or together with Poland. Therefore, Germany would inevitably gravitate toward the Soviet Union.

Such a conclusion does not necessarily follow from this premise. In the first place, Germany's shift into the Soviet bloc could be presumed to be definite, complete, and permanent. It is difficult to see, given the disparity in present power and the known intention of the Soviets to extend Communism in Germany, how any other result could occur. Therefore, such a shift, while possibly of advantage to Germany in that she would nominally have returned to her the lost eastern areas, would be of much more obvious disadvantage, since in the long history of international relations, acquisition of additional territory has hardly ever been considered sufficient reason for a state to sacrifice its very independence.

Granting that the recovery of lost territories will inevitably be one of the aims of any German government, it still appears that the policy adopted to attain that end would far more likely be alliance with the West. When Alsace and Lorraine were stripped from France, the French never thought of regaining them through alliance with Germany. Instead, France sought, and eventually obtained, an alliance with Russia specifically directed *against* Germany. When Italy, angered at French opposition to her aspirations in Africa, allied herself with the Germans (and therefore with the Austrians) in 1882, she found herself in a compromised position, since it was from Austria that *Italia Irredenta* was to be forthcoming. Her subsequent reversal of alliances and her belligerency against Austria was due in no little part to her recognition that it is easier to obtain national territory (or territory considered as such) through the defeat of the power administering it, than through alliance with that power. The proposed East German frontier, far from being an inducement towards Soviet-

German *rapprochement,* is likely to prove a bone of endless contention. While the Polish eastern frontier has been accepted (at Yalta), delimitation of the Polish western frontier specifically awaits the German peace settlement. Whether the final treaty will actually alter the existing status is problematical, but it is premature to regard this issue as definitively settled. Far more satisfactory eastern German frontiers were considered unacceptable by the German government, even though it was forced to accept them nominally, after 1918, and the cession of these territories to Poland was not followed by the establishment of more amicable relationships between Germany and Poland. Rather, in 1939, the Germans, as a consequence of their pact with the Russians, were able to reestablish their sovereignty over these areas by force of arms.

The danger is not that Germany will walk into open Soviet arms but that Germany will seek to draw the West into a conflict with the East, in order to retrieve the lost territories in the East as a minimum goal. While it might be relatively easy for the Russians to return their portions to Germany for purposes of appeasement, it is hardly likely that such partial restitution would satisfy the Germans, and it would assuredly alienate the Poles. So much the more would this be true if, in addition to returning her own portions, the Soviet Union forced Poland to return hers. In the former case, Poland's strategic position would be grievously weakened; in the latter case, she would lose the compensation granted to her in return for her own losses to Russia.

What if, as has been suggested, the Germans prefer alliance with the West? This course, though more desirable in terms of advantage, would scarcely be any better in terms of peace. While there might be strong pressure in the United States to consummate such an alliance, it would inevitably be considered an immediate threat by the Soviets to their vital interests; and while war might not come immediately, the danger of its coming eventually would be greatly increased. The Russians are too well aware of how serious such a power combination would be to allow it to be perfected before they struck in what they would consider to be self-defense. The alternative, from their point of view, would be to sit and watch their position steadily deteriorate. Even should they decide to wait and hope, the tension in the world would continue to grow until peace hung upon a chance incident. While there is, of course, the possibility that the Soviets would be overawed into quiescence by this formidable power bloc and go over to a defensive policy in an effort to avert conflict, it would seem doubtful if the result would be peace. Rather one might expect the Soviets to redouble their efforts elsewhere—in Asia, for example.

The question which is appropriate at this point is: do we seek peace through a settlement of the German problem and a *modus vivendi* with the Russians, or is this a diplomatic (and possibly military) duel to the finish with no settlement but unconditional surrender the goal? If it is a fight to the finish, then the alternatives are Germany in one bloc or the other; if peace is our objective, then Germany can be permitted in neither bloc. Whether this is possible remains to be considered.

So far we have looked at what the power blocs want to have happen and what they can allow to happen in Germany. Now let us see what the German people want, for that, in the end, will be decisive.

What will inevitably appeal to them most compellingly will be the restoration of a unified Reich, and with the example of several hundred years of Polish strivings before us, we may suppose that the Germans will work steadfastly toward a resurrected, revived, and unified nation.

Even the present evidence is sufficient to establish this fact. The newly-promulgated Bonn Constitution contains an express indication that it is considered merely a transitory instrument to be disposed of later when Germany is once again free from alien occupation. It is highly unrealistic to suppose that if two rival German states remain when the armies are withdrawn they will long remain apart. Although much has been made of the tendency to separatism inherent in the "historically separate German states," which were only formally abolished under the Third Reich, it seems unlikely that this force retains much vitality, when we remember that Bismarck, denied military funds by the Prussian Landtag, and opposed by the liberal elements in Germany, was acclaimed by these very elements when by force he created the Second Reich. He was given absolution for his defiant procedure in unconstitutionally arrogating those funds; the unification of Germany was preferred over the liberalization of Germany. Similarly, it can be expected that a reunified Reich would be the principal and primary aim of any German government whether nominally Communist or anti-Communist ideologically.

But an even more important conclusion follows from the premise that the German people will desire unity first and foremost. If Germany were evacuated, leaving behind rival governments in East and West, one of the first things which we could expect to happen would be the attempt of one to dominate the other. In the event this effort were successful and all Germany became Communistic, or alternatively pro-West, the result would differ not at all from the very circumstance which both Russia and the Western powers seek to avoid at present. It would be unacceptable for a self-unified Germany to be in one bloc or the other for precisely the same reasons which make such an arrangement unacceptable now; it would tend to shift the balance of power decidedly one way or the other.

There is one other result which might come from the effort of these rival German governments to absorb and dominate the other: a compromise might be effected which would produce unification without affiliation with either bloc. If the obstacles to successful domination of one government by the other were too great, such a compromise might strongly appeal to both governments of Germany, since it would at least provide unification—which would be the minimum goal and prime moving influence at work in any case. Such a compromise might very well prove more acceptable to the German people as a whole than any other solution. Whether such a compromise would or could be carried out in good faith is a question which merits careful consideration.

The ideological consideration of "Communism" versus "democracy" will prove less important to the German people than will considerations of national unification and a revived Reich. The recent vote in Soviet-occupied Germany is interesting in this respect. Although the ballot offered to the voters did not contain alternative lists of candidates but merely provided a choice of a negative or affirmative vote on the entire slate, one-third of all the votes cast were against the proposed list. Actually, in the conditions under which the vote was taken, such a sizeable opposition vote must be interpreted to mean that a far greater opposition to Communism exists.

This does not mean that a free election in Eastern Germany with secret ballot would result in a pro-Western vote; it would result in a *pro-German vote*—which is not the same thing. To vote for the Communist Party is to vote for Russia under conditions existing in Germany today; there is no equivalent party which is in the same sense an American or Western party. There are parties which observe Western forms and adhere to Western ideas of the bi-party or multi-party state, but the securing of a majority by either the Liberal Democrats, the Christian Democrats or the Social Democrats would not inaugurate a government for all Germany necessarily and permanently dedicated to a slavish adherence to any Western "party line." Quite the contrary is true. Although a Communist government might reasonably be expected to follow closely policies formulated in Moscow, there is no reason to believe that a non-Communist government would be prepared to follow policies created in Washington, London, or Paris, except in so far as these policies were considered to be in the German national interest.

It is true that, should a non-Communist government eventually rule all Germany, and should it be established contrary to Soviet wishes, and encounter active Soviet opposition, it would have to turn toward a close entente with the West in order to survive. However, should such a government be established with the consent of Russia, there is no reason why it would have to or desire to transform itself into an advance Western base and possibly and potentially a battleground *unless* extreme nationalist elements in that government were encouraged to do so by the West. If any such overtures were decidedly repulsed and it was made clear that the West had no intentions of bringing Germany into their bloc, the road to a satisfactory solution would already have been travelled far.

The point which is important in this respect, and one which has been obscured by the over-emphasis on the division of the world into Communist and anti-Communist blocs, is that there is room for a *non-*Communist bloc. The division of power into "for" and "against" is in large part the reflection of the present crisis and would become less obvious and less readily accepted were the present tension to diminish. The fact that the struggle for and against Communism has become all-absorbing to the principal participants has warped their perspective to some extent; but from the point of view of many nations preoccupied with their own interests, the choice is not so simple. Where tension forces choice of sides, a lack of tension can obviate the necessity for such a choice.

This helps to clarify the central issue with which we are concerned: the unwillingness of either West or East to see a unified Germany take its place in the rival coalition stems directly from the assumption that such a choice is inevitable and foreordained. Under the present conditions of tension and distrust, perhaps this is the choice. But if the German problem could be settled, the tension itself could be expected to lessen. It is in part a reflection of the lack of settlement—a result as well as a cause. An initial amount of trust and confidence between East and West is an essential requisite for greater accomplishment than has been effected to date. This minimum confidence can be forthcoming if both blocs are convinced that each desires sincerely to effect a satisfactory settlement, and that the proposed settlement is *feasible* and *workable*.

The only solution under the present circumstances which would reconcile the policies of the powers with the aspirations of the German people is a unified, neutralized, and guaranteed German state. Any plan which hopes to achieve success must take account of this fact.

In seeking the basis for such a plan, we will find that the history of the years following World War I has an abundance of instructive episodes upon which we may intelligently draw for inspiration. Far more than Rapallo, the Pact of Locarno suggests a basis for the settlement of Germany's future. The essential core of the Locarno agreements was the reconciliation of France and Germany and a resulting dissipation of European tension through the collective guarantee of Britain and Italy to rally with armed support to the assistance of either France or Germany, should one be attacked by the other. The Locarno pattern could, with suitable modifications, be used to guarantee both East and West against renewed German aggression and guarantee Germany against aggression from East or West.

The history of Swiss neutrality is instructive in this regard. Swiss independence has been largely the product of an inability of the contiguous nations to agree on a mutually satisfactory division of the country. No possible carving up was considered equal in security value to that which existed with Switzerland intact. The prize was considered by all to be too important to be allowed to slip into the grasp of actual or potential rivals. Thus the operation of the balance of power preserved Swiss independence. In Germany today the situation is much the same. Germany is too important to be permitted, either of her own free choice or as a result of outside pressure, to depart from the role of neutral buffer between two rival coalitions of power. That Germany's power (even at present) is much greater than Switzerland's does not alter the case. It does mean that the arrangement would be more difficult to maintain. This will be true of any German arrangement, no matter what the provisions may be.

These considerations indicate that a settlement for Germany satisfactory to all the parties concerned could be achieved through a collective pact embodying the following provisions:

1) Germany, as a condition of the treaty of peace terminating the occupation, would be declared henceforth neutral. She would be permitted only the minimum armed forces deemed sufficient for defensive purposes, including forces nominally designated for police duties.

2) Should Germany, in defiance of treaty provisions, seek to rearm, depart from neutrality by seeking or consummating any treaty of alliance, or in any other obvious fashion clearly fail to carry out her obligations, she would be punished through the collective action of the powers at present in occupation. Such action would be by unanimous vote.

3) Should a vote taken under the circumstances above fail due to a lack of unanimity, each power would be at liberty to reoccupy its former zone. (This would in effect restore the present situation and would be evidence that sufficient mutual confidence, essential to any real solution of the German problem, failed to exist. Since the present impasse can only yield to unanimous action, it would be realistic to provide that, should unanimity prove transitory, the present state of affairs should be restored.)

4) Should Germany herself become the victim of overt, external aggression (detailed definition of which would have to be included as an integral part of the treaty itself) by any power or group of powers, it would be the duty of the remaining signatories to assist her, in accordance with their respective constitutional procedures, by all possible aid, including, where appropriate, armed force. (If Germany were actually

the scene of armed conflict, war would, of course, have actually begun and there would be no possibility of, for example, American neutrality.)

5) Should Germany become the victim of internal aggression as evidenced by the illegal rise to power of any party or government which endeavored to associate Germany in any but a peaceful sense with any of the signatories to the treaty, then the signatory powers would proceed in accordance with the voting procedure already described. (We cannot prevent, for instance, the possibility of Communists' peacefully coming to power, even though such is unlikely—nor can we prevent them from seizing power. But we could and should then proceed to reoccupy our zone—and Britain and France their zones—in the absence, presumably, of unanimous agreement.)

Once agreement is reached on these major political problems, progress can be made toward consensus on the many minor but vexing issues involved in a thoroughgoing German settlement. The Berlin currency negotiations emphasized the difficulty of reaching agreement on subsidiary issues while the major problems remain unsolved. But the converse is also true. We can expect that, once the basic deadlock is broken, with patience all else will follow. The economic future of Germany will be one of the most important problems. Since it would be unacceptable for Germany to be tied either politically *or* economically to the East or the West, this problem might best be settled through the United Nations. It is worth noting in passing that the Economic Commission for Europe, an organ of the United Nations Economic and Social Council upon which both East and West are represented, has achieved modest but growing success in dealing with economic problems of all Europe. It may very well serve as the vehicle through which Germany will once again be integrated into the European economy.

A settlement on this basis would offer several advantages. First, it would permit the restoration of a unified Germany and thus end the present unnatural division. In return for this, the Germans would necessarily have to accept their frontiers as permanent. Second, any ambitions of the Germans to use one or the other power bloc in an effort to regain former frontiers would become impractical under the proposed voting arrangements, since they would in all probability result in reoccupation and thus renewed division. Third, the dilemma of a restored and united Reich which would at the same time not be a potential addition to a rival power bloc would be resolved by the enforced neutrality of Germany, guaranteed by these voting provisions. Fourth, such an arrangement ought to be acceptable to all the powers concerned since, should it fail to work, the present situation would and could be restored and the security interests of these nations preserved quite as well as they are at present.

Fifth, if the arrangement were successful, the present tension would be lessened and a more hopeful international outlook would develop, and that would in turn make possible greater advances toward a durable peace. The powers might gain much; they would risk little.

This assumes, of course, a willingness on the part of the Soviet Union to accept a solution of the German problem. It might plausibly be argued that, in fact, the Soviets prefer to continue as is. If this is indeed the case, nothing would be lost to the West by a proposal of the kind outlined above. Actually, much would be gained from the standpoint of propaganda, since one of the cardinal elements in the agreement would be a reunited Germany, and it would be clear to all that the West concretely espoused such a policy. Conversely, if, as the Soviets assert, their present attitude results primarily from distrust of Western motives, such a proposal might very well satisfy them. Unless they are seriously misled they cannot have much hope of a Soviet Germany acquiesced in by the West. Were the present condition to continue, Western Germany would be a more powerful acquisition for the West than Eastern Germany would be for the Soviets, since, for one thing, the weight of industry lies on the western side of the present artificial frontier. Such considerations can hardly be lost upon the directors of Soviet foreign policy.

THE PROBLEM OF REVOLUTIONARY ASIA

JOHN K. FAIRBANK *

Our military resistance to Communist aggression in Korea has been entirely necessary and unavoidable, yet it has brought with it the danger that American policy toward Asia may become preponderantly military and so defeat itself. May we again win a war but lose the peace to follow? Win the conflict in Korea but lose most of Asia?

It is significant that our military action in Korea since June 25 has been more vigorous and more fully supported by a united public opinion than was our political action there during the preceding five years. We Americans have learned how to fight, even in rice-paddies. But the political problems of revolutionary Asia have largely baffled us. The use of our China policy as a political football in the contest between the Republican and Democratic Parties has been regrettable, if not indeed disastrous; but

* John K. Fairbank, "The Problem of Revolutionary Asia," *Foreign Affairs*, Vol. 29, No. 1 (October, 1950), pp. 101–113. Copyright 1950, by the Council on Foreign Relations, Inc. Reprinted by permission.

it could hardly have occurred if the American public had been united in its understanding of the revolutionary process in China.

The unity of the American people on the issue of Korea thus gives us a rare opportunity to develop a more comprehensive and positive policy. This opportunity cannot be utilized, as some suggest, by a sole concentration on warfare in Korea and on mobilization at home. Our weakness in dealing with the Asian revolution in the past has not been solely military or material. It has also been intellectual, psychological and political.

We need to agree upon an analysis of the sources of Communist strength in China, as well as in Korea. We must then envisage more fully the role which the American people could play in Asia, if they would, in competition with the Russian influence. How can we relate ourselves more constructively to the forces of social change? How can we forestall the Communist capture and use of these forces for the ends of Communist power?

My own conclusion is that the effort to ally ourselves with "nationalism" in Asia and to use it as bulwark against Communism is a will-o'-the-wisp unless we combine "nationalism" with "reform" in a very specific and sophisticated manner. In the final analysis, "reform" is the more fundamental force. The effort to comprehend the nature of the revolutionary process in Asia is the most pressing necessity in our current mobilization.

II. The Social Context

Any analysis of the sources of Communist strength in a country like China must begin with the social context in which the Communists have risen to power. It is hard, if not impossible, for Americans to appreciate this context of social change. The breakdown of the traditional, self-sufficient farm economy, the loosening of the bonds of the old family system, the rise of national consciousness, the emancipation of women and of youth—these are all abstract and general labels which Far Eastern specialists are accustomed to use but which mean little to the American public. Sympathetic insight into the mainsprings of revolution is not easily acquired from a distance. Too few Americans are tenants dependent upon their own hand labor in the fields to understand the bitterness of anti-landlordism. Few non-Negro Americans belong to racial-cultural-geographical minorities that can appreciate the intense feeling of anti-colonialism. "Feudalism" and "imperialism" do not seem our mortal enemies. Ancient glories in our historical heritage do not contrast with an ignominious recent past—no one has been calling us "natives." In short, we have little basis in our own experience for a sympathetic understanding of the motives and feelings which can be used by organizers of revolution in Asia.

The raw ingredients of social revolution, which lie ready at hand in the villages of China, India and the countries in between, must also be distinguished from the process of revolution, by which they are combined and kindled into explosive activity. The backward technology and low productivity in a Chinese village, the stresses and strains in the old kinship structure and the old class structure, the mounting frustrations of a teeming populace gifted with intelligence and infected with hope of a better life—these are not factors making inevitably for Communism, but merely for change. For us the important question is: How did the Chinese Communists unlock the energy of the Chinese village? How did they crack the traditional structure of these atomic elements in Chinese society and control their chain reaction?

III. The Communist Rise to Power

This deserves our closest study. It is noteworthy that Communism made little progress in China until it found the formula of combining agrarian reform with nationalism. At the end of the first decade of Comintern effort in China, the movement was almost a failure, certainly on the defensive. From 1921 to about 1931 the Comintern's main stress had been laid upon the organization of China's weak city proletariat, since by Marxist-Leninist doctrine only it could lead the revolution. The peasant was esteemed less than the urban worker. When Mao Tse-tung eventually broke out of this doctrinaire cul-de-sac by simply organizing peasants, he called them a "landless proletariat" and used other euphemisms to hide his unorthodoxy. By 1932 he was basing Communist power on the countryside, where most of China lives. Chinese Communism rode to power on the backs of an organized peasantry which provided both the manpower for the Communist armies and the food to feed them, both the local espionage network to frustrate the Kuomintang and the coolie corps to support the Eighth Route Army.

How does one organize peasants? The Communist formula has seemed simple and effective: two classes are needed—the peasant masses of the villages and the intellectual youth recruited from the towns and cities. Once indoctrinated and trained, the latter organize the former and the job is done. But how does one recruit the intellectual and idealistic youth of the nation?

Chinese Communism was at a low ebb in the early 1930's when Mao took over. It remained on the periphery of Chinese politics until Japan struck in 1937. From then on the Chinese Communists became leaders of a patriotic effort in North China, for which Western observers at the time rightly gave them credit. Peasants can never be organized so easily as when foreign invaders are burning and raping in the land: the Japanese army delivered the farming populace of North China into the hands of the Chinese Communist Party, which was ready and waiting to receive them. More important, the Communists found that the intellectual youth of China responded to the call of patriotism, in the war of resistance against Japanese invasion, in a way that they never had to the call of anti-landlordism in the hills of Kiangsi.

Until the war of resistance, the intellectual youth of China had been largely cut off from the peasantry by that subtle but pervasive bifurcation of Chinese traditional society which made it impossible for long-gowned students to mingle with illiterate peasants on a common ground. Getting the literati into direct contact with the villages was the first essential. This process had begun at the time of the Nationalist Revolution of the 1920's, but Japan gave it an impetus that it had never had before. Tens of thousands of Chinese students from the middle schools and colleges went to Free China, where the Chinese Communists soon outdid the Kuomintang in enlisting and training cadres for village mobilization. When the Japanese war ended, Chinese Communism had a grip on the two essentials of power—agrarian revolution as the dynamic of the peasantry and national regeneration as the dynamic of the intellectuals.

The Chinese Communist use of these two elements of power is an object lesson in revolutionary technique. The first stage was the creation of a peasant-supported military force in a territorial base area, such as Ho Chi Minh has in Tonkin, such as the Huks are evidently seeking today on Mindanao. Let us repeat: the peasantry supplied both the manpower and the food supply for the guerrilla armies, the intellectuals of the student class provided the cadres of party-workers necessary to organize the peasantry. In a land which consists of innumerable peasant villages, as most of Asia does, the mobilization and control of the agrarian populace is the key to military power. This activation of the peasantry in turn is achievable only through the devoted work of an élite body of evangelists of the revolution—mainly boys and girls drawn from the esteemed scholar class, imbued with the patriotic fervor of wartime, indoctrinated with the Marxist-Leninist view of the world and trained to use the methods of village organization which Chinese Communism has perfected.

As this new power becomes established in its territorial bases in North China, it proceeded with a second stage, the economic-political-cultural reorganization of the peasant village society. The whole "liberation" movement deserves more careful study by competitors of Communism: its combination of persuasion and coercion, its use of hope and of fear, its remaking of class structure and cultural values, all provide a textbook study in "social engineering." This program unlocked energies which had been for centuries stultified in the old social order, utilized suppressed desires which had long sought expression, and under the slogan of "Liberation" created a new system of power.

It is a truism that in the peasant-based society of China, the surplus for investment, if it is not to be borrowed from abroad or gained through foreign trade, must come in the main from the peasant economy. Thus the new regime must squeeze the agrarian surplus from the farmer just as inexorably as the landlord class ever did. The all-important difference is that the new government not only collects this surplus more efficiently but uses it for wider social ends.

Substituting the government for the landlords has its precedents in Chinese history, but a great deal more has gone with this change-over than the old Confucian literati ever dreamt of. The Communist order in China has fundamentally new ideas and methods, which we minimize at our peril. Among these is its use of the modern technology of communications: the centralized Leninist party apparatus, the monopolistic propaganda machine, and the open and secret police networks. These are familiar features of Communist states elsewhere. They constitute a totalitarian control system more effective and comprehensive than anything in China's past, even when based upon some of the same sanctions as the old imperial administration, with its network of officials, its orthodox Confucian ideology and its monopoly of police power.

Thus agrarian reform is fitted at last into a new pattern of state power. Similarly the patriotism of the Chinese peasant and party worker is channeled into the service of the nation. Increased production, industrialization for defense—these conceptions focus the national effort. They are valid expressions of nationalism.

Let us note one essential step in this Communist rise to power—the capture of the Chinese "liberals," that stratum of unorganized individuals of literary and artistic abilities who have inherited the tradition of scholarship and the position of literati. The Chinese Communist approach to these individuals was in their terms, speaking the language of liberalism, expressing the disgust of the intellectual for corruption and self-seeking in high places, the despair of the patriot over official incompetence, and the hope of high-minded idealists for a better world. Indeed, if these promises of peace, order and plenty should be fulfilled and China not be prostituted for Russian ends, we in America would have no need to fear the course of developments in Asia. Like Pandit Nehru, we cannot rule this happy prospect out of account in China; but neither can we accept it as probable, in view of the Communist record elsewhere.

The desertion of the intellectuals from the old order was a crucial factor in its collapse. As the Nationalist Government sank deeper in a morass of inflation, disinvestment and incompetence, its police and party organizers sought to suppress the disaffection of the intellectuals, and so pushed them directly into the Communist camp. Equally important, however, was the appeal of the Marxist-Leninist view of the world.

The harness and checkrein of the new order is its dogmatic ideology of revolution, which can be manipulated only from the top. In the setting of peasant Asia, the Marxist-Leninist formulas take on concrete meaning. "Feudalism," that ill-defined word, becomes identified with the old order of landlordism. Capitalism becomes an outmoded phase of inevitable world history in which the United States is still backwardly immersed. Most of all, the shopworn thesis of Lenin that imperialism is the necessary final stage of capitalism is used first to explain the aggression of Japan in China (on the theory that the *Zaibatsu* sought profits by war abroad) and then to explain the American support of Chiang Kai-shek (as evidence of the classic tie-up between native feudalism and foreign imperialism). "Feudalism" as the landlord and "imperialism" as the foreign invader make good sense to a peasant or a party worker. After all, even Chiang Kai-shek, in "China's Destiny," showed himself, unconsciously like so many others, a believer in Lenin's theory of imperialism.

It is illusory to think that this made-in-Moscow ideology is incompatible with the sentiment of nationalism, particularly in the early stages of Communist revolution. The Chinese patriot who has felt the humiliation of China's "backwardness" and the "unequal treaties" can rejoice in what seems Communist China's new chance to be in the vanguard of progress.

In practice we outside observers are inclined to overlook the fact that Communist movements are in the main carried on by native converts. It is hard to convince a Chinese Communist who feels himself patriotic that he has sold out to Russia. It is as easy for the Chinese Communists nowadays to suggest that a Chinese Christian has accepted an unpatriotic spiritual tutelage to the West. Like any other faith, Communism is accepted as a way of salvation—national salvation quite as much as human salvation in general.

This brief analysis suggests that the Communist system, with its Russian allegiance, can expand to almost any part of Asia that offers conditions similar to those in China, Korea or Indo-China. An insecure peasantry and a frustrated intelligentsia, the hope for economic improvement and national regeneration, are ready at hand to be organized in the Communist pattern. How can the United States compete with this system in its seemingly inexorable advance?

IV. The Use of Nationalism

Military strength is a first essential for any American policy in Asia, as in Europe, since the Russian threat of force can be offset only by a corresponding threat of force. But to concentrate solely on the creation of military force would be a shortcut to disaster. Communism does not rely on arms alone. Neither can we.

To supplement our rearmament, should we seek to ally ourselves in Asia with the forces of "nationalism"? This is an easy slogan to announce. But nationalism is of many kinds. Let us distinguish two varieties—the conservative and the reformist-revolutionary. Conservative patriots in Asia may have no less love of country than their rivals, and yet have little or no comprehension of the social forces making for revolution. Conservatives in power are of course prone to preserve their power at the expense of change. By some, "nationalism" in Asian countries is taken to mean simply "anti-Communism," on the tenable theory that no real Communist can have the good of his country as the ultimate criterion of his effort. The defect in this kind of "nationalism" is the same as that in any and all "anti-Communism" in Asia—given the context of social change, the key to power lies in active programs of change, not in programs of suppression nor even of maintaining stability.

The true nationalist appeal in backward Asia consists not merely in preserving one's country from outside control, as might be sufficient in the West, but of constructing one's country anew, solving its many problems, uplifting its ragged millions, and remaking its society in every respect where it now is inadequate. Thus the higher patriotism of the modern Orient is compounded of love of country and belief in its potentialities, faith in its future rebuilding, and determination to carry through great social changes. This is the other kind of nationalism—the reformist-revolutionary kind, to be found among most of the Asian leaders who have come to power since the war. Nationalist reformers of this type can lead the Asian revolutionary process, while leaders who identify their own careers with the welfare of their countries and become bent upon holding power lose their following. The nationalism toward which such leaders as Nehru, Soekarno and Thakin Nu appear to be working is compounded of diverse things, many of which are in the realm of the spirit—self-respect and self-confidence, the expression of national culture. We cannot assist this kind of national fulfillment solely by a program of arms and anti-Communism.

The project of stopping Russia by aiding nationalism thus has to be broken down into a more complex series of problems. The peoples of Asia seek to realize their national life in all its many and varied potentialities. Many Chinese today hope to do it under Communist leadership; the Peking Government already claims the usual plethora of achievements, many of which are undoubtedly real. It is the hope of realizing these many potentialities that makes up the real appeal of "nationalism" in Asia—to develop agricultural production, to industrialize for national strength and welfare, to alleviate disease, illiteracy, poverty and ignorance, to build up a genuine "people's democracy" in the proper sense. This expanded nationalism seeks both freedom and welfare, both independence and growth, both political and economic progress—dynamic "reform" in the broadest sense.

V. Leadership in Asia

Since the United States is of all countries the richest in technological and other resources, we have a great opportunity to participate in the remaking of Asia. With a modicum of capital equipment our agricultural specialists can do much to raise Asia's productivity. But this is a political as well as an economic problem. One lesson learned from our private assistance to China's Rural Reconstruction movement in the 1930's—such as the Rockefeller Foundation gave to Jimmy Yen's mass education movement at Ting-hsien in North China—was that the upbuilding of peasant life through programs of literacy, health, technical improvement and cooperative effort sooner or later threatens the established order of tenant-landlord relationships. The local political power must therefore be behind the reconstruction movement and not feel itself obliged to rely upon the landlord interest, as the wartime Kuomintang Government felt obliged to do after Japan had pushed it into southwest China.

The most recent proof of this comes from the successful work of the Sino-American Joint Commission on Rural Reconstruction which was set up by the China Aid Act of 1948 and has been continuing its work in Formosa: the J.C.R.R. program of reducing tenant rents to 37.5 percent and extending landlord contracts to three years really got under way only at the last moment, when the Communists were just over the hill. Only then did the landlord interest, facing extinction, acquiesce in the program; only then could official support become vigorous and adequate. Even today the J.C.R.R.'s main problem is to find peasant associations—those inveterate enemies of the landlord—which are strong enough to carry on the many aspects of the reform. In short, it is plain that American specialists, backed with American technology and some supplies, can help carry through genuine rural reform programs; but they must have the active political backing of the local regime. The Asian government in question must aim at reform, not mere self-defense. In cannot be primarily a landlords' government. This means that agrarian reform, even when helped by us, must depend for its main impetus upon an Asian leadership. Our key problem is, therefore, to find and support those Asian leaders who have the youthful vision and the dynamic idealism to seek a genuine reconstruction of the life of the peasant masses on a non-totalitarian basis.

Here we face the fact that the Communist leadership in Asia has been carefully selected, trained and nurtured by the international movement centered in Moscow. This Russian equivalent to the American program of educating Asian youth has concentrated upon the Marxist-Leninist science of organizing revolutionary power. Our own training of "returned students," on a largely private basis in a variety of subjects at all sorts of universities, has lacked this concentration of purpose. So it is that Chinese trained in the United States are today becoming civil servants under the Communist regime at Peking. We have supplied the trained technicians, the Communists have supplied the new order that makes use of them. This is an index of our own ideological inadequacy to meet the problems of social change in Asia. Students who return to Asia from this country have new skills and insights into the potentialities of modern technology applied to human problems, but they have been given little guidance from us as to how these skills can be applied to the specific problems of Asia. We do not pretend to understand peasant problems, which are beyond our range of study. The American ideology has not yet been applied to the far-different conditions of Asian life. The freedoms of the Anglo-Saxon political tradition are not easily transplanted to alien societies. We have not devoted much attention to making export versions.

Asia thus represents an ideological vacuum in American life. Its problems are not understood by our public, and we lack a comprehensive view and a corresponding will to act in that half of the world. For this weakness the only cure is to foster a greater degree of study and contact, partly in our schools and public life, partly by sending to these new countries of Asia where we still have access a greatly increased number of American students, specialists, travelers and people of good will in all walks of life. As a people we still have the vitality to respond to the intense problems of the Asiatic scene, provided we get in touch with them.

VI. Channels of Aid

Our record in postwar China has a lesson which few Americans have bothered to study. It is significant, first of all, that American influence, which had been exerted for a century through private channels such as the missionary and educational movements as well as private business, suddenly in 1942 began to flow mainly through government channels. The beginning of our large-scale aid to the Nationalist Government marked a departure from the previous century of American activity. Now the United States Government began to carry the enlarged burden of aid to China. As a government it could do this only through the medium of its opposite number, the recognized government of China. This at once brought the United States Government into the Chinese political scene as it had never been before.

This new and greater American influence, however, was even less under our control than the private activity of an earlier day. U.S. Government aid to Free China during the war was given without strings attached in one instance after another. This pattern was set by the first half billion dollars granted to Chiang Kai-shek early in 1942. As the White Paper makes clear, Chiang refused the Treasury suggestion that he state how the money would be spent. The result was that China received an enormous sum outright, and until this day we do not know exactly what happened to it. We did not attach conditions to our gifts in wartime which would ensure that reform programs were undertaken by the Chungking Government. Ambassador Gauss' suggestion that American funds be used in a land reform program, to buy out the landlords, went unheeded. It is a question, of course, how far strings can be attached in our governmental relations with a state whose independence we espouse.

This suggests that a sole reliance upon government channels as the media of our influence will defeat us by stifling our freedom of manoeuvre and flexibility of approach. Throughout the last decade of our intimate relationship with the Nationalist regime, we have been at the mercy of our own principles of international law. The legal sovereignty of the Chinese Government has been further buttressed by the ardent nationalism of its leaders, averse to any semblance of foreign dictation. Finally, when our Government came to the point of formulating conscious programs for domestic reform in China, it was faced by the prior problem of combatting Russian expansion. The growing Communist power forced us into anti-Communism, as distinct from pro-reformism. The Communist success in polarizing Chinese politics put us on the defensive. By making us fearful of Communist subversion, they made us wary of pressing for reforms which the Communists advocated. We thus wound up talking reform but obliged to defend the status quo.

In this context, the Russian example again may be instructive. By the Leninist methods of dual activity in a foreign country—open and secret —Russia was able to maintain relations with the Nanking Government and gain concessions from it, as in Manchuria and Sinkiang. At the same time, the covert and subversive program of the Comintern and its successor system went forward on a different level. By this policy of hitting high and hitting low, both at once, whatever is not gained by formal diplomatic relations may be gained later by Communist-led domestic revolution, as has indeed occurred in China and might sometime threaten in Japan or the Philippines.

Such deception is not possible or acceptable for us. It is not the American aim to subvert foreign governments. We have no intention of pushing them around. But a permissible, honest and open duality of approach on our part might be achieved by an increase of private American contact with Asia, outside of government channels. Private and unofficial American citizens in any country undergoing great changes will include among their number some sympathetic or adventurous individuals who have the genius for participating in the local scene. This participation of private Americans in social movements abroad is part of our tradition. Under our system it cannot be officially organized although it can, by our government's action, be kept within constructive bounds. American support of the Industrial Coöperative Movement in China, the activities carried on under United China Relief and its successor, are recent examples of an established pattern first marked out by the missionaries of a century ago. American education in Asia, for example, has been a result of private activity. This amounts to saying that enterprising individuals must be left free and actively helped to represent us in Asia. American individuals, whether in business or in social services, with all their variety of talents and the multiplicity of organizations which they represent, are the apostles of the democratic idea. To keep them out of Asia is to tie one hand behind us.

American contact cannot be limited to the conservative factions. American students who did not become aware of the currents of social change abroad would hardly be worth sending there. Social scientists whose job it is to study revolutionary movements must have contact with them. We cannot compete with the Communist agents who are in the field against us unless we are willing to let Americans enter the fray and participate in the process of discussion and ideological ferment. If we deny ourselves contact with the welter of conflicting ideas and loyalties in which Communist subversion is making its bid for power in Asia, we will give the game to the Soviets by default.

In Asia, however, it is the governments that must lead in programs of reform and economic development. Many Asians admire nothing in America so much as the T.V.A. Their governmental programs are often called "Socialistic," meaning chiefly that their societies lack the pluralistic institutions which give us our strength. In Asia we must expect to find the state power playing a greater role in the new national life than is the case with us. Private initiative and local capitalist enterprise cannot be expected to do the job in a country like Indonesia or Burma which we expect it to do in our own country. While we may hope that those institutions will have their chance to develop in these new countries, we cannot look to them for immediate results.

This suggests that our competition with Communism in Asia can be mounted most effectively on a basis of increased private American contact arranged directly with the Asian governments. This unofficial American contact, represented on the ideological plane by students, professors, universities and research agencies, can be stimulated and financed in part by expanded State Department programs for educational and cultural exchange. Given the growing facilities of the Voice of America and the United States Information Service, our urgent need is not for outlets toward Asia but for inlets of ideas from Asia. Advertising America does not stop Communism abroad; our information and propaganda work needs an intellectual adaptation to the target audience more than it needs equipment. The great private sector of American education should be enlisted in this ideological effort at home, and mobilized for greater activity abroad.

On the plane of economic and technological aid, the beginnings under our own Point Four program and through the United Nations needs steady expansion—always bearing in mind that undeveloped economies cannot absorb such aid rapidly, and that technology alone, which can be prostituted for political purposes, is no bar to totalitarianism of the right or left.

It is plain that we can neither revive the old "imperialism" and "colonialism" nor escape the problems left in their wake. The new problem of creating a partnership between Eastern and Western states which claim equality in international law but are unequal in economic and military power has not been solved by the Communist system. We have it to solve. It is plain that our doctrine of self-determination for all peoples must be redefined to meet the reality of a world where power is concentrated in big states and the complete independence of small states is impossible. To solve this problem we cannot think purely in political terms, and when we broaden the scope of our thinking, we face at once the social and economic problems of the Asian revolution: how can peasant life be recreated, how can the patriotic intelligentsia be recruited to lead movements of reform, how can we inspire and help them to work out alternatives to the Communist system? We will get no answer, nor will we save Asia from Communism, except by a concerted nation-wide effort of study and action. Our success will depend upon the degree and quality of contact that we can establish, in the immediate future, with the peoples of Asia. In this non-military effort every American agency, from Americans for Democratic Action and the Associated Press to Rotary and the Y.M.C.A., should be enlisted in an all-out intellectual mobilization.

CRISIS IN ASIA

DEAN ACHESON *

The reasons for the fall of the Nationalist Government in China are preoccupying many people. All sorts of reasons have been attributed to it. Most commonly, it is said in various speeches and publications that it is the result of American bungling, that we are incompetent, that we did not understand, that American aid was too little, that we did the wrong things at the wrong time. Other people go on and say: "No, it is not quite that, but that an American general did not like Chiang Kai-shek and out of all that relationship grows the real trouble." And they say: "Well, you have to add to that there are a lot of women fooling around in politics in China."

Nobody, I think, says that the Nationalist Government fell because it was confronted by overwhelming military force which it could not resist. Certainly no one in his right mind suggests that. Now, what I ask you to do is to stop looking for a moment under the bed and under the chair and under the rug to find out these reasons, but rather to look at the broad picture and see whether something doesn't suggest itself.

The broad picture is that after the war, Chiang Kai-shek emerged as the undisputed leader of the Chinese people. Only one faction, the Communists, up in the hills, ill-equipped, ragged, a very small military power, was determinedly opposed to his position. He had overwhelming military power, greater military power than any ruler had ever had in the entire history of China. He had tremendous economic and military support and backing from the United States. He had the acceptance of all other foreign countries, whether sincerely or insincerely in the case of the Soviet Union is not really material to this matter. Here he was in this position, and 4 years later what do we find? We find that his armies have melted away. His support in the country has melted away. His support

* Dean Acheson, "Crisis in Asia—An Examination of United States Policy," *The Department of State Bulletin*, Vol. XXII (1950), pp. 112–115.

largely outside the country has melted away, and he is a refugee on a small island off the coast of China with remnants of his forces.

As I said, no one says that vast armies moved out of the hills and defeated him. To attribute this to the inadequacy of American aid is only to point out the depth and power of the forces which were miscalculated or ignored. What has happened in my judgment is that the almost inexhaustible patience of the Chinese people in their misery ended. They did not bother to overthrow this government. There was really nothing to overthrow. They simply ignored it throughout the country. They took the solution of their immediate village problems into their own hands. If there was any trouble or interference with the representatives of the government, they simply brushed them aside. They completely withdrew their support from this government, and when that support was withdrawn, the whole military establishment disintegrated. Added to the grossest incompetence ever experienced by any military command was this total lack of support both in the armies and in the country, and so the whole matter just simply disintegrated.

The Communists did not create this. The Communists did not create this condition. They did not create this revolutionary spirit. They did not create a great force which moved out from under Chiang Kai-shek. But they were shrewd and cunning to mount it, to ride this thing into victory and into power.

That, I suggest to you, is an explanation which has certain roots in realism and which does not require all this examination of intricate and perhaps irrelevant details. . . .

I hear almost every day someone say that the real interest of the United States is to stop the spread of communism. Nothing seems to me to put the cart before the horse more completely than that . . . people will do more damage and create more misrepresentation in the Far East by saying our interest is merely to stop the spread of communism than any other way. Our real interest is in those people as people. It is because communism is hostile to that interest that we want to stop it. But it happens that the best way of doing both things is to do just exactly what the peoples of Asia want to do and what we want to help them to do, which is to develop a soundness of administration of these new governments and to develop their resources and their technical skills so that they are not subject to penetration either through ignorance, or because they believe these false promises, or because there is real distress in their areas. If we can help that development, if we can go forward with it, then we have brought about the best way that anyone knows of stopping this spread of communism.

It is important to take this attitude not as a mere negative reaction to communism but as the most positive affirmation of the most affirmative truth that we hold, which is in the dignity and right of every nation, of every people, and of every individual to develop in their own way, making their own mistakes, reaching their own triumphs but acting under their own responsibility. That is what we are pressing for in the Far East, and that is what we must affirm and not get mixed up with purely negative and inconsequential statements.

Now, let me come to another underlying and important factor which determines our relations and, in turn, our policy with the peoples of Asia. That is the attitude of the Soviet Union toward Asia. . . .

The attitude and interest of the Russians in north China, and in these other areas as well, long antedates communism. This is not something that has come out of communism at all. It long antedates it. But the Communist regime has added new methods, new skills, and new concepts to the thrust of Russian imperialism. This Communistic concept and techniques have armed Russian imperialism with a new and most insidious weapon of penetration. Armed with these new powers, what is happening in China is that the Soviet Union is detaching the northern provinces [areas] of China from China and is attaching them to the Soviet Union. This process is complete in outer Mongolia. It is nearly complete in Manchuria, and I am sure that in inner Mongolia and in Sinkiang there are very happy reports coming from Soviet agents to Moscow. That is what is going on. . . . this fact that the Soviet Union is taking the four northern provinces of China is the single most significant, most important fact, in the relation of any foreign power with Asia. . . .

All the efforts of propaganda will not be able to obscure it. The only thing that can obscure it is the folly of ill-conceived adventures on our part which easily could do so, and I urge all who are thinking about these foolish adventures to remember that we must not seize the unenviable position which the Russians have carved out for themselves. We must not undertake to deflect from the Russians to ourselves the righteous anger, and the wrath, and the hatred of the Chinese people which must develop. It would be folly to deflect it to ourselves. We must take the position we have always taken—that anyone who violates the integrity of China is the enemy of China and is acting contrary to our own interest. That, I suggest to you this afternoon, is the first and the greatest rule in regard to the formulation of American policy toward Asia.

A CROSSROADS IN FOREIGN POLICY

FREDERICK H. HARTMANN *

We are at a turning point in the foreign policy of the postwar era.

The task of re-evaluating our policies has become imperative. For in a free nation confronted with the formidable problems of our times, involving the future of our very way of life, the issues are too important for the people to permit any policy of doubt, drift and confusion to triumph through inertia. But such re-evaluation, to be intelligent and constructive, must not overly bewail the mistakes that are past but turn to present realities. How well are our present policies equated with our power, and not only our potential but our actual power?

There is first of all our potential. It is enormous and was never more important than in the present era of mechanized and industrialized warfare. Nevertheless a potentiality is not an actuality. The essential ingredient in converting the one into the other is time. In the past that time has been available to us. Our allies held the line until our own effort gradually went into high gear. We reached our maximum effort not only long after war broke out in Europe, but long after we had entered the conflict. But where we are in the front lines from the beginning the tactical and strategic situations and implications are immediately altered. In Korea we have been in that front line from the outset. We are in Japan and Korea, Germany and Austria now. In a third world war we would carry the brunt from the beginning. We must be prepared at the start; more potential power must be converted into actual power.

There is, secondly, the atomic bomb (and perhaps, soon, the hydrogen bomb) and similar weapons of mass destruction. This may be our most important immediate factor in restraining Russia's ambitions. In a war, our atomic weapons would have enormous effect. Yet, it would be foolish to place too much reliance upon them either by neglecting other weapons and large, trained, integrated armed forces, or by assuming that they can prevent the further spread of communism if there is no war. Should communist expansion continue for enough years of nominal peace, the area of democratic freedom and the strength which it can muster will, as the Soviets are well aware, shrink. In our fear of Russia's use of armed forces, we must not forget that thus far the Russians have not had to use their own troops. Atomic bombs are of no avail in this particular context.

* Frederick H. Hartmann, "Away with Unilateralism!" *The Antioch Review*, Vol. XI, No. 1 (Spring, 1951), pp. 3–9. Copyright 1951, by The Antioch Review, Inc. Reprinted by permission.

A third factor in our power is our military manpower. We have created armed forces equipped with potent fire power and with extremely mobile units. At the same time we have tended to overlook a lesson which modern war has to teach us. Far from mechanized and motorized forces being smaller, they have to be larger than ever. Maintenance and rear-echelon details consume large numbers of personnel. In the past we have always been confronted by a shortage of combat divisions. Naturally, in peacetime and under conditions of limited budgets, most funds go into organizational apparatus and into research on new weapons. In meeting future emergencies—that is, for the foreseeable future—we can no longer rely upon these once-tenable procedures. It is time to recognize that a permanent military policy is part and parcel of a permanently important role in world affairs. It is difficult to see how we can be prepared from now on without a policy of calling up annual age groups. Universal service should be planned particularly in terms of military service.

II

One thing is obvious when we compare our policies with our effective and mobilized military power—we have placed our faith in our war potential, the atomic bomb and a relatively small but mechanized army to a much greater extent than has been warranted. This is amply demonstrated by the Korean crisis and the need for declaring a national emergency to make good some of our deficiencies. At the same time we have undertaken a program and policy of resistance to communism everywhere in the world. But we are in danger of forgetting that while Soviet Russia is the real antagonist against which our military power must be ready, communism as a movement and an ideology is not readily susceptible to military force or contained by it. We have been poised to fight Soviet imperialism while the ideology was creating a greater danger. We are fighting the one now in Korea—and this we had to do—but the whole of the Far East and much of the rest of the world is potential prey to the other. Military force is not the answer to this greater problem. Moreover, in our concern over aggression we have been drawn into seeking military support from governments not popularly supported, while intensifying the discontent that sooner or later has broken out, or may break out, into violent revolution. We have done this in part because we have been aware of our low state of military preparedness compared with the universal policy of containment which we adopted.

While it is extremely important that we rearm and sustain our preparations in the years ahead at a much higher level than previously, it is equally important that our policies be formulated within the limits of our actual power. Furthermore, our policies must be calculated not only to cope with the military problem of aggression but also with the conditions under which communism takes root and grows. Each of these two problems, which are at the heart of the power-policy relationship so vital to our national security, are interrelated, yet they must be resolved somewhat differently.

Measures such as European rearmament or economic aid may contribute to the stability of the noncommunist world provided that we are fully aware of the consequences of our actions. There are two extreme views that must be considered. One, held by relatively few, is to place our entire trust in our own forces; to let those who can arm themselves to resist communism do so but without any real help from us. This view is frequently called "hemispheric defense." It is a counsel of despair. Arguing that Europe is low in morale and unprepared for serious opposition to the Red Army, advocates of this view would have America in effect defend herself on her own beaches. On the other extreme are those who hope that foreign armies can do the bulk of the fighting for us, including the potential armies of Germany and Japan which are presumably anticommunist. This view fails to take into account the fact that nations which possess their own armed forces are in a position to insist also on what they want to do with them in terms of their own national interests. In other words, we cannot expect them to do solely what we would have them do. The relationship is reciprocal, not unilateral.

Building up effective allies to contain communist military expansion in Europe and Asia is then not only a military question; it is also a diplomatic question. The other aspect of our policy problem—preventing the further "peaceful" spread of communism as an ideology—is primarily a diplomatic one. The crux of the entire issue is the possibility of losing the military, not alone the ideological, struggle by inept diplomacy. If the attainment of fighting power must be our first concern, the ultimate concern must be with adjusting our approach not only to the power at our disposal but to the diplomatic problems which confront us in the world. Because of our past experience and historical tradition, we often have trouble with this aspect of our policy.

III

As a nation we Americans are often slow in grasping the significance of the political-diplomatic factor as it affects our relations with other nations. In great part this stems not from lack of imagination, but from lack of experience. As a great power among great powers we are only coming of age. After our debut at the turn of the century and our assumption of colonial responsibility at the close of the Spanish American War, we participated occasionally but not regularly in world affairs. Before that time we had lived in semi-isolation, diplomatically speaking. But now we were gradually drawn on an increasing scale into world affairs. Yet we participated reluctantly and sporadically and always with the feeling that such collaboration as we had to have might "entangle" us unless we exercised due caution. After a short adventure in World War I as an "associated" power (not an ally—the choice of word is revealing), we withdrew and girded ourselves round with our own hemisphere, only now and again collaborating and decidedly not participating on any organic or integrated basis.

Actually the term "isolationism," commonly applied to this interwar period, is misleading. We were never isolated as Japan once was isolated. We exchanged diplomatic representatives with many nations; we were concerned over world developments and formulated policies often very similar to those of our former allies, but we pursued these policies on a parallel but separate basis. Our policy was not so much isolationist (denoting withdrawal) as participation on an unintegrated basis—a unilateral participation—we were on our own.

Despite the great events of the past decade and America's assumption of world-wide responsibilities, much of our unilateralist attitude continues to cling to us in an age when it has become obsolete. It is this attitude which is at the root of many of our diplomatic difficulties.

Many voices have been raised in the last year or so expressing concern that isolationism was reviving in America. Confusion has been the keynote of much of this discussion because many of those expressing nominally isolationist views have also called for active intervention in the Far East; many in Congress who have been suspicious of European socialism and reluctant to aid Europe because of it, have called for much more vigorous policies in Asia. It is to be noted that Senators Knowland and Taft, for example, have again and again urged that the United States adopt a forceful policy of its own in Asia. Apart from a few "old-style" isolationists who really advocate abandoning Europe and Asia and relying upon defense of America in America (as, for example, Joseph P. Kennedy and, until recently, former President Hoover), or not defending ourselves at all (the pacifists), Americans today are not split into isolationists versus interventionists, but into those who believe the United States should have a policy which it should pursue by itself and alone if need be (some even say, preferably by ourselves) and those who believe that America must solve its problems collectively with like-minded nations, in close and continued collaboration even though compromises are inevitably entailed. This is a distinction between those who advocate unilateral action and those who are for collective action. In times of tension and confusion the temptation is great for Americans to revert to a unilateralist view because it is so ingrained in our past, while the collective approach is recently learned behavior—a civilized diplomatic veneer—which comes to us only by continued effort.

Yet if the solution of our military problem depends not only upon our own efforts, but upon joint participation in a common plan (as in Western Europe), our joint diplomatic problems are going to bulk ever larger as a possible fertile root of discord between America and her allies. The diplomatic collaboration entailed will be greater than ever and we must be prepared to meet their point of view if we are to expect them to meet ours. If we did not need them, and they us, to oppose communist aggression, the problem would not arise. If we were strong enough to "go it alone," as the extreme unilateralists propose, we would not need to compromise with our allies at all. But this is not the case. The concern of many Americans over "appeasement" is a case in point. It is true that appeasement will not stop a determined aggressor; Britain has good reason to know that this is true. But while Americans remember the Munich agreement, they may easily forget that it was born out of military weakness. The British are concerned that we may become involved in a large-scale war with China which would leave Europe defenseless before Stalin. They are interested not in "appeasement" but in coordinating our still limited joint resources to meet the common threat. Since we are dependent on one another for our mutual defense, it behooves us to work together, thus making compromises inescapable. The diplomatic aspects of the military problem, however, are being worked out. But the diplomatic aspects of the ideological problem remain largely unsolved. The reasons are not hard to find.

As a successful capitalist and democratic nation we are prone to take the merits of our system as self-evident truths which will appeal to all peoples. Many of us prefer, when discussing the causes of communism, to believe that it is a system imposed solely by force upon peoples who, with a free choice, would choose capitalism and democracy. We find it difficult to believe that other peoples have chosen economic systems which are to the left of our own through other than error or sheer force.

The difficulty which we experience in attempting to cooperate with socialist or would-be socialist nations springs out of our different economic beliefs. America's problem so far as the ideological extension of communism is concerned is made extremely difficult because, for various reasons, the world has drifted toward the left. While we are naturally disposed at first thought to meet this threat by exporting a made-in-America capitalism and democracy, private capitalism is not suited to present conditions in large parts of the world.

If we are going to exercise any influence in international relations, it will not be because we emphasize capitalism, but democracy, and it may often have to be social democracy. All this must be done at a time when we have moved further from New Deal ideas and over to the right. Yet the alternative is communism, since as modern ideas born of industrial progress and material benefits have penetrated to the masses of the unindustrialized nations, they have become no longer content to endure their poverty or to accept foreign charity. They are determined on change—and change which will mean improvements now. Gifts and loans are not the answer unless these enable the people themselves to raise their standard of living. If they are poor, they look not to gifts from abroad but to reform at home.

The task of our diplomacy in the contested areas therefore cannot be a mere exhortation to resist communism. We must convince these peoples that we stand for improvement of their condition on terms which they themselves advocate—even though these be socialist terms. We must convince them that they can have this and political independence as well. If the Soviets offer them better economic conditions but political enslavement, we can and must offer them the economic improvements they desire and political independence. It is not a job of selling America. It is a job of bringing effective pressure through diplomacy on governments which are endangering themselves in their short-sighted concern for the interests of a limited group at the expense of the general welfare. Reforms must be insisted upon as a condition for our aid; otherwise we only sow for communism to reap. It is a two-way cooperative task for the benefit of the peoples concerned; it cannot be handled by unilateral determination.

A re-evaluation of American power and policy suggests in conclusion the need to rearm on a rational and permanent basis and to encourage the arming and integration of friendly and allied forces so that we may meet effectively the threat of communist military aggression. This threat can be met, in the final analysis, only by the free nations freely cooperating in the common interest. It is not something which the United States can unilaterally impose as a policy upon allies who have interests and wills of their own. It will come only as the fruit of common, collective and sustained effort. For the larger danger of the ideological spread of communism to nations now free (who are perhaps as powers of small size not a threat in themselves but who would as communist satellites help to tip the balance of power against us), the answer although in diplomatic terms, must again emphasize the collective rather than a unilateral policy. We must realize that other nations and other peoples are not willing to be pawns in our diplomatic chess game but have interests and desires of their own which we cannot ignore.

Finally, we must increase our own power, but we must, more important still, rally the free nations and the free peoples to a collective program of resistance to totalitarianism. If, instead, we insist on our own policy or on our own economic system, we court defeat in our efforts to strengthen the bulwarks of the free world.